State and Society in Eighteenth-Century France

Historical Materialism Book Series

The Historical Materialism Book Series is a major publishing initiative of the radical left. The capitalist crisis of the twenty-first century has been met by a resurgence of interest in critical Marxist theory. At the same time, the publishing institutions committed to Marxism have contracted markedly since the high point of the 1970s. The Historical Materialism Book Series is dedicated to addressing this situation by making available important works of Marxist theory. The aim of the series is to publish important theoretical contributions as the basis for vigorous intellectual debate and exchange on the left.

The peer-reviewed series publishes original monographs, translated texts, and reprints of classics across the bounds of academic disciplinary agendas and across the divisions of the left. The series is particularly concerned to encourage the internationalization of Marxist debate and aims to translate significant studies from beyond the English-speaking world.

For a full list of titles in the Historical Materialism Book Series available in paperback from Haymarket Books, visit: www.haymarketbooks.org/series_collections/1-historical-materialism.

State and Society in Eighteenth-Century France

A Study in Political Power and Popular Revolution in Languedoc

Revised and Updated Edition

Stephen Miller

Haymarket Books
Chicago, IL

First published in 2022 by Brill Academic Publishers, The Netherlands
© 2022 Koninklijke Brill NV, Leiden, The Netherlands

Published in paperback in 2023 by
Haymarket Books
P.O. Box 180165
Chicago, IL 60618
773-583-7884
www.haymarketbooks.org

ISBN: 978-1-64259-996-1

Distributed to the trade in the US through Consortium Book Sales and Distribution (www.cbsd.com) and internationally through Ingram Publisher Services International (www.ingramcontent.com).

This book was published with the generous support of Lannan Foundation, Wallace Action Fund, and the Marguerite Casey Foundation.

Special discounts are available for bulk purchases by organizations and institutions. Please call 773-583-7884 or email info@haymarketbooks.org for more information.

Cover art and design by David Mabb. Cover art is a detail from *Painting 30, Rhythm 69, (William Morris Block Printed Pattern Book, with Hans Richter Storyboard, developed from Richter's Rhythmus 25 and Kazimir Malevich's film script Artistic and Scientific Film – Painting and Architectural Concerns – Approaching the New Plastic Architectural System)*. Paint and wallpaper on canvas (2007).

Printed in the United States.

10 9 8 7 6 5 4 3 2 1

Library of Congress Cataloging-in-Publication data is available.

Contents

List of Figures and Tables   VII

Introduction   1

1 The Peasant Economy, Seigneurial Regime, and State   18

2 The Rewards of Royal Service   44

3 Crown and Nobility in a Time of Financial Difficulties: Royal Policy 1758–89   76

4 Revolutionary Politics 1788–91: Despotism and Equality   105

5 Popular Revolts, Political Authority and the Revolutionary Dynamic, 1789–93   130

6 Politics and Class, 1792–99: Radicalism, Terror, and Repression   161

Conclusion   188

Appendix   203
Bibliography   214
Index   242

Figures and Tables

Figures

1.1 Map of the jurisdiction of the Parlement of Toulouse   22
1.2 Map of the civil dioceses of Languedoc before 1789   23
2.1 Laurent-Nicolas de Joubert, son of Philippe-Laurent de Joubert. Artist: François-Xavier Fabre, a painter of monarchist sympathies, whose studies were funded by Philippe de Joubert. Fabre fled the Revolution to Italy in 1793. Getty Museum   61
2.2 La Promenade de Peyrou, Montpellier. Library of Congress   65
2.3 The arena, Nîmes, France. Library of Congress   66
4.1 Map of the departments of the former province of Languedoc   114
5.1 Dowries of the inhabitants of the Narbonnais and Corbières in the eighteenth century   135
5.2 Assertions of seigneurial rights by department in old regime Languedoc   155

Tables

1.1 Seigneurial levies in Languedoc   32
1.2 Judicial rulings favourable to seigneurs 1750–89   35
1.3 Rulings of the Parlement of Toulouse enforcing seigneurial rights   40
2.1 Gages of associations of office holders   45
2.2 Fees collected by associations of office holders   46
2.3 Average direct tax paid by inhabitants in diverse parts of Languedoc   54
2.4 Revenue distributed in conjunction with the annual meeting of the Estates of Languedoc   71
4.1 Municipal council of Toulouse, February 1790   118
4.2 Capitation of Albi, 1787   119
4.3 Capitation of Montpellier, 1789   125
6.1 Percentage of those arrested in the Gard in 1793 and the year II classified by social and professional group   179
6.2 Percentage of those executed in the Gard during the Terror classified by profession   180
6.3 Percentage of members of the municipal council of Montpellier classified by social and professional group   182
6.4 Percentage of members of the municipal council of Toulouse classified by social and professional group   183

A.1 Recipients of 5,347,859 *Livres* reimbursed by the Estates of Languedoc in 1786 for loans taken out for the king every year since 1775   204
A.2 Creditors of the diocese of Montpellier   206
A.3 Creditors of the diocese of Toulouse, 1787 and 1788   207
A.4 Classification of professions for five Languedocian villages   208
A.5 Peasant revolts in the departments of old regime Languedoc   210

Introduction

> The intermediate, subordinate and dependent powers constitute the nature of monarchical government; I mean of that in which a single person governs by fundamental laws. I said intermediate, subordinate and dependent powers. And, indeed, in monarchies the prince is the source of all power, political and civil. These fundamental laws necessarily suppose the intermediate channels through which the power flows: for if there be only the momentary and capricious will of a single person to govern the state, nothing can be fixed, and, of course, there is no fundamental law.
>
> The most natural, intermediate and subordinate power is that of the nobility. This in some measure seems to be essential to a monarchy, whose fundamental maxim is, no monarch, no nobility; no nobility, no monarch.
>
> MONTESQUIEU, *The Spirit of the Laws*[1]

∴

In stating that kings ruled through the nobility, Montesquieu identified the distinctive attribute of European monarchies. Hereditary nobility set them apart from the republics of antiquity and despotisms of the East. The nobles held positions in the 'intermediate, subordinate and dependent powers' and in this way 'constitute[d] the nature of monarchical government'. They held lordships over peasant villages, benefices in the upper echelons of the Church, venal offices in the high tribunals, and claims on revenue from the tax farms.

These intermediate powers permitted the nobility to take wealth from common subjects. They acquired fortunes 'by taking away a part of the citizenry's physical necessities'. The greater their wealth – 'from ... the wholesale merchant (*négociant*), to the nobles, magistrates, great seigneurs, principal financiers, to the princes' – the more they had to spend on luxury so as to restore to producers the means to survive.[2]

'HONOUR, that is, the prejudice of each person and each condition' is what prompted luxury spending. It was a certain grandeur or dignity of the soul,

---

1 Montesquieu 1949, vol. 1, pp. 15–16.
2 Montesquieu 1949, vol. 1, pp. 15–18, 53–4, 67–70, 163. Quotation vol. 1, p. 98.

which set the social and political forces of monarchical government in motion. Royal subjects were consumed by the ambition to distinguish themselves. Montesquieu argued that public honours increased in proximity to the king and all the riches of his court, and shone downward from this zenith of the state through the nobles to the people. The most honourable pursuit of the realm was to serve the king, particularly in war.[3]

Monarchical government required stable laws and written customs. An arbitrary and capricious ruler could publicly humiliate his subjects and compromise their honour. Accordingly, Montesquieu held that venality of office was a good practice in monarchies, because it made the orders and ranks of the state more permanent. Hereditary owners of offices could not be dismissed for refusing to comply with orders. They thus militated against ill-conceived policies emanating from the royal council. Venality, Montesquieu argued, made governmental tasks a family profession and built up a sense of commitment to official duties. Offices in the sovereign tribunals (the robe nobility of the judiciary) formed key parts of the intermediate powers, recording the properties, honours, ranks, origins, rules, and restrictions applying to each subject. The judges earned the admiration of their countrymen by looking after everyone's rights.[4]

The nobles not only used their positions in the monarchy to uphold their rights to economic resources, public honours and political careers. They also used these positions to uphold royal sovereignty. Kings were undoubtedly 'the source of all power'. Yet they did not exercise power all by themselves. Monarchical government required intermediate powers or 'chiefs', Montesquieu argued, to keep the people from taking things to extremes and to prevent the emergence of seditious elements, which might overthrow the king and instigate revolution. The sovereign tribunals had the confidence of the people, and in difficult times, could set them right, or reduce them to proper obedience.[5]

This book examines the foregoing 'fundamental maxim ... no monarch, no nobility; no nobility, no monarch'. It probes the relationship between the king at the apex of the state and 'the intermediate, subordinate and dependent powers', which imposed his policies on one of the principal provinces, Languedoc. The argument is that scholars must focus on this social configuration to understand the origin and unfolding of the French Revolution.

---

3 Montesquieu 1949, vol. 1, pp. 24–5, 29–32, 57, 115. Quotation vol. 1, p. 24.
4 Montesquieu 1949, vol. 1, pp. 15–18, 23–4, 25–6, 53–4, 55–7, 67–73.
5 Montesquieu 1949, vol. 1, pp. 15–18, 55–6. Louis Althusser called attention to these passages 1972, pp. 85–6.

My approach differs from the one classically adopted by Marxists. Practitioners of historical materialism have long been struck by the increase in industrial output on the order of about 60 percent over the course of the eighteenth century. The value of foreign trade grew from 215 million to 1,062 million livres from 1716 to 1784. Trade increased 300 percent with Europe and 1,000 percent with the colonies from 1716 to 1787.[6] The growth of commerce and industry increased the wealth of the bourgeoisie, expanded the ranks of liberal professionals and public employees, and thus supplied the social strata of readers, *philosophes* and economists responsible for the intellectual and ideological flowering of the Enlightenment. The French nation and bourgeoisie reached social maturity. French thought became conscious of its grandeur and sought to apply its methods of analysis and deduction to all reality, to society as well as to nature.[7]

In 1789, the bearers of this thought, the deputies of the National Assembly invented modern private property separate from the old regime feudal complement of jurisdictional rights and public power. They paved the way for the improvement of this property by facilitating the elimination of seigneurial dues and tithes, and thus gave farmers more freedom to develop agriculture. The establishment of uniform legal standards, a country-wide system of currency, weights and measures, and the removal of feudal obstacles to trade created a national market. Marx argued that the National Assembly enshrined security, or *police*, as the guiding principle of civil life. The Assembly instituted the reign of individual egoism by declaring that the purpose of society was the security of each member's person, rights and property.[8]

Henry Heller, currently the leading proponent of this Marxist view, argues that the bourgeoisie presided over a long process of primitive accumulation, or the expropriation of the rural population from the land. Rural workers of the 1700s could no longer live off their subsistence plots and therefore turned more and more to wage labour. In this way, within a system characterised by the extraction of surplus as rent characteristic of the old regime, profit played an increasingly large role in the economy. The bourgeoisie, which benefited from profit, gained more influence as a result.[9]

The problem with this argument is that, during the period of rising prices in the second half of the eighteenth century – when economic expansion supposedly heralded the rise of the bourgeoisie – primitive accumulation did not take place. Quite the contrary, every well-researched study of rural France

---

6 Soboul 1964, p. 45; Cheney 2010, p. 184; Beik 2009, p. 344.
7 Lefebvre 1988, pp. 1–2, 45, 47, 49, 217; Jaurès 2015, p. 13.
8 Wolfreys 2007, p. 61; Blaufarb 2016, pp. 2, 9–10; Marx 1844.
9 Heller 2006, pp. 4–5, 45–51.

reveals a variegated landholding pattern in which the majority of properties belonged to the peasantry while the majority of the land belonged to the townspeople (the nobility and bourgeoisie). Studies of property holdings from about 1730 or 1740 through the 1800s shows that the nobles lost ground, and the bourgeoisie found itself on the defensive, as peasants racked up debts to acquire land. In the 1780s, the extent of peasant property varied from one region to another and overall totalled 30 to 40 percent of the realm.[10]

According to Pierre Goubert, this spirited and able population of country dwellers produced the wealth of the kingdom. The peasants engaged in myriad economic activities. Specialisation was the dangerous exception, because grain fields were liable to failure. Peasants thus toiled as market gardeners, mixed farmer, vine-growers, day labourers, spinners and weavers, cloth workers, blacksmiths, nail-smiths and innkeepers, and usually poachers and smugglers as well. Their goal was to make a living, pay taxes, seigneurial dues and tithes, and in the best cases, enlarge their holdings and improve their social status. They rarely achieved all of these aims. But their efforts to do so explain both the relative strength of the economy (compared to the other monarchies of the European continent) and their tenacious hold on the land.[11]

Robert Brenner argues that the peasants' parcels of land – a legacy of their success in establishing heritable plots in struggles against the feudal lords during the Middle Ages – deterred productive investment in the economy. Peasants with insufficient land to provide for household subsistence, and thus prone to work harder and longer to obtain tenancies and employment, allowed well-to-do townspeople to secure a share of the national wealth in reliable payments from their property managers and sharecroppers. The mass of micro-proprietors seeking to supplement their income, no matter how poorly paid the work, inclined merchants to put manufacturing out to rural households. Landlords and merchants thus had no need to sink funds into labour-saving capital.[12]

They instead invested their wealth in annuities, seigneurial rights and venal offices. They purchased titles to enhance their rank within the monarchy. The

---

10 Béaur 1984, pp. 270, 336, 339; Tulippe 1934, pp. 110, 161–3, 241, 318–19; Berenson 1984, pp. 9–10, 18, 20, 22–3; Brennan 2006, pp. 183, 186, 189–90, 193, 197–8; Labrousse 1966, pp. 48–51; Bodinier, Teyssier and Antoine 2000, p. 368.
11 Goubert 1970, pp. 34, 46–8.
12 Brenner 1985, pp. 213–327; Brenner 2001, pp. 275–338; Baehrel 1961, pp. 770–1; Le Roy Ladurie 1966, pp. 1:638; Poitrineau 1979, pp. 154, 157–8, 174–5; Bloch 1931, pp. 155, 157, 167–8, 178; Merle 1958, pp. 63–4, 67–9, 71; Jacquart 1974, pp. 104–5, 107, 117, 130, 132, 213, 218, 220, 317, 623, 626, 636, 753–4, 756–8; Venard 1957, pp. 72–3, 83–6, 91, 117–18; Audisio 1993, pp. 68, 148; Larguier and Thirsk 1999, p. 64; Meuvret 1987, pp. 12, 29, 38, 117–18, 124, 150.

nobles used the seigneurial rights to take a second share (in addition to income from their property managers and sharecroppers) of the wealth produced by the peasantry. That is to say, the nobles enforced a slew of minor feudal exactions and rents such as their right to a percentage of the value of land sales (*lods et ventes*). Nobles received a third share of this wealth from the pensions, benefices, offices, governorships and other revenues bestowed by the king on his loyal servants and favourites from royal taxation of the rural population.

The bourgeoisie – consisting of officials seeking ennoblement, state pensioners (especially in Paris), and even some members of trades and manufacturers – took nearly as much revenue from the peasantry. They owned land, only less than most nobles. They also obtained wealth by making loans to the peasantry and by taking up positions as the nobles' property managers. Some of them gained revenue by granting the king the estimated returns from his seigneurial dues and taxes, and then recouping even larger sums from the peasantry.[13]

Little of this revenue returned to the countryside as investment. Successful merchants, landowners and dues collectors habitually purchased land, titles, annuities, seigneurial rights, and judicial offices in an effort to live a noble life of status and stability. The sons of jurists and merchants flooded the law schools after 1750 seeking the training for a career in the judiciary. The value of offices in certain tribunals stagnated or even declined in the eighteenth century. But, overall, the value of venal posts increased more rapidly than did the rate of inflation. The primary impetus for the increase came from the growing ranks of the bourgeoisie whose members purchased offices for profit, prestige, and power. On the eve of the Revolution, venal offices reached their highest prices in decades. The bourgeoisie clearly considered them the best investments in the realm. Offices granted many wealthy townspeople the same exemption as the nobles from the basic tax on commoners known as the *taille*.[14] For these reasons, in towns across France, nobles and venal judges enjoyed the largest fortunes, much larger than those of merchants and manufacturers. The wealth of the nobles and office holders grew relative to that of the commercial classes over the course of the eighteenth century.[15]

The argument of this book, then, is that old regime France did not follow a capitalist logic. There was no tendency toward capitalism's fundamental

---

13   Information in this paragraph and the preceding one is taken from Goubert 1970, pp. 46–8 and Beik 2009, p. 51.
14   Kagan 1975, pp. 38–73; Doyle 1996, pp. 213–14, 220, 222, 224, 226, 228–30, 232–6.
15   Chartier 1969, pp. 165, 172–4, 183; Garden 1970, pp. 190–1, 204, 388–91; Goubert 1959.

precondition, primitive accumulation, or the separation of labour from direct access to subsistence. The upper classes did not contract with abstract labour as a cost in their financial accounts, what Marx referred to as variable capital. To the contrary, the upper classes took wealth from the mostly rural masses. The peasants maintained their communities through toil, solidarity and resistance in the face of the exactions and regulations imposed by the dominant classes. Extra-economic coercion, personal dependence, and the combination of the immediate producer with the means of production remained common to the social relations enforced by the absolutist state, aptly described by Perry Anderson as a 'redeployed and recharged apparatus of feudal domination'.[16]

I therefore challenge not only the classic Marxist interpretation, but also more recent scholarship, opposed to class analysis, which posits the convergence of the bourgeoisie and nobility into a liberal elite. Historians currently argue that, among elites of all three estates, economic growth increased the social estimation of wealth, consumption, and merit and diminished concern for rank and lineage.[17] Yet if one examines the latest research on the salons, one sees that, far from facilitating a common sociability of wealthy and educated members of the nobility and bourgeoisie, they actually restricted participation to those graced with birth, wealth, talent or familiarity with the royal family. Invitees recognised the high nobles' mastery of social codes and customs. The nobility used the salons, like other facets of social and political life, to renew itself and perpetuate its dominance in keeping with changing times and in collaboration with the monarchy.[18]

Montesquieu wrote that 'Monarchy is destroyed when a prince thinks he shows a greater exertion of power in changing than in conforming to the order of things; when he deprives some of his subjects of their hereditary employments to bestow them arbitrarily upon others'.[19] The kings of France repeatedly displayed this destructive propensity when they sold new offices and privileges to raise revenue needed for war. Such policies deprived the traditional incumbents of their jurisdictions and cheapened the rights of established elites. Nobles engaged in conflicts and rivalries to preserve or enhance their privileges relative to one another. Many provincial nobles, some of whom could even be considered poor, no doubt thought they witnessed the destruction of the mon-

---

16 Anderson 1979, pp. 17–20. On the solidarity and resistance of the peasants see Nicolas 2002, pp. 76–7; Kwass 2014, pp. 118–20.
17 Richet 1991, pp. 389–410; Richet 1974, pp. 49–72; Chaussinand-Nogaret 1985; Marraud 2000.
18 Lilti 2005, pp. 81, 236; Beik 2009, pp. 73–4.
19 Montesquieu 1949, vol. 1, p. 113.

archy when they beheld the triumphant display of wealth and power among the courtiers in Versailles.[20]

Yet these conflicts and rivalries are best regarded as the unavoidable expressions of a society of orders and privileges regulated by an absolute monarch. Had the nobles ever united to stabilise the system at the expense of the king, they would have become the focus of the people's attention. Needless to say, they never dreamed of doing so. Their authority had been gravely shaken by the disappearance of serfdom during the twelfth and thirteenth centuries, and then again by the civil wars and rebellions of the sixteenth and seventeenth centuries. Yet, thanks to Louis XIV's absolutist state, the nobles benefited from internal peace and stability relative to the previous century. The reigns of Louis XV and XVI came closer than any previous ones to 'conforming to the order of things', and preserving the nobles' 'hereditary employments'. As William Beik argued, 'after a long evolution involving changing relationships to peasant production, the social reputation which assured domination was guaranteed by seigneurial authority, *plus* economic advantage, *plus* privileged status guaranteed by the crown'.[21]

But the crown's capacity to uphold this social configuration collapsed in 1788 and 1789. In the midst of this crisis, well-to-do townspeople, or the bourgeoisie, attacked the nobility. These urban residents were not the organic intellectuals of a new capitalist mode of production. Antonio Gramsci defined capitalism's organic intellectuals as the deputies or specialised employees – industrial technicians, professional economists, organisers of a new culture and legal system – of the wealthy persons who used money to invest in trade and industry for profit. The intellectuals created the conditions favourable to capitalist accumulation. They gave the capitalists an awareness of common interests. When

---

20   Beik 1985, pp. 98, 158, 177, 219, 257, 332; Jouanna 1989, pp. 12, 62, 114, 116, 267–8, 270; Moote 1971, pp. 54, 118, 159, especially Chapter 4. Blaufarb 2002, pp. 19–20, 33, 38, 42, 44; Mousnier 1979, vol. 1, pp. 121–2, 139–40, 668; Smith 1996, pp. 7–8, 86, 91, 264; Bien 1987, pp. 89–114; Bien 1978, pp. 153–86; Durand 1971, pp. 73, 81, 138, 140–1, 163–4; Goubert and Roche 1984, p. 243; Krause 1999, pp. 469–99; Bonney 1978, pp. 53, 61–4, 224 ff.; Descimon and Jouhaud 1996, pp. 154–5, 159, 173; Hurt 2002, pp. 12, 116, 189; Anderson 1979, pp. 31–3.

21   Beik 1985, p. 335. See also Beik 2009, pp. 4, 51, 63, 73, 135, 138, 161, 332, 356; Mettam 1988, pp. 55–65, 81–101; Parker 1980, pp. 186–7, especially chapter 4; Parker 2003, pp. 91–2; Kettering 1978, pp. 41, 57, 59–71, 213, 220, 330, 336; Kettering 1986, pp. 16, 149, 152, 157, 204–6; Swann 2003, pp. 13, 15–16, 24, 301–2, 322–3, 409; Dessert 1984, pp. 46, 60, 63, 316, 321, 332, 335, 341, 367; Collins 1988, p. 146; Potter 2003, p. 132. Hamscher 1976; Bergin 1985; Lüthy 1998, pp. 2:9–10, 15, 17–18, 23; Campbell 1996, pp. 297–9, 306; Félix 1999, pp. 34–5, 304, 498–9; Bossenga 2003, p. 133; Bossenga 2006, pp. 58–9; Bossenga 2011, pp. 48, 66.

one carefully examines the leaders of 1789, it is clear that one can appropriately classify them, not as capitalism's organic intellectuals, but as ones formed by absolute monarchy. They comprised parish priests, venal jurists, administrators, scholars, and scientists who had pursued careers within the traditions of the old regime.[22]

One can understand this paradox – of intellectuals groomed by the monarchy, who nonetheless turned against its ruling class – by considering one of the differences between capitalist and feudal societies discerned by Gramsci. Under capitalism, the intellectuals have revolutionised the conception of law and function of the state by fashioning a will to conform. Previous ruling classes were conservative in the sense that they did not elaborate a passage from the other classes into their own. Wealthy merchants, to be sure, could purchase the properties and titles required to qualify for the nobility. But they did so with the purpose of joining a closed caste. No one thought the nobles would technically and ideologically expand the parameters of the ruling class. The capitalist bourgeoisie, in contrast, poses itself as an organism in perpetual movement, bringing the entire society up to its cultural and economic level. Capitalism's organic intellectuals inculcate this idea of economic mobility and the non-existence of classes.[23]

François Quesnay and fellow members of the school of economic thought known as Physiocracy hoped to create a capitalist economy. They saw the absolutist state as a legal despotism capable of taking all the fragmented provincial estates, autonomous associations and privileged groups in hand, and forging and sustaining a new economy like the agrarian capitalism they observed in England. Indeed, the prominent Marxist historian Neil Davidson argues that the leaders of the French Revolution hoped to exploit peasants and artisans in new capitalist ways hitherto precluded by the old regime. They therefore used their power at the head of the National Assembly to fully establish a capitalist social and political order.[24]

Yet Physiocracy had little purchase among the deputies of the National Assembly.[25] Diderot articulated this widespread scepticism in his *Observations* for Catherine the Great, who requested his comments on her instructions for a commission named by her to write a law code for Russia. Diderot rejected the physiocrats' economic philosophy. They planned for the producers to reinvest

---

22   Gramsci 1971, pp. 5–7.
23   Gramsci 1971, p. 260. This point about the capitalist bourgeoisie has been made more recently by Johnson 2015, p. 6.
24   Davidson 2012, p. 424. On the physiocrats, see Meiksins Wood 2012, p. 26.
25   Hindie Lemay 1983, p. 286.

surpluses with the purpose of augmenting the total value of goods produced in the kingdom.

> This variety of philosophy tends to hold man in a sort of moronic state, and in a mediocrity of enjoyment and happiness quite contrary to his nature; and all philosophy contrary to human nature is absurd, as well as all legislation in which the citizen is continually forced to sacrifice his taste and his happiness for the good of society. I want society to be happy; but also want to be happy; and there are as many manners of being happy as there are individuals. Our individual happiness is the basis of all our true duties.[26]

Diderot, in this way, spurned the ascetic morality promoted by the physiocrats. He rejected the rational discipline of capitalism. Nowhere does Diderot suggest that wealth should be forced back into farms and manufactures for the purpose of improving production, cutting costs and matching the competitive prices of other investors obliged to do the same for the survival of their enterprises. One does not find in Diderot's work, nor in any other of eighteenth-century France apart from Physiocracy, the assumption common to English writings about the productive use of wealth to impart monetary value to the land.[27] On the contrary, Diderot questioned, in the *Observations*, how

> a society could be happy and radiant? If liberty and property are assured, would it not be permitted to a citizen to employ his wealth according to his taste? Why does one become rich? Is it to be rich? It is to be happy. How is one happy? Is it not through pleasures? What are pleasures? Some are relative to the soul, others to the senses. Why therefore shouldn't I be permitted to employ my superfluous wealth to all of these sorts of needs? Then there would be temples, squares, statues, paintings, tissues of gold … according to whether the rich man will have or will lack good taste …
> Let's see what this rich man, who does not return his surplus directly to the land, does. He makes his nation recommendable to visitors.[28]

---

26 Diderot 1971, p. 123.
27 Weber 1927, pp. 355–6, 366–7. For the physiocratic writings of Turgot and Dupont de Nemours on productive expenditures conducive to development as opposed to extravagant spending see Gustave Schelle 1913–23, pp. 3: 581–6.
28 Diderot 1971, p. 122.

To Diderot, liberty and property meant the pleasurable enjoyment of wealth in ways common to the old regime, which the English gentry found reckless. He conceived of money as use-value. One can only have so many paintings and statues. For capitalists, in contrast, the accumulation of money is an end in itself. Investors seek, and can conceivably obtain, boundless sums of money. Today, billionaires accumulate additional millions every year. This accumulation of unlimited social power constitutes an essential feature of capitalism foreign to Diderot and his French contemporaries. Diderot thought that wealth should go into public edifices, clothes and other things pleasing to the senses and tastes. He did not envision the capitalist use of wealth to procure labour, improve the land, and make it valuable. For Diderot, property and liberty facilitated conspicuous consumption rather than investment to increase labour productivity and make more money.[29]

As Davidson points out, the abbot Emmanuel Joseph Sieyès stated in a speech to the National Assembly in September 1789 that political systems are founded exclusively on labour. Sieyès called men labouring machines. But he did not regard labour as a variable component of capital. Rather, Sieyès argued that the greater the productive activity of the masses, the greater the liberty of the beneficiaries. Labour permitted them to enjoy wealth in the manner indicated by Diderot. Sieyès's triumph was to convince the old regime bourgeoisie of well-to-do officials, merchants, lawyers, professionals, rentiers, men of letters and landowners that they were unjustly deprived of this liberty. He told them that they were the real leaders of the nation but had suffered countless petty humiliations at the hands of the aristocracy. Sieyès harnessed the energies of the bourgeoisie to abolish privileges and lay the groundwork for a constitutional order based on civic equality, a social revolution establishing national sovereignty.[30]

Georges Lefebvre showed, in his classic Marxist book on the origins of the French Revolution, why Sieyès's arguments had such success. The book contains a haphazard analysis of bourgeois wealth but a systematic analysis of bourgeois politics. Lefebvre argued that members of the bourgeoisie owned offices, pursued careers within the customary hierarchy, and valued the established order. The programme of the aristocracy in favour of freedom of expression and the rule of law would have benefited the entire nation. 'It has ... often been thought surprising that [the bourgeoisie], whose spirit' was bound up with 'the social hierarchy' of the time, 'should have been so imprudent ... in attacking the aristocracy'.

---

29   Meiksins Wood 2012, pp. 274–5, 308; Weber 1927, p. 366; Harvey 2010, p. 73.
30   Sewell 1994, pp. 185–6; Davidson 2012, p. 63.

Yet with the convocation of the Estates General for 1789, when the established order was manifestly up for renegotiation, the Third Estate discerned what Gramsci later did in the 1930s, that the ruling class ideologically and technically limited social mobility. Had the Third Estate demanded no more than the programme of the aristocracy, it would have accepted a subordinate place in the state, because the nobility sought to control all estates, both general and provincial. Since at best only a small number of wealthy commoners could become nobles, the rest began to hate what they envied without hope of joining.[31] In this way, the Revolution emerged out of irreconcilable social and economic conflicts. Yet it did not herald the advent of the capitalist class.[32]

In laying out this argument, I first trace the growth of the economy in eighteenth-century Languedoc. The peasants cleared new lands for cultivation and introduced new crops such as maize, vines, potatoes, chestnut and mulberry trees. They farmed grain for the market and manufactured textiles for consumers in foreign lands. This growth mostly benefited the noble and bourgeois property owners in the towns. One of the keys to the economic well-being of landed elites was keeping exact records of their scattered holdings and collecting all of the rents owed to them. Much of their profit came automatically when producers bid up the rents and prices of land.

Chapter 1 shows that in addition to acquiring revenue in this purely economic way, the landed elite also made use of seigneurial rights and local tribunals to collect dues, limit use-rights on their fields, and obtain revenue from land clearances. Seigneurs used the judiciary to monopolise forest products, obtain advantages during the grape harvests, and uphold the free commerce of grain even in times of dearth. Chapter 2 provides a detailed analysis of the ways in which the tax farms and estates of Languedoc channelled another portion of the wealth produced by the peasantry into the private fortunes of nobles, merchants, clergymen and office holders.

Another trend of the eighteenth century was the hardening financial deadlock facing the crown. France's imperial rival had far more resources at its disposal. The gentry landowners of England obtained nearly all of their wealth from yeoman tenant farmers who systematically invested in agricultural improvements. English merchants systematically invested in manufacturing enterprises. Gentry legislators created uniform taxes applicable to all proprietors, including themselves, because, after consolidating their power in the Glorious Revolution of 1688, they knew that the state would pursue their interests as

---

31 Lefebvre 1988, pp. 34–5. The quotation is located on p. 47.
32 Wolfreys 2007, p. 54. My foregoing analysis closely follows the one offered by Comninel 1987, pp. 196–205.

determined through deliberations in Parliament. They thus succeeded in raising taxes without damaging the economy or provoking constitutional crises. Economic development and coherent fiscal laws gave the rulers of England the means to extend their domination over much of the globe.[33]

To meet this challenge, French kings developed the state apparatus. They appointed hundreds of agents to administer the collection of taxes and auctioned off excises to associations comprising thousands of officials. Yet the monarchy still did not raise enough revenue to accomplish its goals. It devoted virtually the entire budget to the military yet lost nearly every war of the eighteenth century.[34]

Previously, Louis XIV had succeeded in aggrandising the realm and holding all of the European powers at bay by utilising traditional, even feudal means of raising revenue. He sold portions of the government, invented tax farms, borrowed from venal officers and provincial estates, and sold and repossessed the royal domains.[35] In the eighteenth century, these traditional means of raising revenue covered less and less of the escalating costs of war. The king and his ministers had to reform the two traditional defects of the financial system. For the short-term loans needed to finance military expenses, the monarchy relied on tax farmers, receivers and treasurers, who reaped profits from fiscal receipts and had powerful allies in the royal court. For its main fiscal stream of revenue, the monarchy taxed the social strata least able to pay. Nobles, ecclesiastics, and many wealthy commoners were exempt from the bulk of the direct taxes.[36]

Political culture and language also developed. Scholarship of the 1980s and 1990s focused on the new beliefs, sensibilities and words that became familiar to the educated classes in the second half of the eighteenth century. Writers appealed to the public as the rational judge of their arguments. Even the king and his ministers sought to claim the mantle of public opinion.[37] They

---

33 Brenner 2003, pp. 649–52, 709–16; Teschke 2003, pp. 252–62; Coleman 1977, pp. 91–172; Horwitz 1977, pp. 311–15; Chandaman 1975, pp. 279–80; Mathias and O'Brien 1976, pp. 601–50; Brewer 1989, pp. 32, 40, 64–87, 89, 95, 129, 257.

34 Kwass 2000, pp. 56–7; Doyle 1996, pp. 71, 99–100; Le Goff 1999, pp. 97, 103; Bosher 1970, pp. 172–3, 175, 178, 190, 280, 303–5, 312; Félix 1999, pp. 40, 43, 298–301, 304, 404–5, 466, 498–9; Stone 1994, pp. 9, 19, 100–2, 158, 160; Skocpol 1979, pp. 48–9, 61.

35 Potter 2000, pp. 599–626; Beik 1985, pp. 38, 137, 160–1, 193, 202, 204, 255, 308, 329; Doyle 1996, pp. 26–57; Parker 2003, pp. 60–96. For an analysis of Louis XIV's absolutism as the stabilisation of noble class rule see Parker 1996, pp. 4, 26–7, 277–8 and Anderson 1979, p. 108.

36 Doyle 1996, pp. 71, 99–100; Le Goff 1999, pp. 97, 103; Bosher 1970, pp. 172–3, 175, 178, 190, 280, 303–5, 312; Félix 1999, pp. 40, 43, 298–301, 304, 404–5, 466, 498–9; Stone 1994, pp. 9, 19, 100–2, 158, 160; Skocpol 1979, pp. 48–9, 61.

37 Van Kley 1984; Baker 1990; Chartier 1991.

imbued royal edicts with universal, standardising language inimical to traditional privileges, seigneurial rights, and venal offices. The physiocrats, for example, affirmed that tax collection would proceed smoothly if landowners obtained a stake in the regime. They proposed a uniform system of assemblies for landowners to administer the tax burden. The physiocrats' publications earned them influence in the highest spheres of government. We will see in Chapter 3 that, in Languedoc, the crown took timid yet unmistakable steps to involve talented commoners in the administration of the countryside, expand the social bases of municipal councils, and reduce fiscal privileges.[38]

Similarly, the nobles perceived such policies through an ideological prism absent from previous centuries. Local magnates, office holders, and seigneurs had resisted the efforts of the king, grandees, and financiers to control the political and economic resources of the country in the civil wars and revolts of the first half of the seventeenth century. These conflicts shattered public order and rent the social fabric of the kingdom. But no innovatory conceptions of sovereignty ever emerged. Nobles ultimately sorted out their respective rights and reconstituted absolutism in a more authoritarian guise.[39]

We will see in Chapters 3 and 4 that the crown again became embroiled in conflicts over the economic interests and public standing of local lords and magistrates in the second half of the eighteenth century. The nobles of Languedoc reacted in similar fashion, protesting against affronts to the honour of the established authorities. Yet the nobles' protests also contained innovative themes absent from former époques. Whereas the most honourable virtue remained service to the king, especially on the battlefield, one also perceives the budding notion of virtuous service to the nation.[40] In the last decades of the old regime, the nobles felt a complex mélange of grievances. Royal policy insulted their honour as the official conduits of the sovereign authority, as it simultaneously closed off honourable channels for serving the public.

The second argument of this book, then, is that the political culture of the period reveals a great deal about the origins of the Revolution but fails to explain why the upper classes actually used ideologies and discourses against the crown. To explain the actual confrontation between cultural currents and absolute monarchy, one must consider the social relations of the period,

---

38 Schelle 1888, pp. 102–3, 108, 119–20, 190–1, 259, 263; Harris 1979, pp. 81, 103; Kwass 2000, pp. 242, 256, 265–6; Félix 1999, pp. 208–9, 231–7, 290–1, 498; Doyle 1996, 103, 107–8.
39 Anderson 1979, pp. 78, 81, 154, 170; Jouanna 1989, pp. 9, 12, 60, 114, 395–6.
40 Shovlin 2003, pp. 224–30; Shovlin 2000, pp. 35–66; Smith 2005, pp. 15–16, 50, 101, 155, 216, 231–2, 263.

namely the reliance of the upper classes on the crown for their authority, honour, and wealth, and the king's reliance on the upper classes to maintain order.

Chapters 3 and 4 show that in the last decades of the old regime, the king and his ministers, as well as a handful of Languedocian potentates, sought to raise more revenue for the state by involving well-to-do townspeople and villagers in local government. To most nobles of Languedoc, such policies represented a threat to their vital interests. They protested against each one of these policies before declaring open revolt in 1788 and 1789. Nobles orchestrated a broad campaign, mobilising all ranks of Languedocian society, against royal ministers and their allies in the province. Pamphlets and public meetings called for representative institutions to put an end to the irresponsible management of state finances. One cannot account for the revolutionary inflection of this campaign without considering the political culture of the time. But by the same token, the tangible confrontation of this culture with monarchical authority only occurred when royal policy imperilled the social standing of the elite.

The second half of this book takes up the bearing of the social relations of the old regime on the course of the Revolution. Since the 1970s, scholars have paid less attention to the social relations of the old regime in their analyses of the conflicts of the 1790s. Instead, one of the more influential theories attributes the conflicts to ideology and language, which rushed into the political void left by the monarchy when the financial crisis obliged it to convoke the Estates General in 1788. Revolutionary militants affirmed the people's will for an abstract ideal order of equality. They had a Manichean ideology, which interpreted events as conflicts pitting the people's natural goodness against the evil intentions of the privileged orders. The effort to impose this ideological construct on an imperfect world led to gratuitous violence and terror inflicted on enemies of the revolutionaries' own making.[41]

Revolutions, by their very nature, are unique historical circumstances in which power is up for grabs. Contending parties use language to mobilise partisans and tip the balance of power in their favour. Yet it is also true that the social relations of the old regime – namely the wealth, honour, and authority enjoyed by the elites through their privileged relationship to the monarchy – shaped people's reception of political arguments.

After all, historians generally agree that the peasant uprisings of the first years of the Revolution arose out of the economic conditions and seigneurial burdens of the old regime. The peasants did not regard lordly rights as legitim-

---

41   Furet 1981, pp. 22, 24–7, 33–5, 48, 50–1, 54, 63, 73–4; Gauchet 1989; Furet and Halévi 1996, pp. 10–11; Gueniffey 2000.

ate and became particularly reluctant to tolerate them in the difficult economic circumstances of the time. They capitalised on the disarray of the authorities in the turbulent years from 1789 through 1792 to put the seigneurial regime definitively to rest.[42]

Chapters 4 and 5 place the popular movement within its economic and political context. A particular mode of economic growth – one which hardly improved the peasants' lot and actually made them dependent on precarious markets – bred anxiety about high prices, seigneurial dues, and fiscal exactions. When royal authority crumbled in 1788 and 1789, the peasants stopped shipments and seized stores of grain, destroyed fiscal offices and refused to pay taxes. These fiscal revolts gave the revolutionary leaders more cause for alarm than did the invasion of châteaux or the destruction of seigneurial titles. In fact, while the Revolution ostensibly involved a conflict pitting well-to-do commoners against nobles, these chapters show that popular uprisings actually created a context favourable to agreement among them. Apart from a handful of barons and bishops of the provincial estates, the upper classes of Languedoc rallied to the defence of the legally constituted government in the capital. Anxiety about unrest led wealthy merchants, jurists, proprietors, and priests to entrust the leadership of political affairs to former nobles with governmental experience in the military and tribunals of the old regime. Nobles, moreover, had defended the common interests in 1788 and 1789 by leading a movement for representative provincial estates. They thus won free elections to national guards and local administrations in 1789 and 1790.

Chapters 4 and 5 explain why this ruling-class unity came undone. The institutional divisions of the old regime eventually set nobles against one another in their reaction to the changes instituted by the Constituent Assembly from 1789 to 1791. While nobles had held positions of authority in all parts of the

---

42 Furet holds that the peasant revolts are not revelatory of the burdens of the old regime but rather of a vast socio-cultural integration of a society dislocated by the expansion of royal authority and the resultant breakdown of the traditional orders. The nobles accentuated the outward signs of rank and precedence to compensate for the loss of real power to the crown. The frustrations of the peasantry, faced with economic difficulties in the second half of the eighteenth century, found an outlet against the symbols of noble snobbishness. Furet 1981, pp. 97, 99, 103. Based on his analysis of the reports of local administrators in 1789 and the actual damage inflicted upon the châteaux of Burgundy, Hilton Root concludes that the peasant revolts never took place at all (1989, pp. 88–102). See also Jones 1989, pp. 106–110. The research presented by Furet and Root pales in comparison to the voluminous research documenting peasant revolts against the seigneurial regime. This research is encapsulated in the works of Lefebvre 1988, pp. 131–51; Lefebvre 1963, pp. 197–238, 279–306, 338–67; Lefebvre 1982, pp. 7–13, 34–46; Jones 1988; Ado 1996; Markoff 1996.

province during the old regime, many of them had had to yield to superiors within the monarchy's hierarchy of precedence and power. In 1789, some of them perceived opportunities within a regime based on civic equality and willingly abandoned their privileges. Yet the monarchy also fashioned an irreducible core of nobles and clergymen reluctant to relinquish their privileged relationship to power. Royalists of Toulouse, Nîmes, and the southern Massif central preferred to oppose the Revolution than to share the political stage with Protestants, merchants, jurists, and landowners of the third estate.

Chapters 4 and 6 show that these nobles and clergymen spread anxiety about a possible return of the old regime. This anxiety intensified amid rampant inflation and war with foreign monarchies in 1792 and 1793. Well-to-do residents of the departments into which the National Assembly divided Languedoc feared that bold measures to defend the Revolution, such as requisitioning grain, controlling prices, arming the populace and broadening participation in government, would undermine property and hierarchy. Master craftsmen, shopkeepers, merchants, farmers, and workers saw this reluctance to defend the Republic as sympathy for the old regime. They believed that the authorities preferred to see royalists triumph and spiralling prices to ruin their livelihood than to extend political participation beyond the upper classes. In 1793 and 1794, when the Convention entrusted local government to militants willing to confront the dangers to the Revolution, some of them used their power to punish former nobles, priests, well-to-do townspeople, and anyone else suspected of opposing democratic rights of participation.

One cannot fully explain this militancy without considering the old regime. Montesquieu believed that honour was the prevailing value prompting individuals to serve the king. Monarchical government 'presupposes ... pre-eminences, ranks, and even hereditary nobility. The nature of *honour* is to aspire to preferments and distinguishing titles; it is therefore properly placed within the government'. He argued that the genius of monarchy was to induce people to perform difficult tasks of state solely for the éclat. For royal officials, 'an action performed without noise is to some extent without consequence'.[43] The nobles' high regard for their official duties led them to uphold the law and defend the liberty of royal subjects from abuses of power. Montesquieu believed that the nobility thus encouraged the rest of the body politic to strive for excellence.

What Montesquieu did not understand was that common subjects regarded the nobles' pre-eminences, ranks, preferments and titles as burdens. In 1789,

---

43   Montesquieu 1949, vol. 1, pp. 23–5.

when leaders of the third estate perceived that the monarchy could no longer defend the nobles' privileges, they determined to extend the opportunity of public service to broader strata of the elite. Some commoners resented the loud assertions of honour characteristic of the old regime and sought to cast them out of the body politic for good. But to understand these revolutionary impulses, we must first look more closely at the distribution of provincial wealth, honour, and authority prior to 1789.

CHAPTER 1

The Peasant Economy, Seigneurial Regime, and State

In 1781, the king's principal agent in Languedoc, an appointed revocable commissioner, known as the intendant, received a report about a series of legal disputes in the diocese of Carcassonne. The litigation began in 1776 when the seneschal court of Carcassonne and the Parlement of Toulouse ruled that the *consuls* (the title of village leaders in Languedoc) of Aragon violated the right of Jean-Marie de Bancalis de Maurel to open the grape harvest and have his grapes harvested before anyone else did. The courts dismissed the consuls' argument that the inhabitants went ahead with the harvest only after Maurel's steward and the steward's friends began gathering their grapes without having given the official notice. A few years later, the noble magistrates of the Cour des Comptes, Aides et Finances of Montpellier granted Maurel's request that the tax rolls of Aragon be invalidated, because the consuls included a herd from his land (*métairie*). The court ignored the consuls' claim that the herd grazed on scrubland (*garrigues*) for which the community paid seigneurial dues.

Maurel secured a judgement in 1780 allowing him to collect fees from the revenue of local limekilns. These fees diminished the income villagers customarily gained by selling scrap wood to the operators of the limekilns. Another ruling forced two inhabitants to pay Maurel a fine for taking their grain to a mill outside of the village and thus evading his monopoly right, known as *banalité*, to have all of the grain of Aragon ground for a fee in his mill. In 1781, Maurel had the provincial commander send a detachment of soldiers to detain three inhabitants for cutting timber in his woods and attacking his guards. He even granted the use of his scrubland to another community offering to pay higher rent than would Aragon. The consuls complained about all of these incidents to the royal council. In the days before the intendant's local agent, known as the subdelegate, held a hearing, Maurel reversed the ranking of the consuls to punish their insubordination.[1]

These events are representative of a trend. Generations of historians have shown that seigneurs garnered additional revenue from their lands and per-

---

1 Archives Départementales de l'Hérault (hereafter ADH) C959.

quisites in the second half of the eighteenth century. This chapter highlights two aspects of the trend that have not received much attention. First, the lords' efforts to increase their incomes had the support of state institutions, particularly the judiciary. Maurel repeatedly enlisted the local courts to enforce levies and to establish his authority. The judges of these courts undoubtedly had high regard for the responsibilities and traditions of the magistracy. But many of them owned seigneuries and assumed that their prerogatives formed integral parts of the legal order. Second, the lords' economic behaviour remained within a traditional mould of institutions and attitudes. Maurel sought not only to amass revenue but also to see village leaders show respect for his seigneurial authority. The legal statutes of the eighteenth century had roots in the Middle Ages and were laden with provisions for seigneurial authority and honorific displays. Royal institutions and laws anchored the country to its feudal past.

In making these two points, this chapter begins with an analysis of the production of wealth in eighteenth-century Languedoc. Landlords took advantage of the inflation of agricultural prices by sponsoring the clearance of new lands for agriculture and the removal of restrictions from the grain trade. Yet they did not invest in their landholdings, accumulate farm animals and capital, or enhance the productivity of labour on their properties. Landlords obtained most of their income from sharecropping agreements. As the peasantry's toil and ingenuity generated economic growth after the 1730s and 1740s, the seigneurs imposed burdens to enhance their share of the output. Merchants played a similar role in the economic expansion by extending networks of textile manufacturing into the countryside. Cottage industry in rural communities provided the merchants with cloths for international markets. Yet the merchants did not gather manufactures together into productive enterprises. The upper classes left economic activity to peasant smallholders, sharecroppers, artisans, and labourers.

We will see in the second part of this chapter that landlords did not benefit from the rising prices and output solely by dint of their property. They also used their privileged relationship to the state. The local judiciary gave the lords advantages during the grape harvests and permitted them to monopolise common lands and woods. The lords obtained verdicts from the judiciary to eliminate use rights on their fields, exempt their lands from taxation, and impose seigneurial dues on peasant communities. The final part is a study of the cultural context. Nobles were the wealthiest members of a society steeped in feudal tradition. They used their influence with the authorities to obtain seigneurial prerogatives and honours consonant with their economic gains.

1   Landowners, Market Opportunities, and Relations of Production

Georges Lefebvre pioneered the study of the social and economic context of the Revolution. One of his most influential discoveries was that nobles secured additional revenue from their landholdings and seigneurial rights in the second half of the eighteenth century. Making use of the most up-to-date research on prices and wages, Lefebvre wrote that population growth outpaced production and caused food prices to rise. Lords, tithe collectors, and other large landowners profited from the rising value of their levies in good and bad years alike, for if bad harvests reduced the volume, they also increased the value. Seigneurs espoused physiocratic doctrines favourable to economic liberalism not only out of principle, Lefebvre suggested, but also because these doctrines cast in a favourable light their efforts to raise rents and end communal rights on their fields and woods. The measures taken in the name of Physiocracy formed part of a seigneurial reaction in which proprietors rigorously enforced rights inherited from the feudal past to take advantage of rising prices.[2]

Scholarly research on the eighteenth-century countryside has borne out many of Lefebvre's findings. In northern Burgundy, liberal economic doctrines influenced lords to rent their seigneuries to a single tenant capable of augmenting production and paying high rent. Burgundian seigneurs extended their landholdings by purchasing peasant parcels and applying the right of *retrait féodal*, which gave them first option to buy land sold within their jurisdictions. They updated the titles detailing their rights so as to benefit from those collected irregularly or incompletely in the past. The lords treated woods and marginal lands more economically by renting them or selling their products for profit. Burgundian lords made use of the royal judiciary to maintain the vitality of their seigneurial courts. They saw their right to administer justice as the soul of seigneurie and a rampart against the potential challenges of disgruntled commoners.[3]

At the end of the old regime, the model seigneurie of the countryside around Bordeaux was a vineyard on the reserve farmed under the lords' management. Seigneurial dues brought in a little more than 11 percent of the lords' landed revenue and sometimes quite a bit more when the lords updated their titles after as many as 29 years of neglect and collected all of the arrears. Tithes amounted to nearly double the sums collected in seigneurial dues. The

---

2   Lefebvre 1963, pp. 225, 227, 232, 350–1; Labrousse 1933, pp. 108–9, 306, 362, 393, 439–40, 493, 599.
3   Saint Jacob 1960, pp. 407, 413–14, 425, 435, 447, 501–2, 569, 572.

seigneurial classes secured most of their revenue, however, by paying a steward to carefully manage their vineyards. The nobles of Bordeaux purchased parcels of land and aggrandised their holdings to gain as much revenue as possible from the expanding market for wine. They took advantage of the exclusive right of urban residents to bring wine into Bordeaux tax-free, the right of first option to buy lands sold within their domains, the right to fees from seigneurial courts, and the right to take possession of uncultivated common lands within their jurisdictions. The nobles saw their seigneurial rights as means of maintaining hierarchy and securing deference from the peasantry. The seigneurial regime framed the lives of the inhabitants of the Bordelais down to the end of the old regime.[4]

Landowners of Languedoc responded to market opportunities like their counterparts in other regions of France. The Canal du Midi, linking the Atlantic Ocean to the Mediterranean Sea, provided the proprietors of upper Languedoc with access to lucrative markets in lower Languedoc, neighbouring provinces, French colonies, and Spain. The price of wheat rose 42 percent in Toulouse, a grain depot along the canal in upper Languedoc, as opposed to 21 percent nationally between 1758–70 and 1771–89. The price of wood rose between 300 and 700 percent in the Sault region of upper Languedoc between the 1730s and the 1770s. The noble judges of the Parlement of Toulouse owned much property in upper Languedoc. They also had the second largest legal jurisdiction of the realm. They used their influence to lead the local landowners in a campaign to implement physiocratic doctrines on free trade. The magistrates repeatedly came into conflict with officials in Versailles over the legality of grain exports in times of high prices and potential shortages. In 1784, the Parlement defied the orders of the king's principal minister, the controller general Calonne, to impose restrictions on the grain trade. Its ruling declared that free trade was part of natural law and the sacred right of property, and was essential to Languedoc's economy and tax-paying capacity.[5]

---

4 Aubin 1989, pp. 180, 186–7, 267–70, 288, 291, 381, 388, 394, 396, 400–1, 445–7, 449; Figeac 1996, vol. 1, pp. 90–1, 93, 106, 120–1, 126.
5 Archives Départementales de la Haute Garonne (ADHG) B 1832. Frêche 1974, p. 692; Fruhauf 1980, pp. 166–7. ADH C2919 contains the administrative correspondence about grain exports.

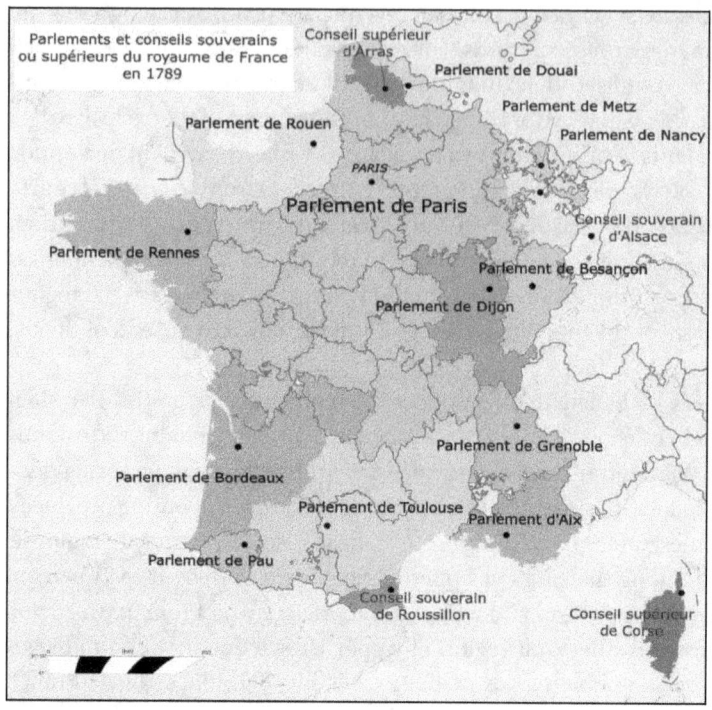

FIGURE 1.1   Map of the jurisdiction of the Parlement of Toulouse

The rising price of grain encouraged the seigneurs of upper Languedoc to purchase parcels of land belonging to peasants. The seigneurs enforced the right of *retrait féodal* to buy land sold within their seigneuries and found pretexts to foreclose on peasant tenures when poor harvests led sharecroppers to borrow money, grain, and seed, and sink into debt. They made use of the royal edict of 1766 (applied to Languedoc in 1770) granting a 15-year exemption from taxes and tithes for land cultivated for the first time in 40 years. Royal policymakers believed the edict would increase incomes, facilitate tax payment, and augment taxable revenue over the long term. The dioceses with a burgeoning population of peasant smallholders, extensive viticulture, and cottage textile production such as Uzès, Narbonne, and Montpellier saw the most land clearances. But in upper Languedoc the nobles sponsored the largest projects of land reclamation. They could afford teams of oxen to clear tracts of land on which grain could be grown for the market. The subdelegate in Albi wrote to the intendant in 1786 that rising grain prices had led proprietors to prepare uncultivated land for the planting of crops.[6]

---

6   Frêche 1974, pp. 208, 248, 264, 267; Forster 1960, pp. 48–9, 51–4, 56, 58. Administrative reports on land clearances are in Archives Nationales (AN) H1/1010.

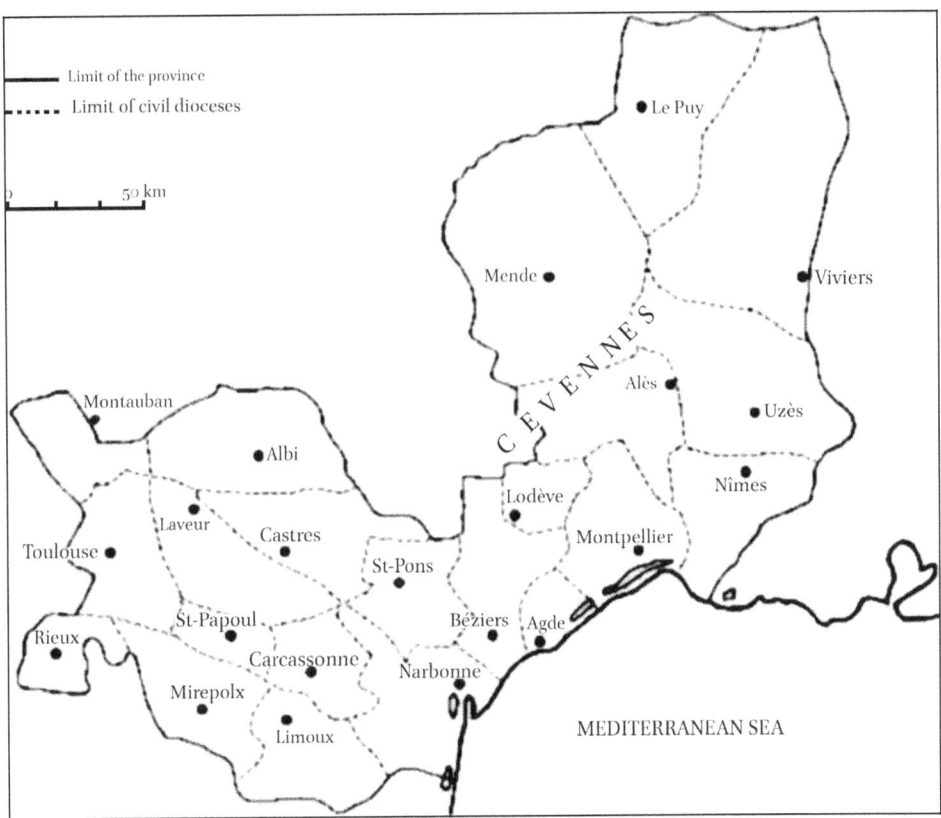

FIGURE 1.2 Map of the civil dioceses of Languedoc before 1789

Landowners, then, clearly sought to profit from the rising prices. Yet it would be wrong to equate the pursuit of profit with the competitive dynamic, intrinsic to capitalism, that forces economic actors to enhance their productivity. Liberalisation of the grain trade and land clearances do not, in and of themselves, improve the farming of crops. In England, gentry landowners obtained nearly all of their income by consolidating and improving their landholdings to attract yeoman tenant farmers liable to increase the value of their estates. The yeomen had to compete with one another to obtain leases and farm these estates. They had to produce for exchange, maximise their price-cost ratio, continually narrow the specialisation of their productive activity in line with market demand, and immediately adopt the latest techniques developed by other farmers. In this way, the yeoman tenant farmers transformed the agrarian landscape of England through the development of convertible husbandry. This term denotes the rotation of tillage on the one hand, with turnips, clover, and other artificial grasses and fodder crops on the other, to improve both arable land and pasture. It allowed farmers to bring fallow land under cultivation, augment the production of fodder, rear a large stock of farm animals in stables, and build up a store of manure fertiliser for the fields. Rested, well-fed, and healthy animals replaced human labour, economised on costs, improved the soil, tilled the land well, and augmented yields.

Convertible husbandry was the single most significant means of enhancing productivity in preindustrial agriculture. It spread over the regions of England with appropriate soils and climates during the 1700s but left hardly any trace in France by the time of the Revolution.[7] French landlords and tenant farmers did not uproot peasant tenures, reorganise the agrarian landscape, or transform the methods of husbandry. Social relations in the countryside did not oblige them to compete, invest, and raise productivity. French landowners did not turn their farms into competitive enterprises. Rather, in Languedoc, the upper classes trusted in sharecropping to appropriate the products of the soil.[8]

The prevalence of sharecropping had roots in the Middle Ages. Dozens of empirical studies have determined that by the end of the thirteenth century, the nobility no longer possessed large demesnes (manorial land) or obtained much labour service from the peasantry. The latter gained de facto propriety rights over much of the farmland of the realm, as rents and dues became immutable, and as their value gave way under the pressure of inflation. The peasants' position on the land subsequently deteriorated as the growth of their numbers led to the subdivision of landholdings into parcels inadequate for their subsistence. From the sixteenth century onward, with the fitful yet relentless consolidation of the absolutist state, nobles used the royal courts to accu-

---

7 Robert Brenner, Christopher Isett and David Parker elegantly describe the English agricultural revolution. Brenner and Isett 2002, pp. 624–8, 634–6; Parker 1996, pp. 223–31. See also Kerridge 1967; Clay 1984, vol. 1, pp. 128–9, 133–5, 137–8, 217–18, vol. 2, 16–21; Cornwall 1954, pp. 48–92; Havinden 1961, pp. 66–79; Jones 1967, the introduction; Jones 1967, pp. 58–71; Thirsk 1978, pp. 162–3, 167, 175; Thirsk 1967, pp. 4:598, 5:511–2; Coleman 1977; John 1965, pp. 19–34; Wrightson 1982, pp. 33, 136, 138. The latest statistical work on English agriculture shows rapid growth of labour productivity after 1500 and the uniqueness of this growth in Europe as a whole. Allen 2000, pp. 1–25; Clark 1999; Crafts 1985; Overton, 1996; Wrigley 1985, pp. 683–728.

8 Léon Dutil wrote that sharecropping was the dominant mode of tenure from one end of the province to the other (1911, p. 75). Frêche and Roger Brunet find that sharecropping was the prevailing mode of tenure in the Midi-Pyrénées and the diocese of Toulouse in the eighteenth century. Frêche 1974, p. 247; Brunet 1965, pp. 357, 360–1. Peter Jones writes that proprietors used sharecropping to profit from their lands in all parts of the southern Massif central (1985, p. 38). Alain Molinier argues that landlords overwhelmingly preferred sharecropping to money leases in the Vivarais in the eighteenth century (1985, p. 161).

mulate property and compensate for the erosion of seigneurial rents. The judiciary provided legal sanction for foreclosures when peasants went into debt from paying dues and taxes or from purchasing basic agricultural supplies. It is commonly estimated that the upper classes reduced the peasants' holdings to between 50 and 30 percent of the land by the time of the Revolution.[9] In Languedoc, the peasants possessed about 20 percent of the farmland of the diocese of Toulouse and a slightly greater percent in neighbouring dioceses. Peasants possessed over 57 percent of the Montpelliérain scrubland and over 37 percent of the entire diocese. They possessed well over 50 percent of the agricultural land of the diocese of Le Puy-en-Velay. The neighbouring diocese of the Vivarais was a labyrinth of properties, over two-thirds of which belonged to the peasantry.[10]

Although the peasants possessed much of the land, few had holdings large enough to assure their livelihood. The population of Languedoc grew anywhere from 26 percent in the Vivarais from 1715–20 to 1801 to 67 percent in the Montpelliérain from 1750 to 1789. This demographic expansion increased the density of the rural population and landholdings. Emmanuel Le Roy Ladurie shows that population growth led peasants to subdivide their properties among multiple heirs and left them with parcels ever less adequate for their livelihood. Proprietors of fewer than four hectares rose from 60 to 90 percent of the population of the area of the future department of the Aude between 1661 and 1789.[11]

The rural population had no choice but to accept low wages and expensive leases from the main owners of the land. The seigneurs of the Toulousain added fees, carting services, and tax obligations to sharecropping agreements, and increased their share of harvests. The lessor's share of harvests mounted to an average of 62 percent in the latter part of the eighteenth century. Leases in the southern Massif central specified an interminable list of services, obligations, and products due to the lessors. The sharecroppers stood in a medieval relation of serfdom vis-à-vis their landlords in all but the legal contracts of the leases specifying the limits of the landlords' rights.[12]

---

9   Lefebvre 1963, p. 344; Fossier 1968, vol. 2, pp. 555–6, 714; Boüard 1970, p. 160; Bloch 1931, pp. 155, 157, 167–8, 178; Fourquin 1964, pp. 175–9; Merle 1958, pp. 63–4, 67–9, 71; Neveux 1975, pp. 9–156, especially page 36; Bois 1976, p. 217.
10 Merley 1974, pp. 159, 320; Brunet 1965, pp. 152–7, 324, 343, 356–7, 360–1; Soboul 1958, pp. 23, 38; Molinier 1985, 58, 161; Dutil wrote that the peasants of the village of Gratens in the diocese of Rieux possessed about 25 percent of the farmland (1911, pp. 70–2).
11 Molinier 1988, p. 139; Molinier 1985, p. 202; Péronnet and Fournier 1989, p. 85; Soboul 1958, p. 49; Le Roy Ladurie 1974, p. 5; Bonnet and Marquié 1980, p. 65.
12 Frêche 1974, pp. 59, 163, 207, 220–2, 248; Forster 1960, pp. 56, 58; Sabatier 1988, pp. 55–6, 187, 202.

The lessors' ability to extract labour and revenue from their tenants no doubt constituted a disincentive to investment. In the Gâtine region of the province of Poitou, for example, the stable returns of sharecropping agreements made landowners leery of experimentation. It made no sense to nobles to replace grain with fodder crops, and thus forgo their principal source of income, in the hope of uncertain profits in the future. Such experimentation flew in the face of the conventional logic that worked to their advantage.[13]

Of course, this regime of low wages and high rents would have led to ruin had the peasantry not augmented production. Evidence from the north of France, where the nobles had had the most success reconstituting domains after the Middle Ages, suggests that the peasant family farm was the most dynamic element of the rural economy. At the end of the seventeenth century, the mass of the population of the Ile-de-France was reduced to small and scattered parcels of land. Wealthy husbandmen leased large farms ranging from 150 to over 200 hectares. These tenants devoted the farms exclusively to wheat for the Paris market. Contiguous farmland permitted them to economise on the costs of ploughing. Tenant farmers added horses to plough the soil more efficiently. They planted sainfoin and alfalfa to obtain revenue supplying all of the horses of Paris with fodder and brought back manure from urban stables to fertilise their fields.[14]

Nevertheless, the tenant farmers did not rotate wheat with nitrogen-restoring crops to augment the acreage of pasture, the production of fodder, and the number of farm animals. Most of the fertiliser for the arable fields came from sheep rather than from cattle and horses. During the eighteenth century, the tenant farmers reserved 35 percent of the soil of the Ile-de-France for fallow land and sheep grazing. They did not systematically substitute the energy of farm animals for that of labourers. The tenant farmers did not lead an agricultural revolution along the lines of seventeenth-century England. Crop yields stagnated in the Ile-de-France between the 1540s and the 1750s. There is much evidence that the tenant farmers pursued profit but little evidence that they experimented with agricultural techniques to enhance the labour productivity of husbandry. It probably made more sense to rely on the work of the mass of peasant micro-proprietors seeking employment and wages than to invest in farm capital.[15]

---

13   Merle 1958, pp. 138, 142, 176, 185; Brenner 2001, pp. 275–338.
14   Moriceau 1994, pp. 622, 629, 631, 635, 640–1, 661.
15   Moriceau 1994, pp. 347–8, 460–1, 640, 642–3, 659–60, 780. François Hincker argues that the growth of the population created a situation favourable to employers. The abundant class of workers allowed employers to pay relatively low wages and gave them little incentive to

In the eighteenth century, the actual landlords, who lived in Paris and the towns of the Ile-de-France, found it more profitable to sell their property to peasant smallholders than to leave all of it in leases with husbandmen. Wealthy townspeople obtained much of the peasantry's property in the Paris basin during the economic downturn of the seventeenth century but then sold land to smallholders during the period of rising agricultural prices of the eighteenth century. Every year of the last three decades of the old regime, apart from the crises of 1761–62, 1767–68, and 1786–87, saw the transfer of property from urban landlords to rural inhabitants.[16]

Peasant farmers made all sorts of efforts to enhance the productivity of the soil in the Pays de Caux of Normandy. Wealthy townspeople of all three estates, owners of about 85 percent of the region's farmland, divided their property into plots of two to 10 hectares and rented it to well-to-do peasants. These tenant farmers benefited from the building of roads and the integration of rural markets after the 1730s. They earned revenue by developing the production of cattle and grain. Peasants experimented with clover, colza, artificial prairies, and green fodder after ploughing. By contrast, the handful of large farms of the region had hardly any fields of fodder crops. The tenant farmers of two to 10 hectares may not have methodically transformed agricultural techniques to economise on labour costs, but they did enhance the yields of crops and augment the productivity of the land. By the end of the eighteenth century, the yields obtained in the Pays de Caux of Normandy equalled the best ones obtained on the large farms of the wealthy husbandmen of the Ile-de-France and surpassed those obtained on the large farms in most of the Paris basin.[17]

The peasantry also took the lead in clearing new land for cultivation. In the second half of the eighteenth century, nobles of Brittany founded an agricultural society and discussed the opening of new lands to modern forms of husbandry. Yet the results were rather meagre. Land clearances were primarily the work of Breton peasants anxious to obtain terrain for their animals to graze and additional parcels for new crops such as buckwheat. In Languedoc, the peasants' efforts to prepare uncultivated lands for farming formed part of the slow mutation of the traditional agrarian structure in the second half of the eight-

---

invest in technologies that would compensate for a human labour force (1989, p. 33). Cynthia Bouton's research suggests that the landlords and tenant farmers of the Ile-de-France obtained their revenue by extracting high rents and low-paid labour from the peasantry rather than from productive investments in agriculture (1993, pp. 57–8, 61, 219, 221, 257).

16 Béaur 1984, pp. 207, 215, 336, 339; Tulippe 1934, pp. 110, 161–3, 241, 318–19.
17 Lemarchand 1989, pp. 72, 268–9, 271–2, 279–80, 290–1, 344, 346, 349, 351–3, 361; Moriceau 1994, p. 468; Jacquart 1974, p. 368.

eenth century. The peasantry had planted grain on hardscrabble land in the fifteen and sixteenth centuries as population growth put pressure on resources. Yields declined with each new hectare brought under cultivation until the economy sank into severe crises in the seventeenth century. But around 1730 or 1740, facing the same type of demographic pressure, the peasants planted vines rather than grains. Vines were better suited to the region's scrublands and generated income with which the peasants could purchase more grain than they could get by farming it themselves.[18]

Vineyards became particularly common in Mediterranean Languedoc. The subdelegate of Montpellier found that the poor quality of the soil meant that half of the fields had to lay fallow to sustain grains. Vines grew better on these soils and permitted the peasants to obtain more income from the land. Artisans and small proprietors planted vineyards near towns and on the hilly and stony land common to the region. A voyager to Montpellier remarked in 1760 that the diocese was covered with vines. In the Montpelliérain village of Pignan, population growth and viticulture on the scrubland increased the number of parcels by over 30 percent between 1750 and 1762, and the number of hectares under vineyards by almost 45 percent between 1750 and 1791. The peasantry's efforts to carve out vineyards from the marginal lands of the Narbonnais doubled the cultivated surface of the diocese in the second half of the eighteenth century. Wine production grew from 2 to 2.5 million hectolitres in Languedoc between 1774 and 1788.[19]

The peasants made similar innovations in the mountainous region north of Nîmes. Poor soils and biennial crop rotations restricted farming to about 15 percent of the Vivarais. The stagnation of grain yields would have made life precarious had it not been for the introduction of new crops. The inhabitants planted chestnut trees on the marginal lands of the area. Chestnut trees yielded nearly as much fruit on hillsides as they did on arable fields and allowed the inhabitants to acquire more resources from the land. The peasants introduced the potato, a crop exceptionally high in calories, in response to dearth in the northern Vivarais at the end of the seventeenth century. As the population grew in the eighteenth century, the peasants sowed potatoes throughout the rest of the diocese.[20]

---

18   Meyer 1966, vol. 1, pp. 538, 554–5, 566, 578, 584; Le Roy Ladurie 1966, vol. 1, pp. 222–3, 225, 532–3.
19   Soboul 1958, p. 49; Tudez 1934, pp. 161–2; Domairon 1920, vol. 4, p. 4; Secondy and Segondy 1980, pp. 181–2, 184, 188; Larguier 1996, vol. 3, pp. 1099–101, 1103–5; Dermigny 1967, p. 397.
20   Higonnet 1971, pp. 48, 51, 58; Molinier 1985, pp. 202, 204–7, 267, 417; Molinier 1988, pp. 139–40, 146–7. Arthur Young noted that peasants cultivated the mountains around Le-Puy-en-Velay all the way up to the summits (1969, p. 182).

The peasants obtained even more resources from the planting of mulberry trees and the rearing of silk worms. They planted mulberries throughout the dioceses of Uzès, Alès, and the Vivarais. The leaves provided nourishment for silk worms, which were vital to the textile industry cantered in Nîmes. The trees generated 20 times more revenue per hectare than did wheat. Like chestnut trees, they grew on almost any terrain and permitted the peasants to extend the ancestral practice of terraced agriculture to the topographical limit and obtain additional resources from the land.[21]

The peasants increased agricultural production in upper Languedoc by introducing maize. The renowned English traveller Arthur Young thought that maize enlivened the villages and towns of the province. It covered between 12 and 20 percent of the arable land of the Toulousain and Lauragais in the 1780s. Maize yielded three to five times more grain per hectare than did wheat. It covered the subsistence of a growing population and permitted the peasants to acquire additional income selling higher quality crops such as wheat, oats, and carrots in markets made available by the Canal du Midi in Narbonne, Béziers, Montpellier, Lunel, and Aigues-Mortes.[22]

Peasant communities were also responsible for the growth of manufacturing. Smallholders and rural artisans around Nîmes and the southern Massif central produced wool and silk stockings for Nîmois merchants, who coordinated a thriving trade of high-end textiles with Spain, the Levant, and other foreign markets for much of the eighteenth century. The merchants did not seek to gather production into factories and manage it directly. The syndic of the stocking manufacturers reported that the number of looms situated in the countryside surrounding Nîmes increased almost six-fold between 1713 and 1754. Merchants provided mulberry leaves, premises, tools, half the silk eggs, and fuel, and later divided the finished silk with rural artisans. Inhabitants used the same term (*métayage*) for these relations of production as they did for sharecropping.[23]

Merchants of Carcassonne and Montpellier did nearly as much business as did their counterparts in Nîmes. Manufacturers put wool out to villages of the Black Mountain (*Montagne Noire*) and the environs of Carcassonne for carding and weaving. The subdelegate of Carcassonne reported in 1787 that 10 percent

---

21   ADH C2250, C2251, C2271; Teisseyre-Sallmann 1995, pp. 222, 224.
22   Young 1969, p. 38; Bonnet and Marquié 1980, pp. 64–5, 69; Frêche, 1974, p. 59; Péronnet 1989, p. 85; Mercadal 1973, pp. 145, 148–9; Jacquemay 1986, pp. 174–5, 300, 304–5, 317, 337.
23   Archives Départementales du Gard (ADG) IV E 22, IV E 31.

of the 30,000 workers in the drapes industry put down their tools three months of the year to work in the harvest and another 40 percent divided the year equally between farming and manufacturing. The merchants of Montpellier put the task of spinning handkerchiefs and cotton cloths out to about 10,000 rural artisans. The merchants set up workshops for weaving and dying on the outskirts of Montpellier, where hundreds of workers supplemented their wages by farming vines and gardens. These semi-urban peasants made up about two-fifths of Montpellier's taxpayers.[24]

Lodève, Mazamet, and Bédarieux were smaller, albeit more vibrant, textile-producing towns. They avoided the deindustrialisation that began to overtake Nîmes, Carcassonne, and Montpellier in the 1770s and 1780s. Their success, however, did not derive from markedly different business practices. The merchant manufacturers of Lodève began to concentrate production in urban factories but still put most of the tasks involved in producing cloth out to rural households. Peasants made up about a quarter of the 9,500 inhabitants of Lodève at the end of the old regime. Mazamet, which was even smaller than Lodève, witnessed a sevenfold increase in output during the eighteenth century. Bédarieux was the smallest of the three. The children and the elderly of its rural hinterland spun wool all year round, while the active population worked in agriculture during the summer months.[25]

The peasants of nonindustrial areas also produced textiles. The subdelegate in Tournon reported in 1786 and 1787 that half of the population of the upper Vivarais divided its time between wool production and agriculture. The women and children of the diocese of Le Puy produced lace all year round and were joined by men during the six or seven months of the agricultural off-season. The subdelegate of the Albigeois reported in 1786, 'Almost all the women and girls of the countryside busy themselves spinning hemp and flax when they are not engaged in agriculture'.[26] Merchant manufacturers probably found it more rational to take advantage of the growing mass of peasant micro-proprietors, anxious to supplement its income no matter how poorly paid the work, than to risk investing in the fixed costs of manufacturing machinery. Languedocian industry was dispersed among the peasantry and left to its supervision.

---

24 The report of the sub-delegate of Carcassonne is in ADH C2599. Tax rolls for Montpellier are in AN H1/292; Marquié 1993, pp. 129, 133–4, 171; Cazals 1984, pp. 134–5; Laurent 1987, pp. 13–15.
25 Cazals and Poitevin 1992, p. 168; Johnson 1995, pp. 9–13; Allaire, 1990, p. 115.
26 ADH C47, C2618; Merley 1974, pp. 124–5; Dutil 1911, pp. 289, 291.

2   Seigneurial Levies and the Royal Judiciary

For all of the efforts of the Languedocian elite to profit from agriculture and manufacturing, its economic behaviour was worlds away from the practices of English landowners and merchants. The gentry granted long-term leases to yeomen farmers, who extended pasture, introduced fodder crops, and augmented the number of farm animals. The value of the leases rose with gains in productivity and economies in labour costs. After 1750, English merchants began to concentrate textile and iron production around some of the key technological breakthroughs of the Industrial Revolution. Tenant farmers and merchants systematically reinvested profits in production in order match the prices of peers faced with the same competitive constraints. The upper classes of Languedoc also sought profit. Seigneurs secured revenue from woods and wheat fields located on their domains. Landlords and merchants gained revenue from microproprietors dependent on them for agricultural land, raw material, and employment. Yet there is little evidence that they invested this revenue to enhance the productivity of agricultural estates and industrial enterprises. Conversely, there is a great deal of evidence that proprietors invested in the political and legal arrangements of the old regime such as titles, seigneuries, and venal offices.[27]

Tithes and seigneurial dues were the oldest arrangement of this sort. They amounted to 13.46 percent of the landed revenue of the diocese of Le Puy at the end of the old regime. Peter McPhee insists that seigneurial dues and tithes, as a general rule, 'were levied at one-eleventh and one-tenth of all produce, including wool and new-born livestock' throughout the Corbières region of Languedoc.[28] Table 1.1 suggests that seigneurial levies were less burdensome elsewhere in Languedoc.[29]

---

27 Robert Brenner was the first to develop this juxtaposition of the political relations of France to capitalist economic relations of England (1976, pp. 30–75). George Comninel makes the same point in comparing the relationship between French landlords and peasant smallholders on the one hand, to the one between the English gentry and their tenant farmers on the other (1987, pp. 189–92).

28 McPhee 1999, p. 28; Merley 1974, pp. 164, 320.

29 Data in these tables comes from Archives Parlementaires 1re série, t. IX discours du 24 septembre 1789; ADH C45. Data on Pouzilhac, Sénéchas, and Castelnau-d'Estrétefonds are probably exceptional and exaggerated, as they were written in parish *cahiers de doléances* in the politically charged atmosphere of the spring of 1789. ADG C1193, C1200. The seigneurial dues of Saint-Victor-de-la-Coste amounted to 21.45 of all taxes, including indirect ones. Pélaquier 1996, vol. 1, pp. 102–3; Pasquier and Galabert 1925, pp. 36–7; Frêche 1974, pp. 507–8, 512, 524; Molinier 1985, pp. 152, 154–5; Rascol 1961, pp. 128, 227; Forster 1960, p. 50; Bastier 1975, pp. 259–60, 309; Cazanave 1999, pp. 14, 20, 57.

TABLE 1.1   Seigneurial levies in Languedoc

Groups of Languedocian lords	Seigneurial dues as a percentage of their income
Nobles of the Toulousain	8 to 18.8
Toulousain parlementaires	10
Ecclesiastics of the Toulousain and the Midi-Pyrénées	2 to 3
Twenty great families of the Lauragais	10

Regions and villages of Languedoc	Seigneurial Dues as a percentage of direct taxes
Toulousain and the Midi-Pyrénées	18.7
Vivarais	10 to 15
Albigeois	23.8
Belpech (diocese of Mirepoix)	13.8
Pouzilhac (diocese of Uzès)	24.1
Saint-Victor-de-la-Coste (diocese of Uzès)	21.45
Sénéchas (diocese of Uzès)	50
Castelnau-d'Estrétefonds (diocese of Toulouse)	184

Regions and villages of Languedoc	Seigneurial Dues as a percentage of the gross product
Vivarais	.44
Albigeois	1.31
Toulousain	1 to 10
Belpech	1.31
Pouzilhac	2.77
Saint-Victor-de-la-Coste	1.89

Region of Languedoc	Tithes as a percentage of the gross product
Vivarais	1.39
Albigeois	3.94
Belpech	3.62
Pouzilhac	9.1
Saint-Victor-de-la-Coste	8.39

Lords periodically increased the value of their seigneurial rights by demanding acts of recognition. In the eighteenth century, the most burdensome aspect of the seigneurial regime of the Toulousain was its volatility. Lords frequently exercised their right to update titles after 29 years of neglect and demand heavy arrears. In the southern Massif central, well-to-do commoners purchased seigneuries to secure prestige and income at the same time as lords sought to extract additional income from their domains. These trends resulted in a rapid turnover of lordships, a confusing proliferation of jurisdictions, and an abusive rewriting of titles, all of which tended to increase seigneurial dues. The Corbières was a web of seigneurial jurisdictions belonging to religious orders, secular lords, and the king. These seigneurs often leased them to other nobles and proprietors eager to draw as much revenue from the rights as possible. In consequence, seigneurial burdens tended to increase in the last decades of the old regime.[30]

Records of the intendant and his correspondence with officials in Versailles contain complaints of peasant communities about abuses of seigneurial authority. Combining these reports with incidents depicted in secondary works on villages in different parts of the province reveals 73 incidents in which lords insisted upon their prerogatives and levies in the second half of the century. The inhabitants of Jonquières et Saint-Vincent, for example, a parish of 181 households in the diocese of Nîmes, complained in the spring of 1789, in their *cahier de doléances* – the list of grievances composed during the elections to the Estates General – that the local lord and his agents vexed the poor with all sorts of fees and repeated demands for feudal recognition.[31]

The lords would not have had success augmenting their rights without the support of the monarchy. The peasants did not docilely bow to assertions of

---

[30] Bastier 1975, pp. 274, 278–9, 310; Jones 1985, p. 163; McPhee 1999, pp. 24–9, 34.
[31] Sources for these 73 incidents are located in the Appendix. The cahier of Jonquières et Saint-Vincent is in ADG C1194.

seigneurial power. The lords had to turn to the judiciary to enforce compliance. The royal tribunals were located in the towns, where nobles were the leading residents. Lords were not a purely rural ruling class. Many held offices in the two sovereign courts of Languedoc. Over 20 percent of the 157 judges who inherited or bought posts in the Cour des Comptes, Aides et Finances of Montpellier after 1750 registered themselves as lords of domains. Of 209 nobles present for the assembly of the second estate of the electoral constituency of Montpellier in March 1789, 24 were officeholders in the Cour des Comptes, Aides et Finances, and 10 were magistrates in other courts. Of 613 nobles present for the assembly of the constituency of Toulouse in March 1789, 81 were justices in the Parlement and two in the local Bureau of Finances. Concrete examples of this milieu were at least seven salons held in châteaux when parlementaire families, friends and other notables sojourned in the countryside. Mme. de Lamothe, the wife of a councillor in the Parlement, held one in Saint-Félix-de-Caraman, and M. de Rességuier, the general attorney, or *procureur general*, representing the king in this tribunal, held another on his domain of Secourieu in the Lauragais.[32]

In short, landlords and magistrates belonged to the same social circles. They presided over urban and rural areas, dividing their time between town and country in accordance with their interests and tastes. Nobles could therefore count on the judiciary to impose their claims on peasant communities. In 1781, César de Malbois, a leading member of the order of barristers associated with the Parlement of Toulouse (*avocat général*), used his influence in the judiciary to halt the corrosive effect of inflation on the value of his levies. He obliged the consuls of Poussan, a village in the diocese of Montpellier, to pay his seigneurial dues in kind. When the inhabitants initiated an appeal of the ruling, Malbois summoned them to his château and forced them to sign a new recognition of his rights with the dues in kind.[33]

The lords also used the judiciary to capitalise on the peasants' efforts to turn hillsides and swamps into vineyards and mulberry groves. Seigneurs of the Corbières enforced their rights to collect dues on parcels of land brought under cultivation by the peasantry and to monopolise other untilled terrains for their cattle and vineyards. The inhabitants of Clarensac, a community of 256 households in the diocese of Nîmes, asserted in their cahier that they had

---

32 Pierre Vialles lists the nobles of the Cour des Comptes, Aides et Finances (1921, pp. 159–229; Donnadieu 1989, pp. 517–29). For the constituency of the nobility of the Toulousain see ADHG 1 L 548. Details about rural salons are in Morère 1991, p. 104; Casteras 1891, p. 15.

33 Négri 1988, p. 70. The lords' efforts to fortify the seigneurial regime benefited from the support of legal authorities within the jurisdiction of the Parlement of Toulouse more than they did in other regions of France (Castan 1980, p. 112).

long enjoyed rights to the local scrubland. They claimed to pay an annual tax to the Crown and a pension to the local lord for the use of it. But when they prepared the land for farming, the lord obtained a verdict from the judiciary obliging them to make a feudal act of recognition and pay seigneurial dues. The lady vicomtesse de Montal, baroness of several communities west of Toulouse, took the brothers Gaillard before the Parlement in March 1783 to force them to recognise that some of their farmland fell within her seigneurial jurisdiction. The Parlement ruled that the land 'will remain in the seigneurial jurisdiction: such that Montal can take real and corporeal possession: the Gaillards are prohibited to give her any trouble ... unless they consent to feudal recognition of the land in favour of Montal'. The ruling forced the brothers Gaillard not only to pay seigneurial dues to farm the land in question, but also to pay all of the baroness's legal fees.[34]

Table 1.2 gives a sense of how lords used the judiciary to impose their claims on peasant communities. It is based on judicial records, litigation described in secondary works, and grievances of peasant communities found in records of the intendant and his correspondence with Versailles. While the table does not present a comprehensive set of rulings, it does show close collaboration between lords and judicial bodies, including the Parlement, Cour des Comptes, Aides et Finances, seneschal courts, Bureaus of Finances, and waters and forests courts (*eaux et forêts*).[35]

TABLE 1.2 Judicial rulings favourable to seigneurs 1750–89

Type of Legal Decision	Number of rulings
Obliging recognition of revised titles and/or forcing peasants to pay dues and tithes	32
Granting lords political prerogatives such as the right to choose village leaders and preside over village assemblies	20
Asserting the lords' property rights over common lands or restricting the peasants' use-rights	17
Obliging peasants to pay fees and fines[36]	14

---

34 McPhee 1999, pp. 22–3; ADG C1198; ADHG B1817. Disputes over common land did more to increase litigation between lords and peasants than did any other issue (Castan 1980a, pp. 67–8).

35 Sources for this table and the 73 arbitrary assertions of seigneurial rights mentioned on p. 43 are in the Appendix.

36 Includes the exclusive rights of *banalité* to operate ovens.

TABLE 1.2 Judicial rulings favourable to seigneurs 1750–89 (*cont.*)

Type of Legal Decision	Number of rulings
Granting lords honorific rights on the village level[37]	11
Exempting lords from taxes or allowing them to consult tax rolls	9
Granting lords sole right to harvest grapes or sell wine during certain periods	5
Foreclosing on peasant tenures or enforcing expropriations	5

3   The Royal Judiciary and the Authority and Honour of the Seigneurs

Table 1.2 makes a neat distinction between rulings. About 75 percent enforced the lords' economic rights, the rest their political and honorific rights. In truth, this distinction is rather arbitrary, for contemporaries did not bracket their relationships into such categories. Seigneurial rights formed an ensemble inherited from the feudal past. The baron de Montesquieu, a seigneur and magistrate in the Parlement of Bordeaux, wrote an illuminating history of French jurisprudence in the final two books of the *Spirit of the Laws*. He argued that the titles to the first fiefs did not exist because the Germanic conquerors of Roman Gaul had simply seized the land. The conquerors eventually emancipated their serfs yet retained various rights in return for providing the peasantry with land. These rights continued to permeate the customary laws arbitrating civil affairs in the eighteenth century. The seigneurs maintained legal recognition of their fiefs and perquisites. Montesquieu lauded this heritage:

> The Germanic nations that conquered the Roman Empire were certainly free … The conquerors spread themselves over the country; they lived in the fields, and little in the towns … As it was necessary for the nation to deliberate on its affairs as it had done before the conquest, it did so by recourse to representatives. Whence the origin of Gothic government among us. At first it was mixed with aristocracy and monarchy – a mixture attended with this inconvenience, that the common people were bondmen. Customary law came to accord letters of freedom; and soon the

---

37 Includes exclusive hunting privileges.

people's civil liberty, the prerogatives of the nobility and the clergy, and the king's power found themselves in such concert, that I do not believe there has ever been such a tempered government ... It is admirable that the corruption of a conquering people's government has formed the best sort of constitution that men could have imagined.[38]

Many nobles of Languedoc felt the same way. François de Boutaric, a lawyer in the Parlement of Toulouse, wrote that feudal rights were imperishable, because one could not alter the terms of what had never been a free contract. The nobles of the constituency of Carcassonne wrote in their cahier, 'this immunity of noble funds and fiefs is not a personal privilege, but a genuine right attached to them by positive laws and the most ancient possessions'. The nobility of the constituency of Béziers demanded that seigneurial privileges be conserved as 'the most sacred form of property'. Jean-Jacques Régis de Cambacérès, a councillor in the Cour des Comptes, Aides et Finances, wrote a draft cahier for the nobility of Montpellier.

> The contribution to public taxation ... cannot extend to the point of including feudal or seigneurial rights; these rights ... are mostly only a representation of a useful property, only a reservation made by former possessors when they gave up their fathers' heritage. Would it be fair to make them share the weight of contributions with those to whom they granted an essential part of their patrimony?[39]

Cambacérès's reasoning resembles that of Montesquieu: the lords furnished the peasantry with tenures many centuries ago, and seigneurial rights were compensation. This interpretation of seigneurial rights speaks of a feudal society in which the nobility enjoyed jurisdiction over all of the land of the realm. The peasants' tenures may not have sustained heavy seigneurial charges at the end of the eighteenth century. Yet they remained central to what the nobles regarded as their fiefs.

The manner in which the Parlement of Toulouse handled the revolt of the armed masks of the Vivarais is a good illustration of this conviction. In 1783, the peasants of the 'honest legion' painted their faces black, put on women's clothing and attacked notaries, dues collectors, and royal attorneys. The attacks

---

38   Montesquieu 1949, vol. 1, p. 163. See also vol. 2, pp. 152–5, 205–7, 266–7.
39   Cambacérès's draft cahier is found in ADH 1 E 1427. Boutaric and Sudre 1751. For the cahier of the nobility of Carcassonne see Archives Départementales de l'Aude (ADA) WB 2062. For the cahier of the nobility of Béziers see AN Ba 21.

revealed widespread resentment toward the local jurists and moneylenders who subcontracted seigneurial rights. The seneschal courts of Villeneuve-de-Berg and Nîmes, and tribunal of the royal military in Languedoc known as the *prévôté* of Montpellier, all moved to assert their responsibility for resolving the region's problems. But the king honoured the Parlement with letters patent to lead an inquiry. The Parlement sent an investigative team of four judges to the southern Massif central. In 1784, after hearing the team's report, the Parlement issued a long denunciation of the insidious means used by lawyers and notaries to drive people into debt and make off with their property. The Parlement admonished notaries for writing excessive bills, lawyers for inventing unwarranted procedures to multiply fees, and other local notables for covertly buying up debts to take hold of properties. What we should notice is that the *parlementaires* sought to correct these abuses by invigorating seigneurial justice. They ruled that henceforth the lords of the region were to draw up lists of lawyers eligible to plead cases in their seigneurial courts. The ruling called on the lords to annually review the lists and replace the lawyers with whom they were dissatisfied.[40]

The Parlement's solution to the problems of the region disconcerted many commoners. A lawyer of St.-Ambroix, a town in the Vivarais, wrote to the controller general in March 1789.

> Those who remain lawyers find themselves obliged to carry out the will of the lords who appointed them, and they often take the side of litigants who are in the wrong. Above all, they cannot take on a peasant's defence in a dispute with his lord without incurring the lord's disfavour. Instead of finding the means, by this measure, of re-establishing order, the Parlement has just re-established the feudal reign, which is the pinnacle of disorder.[41]

The inhabitants of La Calmette, a community of 212 households in the diocese of Uzès, shared this view. They wrote in their cahier that several lords capitalised on divisions within the community to assert fictitious jurisdictions and employ ambitious experts in feudal law to extract revenue from them.

> The abuses of village justice stem from an administration given over to persons who are named and dismissed according to the lords' pleasure

---

40   AN H1/748/187; Molinier 1988, p. 152; Tilly 1986, p. 182; Castan 1980a, p. 187.
41   AN H1/942/2.

and who therefore have no other will than that of the lords. Interested in avoiding a distasteful dismissal, these persons are often the lords' agents, and strive to merit the lords' confidence in oppressing dependent peasants subject to their judicial authority.[42]

The judicial authority of the Parlement of Toulouse constituted the lords' most important means of maintaining the seigneurial regime. Lords brought peasant communities before the Parlement on hundreds of occasions after 1740. The Parlement ruled in their favour each time. A look at one of these rulings shows the rights at stake. M. Jean François Denis d'Albi de Belbèze, councilor in the grand chamber of the Parlement and lord of high, middle, and low justice of Bretx et Thil, a village outside of Toulouse, initiated litigation against his consul and peasants in September 1787. The Parlement ruled that the villagers were forbidden to send animals into his lands, woods, meadows, fields of alfalfa and fodder, vines, shores, wastelands, and other possessions. It forbade them to cut or gather wood on his property. The Parlement granted Belbèze the right to proclaim the start of the grape harvest and have his grapes harvested two or three days before anyone else did. It granted him the right to consult the churchwardens' accounts, as well as those of the administrators of the goods and revenues of the poor. The Parlement's ruling stated that tax assessments would only go into effect after Belbèze's officers had inspected and signed them. It specified that titles, tax assessments, and lists of property transfers were to be locked in the community archives and that three keys were to be made: one for Belbèze's judge, another for the consul, and a third for the clerk (*greffier*).

The Parlement also granted Belbèze the right to exercise justice and enforce it with officers. The Parlement entitled him to choose one of two candidates presented by the community for the position of consul. It obliged the consul to notify Belbèze's officers and give them the subjects for deliberation 24 hours before holding community assemblies. It gave Belbèze the right to have his officers preside over the assemblies. The ruling stipulated that the consul would pay a 100 *livres* fine for failing to bring administrative orders directly to Belbèze before showing them to inhabitants.

The most arresting aspect of the ruling is the honorific rights it specified. The consul had to pledge loyalty to Belbèze in his château and wear a hood to processions, mass, and other public functions. The priest had to pay Belbèze homage and put him and his family in public prayers on Sundays and holidays. The Parlement even enjoined the priest to bath Belbèze and his family in incense before the community during mass.[43]

---

42 ADG C1199.
43 ADHG B 1859.

Registers of the Parlement of Toulouse show that this ruling was nearly identical to hundreds of others. A minimum count of the rulings in the inventory of the series B, volume III, in the departmental archives of the Haute-Garonne reveals the following trend. A survey of the registers reveals some gaps in the inventory yet provides an accurate portrayal of the trend.

TABLE 1.3   Rulings of the Parlement of Toulouse enforcing seigneurial rights

Years	Number of rulings
1741–56	87
1757–73	136
1774–89	235

The scholarship on the seigneurial regime of Languedoc indicates that relations between lords and peasants remained relatively peaceful until the 1730s. The Parlement of Toulouse then began issuing judgements in favour of lords and did so more frequently as the century wore on.[44]

There are several explanations for this rising tide of litigation. Many merchants of the Carcassonnais purchased seigneuries in order to leave wool manufacturing for the noble life of a seigneur. They did not care much about agricultural techniques but kept a keen eye on their privileges. Joseph II Airolles, a descendent of a family of textile manufacturers, bought the domain of Villefloure. Villagers did not recognise his jurisdiction, claiming instead that they depended on royal justice. In 1760, a seigneurial guard caught an inhabitant pasturing animals on what the guard claimed to be his master's fief. Airolles won the ensuing litigation at the Parlement of Toulouse in 1766. Some years later, an agricultural worker presented Airolles with an oath of loyalty for use of a field within his jurisdiction: 'Romieu promptly went to his knees, with nothing covering his head, without any implement of war, and swore and promised to be a good and loyal vassal'.[45] Social-climbing merchants such as Airolles initiated many legal proceedings against communit-

---

44   Bastier 1975, p. 286; Castan 1969, p. 233.
45   Marquié 1993, pp. 248, 250, 254; ADA B604.

ies. Yet it is unclear whether they were responsible for increasing the number. The Languedocian textile industry declined in the last decades of the old regime. The merchant manufacturers may have shifted capital to more stable investments such as seigneuries or may simply have lost the means to acquire them.

Another source of litigation was the alienation of the royal domains. The Crown traded away nearly all of its Languedocian seigneuries between the sixteenth century and 1789. It alienated the highest number toward the end of the old regime. Those who obtained the domains often turned to the Parlement to gain recognition of their newly acquired rights. In 1771, for instance, the king gave his lordship over Buzet-sur-Tarn, a village in the Albigeois, to the comte de Clarac, owner of an adjacent domain, in exchange for woods in the Ile-de-France. Clarac turned at once to the Parlement and secured 41 articles of rights. He gained the right to collect a portion of the harvest of certain crops (*champart*) and his own key to the community archives containing the tax assessments. He obtained the right to proclaim the start of the grape harvest and to have his grapes harvested three days before anyone else. The Parlement barred inhabitants from use rights on his lands. It granted Clarac the right to exercise justice in his château. The Parlement obliged the villagers to notify him before holding assemblies and allow him to inspect the minutes. It ordered them to shut up their dogs and poultry between May and the beginning of the grape harvest so that their animals would not diminish local game. The Parlement made the consuls appear in church wearing a hood and granted Clarac a special row and a special place in prayers. It stipulated that failure to comply with many of these articles would result in a 500 livres fine. Clarac hired a feudal expert to update his titles in 1784 and obligated the inhabitants to recognise them in 1787.[46]

The lords' economic gains constituted the principal source of the litigation. The lords of upper Languedoc accumulated properties in order to profit from rising grain prices. The seigneurs of Mediterranean Languedoc obtained income from the extension of viticulture. Lords throughout the province took advantage of the rising value of woods on their seigneuries. Each one of the 458 rulings described above settled economic disputes over grape harvests and use rights, political disputes over the assemblies of villagers and the selection of consuls, and status disputes over public honours in processions and church. The evidence presented in this chapter suggests that lords conceived of wealth, power, and status as integral facets of the noble life. When they turned

---

46   Castan 1980a, p. 105; Sabatié 1971, pp. 176–96.

to their peers in the judiciary to take advantage of the economic conjuncture, they asked for commensurate political and honorific rights as a matter of course.

Cournonterral, a village near Montpellier, provides an excellent example of a lord's efforts to crown economic gain with political and honorific rights. One of the consuls wrote to the Estates of Languedoc in 1787 that a legal decision deprived the community of income from selling wood and rendered it incapable of meeting its fiscal obligation. According to the letter, M. de Portalès succeeded in convincing the judiciary that the local woods had belonged to the prior owners of his seigneurie and that he therefore had the right to keep the villagers out of them. The judges imposed a heavy fine on the villagers for the wood they previously had taken. Two years later, the consuls complained of new regulations of a different nature. They expressed indignation over Portalès's demand that they appear at public functions in hoods bearing the same insignia as the one appearing on the uniform of his domestic servants.[47] Honorific rights, it seems, made economic gain satisfying and worthwhile.

Property owners of Languedoc sought to benefit from rising agricultural prices in the second half of the eighteenth century. They sponsored land clearances to create additional wheat fields. Parlementaires used their judicial authority to lift restrictions on the grain trade. Yet they did not benefit from rising prices and output solely by means of their landholdings. Members of the upper classes availed themselves of the authority of their peers in the judiciary to abolish use rights to their fields and woods and to secure advantages during the grape harvests. They obtained judgements permitting them to collect seigneurial dues, exempt their properties from taxation, and assert rights over newly cleared lands.

Montesquieu determined that the French monarchy inherited its legal codes and governing structures from the feudal past. Its laws and institutions maintained traditional modes of thought. Lords not only prized their property for its economic value, but also for the political and honorific rights it conferred. They set great store by their rights to authority and honour on the village level. The origins of offices in the magistracy post-dated feudalism yet preserved one of its fundamental characteristics: private ownership over a system of public authority and honour. Whether seigneurs, officeholders, or both, the nobles placed inestimable value on the symbolic trappings of lordship. As the seigneurs gained more wealth in the second half of the eighteenth century, they

---

47   AN H1/940; Saumade 1908, pp. 79–80.

took care to subject village leaders to their authority and oblige entire communities to pay them honours in public ceremonies.

The upper classes' private rights to public authority sometimes put them at odds with royal ministers and intendants. The king's finances depended, in the last analysis, on the wealth produced by sharecroppers, smallholders, and artisans. The claims of tax-exempt landowners to the resources of peasant communities diverted fiscal resources from the royal treasury. In times of financial difficulty, seigneurial rights led to conflict with royal ministers and appointees intent on keeping the monarchy solvent. But before we investigate such conflict, we must examine more closely the governmental institutions of the towns. The upper classes did not obtain all of their wealth from the domination of landed property. They also gained income from venal offices, tax farms, provincial estates, and government bonds. These institutions are the subject of Chapter 2.

CHAPTER 2

The Rewards of Royal Service

Thomas Hobbes determined that people need a state to live in society. A single legitimate source of violence prevents civil strife, private armies, social dissolution, and terror. The state provides security. Yet it has never benefited all members of society equally. States have always imposed order on societies characterised by civil inequality or an unequal distribution of property and power. The last chapter demonstrated that the old regime monarchy of France maintained inequality by permitting seigneurs to enlist the royal judiciary and dominate landed property. This chapter explores the other instances of public authority in the province. Who staffed the state institutions of Languedoc? Did these institutions govern all of the inhabitants according to the same standard regardless of their offices, titles, and wealth? Which social classes or ranks obtained the benefits of the old regime monarchy, and which ones faced the burdens?

In answering these questions, this chapter begins with a study of the judiciary. Royal magistrates not only settled disputes and dispensed justice, but also secured various payments, and shared the authority and prestige of the king. The second section is an analysis of the manner in which the crown raised revenue to finance other services such as security and religion. The monarchy farmed tax collection out to private companies composed of provincial elites. These companies took a portion of the revenue for their members before transferring the rest to the various branches of the state. The religious and military officials responsible for managing provincial finances form the subject of the final section. Bishops, barons, the intendant, the military governor, and other potentates met once a year for the grandiose ceremony of the Estates of Languedoc. They allocated taxes, organised public works, composed the provincial budget, saw to the maintenance of royal troops, and determined the annual subsidy to offer the king. The Estates raised more revenue for the king in the last decades of the old regime and distributed a proportionate amount to the elites of all three estates.

1 The Royal Judiciary: The Police of Hierarchy and Rank

Venal offices in the judiciary attracted buyers for their public responsibilities and honours rather than their economic returns. Many of the seneschal

TABLE 2.1 Gages of associations of office holders

Associations of Languedocian office holders	Annual gages
Cour des Comptes, Aides et Finances of Montpellier	318,810
Bureaus of Finances of Toulouse and Montpellier	163,179
Parlement of Toulouse	156,008
Divers diocese office holders	25,403
All twelve seneschal courts of Languedoc	14,266

courts of Languedoc were burdened with debt and offered the judges hardly any income. These office holders had a hard time finding buyers for their posts. Other magistrates secured steady revenue from their offices. Jurists accumulated more wealth between marriage and death than did other liberal professionals of Toulouse. Some of this wealth came from the annual sum, known as *gages*, paid by the king to show appreciation for royal service and to provide returns on the capital invested in offices. Table 2.1 shows the annual gages accruing to associations of office holders in the last years of the old regime.[1]

These magistrates obtained additional revenue directly from litigants. Royal subjects had to pay fees to jurists to use the royal courts. Table 2.2 gives an idea of what associations of jurists might collect annually for their services in the 1780s.[2]

---

1 Sentou 1969, p. 225. The sums in Table 2.1 correspond to entire groups of office holders, not individuals. The *gages* are found in Archives Nationales (hereafter AN) P5817, P5538. The gages for 'Divers diocese office holders' are an extrapolation based on the gages paid to various office holders of the Toulousain and Montpelliérain. My sources only listed gages for the seneschal courts of Toulouse and Montpellier. I extrapolated for the other 10 seneschal courts using evidence from Dawson 1972, p. 37; Castan 1980a, pp. 124–5, 168–9; Gégot 1974, vol. 1, pp. 22–4. I did not find the gages paid to Montpelliérain barristers, a corps of venal officers. Vialles 1921, p. 234.
2 The figure for the parlementaires comes from a tabulation of the fees listed in all the cases adjudicated in 1783. Archives Départementales de l'Haute Garonne (ADHG) B 1816-24. The figures for the other associations of jurists are estimates based on evidence found in AN H1/748/278; Vialles 1921, pp. 113–4, 230; Puntous 1909, pp. 406–7; Dawson 1972, pp. 82–3; Berlanstein 1975, pp. 2, 68; 'Montpellier en 1768' 1920, vol. 4, pp. 30–1. The figures for attorneys and the director of the general provostship of the province include gages and fees. Doyle finds that the office of attorney yielded annual returns of 10 to 13 percent. Such returns would mean that Languedocian attorneys together earned a total of 396,000 livres or even 528,000 a year (Doyle 1996, p. 204). I did not locate the gages and fees accruing to the judges of the Royal

TABLE 2.2 Fees collected by associations of office holders

Languedocian magistrates	Fees
Cour des Comptes, Aides et Finances of Montpellier	170,452
Parlement of Toulouse	121,545
All twelve seneschal courts	84,600
Barristers of Toulouse and Montpellier	79,200
Royal attorneys (*procureurs*) of Toulouse and Montpellier	73,920
Bureaus of Finances of Toulouse and Montpellier	60,000
Director of the provincial provostship (*prévoté générale*)	8,000

The economic returns of judicial offices were significant but certainly not excessive when one bears in mind that these tribunals upheld the law for nearly two-million provincial inhabitants. The magistracy sustained the laws of the province, maintained public order, and protected the rights of the residents. The judges possessed these responsibilities as inheritable property. Although some sold their posts on the market, most passed on their official duties to their heirs as a family profession.[3] The judges saw themselves as legal authorities whose primary interest was to uphold and develop a body of jurisprudence and defend their respective jurisdictions. They strove to inspire confidence in their professionalism and respect for their sense of responsibility.

The Parlement of Toulouse was the king's supreme judicial authority over a vast region in southern and southwestern France. It issued over 1,200 rulings in 1783. Nearly half of these validated the civil authorities and religious institutions of the province and provided for the spiritual and physical health of the population. Consanguineous couples had to obtain a ruling from the Parlement to marry one another. Their cases made up slightly over seven percent of the Parlement's rulings. Office holders of judicial associations required a ruling of the Parlement to take up their public duties. Municipal councils had to obtain the Parlement's authorisation to appoint commissioners. Lords had to obtain the Parlement's authorisation to appoint seigneurial judges. This type of legal work represented nearly 10 percent of the Parlement's cases.

The Parlement upheld the laws preserving the spiritual sustenance of the provincial inhabitants. Nearly 30 percent of its rulings certified the rights of

---

Waters and Forests, municipal tribunals, coinage courts, salt-tax courts, merchants' tribunals, and numerous others.

3 Vialles 1921, pp. 159–229.

priests to succeed one another at the head of parishes, the rights of canons to administer cathedrals, and the rights of all members of the clergy to receive pensions.[4] One of these ruling from 1783 obliged the *sieur* Rouchés to abide by his agreement to provide Miss Fouraignan with a pension and clothing upon her taking the vows to enter a convent. For her part, Fouraignan was 'to stay in the convent she had chosen and remain withdrawn, and cease her continual leaves, or be compelled by all due and reasonable means'.[5] The Parlement heard an appeal of a ruling of the seneschal court of Pamiers, which had allowed a priest to discontinue religious services in St.-Pierre-de-Rivière on account of 'atrocious imputations and calumnies' in a memorandum of the village syndic. The Parlement ruled that the injurious terms be blotted out and that the priest resume the performance of his duties.[6]

By upholding public order in this way, the Parlement of Toulouse made it possible for the provincial inhabitants to produce wealth, trade goods, and sustain their material existence. Over 40 percent of the Parlement's rulings determined the legality of contracts and debts, often on appeal from subordinate legal bodies such as the seneschal courts and merchants' tribunals. In short, the nobles of the Parlement played an indispensable role in resolving the disputes of the provincial inhabitants.

Notwithstanding these essential services, provincial inhabitants harboured grievances against the judicial system headed by the Parlement. The *cahiers de doléances* – or lists of grievances composed in rural parishes and urban associations in the spring of 1789 as part of the elections to the Estates General – are replete with complaints about delays and lengthy procedures, and especially about the fees charged by jurists. In the spring of 1789, an anonymous 'good citizen from the province of Languedoc' wrote a tract describing the magistrates as 'an innumerable swarm of leaches' that could only be eradicated by abolishing venality of office. 'If ever there is such a chance it is now [with] the holding of the Estates General'.[7]

People had an understandable aversion to paying judges for an official resolution of their disputes. Yet the tenor of their grievances suggests that the problem lay at a deeper level, in the inherent unfairness of the system itself. We saw in Chapter 1 that the jurisprudence of the Parlement of Toulouse permitted seigneurs to secure political and honorific rights left over from the feudal

---

4 These rulings have been tabulated from ADHG B 1816–24.
5 ADHG B1816.
6 ADHG B1817.
7 AN H1/942/2. For similar complaints see ADHG C2161; Archives Départementales du Gard (ADG) C 1193, C1194, C1196, C1199; Jean-Pierre Donnadieu 1989, pp. 104, 133, 216, 739, 762.

past on hundreds of occasions during the eighteenth century. Seigneurs, for instance, had the legal right to rear game, even though it harmed the crops of rural inhabitants. The parish cahiers show that the exclusive hunting privileges of the nobility caused resentment among the peasantry. Many rural inhabitants called for restrictions on the time and place of hunting, and demanded the right to kill destructive animals and birds.[8]

Thus, in upholding the law, the Parlement of Toulouse often forbade common subjects to enjoy sports reserved for seigneurs. In 1783, the Parlement heeded the request of local judges and proprietors and prohibited the playing *mails et boules* on roads leading out of the Boutonnet, a manufacturing suburb of Montpellier. The inhabitants of Rochegude, a community of 80 households in the diocese of Uzès, complained in their cahier that a ruling of the Parlement in 1784 awarded scores of seigneurial rights to M. Chalbos, including the right to protect the eggs of game by obliging them to keep their dogs on leashes. The inhabitants affirmed that they needed to leave their dogs on the loose to protect shepherds and herds from flesh-eating animals. Residents of Launac, a commune of 153 households west of Toulouse, averred in their cahiers that the legal system privileged the powerful over the unfortunate. They stated that their lord's hunting guard shot dead a villager in front of many witnesses yet was exonerated by the judiciary. The inhabitants argued that the seigneurial classes owned the local judiciary and used it to their advantage, 'from now on, there should be only two levels of jurisdiction: the first level composed, like the second, of officers named by the king and entirely independent of all the intermediate powers'.[9]

The Parlement of Toulouse defended laws regarding royal and religious ceremonies, which some provincial inhabitants found tedious. In 1776, master craftsmen and members of the trades sought to evade their traditional duties in Toulouse's religious processions. They claimed that the suppression of the guilds, carried out under the controller general Turgot, did away with their public obligations. But the Parlement ruled that the artisans accompany the processions with their horns, candles, and the reliquaries of Saint-Sernin in accordance with established custom.[10]

After the harvest of 1781, the poor quality of local grains led the Parlement to grant the guild of Toulousain bakers a dispensation from its annual ceremonial obligation to distribute cakes on behalf of the king (*gâteaux des rois*). Two

---

8   Markoff 1996, pp. 45–6, 74.
9   ADHG B1816. ADHG C2161. For Rochegude see ADG C1200.
10 ADHG B1816.

years later, the Parlement ruled that the bakers resume their duty, for they had no right to establish a precedent from a dispensation granted under special circumstances.[11]

In seeking justice from the tribunals, royal subjects not only faced antiquated laws and fees, but also entered an environment requiring deference to the representatives of royal sovereignty. The interior design of Toulouse's palace of justice situated the parlementaires in prominent positions. Strict etiquette, such as the barristers' duty to wear a hat when addressing the magistrates, upheld the dignity of royal justice. The ceremonies marking the fall of Maupeou and the restoration of the sovereign courts in February 1775 illustrate the lofty place held by the parlementaires in Languedoc's official hierarchy. All of Toulouse's official associations turned out for the ceremonies in the traditional attire of their rank. The intendant and the military governor escorted the magistrates into the palace of justice for the latter to regain their seats. The bourgeois guard and the order of barristers followed behind. After registering the edict re-establishing their powers, the parlementaires toured the city in a cavalcade of 40 coaches. The order of barristers then presented them with a marble obelisk on top of which rested a golden sphere adorned with a medallion of the king.[12] The president Puivert supposedly shed tears when he heard the following passage in an address from the barrister Désirat:

> The order of barristers ardently wished for this happy revolution. Its interests alone would have determined its stance. The glory of the magistracy belongs to us in a way: our honour is conjoined to that of the magistracy. Please consider these attachments, sir, at a time when our virtue was tested by such terrible disgraces.[13]

That night Toulousains were treated to firework displays in different parts of the city.[14]

The other sovereign court of Languedoc, the Cour des Comptes, Aides et Finances of Montpellier, had nearly as much responsibility as did the Parlement of Toulouse. The Montpelliérain judges verified titles of nobility and the accounts of financial establishments and tax farms, and heard appeals from

---

11   Dulaurier, Molinier and Barry 1876, vol. 13, p. 1279.
12   Berlanstein 1975, pp. 7–8; Ramet 1935, p. 579.
13   Dubédat 1885, p. 639.
14   Dulaurier, Molinier and Barry 1876, vol. 13, pp. 1270–1.

inferior tribunals such as the salt-tax courts, seneschals, and bureaus of finances. They heard litigation relative to seigneurial titles and financial disputes, including those over tax assessments.

The magistrates of the Cour des Comptes, Aides et Finances took pride in upholding the distinctive tax codes of southern France, the *pays de taille réelle*, where the land itself bore the designation noble or common regardless of the titles of the owner. The nobility of Languedoc derived no fiscal benefit from its personal status. The Cour des Comptes, Aides et Finances meticulously verified the financial claims of litigants and sometimes obliged noblemen to fulfil their fiscal duties. Alexis de Tocqueville recognised the merit of this system. He argued that it did not divide the province into competing associations, arouse resentment against the nobility, or hinder the citizens from cooperating in the management of public affairs. The role of the Cour des Comptes, Aides, et Finances in enforcing the fiscal laws of Languedoc may help to explain why the judges continued to enjoy the confidence of local residents after 1789. We will see in Chapter 4 that nobles of Montpellier won elections to positions of leadership throughout the 1790s.[15]

Nevertheless, one must not imagine that the law codes established civil equality among the populace. In upholding the jurisprudence of the pays de taille réelle, the Cour des Comptes, Aides et Finances still protected tax-exempt property. This property included seigneurial perquisites and tithes, and the vast majority of it belonged to local lords and religious establishments. The remaining village property, the non-privileged land, had to cover community tax quotas. In this manner, the privileged property augmented the tax assessments of the majority of rural inhabitants.

The Cour des Comptes, Aides et Finances upheld its own rights to an honourable rank in the public life of Montpellier. The judges possessed privileges permitting them to pass in front of the members of other royal associations in processions and held seats in the upper echelon of the municipal assemblies. They initiated litigation in the 1770s to put an end to the indecency with which the metropolitan clergy received them in the cathedral. Their benches did not offer a view of the choir. The judges pursued the case through a number of tribunals before the royal council finally ruled in their favour. Members of the Cour des Comptes, Aides et Finances then held a special meeting to discuss their next appearance in the cathedral. They wanted to perform a splendorous entrance for everyone in Montpellier to see that the king had taken their side.[16]

---

15   'Montpellier en 1768' 1920, vol. 4, p. 30; Tocqueville 1955, the appendix 'The pays d'états, with special reference to Languedoc', pp. 212–21.
16   Vialles 1921, pp. 52–5, 67.

2   Tax Farms: The Provincial Fountains of Wealth

Fiscal institutions offered far more opportunities for wealth than did the judiciary. One loses sight of these opportunities when studying royal taxation from the summit of government. James Riley analyses foreign governments' estimates of the finances of French kings. These governments were imperial rivals of France and gathered information about its military capacity. Their information shows that the overhead costs of tax collection did not exceed those in England. Much of the revenue that did not reach the royal treasury of France was spent on government services in the provinces. Another part of overhead costs went to the general farmers of indirect taxes on merchandise. The general farmers charged more revenue for their services than did the general receivers of direct taxes on the land. Their work required greater expenses. They gleaned much revenue from the crown's finances but contributed more than did other officials to the growth of its budgets over the course of the eighteenth century. And the failure of this growth to keep pace with inflation actually reduced the tax burden. Riley concludes that the French fiscal system was no more burdensome than was the English.[17]

There are drawbacks to such a straightforward comparison of France and England. The two countries had profoundly different state structures. The French monarchy did not evolve toward the 'rational bureaucratic' state defined by Max Weber. The ruling dynasty did not organise a hierarchical bureaucracy subject to central direction. To the contrary, the king's formal ownership of the state entitled him to create and sell public functions for revenue. This practice, known as venality of office, permitted kings to build an administrative apparatus without seeking the consent of the governed. Kings induced regional potentates to join the realm by granting them political responsibilities and fiscal privileges. Taxation belonged to purchasers of offices and varied between provinces. State debt was dispersed among the tax farmers, office holders, and provincial estates. In England, Parliament gained control of public finances during the seventeenth century and prohibited the crown from selling government functions. It abolished the tax farms in the 1670s and 1680s and turned the fiscal administrations into tractable bureaucracies. Law, rather than the royal will, regulated public affairs. Parliament succeeded in consolidating its debt, bringing down interest rates, and raising the funds needed to accomplish its foreign-policy goals.[18]

---

17   Riley 1986, pp. 38, 42, 50, 56, 60–1, 64–6, 70, 234.
18   Descimon and Jouhaud 1996, pp. 192–4; Hill 1982, pp. 186–7; Teschke 2003, pp. 126, 175, 231, 253–4.

French absolutism arbitrated competition between the king, landowners, financiers, and office holders for the agricultural and artisan/merchant surplus of the realm. Land and state bonds generated returns of about five percent in the second half of the seventeenth century. The crown tried to attract investors to offices by keeping yields at 10 percent, but financial exigencies, requiring the reduction and taxation of yields, brought them well below this rate. Office holders made up much of the difference by charging fees for their services. The profits of office therefore varied according to the post and the owner's manner of performing its duties.[19]

In sum, comparing British fiscal receipts to the contracts between French kings and their general receivers and tax farmers does not offer an accurate appraisal of the two systems.[20] What office holders took from the economic life of France was a private affair outside the purview of royal ministers. General receivers and tax farmers subcontracted taxation down to the regional level, where it was further sold to local collectors. Thousands of office holders secured income from tax collection on the regional, town, and village levels. Their profits did not figure into the financial balance sheets drawn up in Versailles and the royal courts of Europe.[21]

In Languedoc, the Estates oversaw a budget of 14,346,233 livres in 1789. This sum included three million for the annual subsidy, known as the *don gratuit* or free gift, to the king. It included revenue from taxes on all subjects regardless of their privileges: 3,261,741 from the two *vingtièmes* and four *sols pour livre*, and 1.6 million from the capitation. The budget comprised 229,333 from the provincial tax farm called *l'équivalent* and 6,255,159 from inspectors of butchers' shops, subsidies from towns, levies for the mounted constabulary, and several other designations for which the Estates raised a lump sum rather than allow the king to impose the taxes himself. Of these 14,346,233 livres, 12,791,010 were designated royal deniers and 1,555,223 provincial.[22]

---

19 Descimon and Jouhaud show that office holders also profited from the market value of their posts. The price of some offices increased 900 to 2,000 percent between 1590 and 1660 (1996, pp. 189–92, 195).

20 John Brewer shows that the eighteenth-century states of England and France were fundamentally different (1989, pp. 64–87, 129). Teschke provides a convincing description of the differences (2003, pp. 253–61).

21 John Bosher and Joël Félix paint much the same picture of the early modern French state as do Descimon and Jouhaud (Bosher 1970, pp. 166, 175, 180, 190, 280, 304–6, 317; Félix 1999, pp. 34–5, 40, 43, 304, 404–5, 498–9).

22 AN F4/1245; H1/748/62; H1/748/278; H1/942/1; H1/1105; ADHG C2424, C2430; Petot 1958, p. 314; Duval-Jouve 1974, vol. 1, p. 20; Rioufol 1904, p. 15.

In practice, none of these figures tell us much about the flow of tax revenue. The king never took 12,791,010 from the province. Nearly four million were earmarked for the intendant, the military governor, garrisons, public works, and other establishments indispensable to the crown and the province. Moreover, the king ceded a growing portion of his remaining revenue to service loans taken out by the Estates of Languedoc for the royal treasury. This entanglement of the treasuries of the king and Estates, observable in Burgundy, Artois, Walloon Flanders, and other pays d'états, makes it impossible to distinguish the financial interests of the king from those of the provincial estates.[23]

The budget of the Estates of Languedoc bears little relationship to the amount of taxes actually levied in the province. Royal ministers recognised as much when they gathered information for financial policy. Jacques Necker, the director of royal finances, estimated in 1784 that Languedoc was the ninth most heavily taxed of the 27 généralités in his survey, each inhabitant paying an average of over 22 livres for a total of 37.5 million. A decade and half earlier, the controller general Terray asked the intendants to calculate the tax burden of their *généralités*. Terray determined that Languedoc was the tenth most heavily taxed généralité of the 32 of the realm, each inhabitant paying an average of nearly 20 livres.[24] Table 2.3 lists the average quota of direct tax paid by an individual inhabitant of various communities and dioceses of Languedoc at the end of the old regime.[25]

Necker, Terray, and other royal ministers had fairly accurate records to chart the destination of these direct taxes. The taille, capitation, vingtièmes, *taillons*, and sols pour livres raised upward of 17 million livres a year in Languedoc. Over 11 percent of this revenue remunerated 66 diocese receivers and thousands of parish collectors. The receivers belonged to the upper strata of Languedocian society. Noble Rivals de Gincla, one of the diocese receivers of Carcassonne, was the town's wealthiest resident according to the capitation rolls of 1787. A survey of about 100 after-death inventories of the magistrates of the Parlement of Toulouse reveals three offices of diocese receiver. Another diocese receiver

---

23   Legay 2001, pp. 343, 346, 517.
24   AN H1/1588/47; Necker 1784, vol. 1, p. 226. A pamphleteer wrote in 1789 that the province's 1,800,000 inhabitants paid 36,000,000, or 20 livres a piece, in taxes. Donnadieu 1995, p. 241.
25   ADHG C1516; ADG C1193, C1199, C1200; Pasquier and Galabert 1925, pp. 3, 9, 16, 23, 28, 36, 38, 50, 55, 63; Pélaquier 1996, vol. 1, p. 102, vol. 2, p. 86; Yché 1985, pp. 39, 50; Saumade 1908, pp. 36, 529; Secondy and Segondy 1980, p. 204; Cazanave 1999, p. 57; Molinier 1985, pp. 149, 202. Louis André and the intendant Ballainvilliers came up with very different calculations for the tax burden of the diocese of Mende (André 1894, p. 3; Ballainvilliers 1989, p. 213). Nicole Castan and Jean Merley come up with very different calculations for the tax burden of the diocese of Le Puy (Castan 1980a, p. 74; Merley 1974, vol. 1, p. 89).

TABLE 2.3   Average direct tax paid by inhabitants in diverse parts of Languedoc

Communities (diocese)	Average direct tax burden of an inhabitant
Nine communities (Toulouse)	14.23–6.38 livres
Five communities (Nîmes and Alès)	53.08–29.42 (per household)
Saint-Victor-de-la-Coste (Uzès)	8.53
Capens (Rieux)	5.11
Gruissan (Narbonne)	5.96
Fabrègues and Pignan (Montpellier)	18.19 and 10
Belpech (Mirepoix)	19
The diocese of the Vivarais	11.1 (all taxes, including indirect)
The diocese of St.-Papoul	10.79
The diocese of Mende	26.05 (all taxes, including indirect) – 7.95
The diocese of Le Puy	37.73–5.2

combined the revenue of this office with the proceeds of a lease to collect the seigneurial dues of the archbishop of Toulouse. His services to this clerical potentate put him in line for an ennobling post of *capitoul* at the head of the municipality in the last years of the old regime. Two other receiverships belonged to a lawyer in the Parlement and a judge in the Bureau of Finances of Montpellier. At least eight judges of the Cour des Comptes, Aides et Finances owned diocese receiverships.[26]

The involvement of the nobility in the handling of direct taxes did not escape anyone's attention. In 1784, the controller general Calonne asked the intendant to investigate whether it was an abuse of royal finances that magistrates of the Cour des Comptes, Aides et Finances collected and audited the same accounts. Rural inhabitants, of course, had even greater reason to hope for reform of the system. Many contended in parish cahiers that the king would obtain more revenue and spare them senseless burdens, if he suppressed the receiverships and allowed communities to deposit their taxes directly in the royal treasury.[27]

---

26   AN H1/944/1; Sentou 1969, pp. 90, 92; Larguier 1989, pp. 100–1; Marquié 1993, p. 219; Appolis 1951, p. 318; Vialles 1921, pp. 159–89. Rocqueplan d'Orby owned an office of diocese receiver in the Vivarais in the early 1760s. Reynier 1943–51, vol. 2, p. 251. Jean Jourdan, a merchant manufacturer, and son of the first consul mayor of Lodève, the agent of the bishop, was one of the diocese receivers. The other was Germain Pellet, an owner of financial offices in other dioceses and an investor in the provincial company providing for the upkeep of royal troops. Appolis 1936, pp. 15–16, 33; Biloghi 1998, p. 409.

27   AN H1/944/1. For parish cahiers see ADG C1193, C1194, C1199, C1201. The municipality of

Royal ministers had far less information about indirect taxes. The king's salt monopoly, for instance, known as the *gabelle*, brought in less revenue from Languedoc than it did from other provinces. In 1789, of the 58.5 million livres which entered the royal treasury through the gabelle, about 1,638,000 came from Languedoc. Languedoc was a province of *petite gabelle* in which the inhabitants had to purchase 11.75 pounds of salt at 33 livres 10 *sous* the quintal, a cost of about five livres a head. Thus the gabelle raised over eight million livres in Languedoc. Much of the difference between what entered the royal treasury and was raised in the province must have accrued to the office holders in the salt-tax administration. One of these was François Joseph Catanie, a lawyer in the Parlement of Toulouse and triennial verifier of the gabelle in Montpellier. Another was the intendant Saint-Priest's son-in-law, Bocaud. He was a lessee of the salt marshes of Peccais, an integral part of the gabelle. Jacques-Joseph Boussairolles père, councilor in the Cour des Comptes, Aides et Finances of Montpellier, was the syndic of the lessees of Peccais, and several of his fellow judges were shareholders.[28]

The investment of robe nobles in the gabelle may be the reason Jean-Gabriel Murat, lord of Montai and councilor-auditor in the Cour des Comptes, Aides et Finances of Montpellier, defended it in March 1789 despite the wish expressed in countless Languedocian cahiers for its abolition. Murat wrote to royal ministers that they should not forgo such a lucrative tax at a time when the monarchy struggled with budget deficits. Common subjects, however, refused to go on paying monopoly prices to tax farmers. In 1790, an angry mob assaulted Jacques Archinar fils, a wholesale merchant (*négociant*) from Nîmes and a lessee of Peccais. The rioters threatened to hang him for profiting from such a basic and essential product.[29]

The king's properties and seigneuries generated about 50 million livres a year for the royal treasury at the end of the old regime. Like the gabelle, they undoubtedly cost the populace much more. The most lucrative office in the royal domains of Languedoc, yielding 40,000 a year, was the receiver of the

---

Toulouse had a particular statute according it control over patrimonial revenues and direct taxes. It sold management of this treasury to a consortium made up of a master of surgery, a notary, an attorney, a chevalier from Albi, and a candidate at the stock exchange (*postulant à la bourse*) in 1788. They obtained profits of over 15,000 livres a year. ADHG C290, C357; Lamouzèle 1910, pp. 37, 41.

28 Figures for the *gabelle* come from ADHG 1 L 701; Dupâquier 1988, p. 76; Puget 1990, p. 90; Marion 1927–31, vol. 1, pp. 17–18. For the lessees of the gabelle see ADG L420; ADHG C365; Archives Départementales de l'Hérault (ADH) B44; Michel 1980, vol. 5, 68, 70.

29 AN H1/942/2; ADG L420; Donnadieu 1995, pp. 88, 220, 251, 279, 294, 301, 484, 488, 549, 561, 581, 588, 591, 604, 636, 666, 691, 756.

receipts of the mobile controllers who gathered revenue from various royal levies in the province. Necker reformed the royal domains in 1777, suppressing 506 offices, about a third of the total, in the royal waters and forests. A document from royal accounts generated by the reform, a record of 136 offices to be reimbursed, listed eight in Languedoc. The value of these ranged from 114,886 for the office of former alternative and triennial general receiver of domains and woods of the généralité of Toulouse and particular receiver of the royal lordship of Mazamet to 400 for the office of receiver of fines, restitutions, and confiscations in the royal lordship of Quillan. The average value of these eight offices was over 30,000 livres. If they enjoyed the eight or nine percent returns common to other financial offices, then they generated about 2,700 a year for each of their owners. This sum amounts to almost half of what a great noble family of the grain-growing region of upper Languedoc typically made from its landed and seigneurial properties.[30]

Pierre Joly, director of the Registration and Domains at the end of the old regime, married a woman with seigneurial and landed property around Toulouse worth about 2,500 livres a year. Picot de Lapeyrouse, a wealthy seigneur of upper Languedoc, owned an office in the king's waters and forests in the diocese of Toulouse. A noble judge of the Cour des Comptes, Aides et Finances owned an office of receiver of domains and woods in Montpellier yielding about 10,000 a year in the 1760s.[31]

Louis XIV added a tax, known as *contrôle des actes*, on all notarised documents – including writs, leases, processes, property sales, and arrests carried out by bailiffs – to the royal domains in 1693. The growth of commerce and the multiplication of economic transactions in the decades following 1740 augmented the revenue generated by this tax to about 30 percent of all the proceeds of the royal domains in 1789. The value of the notaries' practices, a reflection of the amount of business they contracted, suggests the magnitude of the sums raised by the right of control. Notarial offices in Toulouse yielded about 4,000 livres a year and sold for about 20,000 in the 1780s. Notaries from Montpellier, however, did not believe such yields were sufficient. They contended that

---

30 For royal budgets see Marion 1927–31, vol. 1, pp. 467–8. For the value of offices in the royal domains of Languedoc see 'Montpellier en 1768' 1920, vol. 4, p. 75; AN F4/1003. Returns on financial offices ranged from 3.75 to 40 percent, and were generally around eight or nine percent. Démeunier 1782–1832, vol. 4, chapter 'Trésorier', and p. 12n; Descimon and Jourhaud 1996, p. 173; Bruguière 1989, pp. 100–1; Riley 1986, pp. 60–1; Dessert 1984, pp. 43, 63; Harris 1979, p. 113; Durand 1971, p. 163. For the landed and seigneurial income of the noble families of the Lauragais region of upper Languedoc see Frêche 1974, pp. 564–5.

31 Sentou 1969, p. 267; Amanieu 1959, p. 146; 'Montpellier en 1768' 1920, vol. 4, p. 72; Vialles 1921, p. 83.

high prices in the provincial capitals, and the 'decency of their station', created expenses unknown to rural notaries. The Estates and intendant of Languedoc responded with an ordinance in 1786 augmenting the fees paid by communities to notaries of Toulouse and Montpellier when the communities reimbursed debts. These new fees ranged from four livres for reimbursements below a 1,000 to 36 for ones exceeding 15,000.[32]

The *contrôle des actes* weighed more heavily on rural areas. One of the many rights of control incumbent upon peasant communities was the four *sols* for each livre charged by notaries for writing the minutes of deliberations into official registers. We saw in Chapter 1 that these types of fees played a part in provoking the revolt of the armed masks in the Vivarais in 1783. The magistrates dispatched by the Parlement of Toulouse to sort out the problems of the region reported that lawyers, notaries, and royal attorneys preyed on the inhabitants' ignorance by inventing unwarranted procedures and fees. Many parishes bemoaned the right of control in their cahiers. Residents of Rousson, a community of 128 households in the diocese of Uzès, declared that there were many illiterate inhabitants in the village who could not forgo the notaries' services. They were exposed to 'exorbitant rights of control and other levies collected by publicans in a harsh and arbitrary fashion'. They demanded that the crown abolish the tax or fix it at a moderate level, 'and radically destroy ... the tax farmers' (*traitants*) methods, and eradicate the odious practice by which they are judge and litigant in their own cases'.[33]

Every six year, the Estates of Languedoc leased the right to collect revenue on sales of fish, wine, and meat, a tax farm known as the équivalent. The lease sold for 1,442,000 livres in 1782 and 1,376,000 in 1788. The Estates used these proceeds to make an annual payment to the crown and exempt the province from taxes on oil, soap, gold, iron, and other products referred to as *les aides*. The eight companies to purchase the équivalent between 1749 and 1788 comprised nobles, Parisians, wholesale merchants, a few jurists and urban rentiers (*bourgeois*), office holders in the financial system such as diocese tax receivers, and an agent named by the archbishop of Narbonne, president of the Estates, to oversee the interests of the province. The companies received investments from office holders in the judiciary, such as treasurers of France in the Bureaus of Finances, and townspeople, such as wholesale merchants and landlords.

---

32   Doyle 1996, p. 227. For the ordinance on the notaries' fees see AN H1/748/179.
33   R.J. Bernard lists the right of control paid by communities for having their deliberations recorded. 1971, p. 114. See AN H1/748/178 for the ruling of the Parlement. The cahier is in ADG C1193.

They annually subleased the tax farm to middlemen, who passed additional contracts stipulating the sums to be paid by butchers, shopkeeper, and merchants in the localities. A sample of these contracts suggests that all of the companies, shareholders, and middlemen together invested about 4.5 million a year for returns of about 400,000.[34]

The tax farmers of the équivalent, like those of the gabelle and the contrôle des actes, faced resistance in the last decades of the old regime. Rural communities and associations of shopkeepers, artisans, and workers complained in their cahiers that the excessive rates of the équivalent burdened the common people and that the collectors vexed them with threats, arbitrary demands, and recurrent lawsuits. Popular resistance to the équivalent forced the tax farmers to suspend collection in some parts of the province during the 1750s and 1760s. The tax farmers received authorisation to form armed detachments to enforce collection in the 1770s. Continued contraband and violence against the tax farmers obliged the Cour des Comptes, Aides et Finances to grant a request of a syndic of the Estates of Languedoc in 1788 and reaffirm a judgement permitting the collectors of the équivalent to make unexpected visits to private homes and search for illegal stocks.[35]

Other indirect taxes did not figure into the fiscal burden calculated by Terray and Necker. The sub-delegate in Nîmes reported in 1788 that stocking and cloth manufacturers had to pay office holders 450 or 500 livres a year to exempt their products from the requirement of having a red label. They had to pay another one percent of their sales at the regional fair of Alès to the municipal magistrates. The decline of the Languedocian textile industry probably depressed these types of fees in the last decades of the old regime. But in Mazamet, annual production increased from about 5,000 pieces in the 1760s to nearly 30,000 on the eve of the Revolution, and swelled the fees paid to inspectors to about 3,000 livres. Inspectors also received payments from the royal treasury. The sub-inspector of drapes in Lodève, for example, received a salary (*appointements*) of 1,200 livres in 1764. Some of these posts belonged to owners of ennobling

---

[34] For the costs of the lease see ADHG C2424, C2430. For the companies that leased the équivalent: AN H1/748/219; ADH A107, A116, A121, A125; ADHG C2196, C2405, C2424, C2430. For other investors in the company see Vidal 1963, pp. 18, 65, 326, 393. For subleases: Archives Départementales de l'Aude (ADA) 7C8; ADHG C16.

[35] For the cahiers see ADH C878, ADG C1193, C1194, C1198, C1200, C1201; Donnadieu 1995, pp. 212, 243, 245, 255, 790. For resistance to the équivalent see ADH B9081, B9156, C9374; Ado 1996, p. 73; Teissier Du Cros 1944–48, pp. 310, 312. For the ruling of the Cour des Comptes, Aides et Finances see ADH A126.

offices in the magistracy, such as Pierre d'Astruc, councilor/secretary of the Cour des Comptes, Aides et Finances and inspector of cloth manufacturers in St.-Chinian in the diocese of St.-Pons.[36]

Municipal sales taxes were another fiscal burden outside of the crown's oversight. Toulouse leased the collection of its patrimonial revenues and taxes on merchandise entering the city (*octrois*) to François Jacques Campan de Latour for 380,000 livres a year in the 1780s. He made over 50,000 in profit between 1782 and 1787. Those who purchased this tax farm between 1740 and 1781 included landlords from Paris, a tax receiver in the diocese of Mende, and a financier from Montpellier. They subcontracted collection to scores of others. Of the 55 receivers, controllers, visitors, and assistants of Toulouse's indirect taxes in 1747, 22 percent were jurists, 18 percent landlords, and 15 percent merchants. Montpellier's municipal tax farm was reputed to have made the fortune of several of the city's great families. Jacques Barthelemy Noailles, a barrister in the Parlement, was a municipal tax farmer in Beaucaire, a town in the diocese of Nîmes, and a triennial collector of the gabelle in Toulouse. Registers from the seneschal court of Carcassonne contain cases from the 1770s and 1780s involving merchants and a public works contractor who owned offices in the town's indirect tax farm. The popular classes seem to have resented surrendering income to these officials. In 1786, the tax farmer of Carcassonne found graffiti on the shutters of his store threatening him with reprisals if he went on taking revenue from local residents.[37]

Payers and treasurers gleaned an additional percentage of fiscal proceeds when they made disbursements to associations of judges, engineers, professors, letter carriers, and other royal officials. An example of these payers and

---

36   For the sub-delegate's letter: ADH C5481. Pouthas 1934, p. 71n; Cazals 1983, pp. 36–7. For Lodève: ADH C2532. For St.-Chinian: Bergasse 1989, pp. 105–6. The Parlement of Toulouse ruled in 1783 that master tailors and widows owning a boutique had to pay an office holder a sum for every *garçon* and seamstress they employed. ADHG B1817. Cloth merchants of Toulouse made an annual payment, or disbursed between one and three sols per piece, to the bureau of the municipal stock exchange (*bureau de la Bourse*). Marinière 1958, p. 274. In Montpellier, the receiver of lotteries, the receiver of taxes on tobacco, and the director of rights on cards each made thousands of livres a year. 'Montpellier en 1768' 1920, vol. 4, pp. 75–6. The cahiers de doléances contain many grievances of urban merchants and craftsmen about the taxes collected on leather, skins, and tobacco. Donnadieu 1995, pp. 221, 234, 279, 294, 756.

37   For finances of Toulouse's indirect taxes see Lamouzèle 1910, pp. 17, 23. For office holders of this tax farm see AN H1/1014; Gebhart and Mercadier 1967, pp. 18, 138–40. For comment about the fortunes built on the indirect taxes of Montpellier see 'Montpellier en 1768' 1920, vol. 4, p. 80. For the indirect taxes of Carcassonne and Beaucaire see ADA B78; ADH B44; Blanc 1984, p. 157.

treasurers is the contractors, known as *étapiers*, who saw to the lodging and provisioning of troops. The passage of soldiers through Languedoc had long caused inconvenience to provincial inhabitants until the Estates negotiated an arrangement with the crown in the latter part of the seventeenth century. The province set up a tax farm to pay for the orderly upkeep of army units and put an end to all of the problems caused by the soldiery. The tax farm also turned out to be a boon for local investors.[38]

By the end of the eighteenth century, the Estates of Languedoc succeeded in housing royal troops while protecting the livelihood of the provincial inhabitants. The archives of the intendancy do not contain any complaints about royal troops passing through the province in the last decades of the old regime. Few Languedocian cahiers de doléances mention the étape or the soldiers it sustained. The étapiers, who provided this service, annually paid between 100,000 and 1,000,000 livres, depending on military needs, to provision and lodge troops in Languedoc in the eighteenth century. If they withheld the same percentage of royal funds for their services as did other office holders in the financial system, then their profits ranged from 8,000 to 90,000 livres a year.[39]

The authorities sought to bar Protestants from these profits. A ruling of 1754 obliged all of the tax farmers, contractors, and sub-lessees of the étape to present proof of Catholicism to a syndic of the Estates of Languedoc. Those who took up the leases generally hailed from the region of Montpellier. Their professions and ranks typically consisted of wholesale merchants, nobles, jurists, and office holders in the fiscal establishments. One finds a great number of merchants on the last leases of the old regime. The étape, like the équivalent and municipal octrois, seems to have been a lucrative placement for well-to-do merchants and landowners seeking to accumulate wealth and eventually buy judicial offices and obtain titles of nobility. The tendency of wholesale merchants to invest in the étape may also reflect the transfer of wealth to a stable investment, as the textile industry of Languedoc declined in the 1770s and 1780s.[40]

Philippe-Laurent de Joubert's office of treasurer of the Estates of Languedoc yielded the highest profits in the province. He descended from an old Montpelliérain family of the robe. His uncle owned one of the executive posts of

---

38 Beik 1985, pp. 132, 172, 248, 261, 283. For a list of other treasurers and payers see 'Montpellier en 1768' 1920, vol. 4, pp. 72–3, 77–8.

39 For the *étapiers*' expenses see AN H1/748/278; ADH C7240, C7481, C7648, C8622. Biloghi 1998, pp. 329, 487.

40 ADH II E 57/441, II E 57/629, 2 B 29–747; Biloghi 1998, pp. 404, 487; Biloghi 1993, pp. 147–68.

FIGURE 2.1
Laurent-Nicolas de Joubert, son of Philippe-Laurent de Joubert. Artist: François-Xavier Fabre, a painter of monarchist sympathies, whose studies were funded by Philippe de Joubert. Fabre fled the Revolution to Italy in 1793.
GETTY MUSEUM

the Estates (*syndics généraux*), and a cousin married a prosperous local seigneur. Joubert's post of treasurer placed him between the revenue collected in the province and the royal treasury. He received and dispensed provincial taxes and arranged for the annual subsidy to the king. We will see later in this chapter that he organised over 100,000,000 livres in loans for the king on the credit of the Estates in the last decade of the old regime. Joubert held such a crucial place in royal financial networks that he spent most of his time in Paris, where his services were most needed. The meetings held in Paris in 1788 and 1789 by the Privileged Company of the Salt Marshes of Sète, a port near Montpellier, show that 9 of the 10 shareholders, including Joubert, resided in Paris. His post of treasurer for the Estates yielded nearly 800,000 livres a year in the 1780s. The rolls of the capitation from 1789 show that Joubert was the wealthiest resident of Montpellier, paying seven times more taxes than did the councillors in the Cour des Comptes, Aides, et Finances.[41]

Joubert's value to royal finances secured him exceptional leverage over the peasants of his seigneurie. The count d'Eu ceded the barony of Montredon, comprising eight villages and the town of Sommières, between the dioceses

---

41 ADH B23646, C1370; AN H1/748/278, H1/748/279, H1/748/293, H1/944/1; Necker 1784, vol. 1, p. 306; Chéron and Sarret de Coussergues 1963, p. 267.

of Montpellier and Nîmes, to Joubert in 1762. Joubert secured a ruling from the royal council in 1786 forbidding the local peasantry to glean wood and graze animals on the scrublands (*garrigues*) and commons. The peasants submitted to fines in return for Joubert's pledge to abandon further litigation they could not afford. They then informed the controller general that Joubert had stripped them of customary rights enjoyed by other inhabitants of the province. Royal lawyers got hold of titles proving the illegality of Joubert's pretensions. We will see in the next chapter that when these types of disputes came to the attention of royal ministers, the king's council withdrew them from the local courts and defended the communities. But in this case, the intendant moved cautiously, advising the controller general, 'We do not see why the administration should intervene in an affair that is being adjudicated in the customary tribunals'.[42]

The controller general's decision to disregard Joubert's abuse of seigneurial privileges highlights the obstacles preventing substantive reform. David Bien shows that royal ministers often created supernumerary posts to oblige associations of office holders to give the king additional funds and cover the extraordinary financial needs of the crown. Members of associations bought these posts to prevent a glut from bringing down the value of their own offices. They borrowed from private individuals to purchase the newly created posts and used the income and prerogatives of the posts to service their debts. In this way, Bien argues, venality of office became so entrenched in royal finances and private fortunes that it could not be uprooted by anything short of a thoroughgoing revolution. Joubert exemplifies this entrenchment of wealthy individuals in the financial networks of the monarchy. His ability to raise revenue helped keep the regime afloat in the 1780s. The monarchy's dependence on office holders such as Joubert prevented it from shedding venality of office and the seigneurial regime, and modernising the state. Seigneurs and office holders ran the state as their patrimony, exploiting it for their private advantage, as the king did not have much of a bureaucracy to run the state himself.[43]

3   The Estates of Languedoc: The Apex of Provincial Patronage

The Estates of Languedoc distributed the greatest honours and fortunes in the province during the 40 days around the New Year comprising their annual

---

42   AN H1/1105. For the contract between the king and the comte d'Eu see Bibliothèque Nationale (BN), Collection Joly Fleury, 560, dossiers 7432 and 7749.

43   Bien 1987, pp. 89–114.

meetings in Montpellier. They saw to various administrative affairs, managed public works, supervised the allotment and collection of taxes, leased the provincial tax farms, and negotiated the portion of Languedocian resources to offer the king. These functions gave the Estates the capacity to represent the interests of provincial subjects to the crown. But in the eighteenth century, the Estates rarely made use of this capacity. The only year in which the Estates opposed the crown was 1750, when the royal minister Machault sought to impose a vingtième tax on all properties, including those exempt from the taille. Machault suspended the Estates and began assessing the tax through royal agents. Two years later, an agreement was reached whereby the Estates obtained the right to administer the tax in return for making an annual payment to the king. Thereafter the Estates no longer discussed royal demands critically.[44] They presented the king the same grievances year after year as if they merely went through the motions. The minutes of the proceedings leave the impression that the members saw to their tasks in a formulaic fashion. The Estates seemed to suffer from sclerosis.

Then again, one can consider the proceedings from a different angle. The traditional interpretative framework for analysing the provincial estates, a framework measuring regional autonomy against royal centralisation, might not be the best way to understand these institutions. Tocqueville popularised the view that kings and royal ministers of the seventeenth century began to appoint provincial intendants in order to govern the realm more efficiently. Reading Tocqueville, one is left with the impression that revocable administrators, answerable directly to the king and his ministers, circumvented the traditional judges and office holders, raised more revenue for the royal treasury, and modernised the state apparatus.[45]

Yet if one takes a careful look at the pays d'états, one comes away with a different view of royal absolutism. The provincial estates took on additional administrative functions, as the king gained more power. The governmental responsibilities of the Estates of Languedoc, Burgundy, and Brittany actually increased, as they became embedded within the expanding spheres of royal authority. William Beik shows that by 1680 the members of the Estates of Languedoc defended their interests by working within the royal agenda rather than by trying to obstruct it. They used their authority to elaborate programmes mutually beneficial to themselves and the king. Looked at from this angle, the

---

[44] Julian Swann shows that the mid-century dispute followed similar lines in Burgundy (2003, pp. 306–8).
[45] This idea of absolutism is one of the themes of Tocqueville 1955.

monarchy does not seem to have promoted centralisation, efficiency, and modernisation, but rather to have promoted the revival of institutions with origins in the feudal past.[46]

This perspective makes sense of the proceedings of the Estates of Languedoc. In the eighteenth century, most of the pages are taken up with administrative affairs traditionally regarded by historians as the preserve of the intendant. The Estates spent their sessions managing the financial allocations, progress reports, and other administrative business related to public works. The Estates oversaw the elaboration of one of the best regional networks of roads. Arthur Young thought that Languedoc had the most beautiful thoroughfares in the realm, 'stupendous works ... superb even to the point of folly', but that inhabitants seldom used them.[47] In the last year of the old regime, provincial inhabitants commonly criticised the Estates for wasting revenue making the main roads grand. The peasantry needed local roads linking rural communities to the major arteries.[48]

The members of the Estates took particular interest in prominent ventures such as the Canal du Midi, constructed in the 1670s, which left a sense of majesty in the province. In the eighteenth century, they busied themselves in almost every session with plans for the embellishment of the Promenade de Peyrou, located in Montpellier, the city of their meetings. This raised promontory and terraced park extends out from the city centre and offers a view of the Pyrenees, the Mediterranean and the Alps. The Estates adorned the promenade with a statue of Louis XIV and an Arc of Triumph in his honour. The Estates also began the restoration of an amphitheatre of the Roman Empire. This sports ground, located in Nîmes, seats 21,000 spectators.[49]

In 1760, the Estates helped the royal minister Choiseul launch a nationwide campaign to rebuild the king's navy after the defeats of the Seven Years War. The members made great show of offering their pensions and annual revenues to cover the costs of a royal loan for the construction of a warship. The archbishop of Narbonne, president of the Estates, stated that he had difficulty restraining the members' ardour to contribute, for it was a matter of serving 'the cause of the king'.[50] Two decades later, the Estates commissioned the Montpelliérain

---

46 Beik 1985, pp. 140, 145, 296–7; Legay 2001, pp. 11–12, 343, 346, 517; Swann 2003, pp. 24, 409.
47 Young 1969, p. 37; Petot 1958, pp. 313–15.
48 The protests against the Estates are located in many sources, particularly AN H1/748/134; AN H1/748/135; AN H1/748/244; AN H1/942/2.
49 AN H1/748, H1/943; Trouvé 1818, pp. 259–60.
50 *Recueil des Gazettes de France, Supplément de la Gazette du 5 décembre 1761*, 49, pp. 604–6. Edmond Dziembowski describes this campaign to rebuild the navy (1998, p. 458).

FIGURE 2.2 La Promenade de Peyrou, Montpellier
LIBRARY OF CONGRESS

lawyer Jean Albisson to write a seven-volume compilation of the history and laws of the province. At the top of the first volume appeared a dedication to 'The eminent members of the Estates of Languedoc'. Albisson wrote just below the dedication that the work was the fruit of their wisdom, solicitude, and several centuries of experience.[51]

The main reason the Estates of Languedoc retained so much administrative responsibility was their success in raising ready cash for the king. The intendants were fiscal agents above all else, and they were evaluated according to their ability to secure revenue for the royal coffers. Experience showed that the best way to secure revenue was to negotiate with local authority figures rather than to override their jurisdictions. Marie-Laure Legay finds that negotiation permitted the intendants to tap the eight provincial estates for 330,000,000 livres of loans between 1740 and 1789. The crown secured about half of this sum from the Estates of Languedoc. In the last decades of the old regime, the crown gave annual instructions to the intendant and military governor (the other royal appointee in the province) to present the Estates with requests for loans. The king thus borrowed over 100,000,000 livres, or more than 15 percent of all royal borrowing between 1779 and 1789.[52]

---

51 Albisson 1780.
52 Legay 2003, pp. 153–4; Legay 2001, pp. 343–4. For borrowing between 1777 and 1781 see

FIGURE 2.3 The arena, Nîmes, France
LIBRARY OF CONGRESS

Serving the king, then, was honourable work, and the Estates of Languedoc assembled dignitaries appropriate to the task. The members were far more aristocratic than their counterparts in the other pays d'états. In Brittany and Burgundy, abbeys, priors, and deputies of the cathedral chapters had the right to sit in the first estate alongside the bishops. In Languedoc, the bishops alone had the right to form the first estate. These leaders of the province's 23 dioceses had multifarious administrative duties. They presided over the Estates' bureaus for public works, extraordinary affairs, agricultural projects, manufacturing establishments, diocesan finances, the writing of the provincial cahier, the recruitment and lodging of troops, and the verification of community debts and taxes in tandem with royal agents.[53]

The bishops enjoyed additional responsibilities within their dioceses. The Parlement of Toulouse ruled in 1784, for example, that *Monseigneur* Jean Felix, Henri de Fumel, prelate, lord count of Lodève and Montbrun, had the right to continue his oversight of justice – including the appointment of judges, eligible lawyers, and officers filing legal documents – for nine communities and the town of Lodève. The Parlement required anyone who had documents relative to the jurisdiction to turn them over to Fumel's officers. The seigneurial

---

BN Collection Joly de Fleury, 1438, fol. 214. For loans of the Estates from 1782 to 1788 see AN H1/748/62 p. 383, H1/748/65 pp. 314–328, H1/748/138, H1/938; ADH 2E 56/583, 2E 58/141, 2E 58/157, 2E 58/190, 2E 58/193, 2E 58/197, 2E 58/199, 2E 61/107. Marion lists royal loans of the *Hôtel de Ville* of Paris (1927–31, vol. 1, pp. 473–4).

53   AN H1/938. For Brittany and Burgundy see Swann 2003, p. 57; Rebillon 1932, p. 80.

jurisdiction of Monseigneur Vermandois de St.-Simon Rouvoy de Sandricourt covered the entire diocese of Agde and entitled him to name the town's administrators (*consuls*). Jean Arnaud de Catellane, bishop-count of the Gévaudan, named the consuls of Mende and most of the priests, abbots, and priors of the diocese. Languedocian prelates also collected immense seigneurial rents and tithes. These ranged from the staggering total of 500,000 livres accruing to the archbishop of Albi to the considerable sum of 30,000 accruing to the bishop of the Vivarais.[54]

The 23 barons of the second estate formed an exceptionally rarefied group. In Brittany, all titled nobles had the right to attend the estates, and several hundred did so on a regular basis during the eighteenth century.[55] The deputies of the second estate of Languedoc, in contrast, had to establish four generations of lineage and exercise a military profession. The Estates instituted these rules in 1768 to exclude robe nobles. The Parlement of Toulouse invalidated the rules, and the Cour des Comptes, Aides et Finances of Montpellier wrote a remonstrance, but the royal council upheld them following an appeal of one of the Estates' syndic generals. Letters patent of the king from the 1780s show that the Estates carried out painstaking inquiries into the lineage of prospective barons. One of the syndic generals, for instance, rebuffed the comte de Polignac's efforts to grant Georges François de Vachon enjoyment of his seat for the year 1769, because Vachon did not have sufficient lineage.[56]

Such qualifications were not unique to Languedoc. In Burgundy, the Estates took various deliberations over the course of the eighteenth century to reserve the noble chamber solely for those able to prove one hundred years of lineage and a military background. The Estates of Burgundy permitted the nobles meeting these qualifications and possessing a fief to attend their meetings. In an average year, about 75 nobles met these criteria and attended the Estates of Burgundy during the eighteenth century.[57] In Languedoc, in addition to proving the proper lineage and military background, the nobles had to own one of 23 specially designated baronies. The rest of the Languedocian nobility, the overwhelming majority, did not have the right to attend the Estates.

---

54 ADHG B1817; Saurel 1898, vol. 1, pp. 4, 63, 110, xxxvi; Picheire 1966, p. 48; Péronnet 1990, pp. 76–90. For the revenues of bishoprics see Bru 1989, p. 16; Molinier 1985, p. 134; André 1894, p. 4; Hindie Lemay 1991, vol. 1, pp. 91, 236, 361, vol. 2, p. 834.
55 Rebillon 1932, pp. 80, 82, 85, 96.
56 The ordinance obliging barons to exercise a military profession is in ADH C7746. Protests of the sovereign courts are in AN H1/1022. The dispute over Vachon is in ADH C7830. AN H1/748/180 contains the minutes of an investigation into the lineage of a baron in 1786.
57 Swann 2003, pp. 65, 68–9.

Some of these baronies, such as Rouairoux and Florensac, did not confer many seigneurial rights. They probably granted admission to the Estates on account of royal rewards for the loyalty of powerful families in prior centuries. But other baronies afforded wide-ranging prerogatives. The prince de Conti sold the domain of Alès, first barony of the Estates, to the maréchal de Castries for 600,000 livres in 1777. Castries was already the military governor of Montpellier and Sète, and the military commander of Flanders and Hainaut. His newly-acquired barony in Languedoc conferred proceeds from mills and wine presses, and over 20 separate levies on the town of Alès and neighbouring villages. It conferred the first option to buy property sold within its jurisdiction and the right to 10 percent of the product of all privately-owned mines. The barony permitted Castries to preside over the local judiciary, sell magistracies for revenue, and occupy places of honour in churches and festivals. Madame de Rohan Chabot, widow of the count de Lautrec, sold the barony of Capendu to Emmanuel François d'Urre, marquis d'Aubais, in 1781 for 290,000 livres. This barony, located in the diocese of Carcassonne, conferred all of the assets possessed by the baron of Alès except the rights on wine and mines but conferred other assets not found in many seigneuries, such woods, arable fields, and tolls on rivers.[58]

The pageantry surrounding the annual meetings of the Estates of Languedoc probably constituted the most valuable privilege of the barons. It cast a shadow over the Montpelliérain nobility grouped around the Cour des Comptes, Aides et Finances. Ceremonies welcoming the barons to Montpellier lasted several days and included masses in the cathedral and processions through the city, as well as visits and laudatory addresses from the intendant and the provincial governor. Each baron entered the Estates in the company of a bishop and a retinue of followers. The barons wore an extravagant military coat bearing two tails, a white plume, and a diamond.[59]

We will see in Chapter 4 that the Cour des Comptes, Aides et Finances orchestrated a broad movement in 1788 and 1789 to regenerate the provincial administration. In the face of mounting criticism, the Estates of Languedoc published a pamphlet defending their powers. The pamphlet stated that kings had never intended the barons to represent the nobility. Centuries ago, the king convoked a select group of barons and bishops to give him counsel. Over the

---

58   ADH A66. The barony of M. le comte de Bannes d'Arejan cost 80,000 livres. *Lettre de M. l'Abbé de Siran, Vicaire Général de Mende, député du pays de Gévaudan, à M. le Comte de Bannes d'Arejan, baron des Etats de Languedoc, nommé par le cour député de cette province, et en cette qualité notable*, 1789.

59   *Lettre de M. l'Abbé de Siran*; ADH C7649.

following centuries, the pamphlet claimed, this right to assemble in the second estate developed into property worth 60,000 livres beyond each barony's seigneurial perquisites and lands. The membership to the Estates accorded by the barony of Alès, the preeminent seat in the second estate, was itself worth 150,000 livres. The pamphlet stated that the rest of the nobility did not own property distinguishing it from the third estate. Nobles 'have never formed a separate body, have never had the right, and cannot assemble as a body to order anything in this capacity'.[60] By the end of the old regime, the provincial elite no longer tolerated such snobbery. The abbey de Siran, for example, published a letter to M. le comte de Bannes d'Arejan, a baron of the Estates, condemning his overblown arrogance. 'In your eyes, the non-baron nobility is only *peuple*'.[61]

The Estates of Languedoc, then, were not a representative body. The bishops of Languedoc held their seats to the exclusion of thousands of parish priests, and the barons' membership came from property so privileged that not even the prominent nobles of the sovereign courts could own it. Some of the deputies spent more time in the royal court than in Languedoc and only came to the province for their annual meeting between December and February.[62] Sixty-eight deputies of the third estate, their 46 votes, and the practice of counting votes by head rather than by order did not make the Estates any more representative. The deputies of the third estate, like their counterparts of Brittany and Burgundy, owed their seats to the possession of municipal offices or to the favour of bishops and seigneurs. Many of them were nobles.[63] Since they did not represent anyone but themselves, they had no inclination or authority to resist the initiatives of the first two estates. Proposals of the archbishop of Narbonne, permanent president of the Estates of Languedoc, met time and again with unanimous support. When the meeting drew to a close, five members would visit the king in Versailles to present grievances, which hardly any Languedoc had taken part in formulating.

---

60 AN H1/748/244. See ADH A66 for the barony of Alès.
61 *Lettre de M. L'Abbé de Siran.*
62 For the composition of the Estates in 1788 see AN H1/748/190. Present at annual meetings were the count of Polignac, a resident of the St.-Germain neighbourhood of Paris, whose wife was a close friend of Marie Antoinette; the cardinal de Bernis, archbishop of Albi, who had been secretary of foreign affairs under Louis XV; Dillon, archbishop of Narbonne, president of the Assembly of the Clergy after 1785, and neighbour of the count of Polignac in Paris; the count of Périgord, a relative of the King; Loménie de Brienne, archbishop of Toulouse; the maréchal de Castries, the highest military figure of the realm; the baron of Hautpoul, known in Versailles as the magnificent; and de Joubert, the treasurer of the Estates, who as we have already seen, resided in Paris.
63 For Brittany and Burgundy see Rebillon 1932, pp. 80, 82, 121; Swann 2003, pp. 57, 66.

The provincial estates enjoyed more financial autonomy than did other institutions in the realm. They did not have to show the accounts of their treasurers to any royal auditors or intendants. The Estates of Languedoc began to publish their minutes in 1776 but omitted documents deemed unfit for the public. The payments to members appear in internal records or in correspondences with royal ministers about financial outlays of mutual interest. Many of these payments were assigned specifically for honorific display.[64]

Members of the Estates distributed additional sums when they met in diocese assemblies, known as the *assiettes*, to allocate direct taxes among the communities. Bishops presided over these assemblies, and barons and municipal officers were among the members. The assembly of the diocese of Toulouse, for example, met in the episcopal palace and drew together the archbishop, the baron de Lanta, officials from 12 communities with the right to send deputies, and a local envoy to the Estates. In 1789, the envoy was the squire (*écuyer*) M. de Verdier de Port de Guy, and the municipal deputies included two other squires, a baron, a doctor, a lawyer, and a knight of St.-Louis. Générac, Ste.-Anastasie, St.-Hilaire d'Ozilhan, St.-Jory, and Bouloc, communities of between of 1,400 and 560 inhabitants in the dioceses of Nîmes, Uzès and Toulouse, claimed in their cahiers that between 27 and 18 percent of their direct taxes were squandered on fees charged by these assemblies for public works, the reimbursement of loans, the honorariums of auditors, the fees charged by tax receivers, and many other expenses. A local nobleman claimed in 1789 that the deputies of these diocesan assemblies appropriated 217,522 livres a year for their private fortunes.[65]

In four dioceses – Albi, Velay, the Gévaudan, and the Vivarais – *Petits Etats* allotted the direct taxes. The organisation, membership, and ceremony of these estates mirrored the provincial body, albeit on a smaller scale. The Estates of Velay, for instance, assembled the abbey of Monestier, priors of Goudet, Chamalières, Grazac, du Bouchet, and de Devesset, three ecclesiastics of the

---

64 Legay 2001, p. 340. The sums listed in Table 2.4 accrued to groups of officials, not individuals. AN H1/748/62 p. 400, H1/748/100 pp. 274, 1257–308, H1/748/134, H1/748/248, H1/748/278, H1/748/282, H1/748/289, H1/944/1, H1/983, H1/1050, H1/1063, H1/1095; H1/1107; ADHG C2432; ADH A66, C2417; Siran 1789; Dulaurier, Molinier and Barry 1876, vol. 14, pp. 2394–445; Petot 1958, pp. 309–14. Swann finds that the officials of the Estates of Burgundy also received lucrative payments for their work (2003, pp. 110–1).

65 For the composition of the assembly of the diocese of Toulouse see ADHG C970. For the cahiers, ADG C1196, C1200; Pasquier and Galabert 1925, pp. 21, 60. Picot de Lapeyrouse 1789, pp. 13, 15, 52. Emile Appolis calculates that the fees of the assiette of Lodève providing for the deputies, the syndic, the municipal magistrates, ecclesiastic establishments, financial auditors, and public works inspectors amounted to 19.72 percent of the direct taxation of the diocese (1936, pp. 28–9, 28n).

TABLE 2.4   Revenue distributed in conjunction with the annual meeting of the Estates of Languedoc

Members, agents, and associates of the Estates of Languedoc	Emoluments distributed at meetings in the 1780s
Count of Périgord, military governor of Languedoc	157,425
His staff	40,670
Dillon, the archbishop of Narbonne, president of the Estates	143,000
The deputies of all three Estates	130,340
Three lieutenants generals	118,000
Their staff	1,500
Intendant, sub-delegates, and personnel of the intendancy	115,357
Seven military governors	60,000
Four directors and inspectors of public works	51,800
Three general syndics (executive officers of the Estates)	49,350
Commander in chief in Montpellier	24,000
His staff	10,300
Nineteen majors, aide-majors, and major-commandants, etc.	29,900
Two secretary/clerks (*greffiers*)	18,100
State secretaries and their employees	12,000
Two commanders	4,400
Lawyer charged with compiling the laws	3,300
The controller general in Versailles	3,000
The master of music	3,000
The provincial agent in Paris	1,600
The interior decorator	1,000

cathedral of Le Puy, the count de Polignac, 17 other barons, and three members of the third estate, usually overlords of towns. Monseigneur de Gallard de Terraube, bishop of Le Puy, held the presidency. The frequent absence of deputies allowed him to appoint replacements. The bishop's right to fill vacant seats was a source of patronage, as the diocese estates distributed thousands of livres to attendees.[66]

Loans taken out by the Estates of Languedoc for the royal treasury channelled much of the wealth of Languedoc into the private fortunes of the upper classes. The king asked the Estates to borrow more and more funds in the 1770s

66   Bayon-Tollet 1982, pp. 180–1, 180n; Rioufol 1904, pp. 8–9, 16–21.

and 1780s. Each loan was set down in a contract stipulating that the king would relinquish a portion of the royal revenue in the provincial budget to reimburse five percent of the outstanding capital and all of the interest payments. Any investor could make his capital part of the five percent to be reimbursed in a given year. This rule helped the Estates and the crown to maintain the confidence of investors. The Estates held a lottery to determine the loan contracts that would complete the five percent of the principal reimbursed annually. The Estates allotted almost 10 million livres to cover reimbursements and interest payments in 1787.[67]

In Burgundy, the bond market of the provincial estates broadened geographically and socially over the course of the eighteenth century. Between 1660 and 1713, local magistrates represented the most significant group of investors. But as the eighteenth century wore on, inhabitants of other parts of France bought a substantial share of the Burgundian debt. Members of the trades, crafts, and professions had bought few annuities from the Estates between 1660 and 1713 but owned 27 percent of the debt between 1727 and 1789. Office holders, military men, nobles, and financiers purchased 57 percent of the Burgundian loans between 1727 and 1789. The Estates of Artois and Walloon Flanders took out far fewer loans than did the Estates of Burgundy yet had a similar clientele of nobles, financiers, office holders, ecclesiastics, and well-to-do commoners.[68]

The Estates of Languedoc held a lottery in 1786 to reimburse 5,347,859 livres worth of bonds from loans taken out every year since 1775. These creditors, classified in Table A.1 of the Appendix, provide a sample of the individuals who obtained income from the fiscal system of Languedoc. What stands out about the borrowing of the Estates of Languedoc is how much revenue it transferred to the capital. Nobles of Paris and Versailles owned 32.92 percent of Languedoc's debt. If one adds the creditors of the third estate of the capital, the percentage mounts to 60.46. By contrast, the largest group of creditors of within Languedoc, the nobles of Toulouse, only owned 4.82 percent of the provincial debt.[69]

Dioceses also took out loans. The Estates of Languedoc allotted over 500,000 livres in 1789 to service debts of dioceses totalling 12,500,000. The Estates made a list of the 674 creditors of the diocese of Montpellier at the end of the old regime. These creditors are identified by name, and for 274 of them by status

---

67   AN H1/748/138; AN F4/1245.
68   Potter and Rosenthal 1997, pp. 597, 599, 604; Legay 2003, pp. 162, 164; Legay 2001, pp. 201, 222.
69   A breakdown of the creditors is found in the Appendix. The original rolls are located in AN H1/748/138.

and/or profession, but the value of their investments is not listed. Nobles comprised 50 percent of these 274 creditors, and ecclesiastics 30 percent. In 1787 and 1788, the authorities paid 93,565 livres of interest for 1,945,084 of bonds purchased from the diocese of Toulouse since 1681. The diocesan assembly had sold most of these bonds in the 1780s. Ecclesiastics and religious institutions received over half of these interest payments, nobles and parlementaires about 30 percent.[70]

The upper classes clearly benefited from the monarchical institutions of Languedoc. The sovereign courts and the Estates provided hundreds of nobles with careers, revenues, privileges, and the honours of serving the king. The provincial estates and tax farms distributed revenue to landed magnates and investors. Seigneurial dues and tithes, and all of the fees and revenues documented in this chapter, excluding justice fees, provided the state, the church, and local lords with 12.73 of the economic product of the Vivarais. Of course, the inhabitants of the Vivarais were among the poorest in the realm and had little income to spare for fiscal officials. In other parts of Languedoc, direct taxation alone amounted to as much as a third of the gross product. The district of Montpellier made estimates in 1791 of the charges weighing on the old regime diocese. Its estimates excluded tithes, seigneurial charges still obligatory after 1789, and the tax on notarised documents, but included 200,000 livres for 'the legal fees resulting from useless degrees of jurisdiction'. The district estimated that the charges had amounted to over 25 percent of the combined income of the inhabitants of the Montpelliérain.[71]

The evidence presented in the first two chapters of this book indicates that the seigneurial regime, the church, the judiciary, the tax farms, and the Estates of Languedoc together appropriated about a third of the provincial wealth. The monarchy actually had additional funds at its disposal, because the annual loans it obtained from the Estates exceeded the service charges paid out of taxation. My calculations suggest that a little over 42 percent of all this revenue left the province for Parisian creditors, financiers, the royal treasury, and the elite nobles who came to Languedoc once a year to preside over the Estates. The

---

70 For total loans of dioceses and the creditors of the diocese of Montpellier see AN H1/748/289. Creditors of the diocese of Toulouse are in AN H1/982, H1/983; ADHG C1039. The creditors of the dioceses of Montpellier and Toulouse are classified in the Appendix.

71 ADH L3417, C46, C47; Molinier 1985, p. 155; Fournier 1978, pp. 173–4. Elie Pélaquier calculates that seigneurial dues and tithes, direct taxes, and the équivalent together appropriated 19.12 of the gross product of Saint-Victor-de-la-Coste in the diocese of Uzès at the end of the old regime (1996, vol. 1, pp. 102–3).

rest went to judges, seigneurs, clergymen, creditors, and tax farmers to fund the public services and officials of the province.[72]

Peasants understood that the upper classes benefited disproportionately from the regime. They contended in parish cahiers that taxes should be simplified and paid directly to the king. We will see in Chapter 5 that peasants attacked fiscal bureaus and tax collectors as royal authority disintegrated in 1789 and 1790. Many historians of the sixteenth and seventeenth centuries maintain that revolts against fiscal officials and royal agents represented an antediluvian reaction of communities against the inevitable process of state modernisation. This chapter suggests that the revolts must be set against the backdrop of the social relations of the time. Landlords benefited from the extension of the state's coercive capacities and the growth of its officialdom. They became office holders in its tax farms and confidants of royal commissioners. Peasants knew that their social superiors benefited from an unjust fiscal system. Popular revolts against fiscal agents were clear expressions of class antagonism.[73] Listen to how the inhabitants of Vénézobre, a community of 206 households in the diocese of Uzès, expressed their grievances in the spring of 1789.

> The tax burden will ease by three quarters once the Estates [of Languedoc] will have been regenerated, because new administrators, chosen and named by their equals ... will do without the disastrous services of treasurers, receivers of the taille, general syndics, this breeding ground of engineers, this legion of inspectors and directors of public works for whom revenue turns to particular utility, and of whom the magnificence and luxury are an insult to the Nation they oppress.[74]

In the sixteenth and seventeenth centuries, Protestants of manufacturing towns in the Black Mountain and Massif central accumulated revenue from textile production and the royal salt monopoly to buy offices of diocese tax receiver, judgeships in the Cour des Comptes, Aides et Finances, and posts in the financial establishments of Montpellier. Such offices provided stepping stones from the provincial nobility into the king's elite financial networks and the lofty social circles of Paris and Versailles. At the end of the 1770s, these centuries-old channels of upward mobility broke down, as financiers no longer raised enough revenue for the needs of the regime. The monarchy could not

---

72   Parker 1996, pp. 100–1. Parker especially criticises the work of Bercé 1974.
73   ADG C 1193.
74   Chaussinand-Nogaret 1970, pp. 11, 55, 58, 217, 312–13.

maintain all the streams of income sustaining the governmental services and private fortunes of the upper classes.

The efforts of the king and his ministers to forestall the breakdown of these channels turned groups of provincial elites against one another. The monarchy did not assign its officials equal access to the benefits of the regime. Toulousain nobles secured most of their wealth from landed property, and supplementary income from seigneurial rights, justice fees, and annuities sold by the provincial estates and diocesan assemblies. The province's main financial institutions were located in lower Languedoc and benefited the upper classes of Montpellier. The prime benefits of royal authority accrued to the oligarchs of the Estates. Their treasury was enmeshed in the financial networks of the crown, and they allocated much of their budget to the provincial creditors among the Parisian nobility. The crown relied heavily on the Estates for loans, as its financial situation deteriorated in the second half of the eighteenth century. The crown granted the Estates additional power over provincial subjects to enforce its financial demands, increasing the Estates' spheres of authority to the detriment of the majority of the provincial nobility. We now turn to these conflicts within the Languedocian elite.

CHAPTER 3

Crown and Nobility in a Time of Financial Difficulties: Royal Policy 1758–89

The upper classes clearly benefited from royal authority. Nobles and affluent commoners acceded to the official positions of the old regime in the royal tribunals, tax farms and provincial estates by means of their status, titles and venal offices rather than by means of their seniority, experience or talent. The judiciary upheld the seigneurial regime, the tax farms offered private profit from the fiscal system, and the Estates of Languedoc provided stable yields on annuities. Royal institutions also sponsored honorific displays celebrating the rank of seigneurs, judges, bishops, and barons.

Though these elites benefited from royal authority, they traditionally had to negotiate, even do battle with the crown to maintain the benefits. The crown periodically made use of the seigneurial regime to fill royal coffers. The jurisprudence of early modern France originated in the feudal past and was laden with provisions for customary rights and seigneurial law. In the seventeenth century, crown jurists asserted that the whole kingdom formed part of the direct domain of the king and was subject to his lordly rights. The king sold exemptions to the nobles and large proprietors threatened by his seigneurial claims. The landed classes may have drawn on this lesson in feudal law to use the seigneurial regime to their advantage in dealings with peasant communities during the eighteenth century.[1]

Royal ministers traditionally regarded the elites' venal offices as sources of revenue to be exploited in times of war and financial need. They regularly created supernumerary posts to force loans out of associations of office holders. Stockbrokers, attorneys, notaries, and other office holders ceded funds to the monarchy to protect the value of their public functions. The annual gages paid by the monarchy for these funds stood below the market rate of interest. This type of financial manipulation drove several magistrates of the Parlement of Paris into serious financial difficulties in the final decades of Louis XIV's reign. The crown did not make many financial demands of this sort between 1723 and

---

1 Kaiser 1994, pp. 309–10, 312; Parker 2003, pp. 91–2. For comment on the longstanding tension between the monarchy on the one hand, and the nobles and office holders who benefited from it on the other, see Anderson 1979, pp. 18–20, 33, 53–5, 101, 107–8; Bloch 1966, pp. 99–101, 128–32, 134, 140–3; Collins 1988, pp. 66, 103–4, 111, 138, 146, 155, 221.

1743. But when war broke out in the 1740s, the crown reverted to the usual means of exploiting office holders, forcing all the richest associations to advance large sums.[2]

Subsequent wars proved that this expedient no longer raised sufficient revenue. Whereas Louis XIV had relied heavily on office holders to cover the costs of his interminable campaigns, Louis XV was only able to get office holders to fund five percent of the costs of the Seven Years War. After 1750, royal ministers began to regard office holders less as sources of ready cash than as obstacles to the establishment of an effective financial administration.[3]

Two historical forces intervened to cause this change of policy. First, imperial rivalries proved a disaster for the monarchy. England had a dynamic economy and a rapidly growing tax base. It had a parliamentary system endowing its rulers with the legitimacy to tax the national wealth. England thus had the means to extend its dominion over foreign lands.[4] Royal ministers of France had to institute fundamental reforms to meet this challenge. They began to make efforts to investigate the landed revenue of the privileged orders so as to bring in a portion of it to state coffers. To obtain some of the landed revenue of the privileged orders, royal ministers recognised that they had to overhaul the venal judiciary, because it provided legal protection to fiscal privileges. Reformist ministers also sought to replace the tax farmers, receivers, and financiers, who profited from the streams of royal revenue, with modern bureaucrats appointed by the sovereign.[5]

Second, the political culture in which the royal ministers developed their financial policies differed from former periods. Around 1750, the Parlements began to baulk at the crown's efforts to implement edicts without consulting the governed. Certain officials in the highest spheres of government listened to the Parlements and tried to build public support for royal policy. The Choiseul ministry made a conscious effort in the 1760s to arouse patriotic sentiment and turn it to the advantage of the regime. A decade later, the controller general Turgot, and his aide Du Pont de Nemours, made a case for administrative assemblies of landowners. They argued that provincial assemblies would give the upper classes a stake in the system and inspire a willingness to pay taxes.[6]

---

2 Bien 1994, pp. 23–71; Hurt 2002, pp. 12, 116, 189; Doyle 1996, pp. 92, 94, 97.
3 Doyle 1996, pp. 99–100, 103, 107–8; Le Goff 1999, pp. 377–413; Riley 1986, p. 181.
4 Brenner 2003, pp. 649–52, 709–16; Teschke 2003, pp. 252–62; Coleman 1977, pp. 91–172; Horwitz 1977, pp. 311–5; Chandaman 1975, pp. 279–80; Mathias and O'Brien 1976, pp. 601–50; Brewer 1989, pp. 32, 40, 64–87, 89, 95, 129, 257.
5 Bosher 1970, pp. 166, 174, 180, 279, 303, 307; Félix 1999, pp. 300–1, 304, 498; Le Goff 1999, pp. 377, 401, 410; Doyle 1996, pp. 137–8; Kwass 2000, pp. 56–7, 95; Stone 1994, pp. 9, 19, 100–2, 158, 160.
6 Doyle 1988, pp. 76, 92; Dziembowski 1998, pp. 458, 469, 479–80, 482; Schelle 1888, pp. 190–1, 259; Du Pont 1913–23, vol. 4, pp. 577, 581–2.

This chapter, then, examines the evolution of royal policy toward Languedoc in the last decades of the old regime. The first section shows that the king and his ministers collaborated ever more closely with the Estates to govern the province. The royal treasury obtained over a hundred million *livres* of loans from the Estates in the 1770s and 1780s. To support this crucial source of credit, the crown granted the Estates authority over the villages and towns of the province. The second part of the chapter shows that the king's intendant and the Estates' executive agents (*syndics généraux*) helped peasant communities obtain rulings from the royal council to quash the judgements of local courts and protect village revenues from the claims of privileged landlords. Royal rulings stripped lords of honorific rights and diminished the humiliating shadow cast by seigneurial suzerainty in order to encourage competent villagers to take part in, and improve, local government. The third part shows that the crown scaled back the jurisdictions of municipal magistrates and office holders. The crown sought to reduce their privileges in order to improve the administration and augment the tax yield. Such policies threatened the nobles' material interests, degraded their public standing and professional activity, and led them to question the legitimacy of absolute monarchy.

1   State Finances and the Royal Chain of Command in the 1770s and 1780s

The monarchy borrowed about 330,000,000 livres from the Estates of Artois, Cambrésis, Flandre, Brittany, Burgundy, and Languedoc between 1740 and 1789. The king obtained the loans at an interest rate of five percent, while his own credit obliged him to pay as high as nine or 10 percent. What is more, loans from provincial estates did not pass through the volatile process of registration in the Parlement of Paris. They allowed royal ministers to raise revenue without disparaging discussion of their administration. The monarchy could have exploited this source of credit even more thoroughly than it did. The *pays d'état* provided about 25 percent of the king's fiscal receipts yet raised only about 10 percent of all royal loans. The king borrowed large sums from the Estates of Burgundy but raised only 42.5 million livres from Brittany despite it having the largest population of all the *généralités* of the realm. The Estates of Artois raised a measly three million.[7]

---

7   Legay 2003, p. 153; Legay 2001, pp. 200, 220, 343–4, 346; Swann 2003, pp. 295, 300–1, 320–3, 327–8; Potter and Rosenthal 1997, pp. 586, 604, 609–10; Velde and Weir 1992, pp. 33–4; Necker 1784, vol. 1, p. 306.

Languedoc seems to be the one pays d'état in which the king exhausted his credit. Nearly half of the loans borrowed by the provincial estates came from Languedoc. The crown used the credit of the Estates to borrow less than 30 million livres between 1733 and 1777, and then over 40 million during the next four years. Necker, the director general of finances, raised almost 10 per cent of the loans taken out to finance French involvement in the American War of Independence on the credit of the Estates of Languedoc. Royal ministers used the credit of the Estates to borrow another 70 million over the next seven years. The monarchy serviced the loans by allowing the Estates to deduct from their annual subsidy to the royal treasury. The Estates deducted the revenue needed to cover five percent of the accumulated principal and all of the annual interest payments.[8]

We saw in Chapter 2 that the budget of the Estates amounted to a little over 14 million livres at the end of the old regime. Of this sum, the king could devote no more than about nine million to service his debts. The rest of the budget was set aside for indispensable services such as the military, the intendancy, and public works. Though the king and the Estates progressively raised taxes to enlarge the provincial budget, the service charges eventually overran the revenue available to cover them in 1787. The interest payments and scheduled reimbursements amounted to 9,716,160 livres, while the royal revenue available to cover them amounted to only 8,808,718. The monarchy had to obtain a loan from the Royal Military Academy to avoid default.[9]

This imbrication of provincial finances in the budgetary policies of the monarchy made the Estates of Languedoc a vital part of the regime. It would be wrong to imagine that the king imposed his policies on Languedoc through his intendant and the military governor. The monarchy secured such valuable credit from the Estates that it made the leading members of this body a part of its administration. If it had bypassed the Estates, run the province through the royal appointees, and centralised authority, it would have cut off this cash flow. The logical course, which the crown followed, was to rely on the president (the archbishop of Narbonne) and the syndic generals of the Estates, the intendant, the military governor, and occasionally a leading baron of the Estates such as

---

8 For royal borrowing through the Estates prior to 1777 see Rives 1885, pp. 95, 103. For borrowing between 1777 and 1781 see Bibliothèque Nationale, Collection Joly de Fleury, 1438, fol. 214. For loans of the Estates from 1782 to 1788 see Archives Nationales (hereafter AN) H1/748/62 p. 383, H1/748/65 pp. 314–28, H1/748/138, H1/938; Archives Départementales de l'Hérault (ADH) 2E 56/583, 2E 58/141, 2E 58/157, 2E 58/190, 2E 58/193, 2E 58/197, 2E 58/199, 2E 61/107.
9 Royal accounts for Languedoc in 1787 are located in AN F4/1245.

the comte de Polignac. Between 1774 and 1789, the correspondence between Versailles and Languedoc was limited to these individuals. The crown protected its key administrators from judicial pursuits. Every year, the king's council of state heeded a request of the deputies of the Estates to suspend all lawsuits against them and their officials 15 days before the assembly, during the proceedings, and 15 days after their separation. The crown actually enforced this policy in 1786 and 1788, when it granted the requests of a syndic general and overturned verdicts of the Cour des Comptes, Aides et Finances of Montpellier summoning him to pay debts.[10]

The crown granted the Estates of Languedoc extensive governmental responsibility over peasant communities in return for their aid in financial matters. Royal reports of the 1780s make clear that the intendant and the Estates jointly monitored the debts and taxes of villages. Judicial bodies could not force communities to pay debts without prior verification by the Estates and the intendant. The royal council overturned judgements contrary to this regulation.[11] According to a royal ruling of 1787 concerning community woods,

> Taxes are the first and principal task of communities ... For a community to always be capable of meeting this obligation ... it is necessary to facilitate the collection of revenue from common lands and resources that circumstances might offer the community to succeed in paying its tax burden. All the regulations made in Languedoc ... for the administration of local taxes have been aimed toward this goal. These regulations are the work of a commission composed of the intendant and the Estates to which the jurisdiction of all that concerns community taxes ... is attributed.[12]

2   The Central Administration, the Estates, and the Seigneurial Regime

In the eighteenth century, royal ministers began to see medieval rights as obstacles to royal policy. In Burgundy, the objectives of the crown and the intendants often brought them into conflict with local lords and tribunals. The intendants defended the integrity of peasant villages, their common property, self-government, and tax collection. The intendants mitigated seigneurial

---

10   AN H1/748/179; AN H1/1050; AN H1/1054.
11   AN H1/748/283; AN H1/1063. Fournier 1994, vol. 1, p. 45.
12   ADH A125.

authority over Burgundian communities so as to establish administrative control and efficient tax collection. Seigneurial dues competed with royal taxes for peasant resources. The intendants encouraged villages to contest seigneurial rights in court and even tried to introduce jurisprudence that did not recognise feudal, extra-economic, property. These policies threatened the fusion of property and public authority, which was the essence of lordship. Seigneurs did not distinguish their landholdings from their rights to administer peasant communities. The intendants therefore seemed to violate the right of property itself.[13]

The crown sought to disentangle the confusion of seigneurial and landed property in Provence and the pays d'Auge of Normandy in the second half of the eighteenth century. Reform-minded ministers wanted proprietors to improve marginal land and increase agricultural output. They believed that indisputable property rights would induce landowners to go forward with profitable drainage projects. But their endeavour to sort out the overlapping claims to the land faced the insurmountable obstacles of the seigneurial regime and its champions in the local judiciary. The Parlements continually upheld medieval privileges over wetlands. The central administration could not end litigation arising out of privileged rights of eminent domain, and improvements did not materialise. Unwieldy judicial procedures inherited from the feudal past were part and parcel of the old regime monarchy and continued to trouble ministers of state until the revolutionary legislators rationalised the administration and judiciary and made it impossible to interminably appeal decisions and block the execution of policy.[14]

In Languedoc, the intendant and the provincial estates came into conflict with local seigneurs and magistrates over the administration of peasant communities. The general councils of many communities permitted anywhere from a quarter to two thirds of village property owners to partake in the management of communal lands, the elections of village leaders, the planning of celebrations, and other local affairs. These assemblies could generally rely on the support of the intendant and the Estates. But in the second half of the eighteenth century, the intendant and the leaders of the Estates seem to have determined that political councils composed solely of local notables would manage village affairs more effectively. Their efforts to establish stable village institutions caused conflict with the Parlement of Toulouse whose magistrates

---

13 Root 1987, pp. 2, 15, 45–7, 197–8.
14 Rosenthal 1992, pp. 14, 73, 94–5, 133–5.

held that the only way to bring order to communities was to shore up the rights of lords and seigneurial judges.¹⁵

The intendant and the Estates of Languedoc sought to prevent local lords from subjecting well-to-do villagers to seigneurial rights. The crown relied on these villagers to administer communities and keep them solvent. Besides, the extension of seigneurial rights depleted the fiscal resources of tax-paying subjects. The intendant and the Estates therefore accorded favourable hearings to complaints about all types of seigneurial burdens. When peasants had sufficient resolve and resources to inform a sub-delegate of the intendant or a syndic general of the Estates of a judicial decision favourable to a seigneur, their perseverance was frequently rewarded with a verdict from the royal council overruling the local court and redressing their grievance.

One of the first verdicts of this sort arose out of a dispute between the peasants of Ste.-Eulalie and Jean Baptiste Pech, a stockbroker (*agent de change*) from Carcassonne and the largest local landowner. Pech provoked the dispute in 1754 by claiming property rights over land used as a path (*parcours*). Several courts heard the peasants' objections before a lawyer of the Parlement of Toulouse decided the case in Pech's favour in 1764. But the peasants refused to accept the decision. They asked the intendant to arbitrate, and his sub-delegate eventually settled the dispute in their favour in 1777. The intendant also overturned a ruling of the seneschal court of Carcassonne in favour of the Abbey Mary and freed Ste.-Eulalie's village leaders (*consuls*) from the indignity of wearing red-hooded costumes to escort Mary from the church to the presbytery on days of festivals.¹⁶

In 1775, 1777 and 1781, the royal council quashed judgements of the Parlement of Toulouse, and the seneschal courts of Castelnaudary and Toulouse, which had subjected the consuls of Plaisance to local office holders and seigneurial judges. The royal ruling of 1781, obtained at the request of a syndic general of the Estates, overturned a judgement of the seneschal court of Toulouse, which had obliged Plaisance to hold elections in the presence of one of the court's councillor-magistrates. The royal council accused the seneschal court of subordinating political councils, altering the liberty of consular elections, and degrading community leaders. It made a similar ruling in 1783, overturning a judgement of the seneschal court of Béziers and stripping the *Sieur* Bonnal, the seigneurial judge, of his jurisdiction over the village of Aniane.¹⁷

---

15   Fournier 1994, vol. 1, pp. 49, 52–3, 343–8.
16   Nègre 1970, pp. 191, 207, 219, 231, 233–5.
17   Plaisance: AN H1/748/177; Anaine: AN H1/748/178.

The royal council paid special attention to the solvency of peasant communities. In 1782, it upheld a decree of the intendant against contrary rulings of the seneschal court and Parlement of Toulouse, which had ordered the first consul of Rabestens to repay the Sieur Moisset, councillor in the seneschal court, a debt of 2,000 livres incurred for the building of a quay. The royal ruling stated that Moisset had to appeal to the agents of the king and the Estates to seek repayment.[18]

Letters patent of the king, given in Versailles in 1783, prevented the Parlement from introducing jurisprudence favourable to tithe collectors. The Parlement attempted to prohibit proprietors from demanding proof of a tithe collector's right to a portion of the harvest of large millet and other small products of the soil (*gros millet et autres menus fruits*). The crown, however, pointed out that according to royal regulations, if a crop was not subject to the tithe in surrounding areas, then the proprietors were exonerated unless the tithe collector could document receiving payment for the previous three decades.[19]

The same year, a syndic of the Estates had the royal council invalidate a judgement of the seneschal court of Limoux and an appeal to the Parlement, which had authorised the Sieurs Moreau and Chambert to collect a debt from the consuls and inhabitants of Fanjaux, a community in the diocese of Mirepoix. The judgement had contravened regulations stipulating that the intendant and the Estates verify all debts prior to their repayment. The royal council not only obliged Moreau and Chambert to reimburse all the sums they had collected, with interest, and all of the legal fees, but also condemned them to pay 150 livres to the Mendicants of the Diocese Hospital for defying the intendant and appealing his decision to the Parlement. In a similar case settled in 1787, the royal council quashed a ruling of the Parlement and forced the Sieur de Prades to restore property seized from inhabitants of Marvéjols, a town in the diocese of Mende, when they refused to abide by a verdict of the Parlement from 1767 granting him a special seat in church.[20]

Calonne wrote to the intendant in 1784 that the marquis de Nérestang failed to comply with a decision of the royal council according him three months to present the titles documenting his right to collect revenue on the grain sold at the market of St.-Didier in the diocese of Le Puy. Calonne instructed the intendant to verify that the inhabitants no longer went on paying this right. The same year, the royal council granted appeals of the consuls of Bérat, a community in the diocese of Rieux, and quashed a ruling of the Parlement in favour the Sieur

---

18   AN H1/748/177.
19   Archives Municipales de Toulouse (AMT) AA312.
20   Fanjaux: AN H1/748/178; Mirepoix: AN H1/748/180.

Comte Dufaur-Coaraze. The Parlement had ruled in 1766 that the consuls show all royal regulations to Dufaur's officers before communicating them to inhabitants. It had ordered the consuls to present items on the agenda of community assemblies to seigneurial officers 24 hours before the assemblies took place. In overruling the Parlement, the royal council declared that the officers had no right to challenge the consuls' administration of community affairs.[21]

In 1785, the inhabitants of Bérat appealed another judgement obliging each one of them to go individually before Dufaur and make a new declaration of recognition (*reconnaissance*) of his seigneurial rights. Calonne wrote to the intendant a year later that he would grant the peasants' appeal in order to save them money and workdays, and spare them a vexatious procedure. In 1786, the intendant followed a similar line of policy in a dispute between the inhabitants of Fronton, a community near Toulouse, and their seigneur the Grand Prior. The intendant encouraged the inhabitants to defend their right to elect their own consuls to administer the village by authorising them to borrow the funds needed to finance a lawsuit. The Grand Prior then abandoned his pretension.[22]

Litigation from Bédarieux illustrates the type of issues that most commonly embroiled the royal council in seigneurial affairs. Rulings of the seneschal court of Béziers and the Parlement of Toulouse granted the Abbey de Villemagne, lord of Bédarieux and Taussac, control over the local administration, the right to review royal statements before communicating them to inhabitants, the right to preside over the lighting of ceremonial bonfires, and an honorific escort to church during festivals. The royal council quashed these rulings in 1775. Three years later, the Sieur Escalle became the seigneurial judge and revived the claims to the Abbey's rights. The Parlement and seneschal court granted him more rights than the Abbey had previously enjoyed. They permitted Escalle to consult the community's accounts, preside over its assemblies, verify weights and measures, and bar inhabitants and farm animals from woods and pastures. The courts also granted him exclusive hunting and fishing privileges. But Escalle soon discovered that local residents and the central administration had not abandoned their opposition to the extension of the Abbey's seigneurial rights. Further litigation ended in a decision of the royal council annulling the judgements of the seneschal and Parlement.[23]

The royal council intervened in a similar dispute between the Sieur de Ferrant and the community of Tharaux in the diocese of Uzès. Ferrant petitioned

---

21 St.-Didier: ADH A125; Bérat: AN H1/748/179.
22 AN H1/1054; Escudier 1905, pp. 198–200.
23 AN H1/748/180; Allaire 1990, pp. 69–71.

the Parlement of Toulouse for a set of seigneurial rights in 1784. The Parlement granted Ferrant's judges control over the local administration (*police*). It obliged the consuls to present official regulations to his judges before communicating them to inhabitants. The Parlement permitted the judges to review the topics for community assemblies before they took place. It granted the judges unlimited access to the minutes of community deliberations. The Parlement obliged the consuls to pay Ferrant honours in all public ceremonies, assemblies, processions, and religious services. Its ruling stipulated that three keys to community archives – containing titles, cadastres, and registers of property transfers – would belong to the first consul, the seigneurial judge and the secretary-clerk (*greffier*).

A syndic general of the Estates brought the Parlement's ruling to the royal council, where it was quashed in 1785. The royal council stated that the local tribunals should not adjudicate these types of cases, because they caused delays and expenses, and were often interested parties. According to the royal council, the Parlement's ruling,

> could only prejudice the administration of communities, in degrading the dignity of consulships, and in imbuing notable inhabitants with a just estrangement from these posts, while it is, on the contrary, in the interest of communities to maintain the glamour of the posts so that they will be filled with capable and distinguished subjects and their responsibilities will be regarded as an honour.[24]

The royal council overruled the Parlement and other local courts in nearly identical cases involving honours, assemblies, elections, administrations, and archives in Vias, St.-Thibéry, Saissac, Revel, Sauve, Salles, Cahuzac, Vagnas, Montgaillard, Bezousse, St.-Félix, and Le Cailar between 1773 and 1787.[25]

These rulings of the royal council challenged the assumptions underlying the honour of noble families. Montesquieu argued that the jurisprudence of the realm took shape when the lords established their hold on fiefs and enserfed the peasantry toward the end of the tenth century.[26] Fiefs constituted tangible

---

24 AN H1/748/179.
25 AN/748/178; AN H1/748/179; AN H1/748/180. Vias and St.-Thibéry were both near Agde. Saissac and Revel were located in the diocese of Lavaur. Sauve was in the diocese of Alès. Salles was in the diocese of Rieux. Cahuzac and Montgaillard were in the Albigeois. Vagnas was in the Vivarais. Bezousse and Le Cailar (not to be confused with Le Caylar in the diocese of Lodève) were in the diocese of Nîmes. St.-Félix was in the Lauragais.
26 Montesquieu 1949, vol. 2, pp. 218–67.

signs of this history, communicating an oath of loyalty to the king, and enjoining their holders to defend the glory and sanctity of the feudal monarchy. One can therefore understand the disillusionment of the Dame Rouch de Zébel in 1784, when a joyous popular celebration greeted the royal council's decision to overrule the Parlement of Toulouse and abolish her seigneurial rights over the Carcassonnais community of Villasavary. She closed the doors and shutters of her residence, while the peasants brazenly proceeded to the free election of consuls and the seating of their officials on her former bench in church. The celebration included a concert, a fireworks display, and patriotic speeches in acclamation of the king. Zébel later wrote to the king beseeching him to repeal his council's decision, 'this ruling has caused the wildest licentiousness, exposing the suppliant to humiliations she should not have feared in an affair where the king's rights are even more at stake than her own'.[27]

The emotions stirred in the diocese of Carcassonne assured that the next round of litigation would attract wide interest. Local nobles determined to make a stand in 1785, when the peasants of Pouget, a community in the diocese of Béziers, asked the Parlement to review its decision to grant the vicomte d'Alzon seigneurial rights. The vicomte explained to his peers in the judiciary that 'vanity and caprice ... have spread the spirit of insubordination in the community ... The first Consul has too often forgotten the consideration he owes his lord'. The Parlement sided with d'Alzon and upheld its original ruling. But the inhabitants of Pouget entered an appeal, and the royal council decided in 1787 that d'Alzon had no right to impose his choice of consul. A syndic of the Estates of Languedoc then intervened and advised the royal council to elaborate on its decision. It thereupon issued a new ruling specifying that the community need not inform d'Alzon before holding assemblies, give him the minutes of deliberations, or grant him a key to archives containing the tax assessments. The royal council clarified that d'Alzon had to reimburse all of Pouget's legal expenses.[28]

This ruling prompted Rességuier, the Attorney-General (*procureur général*) of the Parlement, to write to the controller general in 1787.

> The Estates of Languedoc have long planned to establish a new hierarchy in the judicial order, raise a wall of separation against the Tribunal of the Laws, and emancipate the communities composing the jurisdiction of the Parlement. Various rulings of the royal council, granted upon the requests

---

27 AN H1/748/180; Borrel 1944–46, pp. 184–94. For conceptions of honour see Montesquieu 1948, pp. 24–5, 29–32, 115. See also Mousnier 1979, vol. 1, pp. 122, 139–40.
28 ADH C2018; Delouvrier 1990, pp. 206–32.

of the syndic of the Estates of the province, without hearing a contradictor, have progressively and insensibly consolidated this plan.[29]

The Attorney-General's appeal fell on deaf ears. The very next year, the royal council quashed a ruling of the Parlement of Toulouse and freed the peasants of the Albigeois community of St.-Michel-de-Vax from obligations to M. Jean Pierre de la Combe and his son and heir, captain of the royal corps of artillery, the local seigneurs.

> Although the Parlement of Toulouse and all the other courts and judges of the province have been prohibited from hearing cases pitting ... communities against officers of seigneurial justice, this court has nonetheless persisted in hearing cases and in ruling in favour of lords and their officers ... Although all of our prior rulings had been made on the express orders of His Majesty to his Attorney-General of the Parlement of Toulouse, with prohibition to render such judgements in the future, this court has still ruled in favour of the sieurs de la Combe.[30]

3   Royal Policy toward Town Governments and Fiscal Administrations

All of these royal interventions on the side of peasant communities took place concurrently with a stream of initiatives to curtail the rights of municipal magistrates and office holders. The royal council, the intendant, and the Estates of Languedoc sought to prevent office holders and municipal magistrates from siphoning off the resources of taxpayers. The royal council ruled in 1785, for example, that the squire (*écuyer*) Sieur Jean-Francis-Joseph Faure, sub-lessee of the royal mail-coach service from Narbonne to Perpignan, had no right to collect fees from coach drivers of Montpellier. The ruling obliged Faure to reimburse all the fees he previously had collected.[31]

Royal initiatives of this sort threatened the authority of the treasurers of France of Toulouse and Montpellier more than they did any other office holders of the province. The treasurers of France, judges in the 29 Bureaus of Finances of the realm, gained the status of permanent royal office holders in 1577 and

---

29   AN H1/1431.
30   Archives Départementales de la Haute-Garonne (ADHG) B1859 for the original ruling of the Parlement in 1787. AN H1/748/180 for the decision of the royal council to quash this ruling.
31   AN H1/748/179.

enjoyed hereditary nobility after two generations of service. Over the following two centuries, they worked closely with the intendants to audit the accounts of financial office holders and the royal domains, uphold the king's seigneurial rights, oversee highway maintenance, allocate taxes, survey taxpaying capacities, auction off the leases for municipal indirect taxes, register letters of nobility, and carry out many other official duties. In the 1770s and 1780s, the monarchy took road maintenance and tax collection out of the jurisdiction of several Bureaus of Finances, as it transferred authority to provincial estates and the assemblies of landowners of the Berry and Haute-Guyenne. Then, in 1788, the monarchy abolished the Bureaus of Finances, after it extended the assemblies to all the généralités that did not have provincial estates.[32]

The treasurers of France of Toulouse published a ruling in February 1789 stating that they would defend the rights inherent to the dignity of their posts. They argued that their rights mattered more to the public than to themselves. The most precious privilege of their offices was the opportunity to set an example of

> disinterestedness, love of the state, zeal for the maintenance of the laws, and for the glory and happiness of the homeland ... The Bureau of Finances declares that the love of the laws and the ambition to re-establish their empire in place of arbitrariness are the unique motive for its demands concerning the objects that have been successively dismantled from its original jurisdiction.[33]

The monarchy also sought to curtail the rights of the landowning oligarchs of Nîmes. Economic growth had made merchants of the silk and stockings industries the wealthiest residents of Nîmes as early as the 1730s. Yet they did not play a role in local government, because many of them were Protestant. Religious tolerance directly challenged the legitimacy of divine-right monarchy and indirectly challenged the privileges of elites depended on the monarchy's ability to defend them. The merchants' exclusion from office made them natural allies of reform-minded officials. In 1775, after considering a petition of a syndic of the Estates, the intendant decided to expand membership in the political council of Nîmes beyond the narrow circle of rentier landowners, office holders, and attorneys of the seneschal court. The highest taxpayers would henceforth have seats in the political council. The royal council then rescin-

---

32   AN H1/1596; Bossenga 1986, p. 614; Girardot 1845, pp. 86–7.
33   AN H1/942/2.

ded the reform two years later for fear that Protestants would gain control over the largest town of a region historically troubled by religious strife.[34]

The crown re-examined the exclusion of the merchants from the political council during the financial troubles in the 1780s. The Parlement of Toulouse registered a deliberation of the mayor and consuls appointing Pierre Froment, the lessee of the cathedral chapter's seigneurial dues and tithes, to the post of municipal secretary-clerk and guard of the town archives in 1783. The commercial association (*corps de commerce*) wrote a memorandum to the king in 1785 accusing Froment of abusing the power of his post to undervalue the property of local landlords and increase the direct taxes on merchants and manufacturers. The memorandum stated that the Cour des Comptes, Aides et Finances of Montpellier found fraud in Froment's management of municipal finances but that the town council used its influence with the Estates of Languedoc to suppress the affair. The memorandum claimed that Froment imposed the despotism of the local nobility.[35]

Jurists of the seneschal court wrote to the controller general to rebut these charges and defend their administration of Nîmes. They claimed that they alone understood the complex laws governing town politics, whereas merchants had a stake in local affairs and could not adjudicate disputes impartially. An anonymous letter received by the controller general asserted that Protestants sought to infiltrate the municipality and seneschal court but that, thanks to the vigilance of the local lawyers and judges, the 'bad subjects' would not enjoy the honour of serving the king. The crown permitted the Cour des Comptes, Aides et Finances to settle these disputes. The court convicted Froment of dishonest bookkeeping, despite appeals of the cathedral chapter to the Estates to have him exonerated, and Froment voluntarily went into exile. Yet the municipality still suffered from internal strife. Royal regulations of 1788, granting the commercial association a third of the seats on the municipal council, did not satisfy either of the opposing parties. Catholic proprietors felt betrayed, while Protestant merchants thought that their contribution to the economy entitled them to a greater voice in local affairs.[36]

The magistrates of the Parlement of Toulouse believed the monarchy ought to support the Catholic notables of Nîmes. They conscientiously served the monarchy when it looked after traditional rights. The parlementaires paid

---

34   ADH C965; ADHG C47. Line Teisseyre-Sallman charted the economic ascendancy of the textile merchants of Nîmes. Office holders in the local judiciary paid the largest dowries until the 1730s, when merchants started paying even larger ones (1980, p. 970).
35   ADHG B1816; AN H1/801.
36   AN H1/801; Gutherz and Huard 1982, p. 216; Félix de la Farelle 1841, pp. 129–30, 133–4, 140–8.

attention to the minutest points of jurisprudence when reviewing cases concerning the rights of lords and ecclesiastics. In 1784, before registering royal letters patent for the St.-Ursule monastery of Nîmes to acquire six houses, the Parlement instructed the local seneschal court to consult the seigneurs in whose domains the houses were located to find out about the relevant customs. But in other cases, when the crown seemed to threaten the traditional order, the Parlement demurred. The magistrates remonstrated against the edict of 1787 granting civil status to Protestants. The Parlement wanted the crown to spell out all of the offices of the magistracy that Protestants would never have the right to hold. The crown dismissed the remonstrance, maintaining that the edict clearly barred Protestants from royal service and office holding and that no additional proclamation was necessary.[37]

The Parlement showed particular concern for maintaining the status quo in upper Languedoc, where its members enjoyed considerable privileges. The city of Toulouse reimbursed the sales taxes (*octrois*) collected on the consumer goods of the first president of the Parlement. All the judges enjoyed exemption from the *gabelle*, receiving enough untaxed salt for themselves and their associates. They had a say in who would join the eight officials, known as *capitouls*, who presided over the municipality. Admission into the *capitoulat* was a momentous event for lawyers and royal prosecutors (*procureurs*) of the third estate, for in addition to conferring public responsibilities, the posts also conferred hereditary nobility. The capitouls consequently performed elaborate displays of deference for the parlementaires and submitted to their judgement in municipal affairs. The parlementaires also presided over the municipal council in which lawyers, capitouls, and judges of the seneschal court met to oversee the town affairs.[38]

The king and his ministers frequently threatened these privileges in the period from 1680 through the first half of the eighteenth century. The royal council announced the king's intention to revoke the capitouls' nobility, their exemption from taxes, and their authority over municipal government. The royal council threatened to make their posts venal and thus deprive the local elite of the power to ennoble its supporters. The crown brandished all of these policies in order to oblige the elite to raise loans on the credit of the municipal budget. It thereby succeeded in obtaining millions of livres.[39]

1763 marked a dramatic change of policy toward the elite. The crown amassed short-term debt during the Seven Years War and needed to raise taxes to

---

37   ADHG B1817, B1861.
38   Casteras 1891, pp. 153–5; Dulaurier, Molinier, and Barry 1876, vol. 13, p. 1315.
39   Schneider 1989, pp. 277–83; AMT BB 283.

avoid financial collapse. It promulgated edicts for an additional vingtième tax on all revenues, including those of the privileged orders, and for new tabulations of landed incomes to make the tax effective. The Parlement of Toulouse made clear that it would not register edicts permitting the investigation of landed revenues or a tax of unlimited duration on the nobility. The military commander, the duc de Fitz-James, ringed the Parlement with soldiers and compelled registration. The Parlement responded by taking the extraordinary step of remaining in session beyond its official date for vacation and annulling the edict. Fitz-James then put the magistrates under house arrest. But without the Parlement's authorisation, the tax proved impossible to collect. The opposition of the Parlements in other regions threatened the stability of the regime. To halt the deterioration of royal authority, the crown released the Toulousain magistrates from house arrest and withdrew the proposal to investigate landed revenues in December 1763. The Parlement of Toulouse then registered the vingtième with the proviso that it expire after ten years. The Parlement ordered the arrest of Fitz-James and expelled its first president, François de Bastard, for having worked too closely with the ministry. It did not have the legal right or power to enforce the arrest of a peer of France such as Fitz-James but did have enough clout to convince the crown to withdraw the military commander from the province.[40]

This conflict heralded a change in royal policy toward the upper classes of Toulouse, especially the parlementaires. The crown no longer regarded them solely as a source of credit to exploit in times of war but also as an obstacle to effective governance. In 1770, the Parlement adhered to the tenet of *union de classes*, the solidarity of all the Parlements, and stood by the courts of Rennes and Paris in calling for the arrest of the duc d'Aiguillon, the military governor charged with enforcing fiscal policy in Brittany. Louis XV, and his ministers Maupeou and Terray, then began to suppress the Parlements and replace them with pliant courts. The suppression of the Parlements represented such an extraordinary act that the military governor of Languedoc, the Prince de Beauvau, resigned rather than carry it out, and the king appointed the loyal count of Périgord in his stead. The Parlement of Toulouse issued a series of public letters, judgements and remonstrances, arguing that its right to review and comment upon edicts before registering them into the law books formed a part of the French constitution and a guarantee against arbitrary power and despotism.[41]

---

40 Schneider 1989, p. 286; Dubédat 1885, pp. 457–9, 463, 506, 511–13; Ramet 1935, pp. 573–4; Swann 1995, pp. 230, 240, 245–6; Hudson 1972, pp. 97–117; Egret 1970, pp. 101, 153–5, 194–5, 230; Bastard d'Estang 1857, vol. 2, 219–20, 222, 331–2.
41 Schneider 1989, pp. 282–3, 287; Ramet 1935, pp. 575–9; Swann 2003, 358; Egret 1970, pp. 194–

> The authority of both the prince and the laws has the same source and the same origin; one cannot weaken one without striking a blow against the other ... the tranquillity enjoyed by monarchs is principally due to the confidence, which the laws and their guardians inspire in the people.[42]
>
> When the law of registration ... will be reduced to a mechanical formality, what will protect the property of individuals, the legitimate liberty of citizens, the rights of the peers, the privileges of the clergy, the prerogatives of the nobility, and the irrevocability of offices?

The judges called for a meeting of the Estates General to re-establish the rule of law.[43]

To implement such a far-reaching alteration of the judicial system, the king and his ministers realised that they needed to win some of the parlementaires to their side. The judges were wealthy influential nobles and, apart from a handful of knowledgeable barristers, the only ones versed in local laws and customs. Most of the seats in Toulouse's new superior court went to the jurists who had supported the crown against their rebellious colleagues in the disputes of the preceding decade. The first president de Niquet had held the same post in the former Parlement. The crown, however, prevented these magistrates from taking their yearly vacations to attend to their seigneuries and estates. It also transferred much of their jurisdiction to the seneschal courts and a superior court of equal rank in Nîmes. The magistrates felt loath to serve the new tribunals and shared with their former colleagues, who were excluded from the new legal organisation, a dour attitude toward this judicial reform.[44]

Louis XVI restored the former Parlements in 1775 after assuming the throne. He sought to bring public opinion behind the monarchy and begin his reign on the right foot by re-establishing the distinguished magistrates at the head of the judiciary. Financial difficulties, however, assured that the crown continued to amend the administration and attenuate the power of the Parle-

---

5; 'Le 9 février 1771, le parlement de Toulouse arrêta qu'il seroit écrit au roi. La lettre fut rédigée ainsi qu'il suit' 1775, vol. 2, pp. 180, 185.

42   'Arrêt de la cour du parlement, du 18 mars 1771, qui fait inhibitions & défenses de mettre à éxecution, dans son ressort, aucuns actes émanés des Juges établis par lettres-patentes du 23 janvier, & édit de Février derniers' 1775, vol. 2, pp. 192, 196.

43   'Arrêt de la cour du parlement, du 18 mars 1771, qui fait inhibitions & défenses de mettre à éxecution, dans son ressort, aucuns actes émanés des Juges établis par lettres-patentes du 23 janvier, & édit de Février derniers' 1775, vol. 2, pp. 209–10.

44   Dulaurier, Molinier, and Barry 1876, vol. 13, pp. 1213–14, 1216, 1266, 1268; Bastard d'Estang 1857, vol. 2, pp. 454, 462, 464.

ment. Reports and letters sent between the intendant, sub-delegate, Estates of Languedoc, and Versailles in the early 1770s alleged that the municipality of Toulouse wasted revenue and did not maintain infrastructure and public order. The intendant and sub-delegate wrote that the ennoblement of capitouls encouraged a wasteful system of patronage and placed incompetent novices at the head of local affairs. To rectify these problems, royal edicts of 1778 and 1783 stipulated that the eight capitouls would henceforth belong to three classes of inhabitants: two nobles of long lineage (*gentilshommes*), two former capitouls, and four lawyers, doctors, merchants, notaries, or landlords (*bourgeois*). The edicts stripped the parlementaires of the presidency of the municipal councils and gave it to the capitouls of noble lineage. Policymakers placed these nobles at the head of the municipality in the hopes of increasing the leverage of the intendant and the Estates. Everyone knew that the nobles would rely on the intendant and the Estates to avoid subordination to the parlementaires.

The edicts also assured a more equitable representation of the different classes of inhabitants in the municipal government. They expanded the political councils to include the municipal tax receiver, the archbishop, canons, vicars, notables, landlords, and wholesale merchants (*négociants*). Some of these figures hailed from social strata below Toulouse's landowning and judicial elite. A few did not even own rural property. They were not as beholden to the Parlement as were the associations of jurists. The Parlement declared in 1783 that it had not verified the edicts' concordance with local customs.

> To not cry out against edicts, which change permanent establishments, would precipitate moderate government into despotism, not that of the prince, but of the lower orders, a despotism more harsh and degrading, which would suffocate all sentiment of virtue, patriotism, and public good in his subjects' souls.[45]

The reorganisation of the municipality had fiscal implications. Local elites traditionally had control over the office of municipal treasurer. This office received the property taxes destined for the provincial treasurer as well as the indirect taxes collected for municipal expenses. The Toulousain elite had worked out an arrangement mutually beneficial to the tax receiver and local proprietors. The receiver did not have to pay obligations incumbent upon the king's venal

---

45 The quote is in Dubédat 1885, pp. 661–3. Information on the edicts of 1778 and 1783 is in ADHG C284, C285, C290; AN H1/1014; Nelidoff 1996, pp. 14–16, 29–30; Lamouzèle 1910, pp. 4–5, 12–13.

officers such as extraordinary fees of reception, presentation of accounts, and various other royal charges (*centième denier* and *dixième d'amortissement*). For their part, the local proprietors enjoyed a relatively light tax burden, because municipal statutes did not permit the receiver to charge as heavy fees for his service as did the diocese receivers of Languedoc. The receiver of Toulouse relied on indirect taxes to meet the city's quota for the provincial treasurer. He took out loans to pay the provincial treasurer while allowing time for indirect taxes to enter his till. The receiver permitted local proprietors to accumulate arrears.

A deliberation of the Estates of Languedoc criticised these practices in 1782. One of the general syndics reported to Versailles in 1783 that the parlementaires set a bad example by paying their direct taxes 18 months, and sometimes even two years late. To reform these practices, an edict of 1783 took the fiscal administration of Toulouse away from the municipal elite and brought it in line with the rest of the province. The edict separated the administration of direct and indirect taxes into distinct offices, integrated the municipal receiver into the association of diocese receivers, and obliged him to deposit his funds directly into the treasury of the Estates.[46]

The parlementaires were particularly troubled by the crown's disregard for their judicial competence. As we have seen, the intendant and the Estates repeatedly withdrew litigation pertaining to rural communities from the Parlement's jurisdiction. They sought to prevent the communities from going into debt over costly legal battles. To this end, the king and his ministers organised a committee of lawyers to work under the intendant and give free advice to communities on the practicality of lawsuits. The intendant, however, reported to the controller general that local judges would oppose this committee, because it would reduce the volume of litigation passing through their courts. Less litigation meant fewer fees and less of the intangible satisfaction of providing justice for the king and his subjects. The intendant especially feared that lawyers would be unhappy to see their caseloads diminish and would persuade the Parlement to raise objections. According to the registers of the municipality of Toulouse from September 1786:

> A council composed of citizens who were the most recommendable for their integrity and their wisdom administered the city of Toulouse. Deputies of the Parlement headed this council and the most famous lawyers were among its members ... Would it be fair? Would it be reasonable? To

---

46   AN H1/944/1; AN H1/1014; ADHG C357.

subordinate the decisions of this council to the personal sentiments of a few lawyers in whom the intendant is obliged to have confidence.[47]

The magistrates of the Cour des Comptes, Aides et Finances had almost as much privilege to defend as did their peers in Toulouse. They laid claim to the arbitration of all of the province's financial litigation. The magistrates also had important powers in Montpellier. They held 2 of the 24 seats of the political council, and along with dependent jurists, controlled over 40 percent of its membership. The political council periodically submitted a list of candidates to the marquis de Castries, the military governor, who chose six consuls to preside over the municipality. Rolls of the capitation, a tax falling on all proprietors regardless of their privileges, show that the judges of the Cour des Comptes, Aides et Finances were the wealthiest residents of Montpellier, paying assessments second only to M. de Joubert, the treasurer of the Estates, and the comte de Biffy, a military general. The judges received a free provision of salt from the royal monopoly and enjoyed exemption from municipal taxes. Louis XIV added to the magistrates' gages after they paid the royal treasury for extra offices in 1683, 1690, and 1704. Thereafter, the magistrates enjoyed undisturbed tenure over all of the responsibilities, revenues, and honours of their positions.[48]

Toward the end of the old regime, the crown began to scale back the magistrates' privileges. The royal council ruled in 1780 that the Cour des Comptes, Aides et Finances, the Bureau of Finances, and the presidial seat would no longer send deputies to the assembly composed of the representatives of Montpellier's official associations. The ruling established that this assembly would henceforth select the 24 members of the political council. To establish these regulations, the royal ruling quashed a judgement of the Cour des Comptes, Aides et Finances, as well as deliberations of the Bureau of Finances and the presidial seat. The regulations eventually permitted the crown to exclude local judges from the administration of municipal tax collection. In 1787, the royal council created a commission comprised of the consuls and political councillors – officials, that is, whom the Cour des Comptes, Aides et Finances no longer selected – to draw up the municipal tax rolls, examine the local treasurer's accounts, and discuss legal and economic affairs.[49]

The magistrates might have resigned themselves to this lack of confidence in their administration of municipal affairs had the crown not infringed upon

---

47   ADHG C265. Information on the committee of lawyers is also located in AN H1/1107.
48   H1/748/292 contains rolls of the capitation from 1789. Vialles 1921, pp. 75, 113.
49   AN H1/748/177; Duval-Jouve 1879–81, vol. 1, pp. 28–9; 'Montpellier en 1768' 1920, vol. 4, p. 35.

their principal jurisdiction. The crown sought to reduce provincial expenditures by making the fiscal administration the exclusive responsibility of the Estates of Languedoc. A royal declaration of 1758 stipulated that the provincial treasurer only had to present his accounts to the Estates, not to the Cour des Comptes, Aides et Finances. The declaration established that the provincial tax receivers did not have to show the tribunal the expenses of the diocese assemblies charged with distributing direct taxes among the communities. It prohibited the magistrates from attending these assemblies or reviewing their minutes. The declaration affirmed that the Estates and their syndic generals would control the administration of dioceses and communities.[50]

Royal interventions of this sort reduced the fees gleaned from the streams of tax revenue by the magistrates. In 1779, the archbishop of Narbonne wrote to Necker of his efforts to fulfil Necker's wish to see the Estates of Languedoc diminish expenses. The archbishop claimed that one expense he had reduced was the fee (*épices*) collected by the Cour des Comptes, Aides et Finances when it registered letters patent for the salt marshes of Sète. He convinced the court to reduce the fee from 25,000 to 15,000 livres.[51]

The crown encroached upon the right of the Cour des Comptes, Aides et Finances to arbitrate disputes over tax assessments in 1770, when it extended to Languedoc the declaration granting fifteen-year exemptions from taxes and tithes to proprietors for land brought under cultivation for the first time in 40 years. The purpose of the declaration was to increase incomes, facilitate tax payment, and augment fiscal resources over the long term. But the Cour des Comptes, Aides et Finances ruled that the declaration transferred its jurisdiction over leases of abandoned lands and other relevant properties to the king's intendant and the Estates' syndics. The judges claimed that the royal declaration did away with the right of provincial inhabitants to be amenable only to ordinary courts. When the monarchy did not respond to the ruling, the Cour des Comptes, Aides et Finances obstructed declarations of 1775 and 1777 meant to clarify local rights with respect to land clearances. In these declarations, the monarchy offered tithe collectors the opportunity to contradict the claims of land-clearers that terrains had not born fruit in 40 years. But the Cour des Comptes, Aides et Finances dug in its heels and refused to register the declarations.[52]

The position of the Cour des Comptes, Aides et Finances was clear: local magistrates, rather than the intendant or the royal council, should arbitrate

---

50   Dulaurier, Molinier, and Barry 1876, vol. 13, pp. 1146–7.
51   AN H1/944/1.
52   AN H1/1010.

fiscal disputes. The position involved more than a simple conflict of jurisdictions. It directly affected the monarchy's ability to obtain taxes from the nobility. In Brittany and Burgundy, the nobles succeeded in thrusting fiscal burdens onto the rest of the population through their control over the provincial estates. The nobles of Languedoc could not do the same, because they resided in a province of *taille réelle* in which the land itself bore the designation common or noble regardless of the status of the owner. Tax increases fell on all of the non-privileged land even if it belonged to nobles and clergymen. A sample of 12 communities in diverse parts of the province shows that the monarchy increased the taxes by over 46 percent between 1712–49 and 1775–89. The vingtième tax of the diocese of Limoux rose from 6,094 livres in 1777, to 6,877 in 1780, to 10,942 in 1784 after the establishment of a third vingtième, and then down to 7,687 after its expiration in 1788. This sum exceeded the one paid in 1777 by over 20 percent.[53]

While the rising price of grain gave proprietors additional revenue with which to cover these tax increases, many sought to retain these profits rather than turn a portion of them over to fiscal officials. We saw in Chapter 1 that hundreds of rulings of the Parlement of Toulouse gave seigneurial officers the keys to community archives. The rulings made it possible for seigneurs to contest tax assessments before their peers in the local judiciary and administration. They thereby evaded fiscal burdens weighing on other inhabitants. Government inquiries, for example, revealed that noble properties did not bear the official rate of the capitation in most parts of the Vivarais.[54]

These under-evaluations thrust an additional part of the land taxes on the other proprietors. Villagers therefore had an interest in redrafting tax registers and forcing landowners to show their titles. Over a quarter of all Languedocian communities had their tax registers rewritten between 1700 and 1789. Redrafting the registers led to litigation at the Cour des Comptes, Aides et Finances. Inhabitants of Fabrègues, a community in the diocese of Montpellier, updated their registers in 1776 and asked landowners to prove the privileges of their

---

53 Collins 1995, p. 10; Swann 2003, pp. 308–9. The figures for the 12 communities in diverse parts of the province are located in Reynier 1943–51, vol. 2, p. 249; Gorlier 1955, p. 152; Peyriat 1990, p. 267; Cazals 1883, p. 199; Yché 1985, pp. 49–50; Saumade 1908 p. 529; Segondy 1949, pp. 508–9; Contrasty 1936, p. 324; Pasquier and Galabert 1925, p. 28; Pélaquier 1996, vol. 1, pp. 96–7. The vingtième of Limoux is in the Archives Départementales de l'Aude 29 C 1.

54 The price of grain rose about 40 percent between 1752–61 and 1779–88 in the markets of Montpellier, Béziers and Toulouse. Geraud Parracha 1957, p. 339. Molinier 1985, p. 150; Reynier 1943–51, vol. 2, pp. 252–4; G.J. Cavanaugh comments on the nobles' ability to use their influence to escape taxation in the pays de *taille réelle* (1974, p. 685).

properties. Several landowners saw their properties included in the tax rolls. The countess of Bassy turned to the Cour des Comptes, Aides et Finances to dispute the inclusion of her scrublands (*garrigues*). Although the court confirmed that the lands did not enjoy privileges, the fines it placed on the community for overtaxing them amounted to such a burden, an annual annuity over 500 livres, that the countess came out ahead, and the community lost revenue.[55]

As we have seen, the king and his ministers disapproved of rulings like these, which diminished the fiscal resources of peasant communities. Yet they had few means of forcing local authorities to execute policy. Venal office holders, such as the magistrates of the Cour des Comptes, Aides, et Finances, had proprietary rights to their posts and could not be replaced for their reluctance to follow the agenda set in Versailles. The drafting of cadastres fell within the administrative ambit of the Cour des Comptes, Aides et Finances. The king and his ministers had no right to monitor the fees charged by land surveyors or those charged by the Cour des Comptes, Aides et Finances to make new assessments legally binding. They lacked the legal oversight necessary to assure the solvency of tax-paying communities.[56]

To compensate for this administrative deficiency, the crown decreed in 1784 that the intendant would oversee all of the procedures for the drafting of new cadastres. The judges of the Cour des Comptes, Aides et Finances, however, had no intention of surrendering the principal part of their jurisdiction to the king and his agents. The president M. de Claris informed the controller general that he and his fellow judges refused to register the edict. They remonstrated that the edict did away with the last vestiges of their authority despite the solemn pledges of previous kings. The Cour des Comptes, Aides et Finances modified the edict to preserve its prerogatives several months later. The controller general then tried to settle the dispute once and for all by having the chancellor overrule the tribunal and undo its modifications.[57]

In the 1770s and 1780s, Norman magistrates objected to the efforts of royal appointees to look into the assets of landowners and verify that they paid their share of the vingtièmes. The nobles thought that these investigations expanded the authority of the crown beyond the limits proscribed by the customary laws and practices of Normandy. The investigations raised fears that the monarchy tended toward despotism. Continual protests against the crown's efforts

---

55 Frêche 1971, pp. 324–5, 334–40; Saumade 1908, pp. 417–19.
56 Faucher 1948, pp. 18–19.
57 AN H1/1050; Vialles 1921, p. 69.

to increase taxation on landowners helped fashion a political culture inimical to royal absolutism.[58]

In Languedoc, the magistracy mounted a similar sort of resistance to the meddling of royal agents in the financial accounts of landowners. The Cour des Comptes, Aides et Finances did not resign itself to seeing the king's commissioners assume control over the composition of tax registers. The magistrates continued to judge disputes over fiscal assessments, even after the king placed the disputes within the intendant's jurisdiction. They ruled in 1786 that properties near the chapel of Notre Dame de Vals belonging to the Sieur Ranbaud, priest of Ginestas, a parish in the diocese of Narbonne, were privileged lands exempt from direct taxation. The intendant helped the community and consuls bring the case to the royal council where the ruling of the Cour des Comptes, Aides et Finances was quashed in 1788. The royal council instructed the intendant to reinsert the properties in the village tax rolls and oblige Ranbaud to reimburse all of the community's legal expenses.[59]

4   The Locus of Power: The King or the Provincial Nobles?

The foregoing disputes bear directly on the longstanding and well-known debate between Robert Brenner and David Parker about the state and the nobility. Brenner argues that the peasantry established inheritable tenures owing negligible dues to the lords between the thirteenth and sixteenth centuries. The lords turned to state offices and taxation to maintain their authority and income. As nobles came to rely on the monarchical administration and jurisdiction, they helped the crown to lessen the remaining seigneurial burdens limiting its fiscal capacity and authority. The crown protected peasant tenures, liquidated the remnants of serfdom, multiplied royal courts to the detriment of seigneurial justice, and increased state taxation to the detriment of seigneurial levies. Lords lost control over peasant communities as a new ruling class, comprising many of the same lords, integrated itself into the absolutist state through offices, pensions, and grants of land. Many nobles periodically opposed the rise of absolutism, but failed to halt its development, because the king could ally with feudal magnates and incorporate them into the regime.[60]

---

58   Kwass 2000, pp. 85–9, 159–65, 206–8.
59   AN H1/1054.
60   Brenner 1985, pp. 213–327.

David Parker does not believe that the state insinuated itself between seigneurs and peasants to develop its fiscal capacity. The landed elite controlled royal offices and institutions and thus had influence over the state. Magistrates, bishops, military nobles, and municipal leaders diverted an inestimable proportion of royal revenue into their private fortunes. Parker argues that it would be difficult to find a clearer case of 'unmediated cohabitation' of power and wealth. The king appeared to have independent authority, but actually only arbitrated rivalries between noble families, kin-groups and clienteles, while never freeing his authority from theirs. Versailles and the state apparatus were forums for the regulation of disputes within the nobility. 'Whatever had been the case in the later Middle Ages, by the early modern period the notion that the state existed as an independent competitor of the nobility for the revenues of the peasantry will not stand scrutiny'.[61]

The first three chapters of this book support the broad outlines of Parker's argument. Landlords and office holders were often the same people and belonged to the same milieu. They could count on sympathetic hearings from peers in the local judiciary to enforce seigneurial levies, protect tax-exempt property, and show their rank in public events. State offices enabled the upper classes to lay claim to much of the national wealth, which they did not secure from their landholdings and seigneurial rights alone. Their privileges posed problems for the monarchy by putting much of the kingdom's economic resources out of its fiscal reach. But the monarchy did not have the means to put an end to these problems for two reasons.

First, the wealth and authority of seigneurs and office holders made them insurmountable obstacles to substantive reform. Royal ministers and their agents sought to introduce jurisprudence untainted by the feudal past in order to establish more modern forms of property and improve the finances and administration of rural communities. They used the royal council to overrule local courts and limit seigneurial rights. Yet as we saw in Chapter 1, local courts issued far too many rulings for peasant communities and royal appointees to challenge anything but a small proportion of them. The peasants had a hard time making their grievances known, because they had to overcome internal divisions, raise sufficient funds to cover legal fees, and brave the enmity of their seigneurs. In the same way, 30 years of initiatives aimed at enhancing royal control over the fiscal administration did not overcome the authority of the Cour des Comptes, Aides et Finances. This court continued to assert its jurisdiction over financial litigation and continued to protect tax-exempt land down to the

---

61 Parker 1996, p. 265. See also pp. 21, 181–2, 263–6, 268.

end of the old regime. Even the treasurers of France succeeded in winning the restoration of their tribunals (the bureaus of finances) after a fierce round of protests at the end of September 1788.[62]

Second, the monarchy could not offer an alternative form of rule. Although the king possessed sovereignty over the realm, he did not have much of a bureaucracy to enforce it. The crown relied on local elites to maintain order, because its intendants did not have the administrative capacity to do so themselves. The monarchy could have appealed to the civic pride of the governed. It actually made efforts to involve well-to-do villagers and townspeople in the public affairs of Languedoc in the 1770s and 1780s. Yet it never made these appeals explicitly and consistently, because popular involvement in politics posed a threat to royal sovereignty.[63] Thus, to reduce the parlementaires' influence over Toulouse, the crown tried to elevate the authority and honours of sword nobles. To loosen the grip of seigneurs and venal magistrates on the countryside, it sought to transfer administrative responsibility to the provincial estates. What the monarchy gained in financial capacity, it lost in legitimacy, for the Estates of Languedoc were controlled by an aristocratic oligarchy, which did not enjoy the loyalty of provincial inhabitants.[64]

Nevertheless, Brenner's argument retains a kernel of truth. In England, the seigneurial classes maintained control over unusually large demesnes by western European norms through the feudal crises of the late Middle Ages. Farms of fewer than 30 acres all but disappeared from the agrarian landscape. Holdings of hundreds, even thousands of acres covered nearly all of the land. After the demographic downturn of the fourteenth century, the upper classes could only gain value from their lands by leasing them out to tenants, who had to pay the going market rate for leases to farm the land. Yeoman tenant farmers had to produce for exchange and compete for markets to survive economically. They had to systematically maximise their price/cost ratio by cost-cutting through ever deeper specialisation and automatic adoption of the latest techniques adopted by competitors. Farmers, in a word, had to generate earnings and reinvest them. To maintain this capitalist dynamic, which assured rising profits from the land, the gentry did not demand much from the state beyond the enforcement of private contracts negotiated in a free market.[65]

---

62   Bossenga 1986, pp. 628–30.
63   Schneider, 1989a, pp. 216–17.
64   The Estates of Burgundy also lost legitimacy as they obtained more responsibility for governmental affairs, because such responsibility came within a system based on hierarchy and absolutism (Swann 2003, pp. 24–5).
65   Allen 1992, pp. 62–3, 73–4; Larguier and Thirsk 1999, pp. 18–19.

In France, the countryside emerged from the Middle Ages in countless parcels of land, most of which belonged to the peasants. We saw in Chapter 1 that peasant tenures covered from 20 to over 50 percent of the arable land of the different regions of Languedoc. Few peasants, of course, had enough land to be self-sufficient. Most had to become sharecroppers, leaseholders, and labourers for large proprietors and merchants. Landlords obtained handsome profits from their properties, as the population and prices rose in the second half of the eighteenth century. Likewise, merchants extended textile manufactures into the countryside to gain profit from international trade networks. Landlords and merchants secured revenue from rural inhabitants in need of tenancies and employment, and willing to work for low returns. The dense rural population facilitated the accumulation of wealth through these extractive methods and thus discouraged productive investment in agriculture and manufacturing.[66]

The monarchical state, conversely, offered opportunities for investment in titles, offices, seigneuries, government bonds, and other juridical arrangements of the old regime. The nobility and bourgeoisie sunk much of their fortunes into the political institutions of the monarchy. They thus relied on the state for more than the enforcement of private contracts negotiated in a free market. They relied on the state to make seigneurial levies binding, to secure the rights of office holders to fees, to distribute emoluments in aristocratic bodies such the provincial estates, to pay interest on its loans, and to compel common subjects to defer to the authority and honours of lords and office holders. The king's military glory and religious mission made the system effective. He had to wield personal authority, because the upper classes lacked legitimacy.[67]

Personal authority, however, was not entirely consistent. The king was apt to pursue his own interests when faced with financial difficulties. In the second half of the eighteenth century, the monarchy relied heavily on the Estates of Languedoc for revenue. It increased the authority of the oligarchs of the Estates to the detriment of the majority of the provincial nobles. Royal ministers sought to improve the administration and finances of municipalities and parishes by involving well-to-do commoners in local affairs. These measures

---

66   In the Ile-de-France, where proprietors residing in the towns owned farms on the same scale – indeed larger in many cases – as the large capitalist farms of eighteenth-century England, the peasants' parcels of land, often just an acre or two, still occupied about five to 15 percent of the arable fields, even in times of land concentration such as the crisis years of the end of the seventeenth century. Jacquart 1974, pp. 118, 213–15, 623, 626, 636, 733, 753, 756–8; Tulippe 1934, pp. 97, 146, 156, 237, 240, 263; Brunet 1960, pp. 280, 282, 284.

67   For Brenner's comparison of France and England described in the preceding three paragraphs see 1985, pp. 242–46, 253–64, 299–307, 312–19. One should also consult Brenner 2001, pp. 275–338.

not only deprived lords and magistrates of their privileges, but actually called these privileges into question. The monarchy challenged the vital interests of its traditional allies and thereby undermined the social basis of its existence.

Nobles acquired distinguished honours by serving the king in the public institutions of the monarchy. Some of these institutions only displayed the authority and honours of the nobles intermittently. The elite bishops and barons of the province spent little more than a month in Montpellier at the annual meeting of the Estates. Many nobles lived in the towns and only made use of their seigneurial rights on periodic visits to their rural domains. But the nobles of other institutions had to pay constant attention to the public affairs of the monarchy. The magistrates of the sovereign courts prided themselves on defending the law and protecting the liberties of the king's subjects. Their honour was bound up with their professional responsibilities. According to Montesquieu,

> There is nothing, in monarchical government, that laws, religion and honour prescribe as much as obedience to the prince's will: but this honour dictates to us that the prince must never prescribe to us an action that dishonours us, because it would render us incapable of serving.[68]

Royal policies of the 1770s and 1780s did not permit the nobles to serve their king and countrymen in a dignified manner. The policies tainted the status of the local magistrates and seigneurial classes in the public life of the monarchy. Educated members of the upper classes saw that the crown did not recognise any limits to royal power. The majority of the provincial nobility concluded that it could no longer serve absolute monarchy and determined to resist fresh abuses.

In 1788, the intendant and the military governor made the king's conventional request to the Estates of Languedoc for a subsidy. They also demanded a loan of 12 million livres, an extraordinary grant of nearly a million, the prolongation of the second vingtième, and an increase of the vingtièmes' yield through precise assessments of the properties of the privileged orders. The king's directives looked to continue and reinforce all of the policies of the preceding decades. When the Estates prepared instructions to facilitate the implementation of the king's directives, the provincial nobility revolted.

Picot de Lapeyrouse typifies this revolt. He owned a seigneurie near Toulouse and an office in the royal domains. In the 1770s and 1780s, Picot obtained

---

68 Montesquieu 1949, pp. 29–32.

rulings from the local judiciary entitling him to exclusive hunting rights, fines from the peasantry and dues from the users of common lands. The courts gave him the right to update his seigneurial titles and enhance his prerogatives. In 1789, he published a pamphlet accusing the Estates of usurping the administrative responsibility of local judges and seigneurs. The pamphlet stated that the intendant authorised the syndic of the Estates to put a few poor and illiterate peasants in charge of village affairs. These peasants did not shoulder much of the tax burden and had no qualms about seeing it rise. 'Strange and absurd rules do not allow the seigneurs to have any knowledge of the administrative affairs of their communities, even though they ordinarily own the most land, and many of them contribute a third or even a half of community taxes'. The pamphlet contended that the Estates of Languedoc agreed to taxes on provincial inhabitants but did not offer them representation.[69]

Nobles like Picot de Lapeyrouse associated their own liberty with that of society as a whole. The collapse of royal authority in 1789 brought them face to face with the limited scope of their agenda. As we will see, the political positions taken by nobles in 1789 and 1790 arose out of their background in the old regime. Their decisions about whether to accept the thoroughgoing changes inaugurated by the Constituent Assembly modified the entire course of the Revolution.

69   Picot de Lapeyrouse 1789, pp. 12, 44–5, 58; Amanieu 1959, pp. 146, 148, 176–7; Bastier 1975, p. 57.

CHAPTER 4

Revolutionary Politics 1788–91: Despotism and Equality

Discontent with royal agents and the Estates of Languedoc had been long in coming. Monarchical institutions provided the nobles with careers in the military, judiciary, and administration. They permitted the nobles to dominate landed property, collect revenue from common subjects, and display the honour of royal service in public ceremonies. Financial difficulties of the 1770s and 1780s made it difficult for the monarchy to sustain these institutions. The king found it difficult to permit the nobles to serve his regime in a dignified manner. His ministers sought to raise more tax revenue from the nobility and make the fiscal resources of the province available to royal treasuries rather than to privileged landowners. The bishops and barons of the Estates had become so integrated into royal financial networks that they not only tolerated these policies but also went so far as to initiate their own. When the Estates acquiesced to the king's fiscal demands in 1788, the provincial nobility revolted.

The revolutionary turn taken by this revolt emerged out of the political culture of the period. Scores of deliberations and pamphlets published in 1788 and 1789 assumed the existence of a reading public interested in reforming state institutions. Many of these publications demanded the restoration of the traditional privileges of the judiciary and the province. Many others, however, made use of the innovative language of the period. They appealed to abstract principles transcending historically sanctioned rights. Virtually all of them claimed the right of provincial inhabitants to be represented in government.[1]

The nobles spearheaded this protest movement. They would not have succeeded in making it very broad without the preceding period of economic growth and the emergence of a relatively large urban population eager to participate in government. Yet the actual catalyst for the movement did not emerge out of the private economic sphere but from within the state, among the magistrates who had experience with the jurisdictional conflicts of the old regime and who had official mediums to publicise their views. The nobles of the Parlement of Toulouse and the Cour des Comptes, Aides et Finances of Montpel-

---

[1] Keith Baker (1990) discusses the importance of the concept of public opinion. David Bell highlights the novelty of such appeals to abstract principles. He argues that they first emerged in the second half of the eighteenth century (Bell 1994, pp. 10–11, 210).

lier resented the institutional arrangements of the old regime, which accorded political influence to the Estates of Languedoc, and deprived the rest of provincial society of representation in government.

The purpose of this chapter is to examine the movement for political representation and to uncover the issues which ultimately brought about conflict among local clergymen, nobles, and well-to-do commoners. How did the economic context and social relations of the old regime bear upon the attitudes of provincial elites toward revolutionary change?[2]

To answer this question, the chapter first examines the movement, mobilised by nobles, for representative provincial estates in 1788 and 1789. Priests, jurists, merchants and landowners rallied to the demand that the monarchy make the estates accountable to the governed. They joined the movement while harbouring frustration with the nobles' control over positions of wealth and power. In the spring of 1789, a growing number of townspeople made additional demands for an equitable system for acceding to positions of political responsibility.

The second section of this chapter shows that these demands did not necessarily lead to conflict. Nobles enjoyed the goodwill of other townspeople for having initiated and led the movement against the Estates. As peasants and artisans invaded châteaux and destroyed fiscal bureaus amid the collapse of royal authority in 1789 and 1790, anxious citizens looked to nobles for leadership. Many nobles had been competent professionals in the military and judiciary of the old regime. They had upheld law and order in the province for over a century. For that reason, the active citizens, meeting the property qualifications to vote, elected nobles to the local administrations and national guards.

Yet in upper Languedoc, the nobles of Toulouse refused to depend on the new constitutional system for the right to hold positions of leadership. They had towered over this agrarian region for centuries by dint of their wealth and the power of the Parlement. In 1789 and 1790, they denounced the National Assembly for undermining royal sovereignty and the laws of the realm. To the northeast, the monarchy had placed the local administration under the suzerainty of the archbishop of Albi and had not accorded local nobles much political responsibility. These nobles enjoyed much of the wealth of the Albigeois but cut a poor figure in Toulouse and Montpellier. Never having enjoyed much power under the monarchy, and never having distinguished themselves

---

2 To understand the pervasive aspiration for freedom, popular welfare, collective happiness, and improvement of the government see Bell 1994, pp. 11–12, 15, 163, 203; Darnton 1995, pp. 197, 243–6; Jones 2003, pp. 28, 178–81, 213–14, 264–5, 307, 359, 370, 374; Chartier 1991, pp. 2, 6, 85.

through wealth, the nobles of Albi embraced a society based on equality before the law and consistently won elections during the Revolution.

The third section analyses the economics and politics of lower Languedoc. Protestant merchants of Nîmes coordinated a vast region of textile manufactures extending into the southern Massif central. Political authority, however, belonged to the agrarian elite of Nîmes because of the monarchy's strictures against Protestants. Many nobles were attached to the traditions of royal sovereignty and orthodox Catholicism which upheld their ascendancy. Their peers in the southern Massif central valued tradition even more. Here, the local bourgeoisie consisted of Protestants, petty jurists, and landowners of comparatively minor fortunes, whom the nobles were loath to join in the management of local affairs. Nobles of Nîmes and the southern Massif central exploited the climate of insecurity, caused by economic crisis and fear of the Protestants' influence in political affairs, to organise peasants into armed resistance to the Revolution.

The nobility of Montpellier did not enjoy the same history of leadership. Once a year, some of the most illustrious dignitaries of the realm attended the Estates of Languedoc and overshadowed the city's nobles. What is more, the growth of manufacturing and the abundance of wealthy merchants made any attempt to exclude them from the political arena unthinkable once royal authority collapsed. The merchants' presence testified to the anachronism of privilege. When the National Assembly transformed the principles of government, the local nobility of Montpellier fell in line and, thanks to its professional experience in the judiciary, consistently won elections to positions of leadership.

1   Common Projects and Divergent Perspectives

When Loménie de Brienne and Lamoignon suppressed the leading tribunals of the realm in May 1788, nobles throughout France mobilised protests against the arbitrary authority of the government. Nobles of the Dauphiné rallied all ranks of the upper classes to the town of Vizille to call for the restoration of the provincial estates. The success of the meeting inspired the inhabitants of other provinces to publish hundreds of pamphlets and petitions calling for the restoration of their estates.[3]

Issues differed in the *pays d'état*, where the provincial estates had never ceased to meet. The residents of Brittany and Burgundy focused their atten-

3   Doyle 1999, pp. 133, 138–9.

tion on the balance of power within the provincial estates. All of the titled nobles of Brittany had the right to attend their estates. In Burgundy, all fiefholdings nobles with proof of lineage had the right to attend. The efforts of law students of Brittany to break the nobility's grip on the provincial estates degenerated into violent clashes against paid lackeys of the privileged orders in the streets of Rennes in January 1789. The deputies of the third estate of Burgundy voiced disapproval of the nobles' fiscal exemptions and their control over voting procedures. These protests persuaded the king and his ministers to decline the appeals of the Burgundian nobility for a special meeting of the provincial estates in the spring of 1789. The king and his ministers feared a repetition of the violence in Rennes.[4]

Languedoc and Walloon Flanders were not prone to such internecine conflict, because all of the ranks of the upper classes faced exclusion from the estates. The seats in the Estates of Walloon Flanders belonged to a coterie of Lillois oligarchs and the foremost provincial seigneurs. In Languedoc, the highest spheres of the French nobility and royal court controlled the 46 bishoprics and baronies furnishing entry into the Estates. The 73 seats of the third estate went to nobles and town councillors enjoying exclusive rights to their posts. They consistently sided with the bishops and barons. The common aspiration of all Languedocian elites for representation in the Estates delayed the emergence of conflict between the privileged orders and the rest of provincial society.[5]

The inhabitants of Languedoc began to show their aspiration for representation after the penultimate meeting of the Estates in January and February 1788. The intendant and the military governor presented the king's request for an extraordinary supplement of about 10 percent to the annual contribution to the royal treasury and a loan of 12,000,000 *livres*. They presented another request for a prolongation of the second *vingtième* – a tax on all land, regardless of whether the owner was noble or commoner – and an augmentation of the yield by about 25 percent through official evaluations of tax-exempt land.

When the Estates set to work to fulfil the king's wishes, the Parlement of Toulouse and the Cour des Comptes, Aides et Finances of Montpellier demurred. The sovereign courts of Languedoc, like their counterparts in other provinces, refused to write the king's edicts into the legal registers. The Cour des Comptes, Aides et Finances published a remonstrance in February 1788, stating that the Estates profited from provincial taxes, spent vast sums on luxury, and did not represent the three orders of the province. A month later, the Parlement

---

4 Egret 1955, pp. 189–215; Swann 2003, pp. 24, 368, 371, 373, 377, 379–80, 388.
5 Bossenga 1991, pp. 18, 24, 78, 90, 93.

issued a remonstrance making similar charges. The crown suppressed the Cour des Comptes, Aides et Finances and Parlement, along with the other sovereign courts of the realm, in May. This coup sent the whole province into an uproar, except for the Estates, which remained silent.[6]

The sovereign courts intensified their campaign against the Estates of Languedoc upon their restoration in the fall of 1788. The Cour des Comptes, Aides et Finances published a statement in December, 'that a century of reason and justice must no longer allow the spirit of barbarism and superstition to subsist'. The court avowed itself 'terrified by the rapid pace at which this imperfect constitution [of the Estates] has proceeded toward the last degree of degeneration'. It labelled the archbishop of Narbonne a 'despot'.[7] Nobles and magistrates published dozens of pamphlets denouncing the Estates over the course of 1788 and the beginning of 1789. The pamphlets led to scores of assemblies of nobles, clergymen, and leaders of the third estate, usually meeting together, between the end of 1788 and the beginning of 1789. The assemblies published deliberations calling for a provincial constitution, which would ensure responsible management of finances and representation for the three estates. The marquis de la Tour-Maubourg, for instance, chaired an assembly of over 300 clergymen, nobles, and commoners of the Velay at the end of 1788. It ruled:

> The orders originally obtained representation through free elections ... Yet the principal lords, ecclesiastic and lay, have succeeded in bestowing on their posts and estates the right of representing the clergy and the nobility ... Nor can the deputies of the third estate legitimately carry the wishes of this order, since they are taken in the class of noble mayors, owners of offices, or town leaders who are chosen by certain inhabitants of their towns and not by the generality of the people living under them.[8]

---

6 For the meeting of the Estates of Languedoc in 1788, and the protests and remonstrances of the following months, see Archives Nationales (hereafter AN) H1/748/65 pp. 522–3, H1/748/135, H1/748/165, H1/748/244, H1/1063, H1/1105; Archives Départementales de l'Hérault (ADH) C6546; *Rapport de Messieurs les commissaires nommés par déliberation des États de Languedoc, du 18 Janvier 1788. Précédé d'une lettre des commissaires des trois ordres du diocèse d'Alais à M. l'Évêque d'Alais; et suivi d'une lettre du Roi à M. l'Archevêque de Narbonne*, 1789.
7 AN H1/942/2.
8 Rioufol 1904, pp. 37–8. Other pamphlets and assemblies are found in AN H1/748/65 p. 419; AN H1/748/134; AN H1/748/135; AN H1/748/244; AN H1/942/2; AN BIII, 92; ADH C4685; Archives Départementales de la Haute-Garonne (ADHG) 51B29; Archives Municipales de Toulouse (AMT) AA 116, AA 319; Archives Départementales de l'Aude (ADA) 4E 206 AA 85; *Arrêté des habitants de la ville de Mende, capitale du Gévaudan; Lettre de M. L'Abbé de Siran, vicaire général de Mende, député du pays de Gévaudan, à M. le comte de Bannes d'Arejan, baron des Etats de Languedoc, nommé par la cour député de cette province, & en cette qualité notable,*

The three orders of Cintegabelle, a town near Toulouse, assembled in February 1789 to publish a deliberation. They elected the marquis du Villiers, seigneur of Lissac, president of the assembly by acclamation. The deliberation stated that the deputies of the Estates of Languedoc owed their positions to the episcopate, baronies, and municipal and diocesan oligarchies. The deputies did not have a mandate from provincial inhabitants and consequently did not have a legal mission.

> Emoluments are excessive. Certain representatives have only pecuniary titles ... Certain despotic members distribute large sums in bonuses and useless projects of beautification. This administration has forced the province to borrow without even obtaining the consent of any of the orders. Consequently, local taxes, progressively augmented by superfluous expenses, exceed taxes for the king several times over.[9]

A month later, nearly every *cahier de doléances*, whether written in the assemblies of the clergy or rural parishes, demanded representative provincial estates. To take a case in point, the chamber of the nobility of the electoral constituency (*sénéchaussée*) of Béziers published a ruling in March 1789.

> The existence of the current administration qualifying itself the Estates of Languedoc has profoundly injured the honour of the nobility; the nobility's civil existence is ignored, and its liberty annihilated ... Twenty-three *Gentilshommes* supplant and push aside the nobility of 23 dioceses ... They dare dispose of the property of all ... and do not fear keeping control of what is as abusive as it is unjust by smothering the protests of the dispersed nobility ... The first article of the cahier will develop this most crucial grievance to obtain ... truly constitutional estates ... composed of deputies from each order ... freely elected in each diocese.[10]

Parish priests had good reason to seek reform of the Estates, for as we saw in Chapter 2, the 23 bishops of Languedoc controlled all of the clergy's seats, as well as its authority and wealth. The bishops had secular authority over their dioceses and obtained millions of livres from seigneurial dues and tithes. By contrast, about 75 percent of the priests of the diocese of Montpellier lived on

---

1789; Nielidov 1989, pp. 602–3; Gorlier 1955, pp. 205–6; Falgairolle 1897, pp. 9–10; Allaire 1990, p. 129.
9   AN H1/942.
10 AN H1/943. For a survey of the cahiers see Vidal 1979, pp. 225–7.

a stipend of between 300 and 600 livres a year until the crown raised it to 750 in 1786. Priests usually came from families of office holders, professionals, and merchants. Only about one percent was of noble origin.[11]

Between January and March 1789, priests all over the province published tracts condemning the upper clergy's control over church wealth. As an illustration, the priest Magalon of St.-Gervais, a village in the diocese of Uzès, wrote a letter to Necker in March 1789 stating that, 'it is truly a strange thing to perceive such a disproportion in the distribution of ecclesiastical property'. He wrote that priests had reason to feel indignant at seeing the accumulation of benefices by bishops and archbishops who did little work for the first estate. The church should instead allocate the revenues of abbeys to priests who have shown merit and talent. 'It is through this equitable sharing of church revenue that the greatest number will be made happy'.[12] The lower clergy organised to win control of the first estate in several constituencies during the writing of cahiers and the elections to the Estates General. When the clergy of Béziers assembled in March 1789, for example, priests overwhelmed the upper clergy, forced the bishop to withdraw, and elected two priests to the Estates General.[13]

These protests within the first estate encouraged commoners to speak out against the privileges of the nobility. The general council of Bédarieux deliberated in December 1788 that 'the vicious organisation of the Estates of Languedoc ... comes from the time of fanaticism and ignorance when the clergy and nobility commanded the third estate like a herd of slaves whose heads had been weakened and shrunken by superstition and feudal anarchy'.[14] Between November 1788 and February 1789, the residents of Cuxac, Castres, Montpellier, Nîmes, and the Cévennes raised their own concerns, independent of the movement against the Estates. They gathered to protest the exclusion of commoners from the honorific and lucrative offices of state. The priest, leaders (*consuls*), and principal inhabitants of St.-Denis, a town in the southern Massif central, replied to a statement issued by the local nobility in February 1789.

---

11 Nicod 1971, p. 153; Tackett 1986.
12 This letter and others are found in AN H1/942/2. François Rouvière described another in 1974, vol. 1, p. 14. Lesser clergy of the dioceses of Mende, Limoux, Mirepoix, and the Vivarias denounced the privileges and prerogatives of bishops in 1788 and 1789. Péronnet 1990, p. 83; Arnaud 1904, pp. 91–3; Cazanave 1991, p. 51; Jolivet 1980, p. 73.
13 ADH C877, C879. Actions taken by parish priests of Languedoc to control elections to the Estates General and the writing of cahiers de doléances can be found in AN Ba 29, AN Ba 55; AN H1/748/292; Arnaud 1904, pp. 87–93; Ladurie 1967, p. 97; Jolivet 1980, p. 74.
14 Allaire 1990, p. 129.

> We have responded ... with a unanimous voice that it would be fair to allow the third estate to enter into the administration; this estate participates the most without dispute in the burdens and taxes: it would therefore be fair for it to participate also in the ... administration of posts and taxes according to the maxim: qui sentit onera sentire debet et commoda. There is no lack of people in this estate who have as much talent, probity and integrity as in the other two. Would it not be a truly excellent means to prevent abuses?[15]

When well-to-do townspeople met in March 1789 to write cahiers and elect deputies to the Estates General, they unanimously demanded that public offices be allocated according to an equitable principle. Every assembly of the third estate of the major towns and constituencies of Languedoc called on the crown to cease reserving official posts for nobles. The third estate of the constituency of Montpellier formulated its first entry, under the heading 'Administration of the Realm; the third estate will be admitted to civil and military posts in abrogation of the ... ordinances and customs that exclude it and deprive it of the liberty to serve the king and nation'.[16]

These demands of the third estate, like those of the lower clergy, reflected a tangible state of inequality. We saw in Chapter 2 that nobles dominated provincial institutions. The military governor, his lieutenants, and the intendant were all nobles of long lineage. Leading dignitaries of the realm oversaw the deliberations of the Estates of Languedoc. The 270 judgeships of the Parlement of Toulouse and the Cour des Comptes, Aides et Finances of Montpellier belonged to local seigneurs. These magistrates had influence over the municipalities of Toulouse and Montpellier. Royal ministers sought to involve commoners in the administration of the towns in 1770s and 1780s but never envisioned elections based on civic equality. The monarchy reserved places for sword nobles in Toulouse and gave the military governor the power to name the consuls of Montpellier. Even in the second-tier manufacturing town of Lodève,

---

15 AN H1/942/2. The Latin is underlined in the original and translates: 'He who bears the burden ought to experience the benefits'. The other four deliberations are found in AMT AA 314; AN H1/1447; M. B ... M ... Avocat au Parlement de Languedoc, members de diverses academies 1788; Combes 2000, pp. 39–41.

16 AN B. III, 92. The same demand for an equitable principle of access to royal offices is in the cahiers of the third estate of the constituencies of Nîmes, Carcassonne, Castres, Limoux, Lauragais, Toulouse, Le Puy, and the pays de Gévaudan, as well as in those of the towns of Mende, Agde, Albi and Pézenas. ADH C877, C879; ADHG 1 L 548; AN B. III, 85; Rioufol 1904, pp. 45, 50; Donnadieu 1989, pp. 104–5, 169–70; Nelidoff 1996a, pp. 214, 222.

the first of the three consuls in 1788 was Pierre-Joseph de Salze, knight of St.-Louis.[17]

Some nobles believed that their control over the provincial instances of government was rooted in a legitimate constitutional order. A Narbonnais nobleman wrote a pamphlet entitled 'Political Problem' in February 1789.

> The most illustrious publicists, notably our dear Montesquieu, advance on principle 'that if it is sometimes necessary to change certain laws, one must observe so much solemnity, and bring so much caution to bear, that the people naturally conclude that laws are sacred, since such formalities are necessary to abrogate them; in altering or abolishing established laws, the people are thrown into disorders inseparable from changes ... whatever the laws, it is always necessary to follow them, and look upon them as the public conscience to which that of particulars must conform'. If a profound knowledge of the human heart and of the goal and motivating forces of social institutions dictated these principles, can one watch without fright the French constitution threatened with destruction?[18]

Such attitudes prevented the three estates from writing common cahiers in several constituencies. The nobles of Limoux wrote in their cahier that the crown should protect privileges and properties, including venal offices, and count votes by order in the Estates General. They demanded that the crown make the Parlement and its right of registration unassailable. The next day, when the three orders assembled to present deputies and cahiers, bourgeois jurists stated that the nobility's deliberation improperly violated the spirit of the Estates General. The count of Latourzelle later wrote to a royal minister that the third estate had treated the nobility and clergy of Limoux in an unseemly manner. Similarly, disagreement among the three estates of the Castrais spoiled efforts to hold a common assembly. The nobles wrote in the preamble to their cahier, 'mustering all of our efforts and wisdom, not to change the constitution, but to affirm it, we demand that the third estate be satisfied with all of the rights it has obtained and the nobility has lost, and that it cease at long last to com-

---

17   AN H1/1014; ADHG C284, C285, C290; Laurent and Gavignaud 1989, p. 35; Martin 1900, p. 293.
18   AN H1/748/292. In 1789, M. l'Abbé de Siran, vicaire-général de Mende and abbé d'Issoire, also wrote against dissolving the three estates into a common body of citizens. He argued that such systematic reform would alter the monarchical constitution. *Plan patriotique, proposé au Gévaudan pour la députation aux États-Généraux*.

plain'. The first article of the cahier demanded that the Estates General count votes by order, not by head.[19]

2   The Toulousain and Albigeois after July 1789

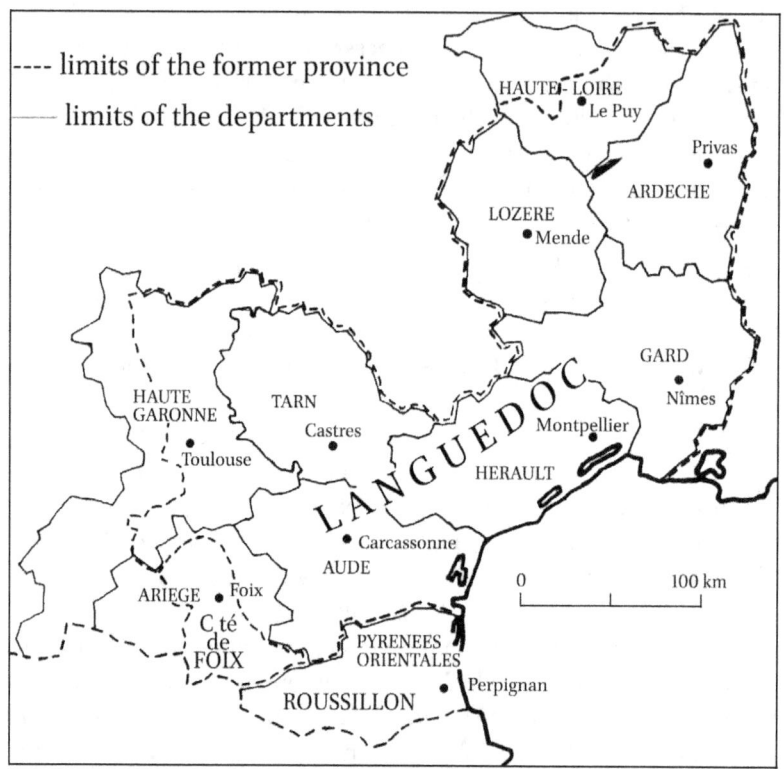

FIGURE 4.1   Map of the departments of the former province of Languedoc
BRU 1989

Nevertheless, these disputes over the nobles' hereditary rights to public positions did not dominate provincial debate. Provincial residents showed more concern about the archaic constitution of the Estates of Languedoc. This issue

---

19   AN B III, 42. Details concerning the assemblies of Limoux are located in Arnaud 1904, pp. 94–8, 102–5. Gilbert Larguier shows a similar dispute between the orders in the constituency of Mirepoix 1989, pp. 33–4, 45–8. The nobles of the constituency of Béziers demanded the right to form a separate provincial corps. They demanded that all tribunals reserve certain seats for nobles. AN Ba 21.

united townspeople under the leadership of nobles. Moreover, popular unrest in 1789 and 1790 made bourgeois property owners fearful of abrupt change. We will see in the next chapter that peasants and artisans seized stores of grain, ravaged fiscal bureaus, and raided private residences in the major towns of Languedoc. Nobles had held public responsibilities as military commanders and judges during the old regime, and seemed to have the experience needed to maintain order.

Patriotic celebrations united the active citizens of Foix in the election of Bertrand d'Artiguières, a commander of dragoons and knight of St.-Louis, to preside over the municipality in 1790. Residents of the manufacturing town of Bédarieux created a militia and repaired town walls after agitation, tumultuous gatherings, seditious chants, and brawls in April 1789. They elected De Vourbezou, a lieutenant colonel of infantry, to command their militia. The active citizens of the Corbières region of Languedoc elected seigneurs and royal office holders to the administrative bodies of the Aude.[20]

Residents of Toulouse had confidence in the Parlement in the first year of the Revolution. The loyalty of barristers to the Parlement, and the general movement uniting the educated and propertied elite against the Estates of Languedoc, forestalled the emergence of conflict between third-estate patriots and traditionalist nobles in 1789. The barristers were among the wealthiest and most respected members of the municipal bourgeoisie. They owned rural estates and relished playing the role of master before their sharecroppers. Their esteemed order formed part of the judicial hierarchy of the old regime. The barristers were fond of what was known as the 'monarchical constitution'. Many of them remained loyal to the parlementaires in the first years of the Revolution.[21]

Popular unrest induced the rest of the municipal bourgeoisie to rally behind the Parlement. Residents of the popular quarter of St.-Cyprien crossed the Garonne into the heart of town, seized stores of grain, and sold them at low prices in August 1789. The rioters threatened to hang a café owner accused of hoarding. They broke into the prisons run by the tax farm for salt (*la gabelle*) and freed detainees. The *capitouls* and the political council of Toulouse asked the Parlement to forgo its annual vacations and remain in session to help restore peace and stability. 'It is in its authority that resides our principal

---

20 Arnaud 1904, pp. 122, 133–4, 151; Allaire 1990, pp. 131–2; McPhee 1999, pp. 56, 91, 111; Larguier 1989, pp. 65–6, 103, 107–8. The vicomte Jean de Lasset was elected commander of the national guard of Mirepoix in 1789 and mayor in 1790. Cazanave 1991, p. 48.
21 Berlanstein 1975, pp. 40, 53, 112, 149, 161–2.

confidence'.[22] Property owners entrusted nobles with the command of 12 of the 15 legions of the Toulousain National Guard. Merchants, jurists and other townspeople failed to press for a municipal revolution, because the parlementaires and capitouls seemed best prepared to provide relief to the urban masses and maintain order.[23]

Many nobles refused to lead in this consensual fashion, dependent on the approval of commoners. They believed in old regime practices entitling them to authority. They published a cahier formally refusing to prepare grievances and elect delegates with the other orders, and swore never to accede to voting by head in the Estates General. They organised a meeting of the first two estates of the region in the fall of 1789 to protest the abolition of feudalism and the privileges of Languedoc. When the National Assembly established a new judicial system in 1790, the Parlement issued a manifesto declaring the National Assembly illegal and disputing its right to destroy the prerogatives of the first two orders, the provincial estates, and the king. The St.-Barthélémy legion of the National Guard, located in the neighbourhood of the Parlement, and led by the president d'Aspe, issued disparaging statements about the Constituent Assembly. Its rivalry with patriotic national guards degenerated into a clash in which two militiamen from the popular neighbourhood of St.-Cyprien lost their lives in March 1791.[24]

The nobility's repudiation of the principle of equality before the law arose out of the social and economic context of the region. The parlementaires had long enjoyed judicial and economic authority over upper Languedoc and political authority within Toulouse. A survey of after-death inventories shows that the Toulousain nobility and bourgeoisie had similar sources of wealth. Almost all the nobles had over 50 percent of their wealth in rural property, and over 50 percent of them had over 75 percent of their wealth in rural property. Manufacturers had over 40 percent, and merchants nearly 70 percent, of their wealth in real estate. Members of other professional groups of the municipal bourgeoisie had an even greater percentage of their fortunes in rural property. Yet while the fortunes of the nobility and bourgeoisie stemmed from the same sources, the two groups hardly formed a cohesive class. Parlementaires had an average of 15 times the wealth of the members of the bourgeoisie. Other nobles had almost six times the wealth. Having long towered over the inhabitants of upper

---

22 AN H1/748/291.
23 ADHG 1 L268; Nelidoff 1996, pp. 97, 113–14. See also Lyons 1978, p. 33.
24 The cahier is in ADHG 1 L548. Details of the meeting of the first two estates are in ADHG L323. See also Johnson 1986, pp. 121, 123. Details about the national guard are in ADHG 1 L268.

Languedoc, the nobles refused to accept a constitution requiring them to solicit bourgeois votes to remain in power.²⁵

The nobles' aristocratic attitudes were their ruin. In view of their influence over the municipal third estate, the residents of the region organised outside of Toulouse during the elections for the Estates General. The judges of the seneschal court did not depend on the Parlement for the value of their official positions as much as the Toulousain barristers did. Registers of the municipal government contain complaints that the judges concerted with the delegates of the five dioceses of the constituency to elect each other's deputies to the Estates General and exclude the bourgeoisie of Toulouse. The third estate elected André de Lartigue, chief justice (*juge-mage*) of the seneschal court and outspoken critic of the Parlement, to the Estates General. While it selected three of the eight deputies among the order of barristers, none of the three were favourites of the Parlement. Active citizens of the Haute-Garonne elected only one Toulousain in 1790 to the first departmental administration. Even within Toulouse, the traditional authorities' flat rejection of the National Assembly led voters to overhaul the municipal government. Only 4 of the 56 members of the first municipality elected in 1790 had been capitouls in the 1780s or councillors in the pre-revolutionary municipality, and none of them had been parlementaires.²⁶ Table 4.1 shows the professions of the first elected municipal councillors of Toulouse.

A few nobles of the Albigeois and Tarn joined their Toulousain counterparts in opposition to the Revolution. The cardinal de Bernis, archbishop of the Albigeois, rejected the civil constitution of the clergy, refused to relinquish his bishopric, tithes, and church property, and emigrated to Rome in 1792. The count of Toulouse-Lautrec had a distinguished military career capped by honours of the royal court. He used his considerable fortune and influence to win election to the Estates General over the objection of many local nobles. He rejected the Revolution from the outset and emigrated to Spain in 1791. Authorities got a hold of letters sent between Toulouse-Lautrec and his seigneurial steward revealing plans to foment an uprising in which rebels would seize châteaux and turn them into military strongholds for the armies of the émigré princes.

---

25 Sentou 1969, pp. 84, 120, 146, 148, 156, 163; Jacques Godechot and Suzanne Moncassin have shown that in 1785, nobles left less than two percent of municipal dowries for 32 percent of their total value, while members of the bourgeoisie left almost 12 percent for 45 percent of their total value (1965, p. 157).

26 AMT BB 61. Berlanstein describes the election to the Estates General (1975, pp. 153–4). A list of capitouls from the 1780s is in Lamouzèle 1910, p. 10. The composition of the pre-revolutionary municipality of 1789 is in AN H1/748/291.

TABLE 4.1   Municipal council of Toulouse, February 1790

Professions[a]	Percentage of the 56 officers and notables
Jurists[b]	29
Merchants/manufacturers	23
Master craftsmen/shopkeepers	20
Professionals[c]	11
Landlords (*bourgeois*)	7
Farmers	5
Military officers	4
Nobles	2

a   AN H1/748/134.
b   Barristers, royal attorneys (*procureurs*), notaries, etc.
c   Doctors, professors, public works contractor (*entrepreneur*), engineers.

The difficulty in executing the plans, Toulouse-Lautrec wrote, was that the local nobles knowledgeable of military techniques were patriots.[27]

The Albigeois nobility's support for the Revolution and its rejection of traditional leaders such as Bernis and Toulouse-Lautrec arose out of the economic and political context. Table 4.2, listing all those who paid over 10 livres of capitation, a tax on nobles and commoners alike, shows that nobles were among the wealthiest residents of Albi.[28] Yet it also shows that their fortunes paled in comparison to those of nobles of the provincial capitals of Toulouse and Montpellier. The nobles of Albi did not have the means to distinguish themselves on the national, or even the provincial, level.[29]

The royal administration did not accord local nobles any of the honours of governmental responsibility. The cardinal de Bernis had titles to the presidency of the *Petits Etats* of the Albigeois, which handled public works, the allotment of taxes, and other administrative affairs. He had seigneurial rights over the town of Albi. Bernis pressed his right to name the consuls and to have his representative chair the municipal council over the protests of local not-

27   Bru 1989, p. 16; Hindie Lemay 1991, pp. 87, 895–6; Combes 2000, pp. 41–4, 77–9.
28   The tax rolls are in Archives Départementales du Tarn (ADT) C573. Historians believe that capitation rolls of Languedoc of the second half of the eighteenth century are fairly accurate measures of wealth. Marquié 1993, p. 218; Marinière 1958, p. 280.
29   Sharon Kettering comments on how expensive it was to attend the royal court, where the most lucrative and prestigious political responsibilities were conferred (2001, pp. 66–72).

TABLE 4.2 Capitation of Albi, 1787

Profession/rank	Assessments (percentages based on 155 taxpayers)			
	10–20 livres	20–40	40–60	60+
Nobles	5	4	2	2
Jurists, office holders and other liberal professionals	8	6	1	2
Bourgeois rentier landowners	11	2	2	
Merchants[a]	14	5	3	1
Commoners with no profession or rank[b]	13	4		1
Shopkeepers/artisans[c]	9	1		
Farmers[d]	5			

a *Marchands, négociants,* and *transporteur.*
b Mostly widows and daughters.
c Includes *aubergist, boulanger, serrurier, orfèvre, maçon,* etc.
d *métayers, paysan,* and *ménager.*

ables during the 1780s. Nobles therefore had special reason to oppose the Estates of Languedoc. They suffered not only from the ban on entering the Estates but also from the tutelage of the cardinal de Bernis, one of the Estates' leading members. At an assembly of the three orders of Albi in January 1789, the marquis de Rochegude, a naval commander, pronounced,

> It is a fact, only too well known, that the members of the first two orders, often foreigners to Languedoc, consent to the taxes we pay and that the third estate is hardly consulted ... Born free like the air ... let us conserve our natural dignity ... the Estates are not our representatives ... It is time to break out of the lethargic sleep in which we are buried, it is time to break the heavy chains ... it is time to overturn a monstrous colossus which arrogantly tramples us ... Let us retake control of our administration.[30]

Never having enjoyed many honours of serving the monarchy, the regional nobility had little to lose from political change. Many local nobles may have sensed bright futures ahead, as active citizens looked to them for leadership amid the unrest of 1789 and 1790. The urban poor of Albi attacked a grain

30   ADT C54; Niélidow 1989, pp. 28, 32.

retailer accused of hoarding in July 1789. In August, inhabitants of Castres destroyed the offices of the tax farmers who collected revenue from grain sales. Labourers armed with axes and picks forced the municipality of Albi to distribute aid and open charity workshops the following spring. Property owners formed the patriotic legion of Albi in July 1789 'to repel brigands who overrun the frontiers of the Albigeois'. They made Durfort, a knight of St.-Louis, the director. Active citizens of Albi chose Raymond Gorsse, the former syndic of the Estates of Languedoc for the diocese, to preside over the municipality, and Delecouls de Cantepau, a lawyer in the Parlement and mayor since 1787, to fill the post of executive agent (*procureur-syndic*) in 1790. Active citizens elected Joseph de Lastours, a noble magistrate of the Cour des Comptes, Aides et Finances, to preside over the general council of the Tarn in 1790. They continued to trust these figures the following years. Voters elected the marquis de Rochegude to the Convention, and Gorsse and de Cantepau to lead the district of Albi. The Convention made Lastours the national agent for Castres in 1793 and 1794.[31]

3 Nîmes, the Southern Massif Central, and Montpellier after July 1789

Lower Languedoc had a unique political and economic context characterised by a large Protestant community and a textile industry that saw extensive growth over the course of the eighteenth century. Wholesale merchants put raw material out to peasants and artisans of the southern Massif central for spinning and then brought the yarn and silk into urban workshops for weaving and dying. The population of Nîmes grew threefold between 1720 and 1780. A tabulation of dowries shows that the fortunes of municipal textile merchants, many of whom were Protestant, surpassed those of the local landowners and jurists as early as the 1730s. The merchants held sway over the mass of urban manufacturers and workers on account its dependence on them for wages. The merchants' influence grew in the 1780s, as the decline of the textile industry left almost 60 percent of looms inactive and made thousands of workers dependent on charity. Royal strictures on Protestants, however, left nobles, lawyers, and judges of the seneschal court in control of the administration. We saw in Chapter 3 that reform-minded ministers failed in their bid to bring Nîmes's wealthiest residents into the municipal council in the 1770s and 1780s on account of the Catholic elite's resistance to change and the monarchy's unwillingness to grant political responsibility to Protestants.[32]

---

31   ADT B805; Bru 1989, pp. 32, 40–1, 69; Faury 1983, pp. 224–7.
32   AN H1/801; ADHG B1861, C47; ADH C965; Teisseyre-Sallmann 1980, p. 970; Lewis 1978, p. 10;

These prejudices looked as if to vanish in the patriotic atmosphere of 1789. The local nobility rallied the residents of Nîmes against the oligarchic leaders of the Estates of Languedoc. In February 1789, after learning that the baron de Marguerittes had spoken out against the Estates, the third estate of Nîmes unanimously deliberated 'to testify its thanks, satisfaction and gratitude to Marguerittes ... for having defended with dignity and courage the cause of the people'.[33]

Anxiety about popular unrest generated even more support for the nobility. After the fall of the Bastille, rumours spread through Nîmes, Vauvert and Alès about armies of brigands. Further to the North, peasants burned chateaux, seigneurial titles, and government registers in the Vivarais. The bourgeoisie formed defence forces amid general panic and turned to the traditional authorities for leadership. The active citizens of Nîmes made Marguerittes the first elected mayor of the municipality in February 1790. They elected Catholic nobles, landlords, and canons to the city council. The residents of St.-Hippolyte-Du-Fort of the Gard elected the lieutenant general and governor, M. de Comeiras, head of their militia in August 1789, and the noble de Bousquet mayor the next year. Active citizens elected five nobles – including a magistrate of the Cour des Comptes, Aides et Finances and the syndic of the Estates for the diocese of Uzès – two magistrates of the seneschal court and a lawyer to be presidents of the eight district tribunals of the Gard in 1790. The residents of Le Puy, capital of the Haute-Loire, elected Roche de Pezouls, the last mayor of the old regime, to lead the city government in February 1790.[34]

The establishment of religious toleration and the deepening of the economic crisis led many residents to reassess their political positions. The Revolution threatened the centuries-old traditions that had assured the nobility's

---

Lepetit 1988, p. 13; Gutherz and Huard 1982, p. 215; Hood 1971, pp. 265, 267, 274; Laurent and Gavignaud 1987, p. 18.

33 Rouvière 1974, vol. 1, pp. 16–17.

34 Rouvière 1974, vol. 1, pp. 11–12, 19, 54–5, 500–3; Riou 1988, p. 165; Gutherz and Huard 1982, pp. 219–20; Peyriat 1990, pp. 280, 282, 290; Bayon-Tollet 1982, pp. 269, 276. Active citizens elected Henri Folcheri de Nizan, knight of St.-Louis, president of the district of Uzès in the Gard in 1790. The baron de Vauvert won election to the post of colonel and his seigneurial judge, François Boissier, lieutenant colonel, of the revolutionary legion Vauverdoise in the Gard in August 1789. Active citizens of Le Vigan chose the baron d'Albignac for mayor after Henry Quatrefage de Laroquète left to join the National Assembly. Jacques Christophe Despeisses, seigneur of six villages and other places, won command of the national guard of St.-Florant in the Gard in August 1789. Nobles and retired military officers won all of the posts of command in the national guard of Annonay in the Vivarais at the end of 1789. D'Albiousse 1978, p. 225; Falgairolle 1897, p. xxxi; Gorlier 1955, p. 214; Bousiges 1988, p. 24; Jolivet 1980, p. 151.

authority over Protestants. The nobles felt unable to compete with Protestants once the collapse of royal authority swept away their institutional support. They suddenly faced the prospect of having to work with, and possibly even obey, the Protestant bourgeoisie. Amid the nobles' electoral triumphs of 1789 and 1790, Protestants gained control of the national guard of Nîmes and won five of the eight seats of the third estate of the Gard in the Estates General.

Economic conditions in the countryside created propitious grounds for the recruitment counterrevolutionary fighters. The infertile soil of the Gard never yielded more than a third of the inhabitants' subsistence. Peasants in the suburbs of Nîmes and the region to the north depended on textile production and part-time work in coalmines to make ends meet. Their life became precarious as a result of the decline of the local textile industry in the 1780s and bad harvests of the revolutionary period. Appeals to religious prejudices resonated in this climate of uncertainty. The history of conflict between the Catholics and Protestants of Nîmes and the mountainous region to the north left a legacy of mistrust. Many believed that the Protestants coveted the chance to seize power and oppress Catholics.[35]

The Catholic elite rallied behind the jurist François Froment in 1790. He owned a local seigneurie and inherited his father's lease of the cathedral chapter's domains and perquisites. Froment's father had earned the ire of local Protestants in the 1780s by using his position as tax assessor to favour the economic interests of Catholic landowners. After attending the meeting of the clergy and nobility of Toulouse to protest against the National Assembly, François Froment returned to Nîmes in the spring of 1790 to recruit a Catholic and royalist militia with the tacit support of the mayor baron de Marguerittes. Froment and his militiamen announced their defiance of the National Assembly, and their support for the rights of the king and Catholicism, in a meeting at the church of the Penitent Blanc in April 1790. Marguerittes held a banquet for the Catholic militia in May. Froment's forces and the Protestant-led National Guard clashed a month later, and about 300 people, mostly Catholics, died.[36]

Nobles then turned their attention to the poor mountainous departments north of Nîmes. Peasants of the Ardèche had incomes 20 percent below the national average. The department had only six towns over 2000 inhabitants and only one over 5000. Members of the local bourgeoisie generally moved to Toulouse and Montpellier once they accumulated some wealth. Those that

---

35 AN F11 458; Archives Départementales du Gard (ADG) IV E 22; Lewis 1978, pp. 14, 16–17; Johnson 1985, p. 110; Hood 1971, pp. 267–8, 274.
36 ADG L 1975; Daudet 1881, pp. 7, 10, 23; Lewis 1978, pp. 10, 17, 20–1; Gutherz and Huard 1982, p. 220.

remained were relatively poor. They commonly bought offices in seigneurial courts conferring precedence in local processions but never came close to sharing the honours of public authority with the nobility. Many members of the local bourgeoisie were excluded from official positions on account of their Protestant faith. The upper clergy and noble owners of certain domains controlled the presidency and most of the seats in the Petits Etats of the Velay, Vivarais, and Gévaudan, the main administrative bodies of the region. The lords helped maintain order through their seigneurial courts. We saw in Chapter 1 that the Parlement of Toulouse invigorated seigneurial justice after rioting in 1783 exposed the lack of royal institutions in the region. The Parlement enjoined the local seigneurs to scrutinise the lists of jurists eligible to practice in their courts and remove the ones they did not like.[37]

Long accustomed to dominance in local affairs, seigneurs and clergymen were loath to share authority with Protestants, merchants, and jurists. They refused to seek votes for the right to hold office. The context of insecurity caused by bad harvests and the decline of the textile industry made it possible for nobles to exploit latent prejudices against Protestants. The populace became especially receptive to anti-Protestant propaganda after news spread of the fighting in Nîmes that left hundreds of Catholics dead. On three separate occasions between 1790 and 1792, bishops, abbeys, nobles, jurists, magistrates, and royal military officers rallied peasants to armed encampments in the châteaux of Bannes and Jalès, where the departments of the Lozère, Ardèche, and Gard meet, to fight for throne and altar.[38] A manifesto circulated at the end of 1790 and the beginning of 1791, 'of 50,000 loyal Frenchmen armed in the Vivarais for the cause of religion and the monarchy against the usurpation of the so-called National Assembly'. It alleged that, 'Protestants seek to impose their laws ... They have obtained military ranks, public employments and honours. Catholics are turned away. Attachment to the apostolic and Roman church is a pretext for exclusion from all the public offices'.[39] Despite the revolutionaries' brutal repression of the instigators of these rebellions (or perhaps because of it), escaped leaders organised another counterrevolutionary rising, Charrier's Catholic army, which marched on St.-Denis in the Lozère in 1793.[40]

---

37 Molinier 1985, pp. 155–6; Molinier 1988, p. 141; Jones 1979, pp. 70, 76; Bayon-Tollet 1982, pp. 180–1; Beik 1985, pp. 69, 297; Castan 1980a, p. 120; Roux 1988, pp. 24, 67.
38 AN BB16 253; AN F1 103; Lewis 1978, pp. 11–13, 22–3, 28, 32, 36, 62; Laurent and Gavignaud 1987, pp. 86–8; Daudet 1881, pp. 32–3, 50, 54–5, 66, 78–9, 136, 179, 195, 221–2; Duboul 1890, pp. 282, 313.
39 Quoted from Riou 1990, p. 114.
40 Delon 1922, pp. 231, 235–9, 288–9; André 1894, pp. 75, 78.

The nobles' refusal to resign themselves to the Revolution resulted in an overhaul of the local administrations. How could the citizenry trust local government to its customary leaders, after these had taken up arms against the principle of equality before the law? The Constituent Assembly dismissed the municipality of Nîmes after the bloody clashes of 1790. Nîmes did not have another Catholic mayor until 1815. Protestants also won control over the department and many districts of the Gard. To the north of Nîmes, the inhabitants of the Haute-Loire organised a committee to root out suspects after news spread that the conspirators of Jalès had planned to seize control of Le Puy. Patriots searched houses, made arrests, and filled the local jails. The department dissolved the committee in July 1791 after the return of calm. But active citizens had grown apprehensive of the traditional leaders. The second and third elections to the municipality of Le Puy in the fall of 1790 and 1791 saw less affluent individuals, and even some artisans, accede to office.[41]

Montpellier and the department of the Hérault did not experience such a radical overhaul of political personnel. The noble magistrates of the Cour des Comptes Aides et Finances initiated the movement against the Estates of Languedoc in February 1788 and were this body's foremost opponents over the following year. In the spring of 1789, the nobles of the electoral constituency of Montpellier renounced their fiscal exemptions. They declared that honour was 'singularly appropriate to monarchical government' and the only privilege worth conserving.[42] Residents of Montpellier formed one of the first bourgeois militias in France after a violent subsistence riot in the nearby port of Agde in April 1789. They elected Jean-François-Antoine Serres de Meplès, president of the Cour des Comptes, Aides et Finances, and the merchant Estorc to the two posts of commander.[43]

The local nobility aligned itself with the Constituent Assembly in the ensuing months. The absolutist state's architecture of authority and honour structured this choice. The nobles of Montpellier were not habituated to the same degree of pre-eminence as were their counterparts in Toulouse. The magistrates of the Cour des Comptes Aides et Finances had political responsibilities and honours in Montpellier, and extensive judicial authority over the province. Yet every year for 40 days in January and February, the public eye disregarded the local nobles and focused its gaze instead on the spectacular ceremonies surrounding the dignitaries of the Estates of Languedoc.

---

41   Lewis 1978, p. 25; Bayon-Tollet 1982, pp. 284–5, 302.
42   The cahier is in AN B. III, 92. It also stated that the crown should conserve seigneurial rights and that the nobility of Montpellier did not intend to renounce them.
43   Laurent and Gavignaud 1987, p. 37.

The economic context also influenced perceptions. The city had a throng of manufactures, some of which housed hundreds of workers. Rolls of the capitation constitute one of the best sources for measuring municipal fortunes. Judges of the Cour des Comptes, Aides et Finances recognised that the rolls for allocating the regular direct tax (*la taille*) had not been renewed for over a century and left out many properties of the wealthy.[44] Table 4.3, listing residents who paid at least 20 livres of capitation in 1789, seven to eight percent of the households, demonstrates that the magistrates of the Cour des Comptes, Aides et Finances were some of the wealthiest inhabitants of Montpellier. Yet it also shows that non-noble landowners, lawyers, and especially manufacturers and merchants formed the most numerous strata of the local elite.[45]

TABLE 4.3   Capitation of Montpellier, 1789

Professions/rank	Assessments (percentages based on 660 taxpayers)				
	20–40 livres	40–80	80–160	160–360	360+
Noble magistrates, Cour des Comptes, Aides et Finances			6.36	11.36	.15
Noble magistrates, *Trésoriers de France* of the *Bureau des Finances*			4.7		
Nobles[46]	1.66	5	3.94	1.97	.3
Military men[47]	.6	.15	.15		.15
Administrative and financial office holders[48]	.60	1.35	.9	.60	.3
Jurists[49]	3.03	1.66	.3		
Common landlords	3.79	3.33	1.06	.15	
Professionals[50]	1.06	.6	.3		

44   One judge asked that capitation rolls be used to establish a new tax on salt to replace the hated royal monopoly. AN H1/848; H1/944/1.
45   These tax rolls are in AN H1/292.
46   Includes many seigneurs, *vicomtes*, chevaliers, barons, *écuyers*, etc., and some with only the particle *de*, who may not have been noble.
47   *Aide-major*, governor De Calvisson, infantry officer, lieutenant colonel, captain, etc. and *le comte de* Biffy, a military general, paying 1370 livres.
48   *Commissaire des guerres*, *le fermier général des étapes*, director of the royal domains, director of the tax farms, *agent de change*, etc. and de Joubert, treasurer of the Estates and de Joubert *fils*, together paying 1718 livres.
49   *Conseillers*, lawyers, notaries, *juge-mage*, royal attorneys, etc.
50   Doctors, professor, engineer, public works contractor.

TABLE 4.3 Capitation of Montpellier, 1789 (cont.)

Professions/rank	Assessments (percentages based on 660 taxpayers)				
	20–40 livres	40–80	80–160	160–360	360+
Merchants/manufacturers[51]	7.12	7.58	5.91	1.66	.3
Commoners, no profession or rank listed	6.52	4.24	3.33	1.36	.15
Artisans/shopkeepers[52]	3.03	1.66	.15	.15	
Farmers[53]	.6	.15			
Workers[54]	.45				

These class relations appeared in the city's social geography. The place de Canourgue and surrounding streets became Montpellier's chic neighbourhood in the eighteenth century. Judges of the Cour des Comptes, Aides et Finances bought residences overlooking the plaza between 1665 and 1756. Members of the bourgeoisie purchased buildings in the surrounding streets in the following decades, as the percentage of peasants and artisans inhabiting the neighbourhood declined. The nobility must have noticed all the wealthy commoners joining the upper ranks of society. Their presence testified to the injustice of the traditional practices of the absolutist state, which reserved governmental careers and honours for nobles. After July 1789, any attempt to bar the bourgeoisie from the political arena probably seemed anachronistic.[55]

Nobles thought their governmental experience and loyalty to the Revolution merited them a place in the institutions created by the Constituent Assembly. President Bonnier d'Alco wrote to the National Assembly on behalf of the Cour des Comptes, Aides et Finances in September 1789,

> We are 128 officers ... It is a fact that the active number is hardly over 30 ... Now this number of useful citizens, of magistrates, is not far from the one with which the National Assembly will probably decide to compose each sovereign tribunal in the new organisation ... All know the proofs

---

51 *Marchands, négociants, bijoutier, commissionaire, droguiste*, etc.
52 *Maître chirurgien, maître serrurier, apothicaire, mangonnier, confiseur*, etc. as well as Bazile *maître orfèvre*, his sons and aunt together paying 178 livres.
53 *Ménager, fermier*.
54 *Fenassiers, teinturier*.
55 Pascal 1994, pp. 400, 405; Thomas 1936, p. 174.

we have given of civic mindedness and devotion to the national assembly and to the good of the state. Where will one find magistrates who are as experienced and loyal, and as attached to their duties?[56]

Residents elected 99 deputies in August 1789 to regenerate the municipality. Twenty-four were judges in the Cour des Comptes, Aides et Finances. The deputies declared it their duty to jettison feudal law and allow 'all interested parties capable of expressing a suffrage, without distinction of rank, station or birth' to write new laws assuring a fair allotment of municipal offices. Twenty-five judges of the Cour des Comptes, Aides et Finances helped form the Club of the Friends of the Constitution and of Equality in February 1790. Minutes of a civic ceremony in 1791 listed elected officials of the directory of the Hérault, the directory and tribunal of the district of Montpellier, the municipality, the general staff of the National Guard, and the Society of the Friends of the Constitution and of Equality. Fifteen percent, including the president of the district and the mayor of Montpellier, were former nobles of the Cour des Comptes, Aides et Finances. Twenty-seven of these judges served the Revolution as elected officials at all levels of government, including district tribunals, presidents of departmental councils and even members of the Convention's committee of public safety.[57]

In conclusion, nobles brought about scores of assemblies of the three estates of Languedoc to demand a representative provincial constitution in 1788 and 1789. The movement created a mood of patriotic cooperation between nobles and commoners and tempered divergent opinions about how far reform should go. In the spring of 1789, priests, lawyers, merchants, landlords, and other members of the bourgeoisie voiced support for a new regime of civic equality and an impartial principle for access to government careers. Yet when given the vote, they entrusted authority to the second estate. Nobles were experienced and respected public figures, and had been in the forefront of agitation for reform. They seemed qualified to pacify popular unrest, which posed a physical and economic danger to all those who enjoyed a certain ease.

Many nobles would not rule in this consensual fashion. The political structure of the absolutist state, together with the economic context, shaped their perception of the new order. Toulousain parlementaires had far and away the greatest fortunes of upper Languedoc. They possessed administrative authority within Toulouse and judicial authority over much of southern France. The

---

56   Vialles 1921, p. 267.
57   Vialles 1921, pp. 159–89, 199–204, 218–24, 256, 259n, 276; AN H1/748/292; Gégot 1974, vol. 1, pp. 94–5.

nobility of Toulouse refused to solicit the support of other citizens for the right to preside over public affairs. The nobles of the Albigeois did not have this legacy of economic and political domination. The monarchy accorded the archbishop of Albi, an influential member of the Estates of Languedoc, a preponderant voice in the diocese and municipality, and left nobles with little role in government. Most nobles of the Albigeois had political rights to gain by siding with the Constituent Assembly. Their support for the Revolution won them the confidence of their fellow citizens and enabled them to carry elections to positions of leadership in the Tarn.

In lower Languedoc, the nobles of Nîmes were attached to the traditions of throne and altar that assured them the upper hand over wealthy Protestant merchants. Nobles were particularly attached to absolutist traditions in the poor mountainous region north of Nîmes. They refused to associate in the political arena with the regional bourgeoisie composed of Protestant jurists and proprietors of relatively modest means. Popular fears of Protestants helped forge a social basis, absent from the Toulousain, with which the nobles of Nîmes and the southern Massif central mounted armed resistance to the Revolution. The nobles of Montpellier, contrary to their counterparts in Nîmes and Toulouse, had not enjoyed political and economic dominance over their region. The Estates of Languedoc overshadowed them from above, while a growing bourgeoisie inundated them from below. The Revolution did not distress them so deeply, and resistance seemed futile. The nobility of Montpellier embraced the Revolution and regularly won elections to government office, whereas the nobility's obduracy elsewhere in the province led active citizens to entrust political affairs to townspeople who had never had much official responsibility under the old regime.

These findings confirm the revisionist argument, advanced three decades ago, that the nobility and bourgeoisie did not have contradictory class interests.[58] Economic forces did not impel the bourgeoisie of Languedoc into conflict with the nobility. Many of the fortunes of merchants and manufacturers came from land rents. Merchants of Nîmes and Montpellier were not particularly impatient with nobles. They worried above all about maintaining class relations vis-à-vis the mass of peasants and artisans. Popular revolts set off fears among property owners and led them to entrust political authority to nobles throughout the province in 1789 and 1790. Nobles had professional experience with government during the old regime and seemed the most qualified to lead the new one.

---

58   Taylor 1967, pp. 469–96; Lucas 1973, pp. 84–126.

My research shows that this confidence in the nobility broke down under the weight of the old regime. A common disgust with the arbitrariness of the old regime monarchy may have brought the nobility and bourgeoisie together in opposition to absolutism but did not imbue all nobles and clergymen with liberal values. Timothy Tackett's work on the National Assembly demonstrates that the economic and cultural legacy of the old regime imparted a profoundly conservative attitude to many nobles. Similar to what we have seen in Languedoc, Tackett finds that nobles provoked conflict with deputies of the third estate by refusing to accept equality before the law. He shows that while bourgeois and noble deputies obtained wealth from the same sources, the nobles' fortunes and political influence were far superior. Nobles of Toulouse and the southern Massif central, like their peers in the Constituent Assembly, had an aversion for sharing the political arena with jurists and merchants of relatively modest means. Tackett's research demonstrates that noble deputies of the National Assembly promoted enlightened reform while harbouring an unshakable belief in orthodox Catholicism and their political prerogatives.[59] Similarly, the nobles of Nîmes and the southern Massif central campaigned for representative and constitutional government, yet recoiled at the idea of participating in politics alongside commoners and according civil rights to Protestants. The absolutist state reproduced inequalities of status and power, and instilled beliefs in hierarchy and rank resistant to the principles of the Constituent Assembly.

The nobles' refusal to accept equality before the law modified the course of the Revolution. As it became clear that many of them held fast to aristocratic values and supported counterrevolution, bourgeois administrators grew tolerant of peasant revolts against the seigneurial regime. Some local authorities encouraged attacks on châteaux to prevent the nobility from using them as military strongholds for counterrevolution. Peasants of the Ardèche, Gard, and Ariège, departments where nobles had come out against the Revolution, destroyed scores of châteaux in 1792. We now turn to this dialectic between popular revolts and conflict within the upper classes during the 1790s.

59 Tackett 1996, pp. 39–41, 108, 304, 306, 308.

CHAPTER 5

Popular Revolts, Political Authority and the Revolutionary Dynamic, 1789–93

The collapse of royal authority in 1789 permitted a renegotiation of all the benefits and burdens of government. We saw in the last chapter that priests, merchants, jurists, and other bourgeois proprietors sought to expand access to the professions, honours, and wealth available through the state. In this chapter, we will see that the lower classes of town and country also sought to take advantage of the breakdown of royal authority. Peasants and artisans fought to put an end to burdens enforced by lords and office holders. They stubbornly resisted seigneurial dues and taxes.

Alexis de Tocqueville and Georges Lefebvre established the paradigms for analysing the grievances that fuelled the popular revolts of the Revolution. Tocqueville argued that the growing role of royal agents in the administration of the country diminished the governmental responsibilities of feudal lords. Seigneurs no longer performed any useful public services for rural inhabitants yet continued to collect tribute from them. The peasants thus found it unfair that they had to go on paying dues to idle parasitic lords.[1]

Lefebvre maintained that the nobles sustained an 'aristocratic reaction' to regain the rights they lost to the consolidation of royal absolutism under Louis XIV. They added to the seigneurial levies weighing on rural communities and, in so doing, intensified resentment among the peasantry. The two paradigms offer divergent assessments of the vitality of the seigneurial regime. Yet both assume that state formation threatened the prerogatives of the lordly classes and that the seigneurial regime was the fundamental cause of the peasants' resentment.[2]

This chapter measures the extent to which the seigneurial regime and the state had a bearing on the popular uprisings of the Revolution. It evaluates the economic growth of the eighteenth century to determine the particular problems facing the peasantry at the time of the Revolution. One of these problems, we will see, a problem that has not received much attention in the literature, was the fiscal burdens imposed by the revolutionary legislators. The peasants'

---

1 Tocqueville1955, pp. 24, 26–7, 29–30, 79.
2 Lefebvre 1963, pp. 225, 227, 232, 340, 345–6, 350–1, 353, 361.

unwillingness to pay led to violent conflict with the authorities. Seigneurial dues, by contrast, did not provoke many rural uprisings. One of the principle findings of this chapter is that the peasantry broke into chateaux and destroyed noble titles because of the overall political context pitting the largely bourgeois defenders of the new order against the suspected enemies of the Revolution.

The chapter begins with a discussion of what I call growth without development. The peasants increased the output of agriculture and manufacturing by taking advantage of the market opportunities of the eighteenth century, yet their standard of living did not improve. Their dependence on the market actually made them vulnerable to economic fluctuations. We will see in the second part of the chapter that an abrupt increase in grain prices after 1788 set off a wave of uprisings. The lower classes held up grain shipments, ravaged fiscal bureaus, and broke into the homes of notables in many parts of the province.

The third part of this chapter analyses popular resistance to taxation. Peasants knew from their experience under the old regime that nobles and wealthy commoners benefited from fiscal exactions. They were sceptical that their tax payments could ever improve their lives. By contrast, many jurists, merchants, manufacturers, professionals, and landowners believed the Constituent Assembly created a rational framework for public life, offering opportunity to talented, industrious, and virtuous patriots. Revolutionary officials deplored resistance to taxation and opposed it with all of the means at their disposal.

The final part shows that they responded differently to revolts against the seigneurial regime. Authorities did not act resolutely to stem this lawlessness and sometimes even abetted it as the Revolution unfolded. The coincidence of royalist uprisings with war against foreign monarchies made patriots wary of potential enemies inside of France likely to be found among the former nobility. By 1792, many revolutionaries were intent on making a show of force against the former seigneurs. The state and its financial sustenance mattered to broad strata of the upper classes, whereas the seigneurial regime mattered to a relatively small group increasingly associated with counterrevolution. The revolutionary elite smothered the peasants' efforts to resist taxation, while it allowed their assaults on seigneurial property to develop in scope.

1   The Eighteenth-Century Economy: Growth without Development

To understand the popular violence of the revolutionary period, we must recall the economic trends described in Chapter 1. The peasants' efforts to produce for the market led to economic growth, but did little to increase their standard of living, and actually made them vulnerable to economic fluctuations. They created vineyards on the hilly and gravelly soils of Mediterranean Languedoc. The peasants of the Cévennes and the southern Massif central planted mulberry trees, used the leaves to nurture silk worms, and earned income from the regional apparel workshops. The peasants of upper Languedoc developed the cultivation of maize. This crop yielded more calories per hectare than did other grains, covered the peasants' subsistence needs, and permitted them to send surpluses of wheat down the Canal du Midi to lucrative markets in lower Languedoc. Many of them also worked as agricultural labourers on the grain-growing estates of the Toulousain and Lauragais. Peasants throughout the province, and particularly around the manufacturing towns, churned out textiles for international consumers. The peasantry's ingenuity in producing for the market expanded the economy.

But was it a source of development? Did market involvement raise the standard of living? Philip Hoffman, author of an influential book on the French countryside, believes that it did. He argues that urban growth stimulated rural inhabitants to increase output and capitalise on the town markets. Improvements to the transportation network lowered costs, created incentives and thus spurred productive farming. The consolidation of plots and enclosures, the resultant economies in farm buildings, new crops such as maize and sainfoin, and new implements like the scythes to harvest grain, all raised productivity. Capital in the land, such as vineyards and arable fields of oats, straw and hay, generated income from town markets for wine and horse feed. All of these trends are proven, Hoffman claims, by a calculation of lease prices relative to the costs of agricultural inputs, particularly in the Paris basin, but also in the vicinity of Albi, although his calculation shows declining productivity around Beziers.[3]

I maintain that economic development occurs when a population obtains greater returns from its exertions. Gains in labour productivity expand the entire economic pie for all strata of the population even if the owners of capital benefit most. I will show that this way of looking at the Languedocian economy casts doubt on Hoffman's analysis. The peasantry increased overall output and lease prices but only through an even greater increase of drudgery and a stagnant or declining standard of living.

Population growth ranged from over 25 percent in the Vivarais to almost 70 percent in the Montpelliérain over the course of the 1700s.[4] This demographic expansion led the peasant households to subdivide their landholdings

---

3 Hoffman, 1996, pp. 39, 91, 94, 125, 127, 134, 144–6, 149, 155, 158, 171, 176, 183, 201–2.
4 Molinier 1988, p. 139; Molinier 1985, p. 202; Fournier and Péronnet 1989, p. 85; Soboul 1958, p. 49; Frêche 1975, pp. 59, 163, 207, 220–2, 248.

among heirs, and left them with plots ever less adequate to provide for their subsistence and occupy all of their family labour productively. In the fifteen and sixteenth centuries, when faced with population growth and the resultant reduction of farm sizes, peasants planted grain on the hardscrabble of hillsides and heaths. Yields declined with each new hectare brought under cultivation until soil exhaustion led to an economic crisis. In the eighteenth century, the peasants began to clear the scrublands for vineyards rather wheat fields. Vines grew well on the hilly and gravely soils of Mediterranean Languedoc and raised revenue with which the peasants could purchase more grain than they could grow themselves. Vines brought more resources into Mediterranean Languedoc.[5]

They did not, however, put the region on course toward an advanced phase of growth. An overview of the landholding-pattern shows a coincidence of viticulture, peasant property, and parcels carved out of the scrublands. It did not require investment in fertiliser, horses, stakes, and ploughs to cultivate vines. But it did require immense amounts of labour to clear marginal lands, sink the roots of vines deeply into the arid soils of the Mediterranean, and undertake the attentive husbandry essential to viticulture. The sub-delegate in the diocese of Montpellier calculated that vines required two and a half times more labour per hectare than did wheat. Peasant micro-proprietors had an advantage in this economic line, because they could draw on their reserves of underemployed family members at rates of return below those paid in the labour market, perform the intensive tasks required for viticulture, undersell vineyard owners, who paid labourers, and thus gain additional resources from their lands. A memorandum written for the intendant in 1768 stated that the vineyards of the hilly parts of the Montpelliérain were farmed by owner operators, because these households had the advantage of being able to deprive themselves of all but the strict necessities of life to make ends meet.[6] They could reduce their costs of production, their own consumption to be precise, lower than could large proprietors obliged to pay for labour.

Thus, the gains to be made from viticulture on the scrublands did not amount to much. The royal edict of 1770, granting fiscal exemptions for newly-cleared properties, encouraged the peasants of the Narbonnais, southwest of the diocese of Montpellier along the Mediterranean coast, to create vineyards on marginal lands that would not go immediately into tax rolls. The exemptions

---

5   Le Roy Ladurie 1966, pp. 223, 225.
6   Archives Départementales de l'Hérault (hereafter ADH) C47, C6; Soboul 1958, pp. 38, 72; Labrousse 1944, pp. 554, 558; Barante 1802, p. 195; Dion 1959, pp. 32, 36–7, 466–7.

lowered the threshold of economic gain needed to make the land clearances worthwhile. The meagre economic resources obtained from the scrublands, however, did not cover the needs of the growing population. About half of the new parcels were of such poor quality that they were abandoned by 1800. The effort to carve vineyards out of the scrublands may even have diverted attention and investment from the best lands which remained within traditional crop rotations.[7]

Dowries of artisans and shepherds of the Narbonnais rose somewhat over the course of the eighteenth century, while those of peasant proprietors and day labourers increased quite a bit. These gains represent a recovery from the crisis years of the end of Louis XIV's reign when rural immiserating and indebtedness led to the transfer of property from peasants to well-to-do townspeople. The years 1709–12 saw harvest failures and economic depression.[8] The recovery of the eighteenth century was due in large part to the expansion of viticulture. But a clear rupture occurred in 1770, thrusting all strata of the rural population into serious economic difficulties.

The effort of so many peasants to clear lands for vineyards and obtain additional revenue from their supply of family labour saturated the wine market and drove down the price. Excessive harvests created a severe recession in Languedoc in the last decade of the old regime. Comparing the dowries in Figure 5.1 to the rate of inflation measured by the price of wheat – an indication of the prices of most items of trade until wine prices collapsed in the 1770s – suggests that the standard of living declined. The price of grain rose about 40 percent between 1752–61 and 1779–88 in the markets of Montpellier, Béziers, and Toulouse, and by over 22 percent throughout the province between 1756–59 and 1785–88. The peasants were caught in a vicious circle in which the rise in the price of grain, the main item in household budgets, left the population less able to purchase wine, and further aggravated the crisis of overproduction for vintners.[9]

The planting of mulberry trees in the southern Massif central formed part of a similar sort of labour-intensive growth. The peasants integrated mulberry

---

7   Larguier 1996, vol. 3, pp. 1096, 1100, 1104. The growth of agricultural output in Mediterranean Languedoc in the eighteenth century amounted to about 22 to 29 percent and did little more than recuperate the level of growth attained in the middle of the seventeenth century (Goy and Head-Köenig 1969, pp. 66–83).

8   The crisis is described in Jacquart 1974, pp. 213, 623, 626, 636, 753. For the crisis in Mediterranean Languedoc see Goy and Head-Köenig, 1969, pp. 66–83.

9   ADH C2920; Labrousse 1944, pp. 175, 292–3, 295–6, 307–8, 335–6, 437–8, 442–3, 540, 541n. The price estimates are taken from ADH C2920; Parracha 1957, p. 339; Labrousse 1933, p. 109; Riley 1986, pp. 12, 20, 108.

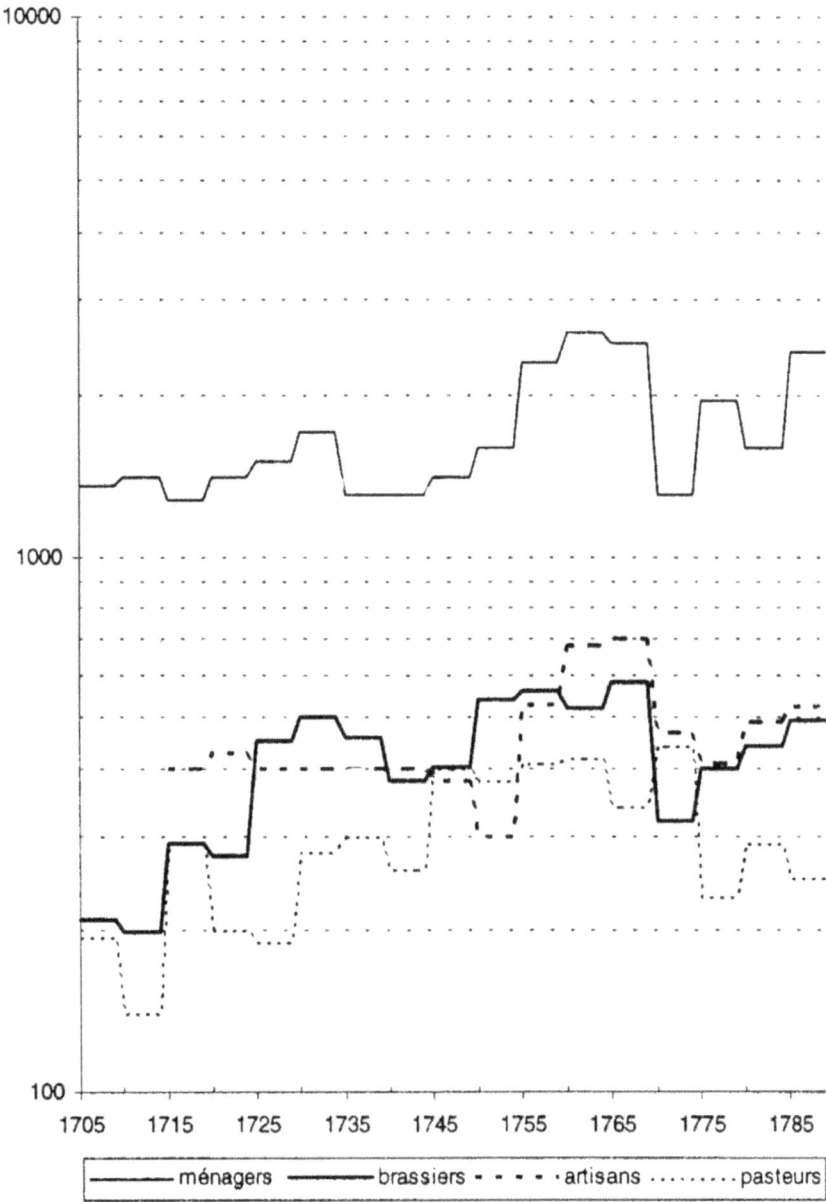

FIGURE 5.1 Dowries of the inhabitants of the Narbonnais and Corbières in the eighteenth century

trees into their traditional crop rotations. A study of Sardan, a village north of Montpellier in the department of the Gard, shows that land clearances augmented the surface of arable fields by 35 percent between 1666 and 1791, as the population of the area grew in the middle decades of the eighteenth century. Peasants cultivated grain on about 80 percent of the arable land in 1666, and barely over 50 percent in 1791. Yet the area sown in grains actually increased and occupied parcels throughout the village. Much of the land cleared in Sardan went to mulberry trees. These appeared after 1666 and claimed more hectares than did any crop except grains in 1791. They permitted the villagers to obtain more income within a traditional system of poly-culture and subsistence farming. The departmental archives of the Gard contain hundreds of *cahiers de doléances* written in rural parishes in the spring of 1789. These cahiers listed the products of the soil and read like a monotonous list of peasant poly-culture: variety of crops within each parish, yet uniformity between parishes. Villages contained mulberry trees, wheat, fodder, vines, woods, pasture, and sometimes olive trees.[10]

The inhabitants of the southern Massif central expended vast amounts of labour to farm subsistence crops, clear hillsides for mulberry trees, and raise silk worms for Nîmois apparel workshops. The intendant Ballainvilliers wrote in 1788 that the worms required constant attention to yield an abundant quantity of silk. The amount they produced was directly proportional to the hours spent nurturing them. Silk worms were an economic line in which the peasants had an advantage because of their plentiful reserves of labour. They permitted a growing number of peasant households to eke out income at the margins with its excess capacity for work but did not drastically increase the returns to peasant labour. The standard of living remained at the same low level of former epochs. The consumption of calories per capita in the Vivarais hardly changed between the end of the seventeenth and eighteenth centuries. Malnutrition remained endemic.[11]

In the Toulousain of upper Languedoc, most of the landholdings were between 1 and 20 hectares and belonged to village micro-proprietors and peasant households, whereas the majority of the land consisted of properties of 10 to 100 hectares and belonged to urban residents of the nobility and bourgeoisie. Many of the peasant parcels resulted from population growth and the subdivision of holdings among heirs. Proprietors of fewer than four hectares rose from

---

10   Savey 1969, pp. 49–51.
11   Ballainvilliers 1989, pp. 359–60. M. B ... M ... Avocat au Parlement de Languedoc, member de diverses academies, also commented on the assiduous labour that went into sericulture. 1788; Molinier 1985, pp. 156, 266, 277.

60 to 90 percent of the population in the area of the future department of the Aude between 1661 and 1789. The introduction of maize represented a crucial advance for these peasants. Maize required meticulous weeding and hoeing, but yielded three to five times more grain per hectare than did wheat. By intensively farming maize for their subsistence, the peasants enhanced output with their reserves of family labour and freed up additional quantities of wheat for the market.[12]

Yet the economic benefits of maize accrued to the proprietors with holdings between 10 and 100 hectares. Maize permitted these landlords to maintain low wages, because it permitted the peasantry to subsist at a lower cost. Large landowners could therefore obtain additional labour from their agricultural valets, raise the rent on their tenants, and demand extra produce and labour services from their sharecroppers. They secured greater returns from their lands by raising rents and tilting sharecropping agreements to their advantage. The introduction of maize permitted the landowners in the towns to obtain revenue from an additional quantity of peasant labour. In the diocese of Toulouse, the price of wheat rose from an index of 100 in 1722–26 to one of 162 in 1784–88, whereas salaries only increased to an index of 125. In the diocese of Lavaur, wheat prices rose from a base of 100 in 1710–19 to an index of 185 in 1780–89, whereas salaries increased to one of 140. Salaries declined 15 percent in the Albigeois, 55 percent around Alet, 46 percent near Castelnaudary, and 3 percent in the Castrais between 1722–26 and 1784–88.[13]

These numbers indicate a decline of real wages in the region of cereal culture of upper Languedoc. They indicate a decline in the marginal productivity of labour. The trend brought on serious economic difficulties in the 1770s and 1780s. Population growth ground to halt in the region of Toulouse and the Midi-Pyrénées. After the early 1770s, disease and bad harvests brought on a demographic crisis which culminated between 1788 and 1792. These years were comparable to the calamitous years of Louis XIV's reign.[14]

Languedocian textile manufacturing also suffered from this precarious, labour-intensive form of growth. The growing population with landholdings ever less sufficient to cover its subsistence and absorb its reserves of family

---

12 Brunet 1965, pp. 152–6, 356; Marquié 1980, pp. 64–5, 69; Mercadal 1973, pp. 145, 148–9.
13 Forster 1960, pp. 56, 58. Between 1722–26 and 1784–88, salaries declined 15 percent in the Albigeois, 55 percent around Alet, 46 percent near Castelnaudary, and three percent in the Castrais. In the diocese of Toulouse, salaries increased from an index of 100 in 1722–26 to one of 125 in 1784–88. In the diocese of Lavaur, prices increased from a base of 100 in 1710–19 to an index of 185 in 1780–89, whereas salaries increased to one of 140. Frêche 1975, pp. 59, 163, 207, 220–2, 248, 561–2.
14 Frêche 1975, pp. 54, 57–8, 110–1.

labour encouraged merchants to put manufacturing out to rural households rather than to invest in manufacturing facilities. Manufacturers of Carcassonne, Montpellier, and Nîmes prospered in the decades after 1750 from the low-paid work of thousands of rural artisans of the Black Mountain (*Montagne Noire*) and Cévennes. They put raw material out to peasant communities and then brought finished silk and wool fabric into urban shops for artisans to make marketable cloth. Even outside of the manufacturing regions, perhaps the majority of households reduced outlays for clothing and obtained extra income by producing lace, spinning flax and hemp, and churning out textiles for the market.[15]

This type of manufacturing ran up against a structural barrier to growth in the 1770s and 1780s. In Nîmes, 58 percent of looms fell into inactivity and 11,000 artisans lost their work in the 1780s. A simultaneous crisis in wool manufacturing reduced thousands of workers to beggary in Carcassonne. The Montpelliérain textile industry began to wane around 1770. None of the three manufacturing centres ever recovered. The sub-delegates of Nîmes and Carcassonne ascribed the crisis to the loss of export markets. They argued that the competition of English manufactures, political and social turmoil in the Levant, and the closing of Spanish frontiers to imports in 1778 dealt a heavy blow to local manufacturing.[16]

From a broader perspective, it is evident that the weakness of Languedocian industry was the lack of domestic demand. The merchants of Carcassonne, Montpellier, and Nîmes did not engage in two-way exchange between town and country. They took wine, cloth, and silk from the peasants but sold the peasants little in return. Languedocian merchants made almost all of their sales abroad. Merchants of Castres, Mazamet, Saint-Pons, Limoux, Levenalet, Chalabre, Bédarieux, Bize, Lodève, and Montolieu oriented production toward the interior market, especially the army. Lodève later saw a boom in textile production under the July Monarchy. These villages pointed the way toward the future development of the national economy but remained negligible compared to the eighteenth-century export manufacturers of Carcassonne, Montpellier, and Nîmes.[17]

---

15 See Chapter 1, pp. xxx–xxx for specifics on the Languedocian textile industry.

16 Archives Départementales de l'Aude (ADA) 9 C 20, 34 C 2599; ADH C5481; Gouron 1939, pp. 112–14; Gutherz and Huard 1982, p. 215; Bonnet and Marquié 1980, p. 71; Cazals 1984, pp. 138, 140, 143–4; Cazals and Valentin 1984, pp. 97, 106; Canonge 1990, p. 14. J.K.F. Thomson shows that the textile industry of Clermont-de-Lodève declined after the 1750s and no longer offered steady employment. Workers became part-time farmers, like their counterparts elsewhere in the province, during the rest of the century (1982, pp. 432–5).

17 Pat Hudson and Joel Mokyr show that most of the commodities produced in England dur-

In these towns, the clusters of workshops lacked the stability of a national market. The overwhelming majority of the inhabitants subsisted in the countryside at a low standard of living. They saw to many of their needs through the activity of family members and thus avoided purchases and the depletion of household income. For this reason, the peasantry did not constitute a stable market liable to sustain investment in labour-saving implement. The manufacturers of Nîmes increased efficiency year by year through piecemeal ameliorations in their shops but never envisioned capital investments that would fructify over the long term. It was only a matter of time before they succumbed to the domestic producers in foreign markets or the more advanced industrialists of England. The loss of export markets signalled the end of local manufacturing, because merchants did not have consumers to fall back on inside of France.[18]

In the last decades of the 1700s, the collapse of manufacturing combined with the depression of the wine market and steady rise in grain prices to create an acute social crisis. The crisis did not result from declining output but from the population's inability to acquire it. The peasants actually increased the production of wine, grain, and cloth by intensifying their labour. The growth of the population led families to subdivide their landholdings and left them with parcels ever less sufficient to cover their subsistence or occupy the labour all of their members. Peasants put their reserves of labour to use cultivating vines and mulberry trees, producing textiles, renting land, and working for wages. The benefits of this economic growth accrued to urban proprietors and merchants with land and employment to offer. Urban consumers benefited from the production of wine, textiles, and wheat. Rural inhabitants, by contrast, found themselves increasingly dependent for their subsistence on grain markets in a period of rising prices.

The latest data on the popular disturbances of the old regime show a sharp rise in grain riots over the course of the eighteenth century. The rise suggests that the peasants became increasingly reliant on markets for their subsistence. In Languedoc, peasants with little land joined suburban inhabitants in grain riots around Narbonne in 1766 and in the southern Massif central in 1783. The same groups rioted in Carcassonne, the area of the Garonne, and the Albi-

---

ing the classic period of the industrial revolution went to the internal market. Hudson 1992, pp. 167–200; Mokyr 1977, pp. 981–1008; Mokyr 1999, pp. 1–127. In 1803, as exports further declined during the Napoleonic Wars, the interior market still did not even absorb 30 percent of the Aude's drapes. Barante 1802, pp. 118, 124, 220, 225; ADA 34 C 2599; ADH C5481; Johnson 1995, pp. 8, 12–14; Cazals and Valentin 1984, p. 106. Minovez 2012, pp. 67, 70, 117–18, 147, 165, 483; Minovez 2012a, pp. 94–96, 113, 214, 219.

18   Teisseyre-Sallmann 1995, pp. 320, 344.

geois after a bad harvest in 1773 and 1774, and again in the dioceses of St.-Pons, Toulouse, and Rieux in 1788.[19]

Prices on the 14 principal markets of Languedoc soared between about 40 and 70 percent following a bad harvest in 1788. Table A.5 of the Appendix, tabulating all of the acts of lawlessness in Languedoc during the Revolution, shows 88 separate subsistence revolts in town and country between 1789 and 1793.[20] Many of these popular revolts coincided with rising prices and had little to do with political agitation and counter-revolutionary activity. Many occurred for ostensibly religious or political reasons, but were ultimately caused by fear of famine and economic collapse. In the context of peasant property and agriculture inherited from the feudal past, the growth of the population and the concomitant spread of market involvement did not improve the standard of living or sustain the economy, but instead resulted in a general social crisis.

2   An Explosion of Discontent

Peasants and artisans banded together to contend with grain shortages and high prices by destroying fiscal bureaus, laying hold of stores of grain, and threatening violence against people and property to force authorities to provide affordable bread. Table A.5 of the Appendix shows that 57 such subsistence revolts took place throughout the province in 1789.[21] The intendant wrote to the controller general in April, for instance, that the popular classes of Agde chased the bishop from his château and harried him in the streets. When the bishop slumped to the ground ill, people forced him to sign an agreement reducing the fees he collected from the town flourmill. The authorities in Agde wrote to the controller general that they had to lower prices when people threatened to burn town hall, the bishop's palace, and the houses of wealthy individuals. Armed with axes and other weapons, people went to the sales-tax offices, stole money, ripped apart registers, destroyed scales and furniture, and threatened to beat the officers if they resumed their work.[22]

Similar revolts broke out sporadically over the next three years. In June 1790, Joseph Raynal, a butcher and the self-styled mayor of Mende, led a crowd to the sales-tax office, where they stole registers, destroyed equipment, and chased

---

19   ADH C6847, C6856, C6886; Lemarchand 1990, pp. 32–48; Bourderon 1954, pp. 155–70.
20   ADH C2927, C2942–5; Johnson 1986, pp. 38, 40, 55.
21   See Appendix A.5 for a breakdown of all the popular uprisings in the province during the Revolution.
22   Archives Nationales (AN) H1/1063, H1/1453.

out the employees. Butchers slaughtered animals in front of the tax offices amid a general refusal to pay such indirect levies. Women rallied peasants of the region to force the municipality to imprison a lawyer, the judge of the cathedral chapter, for hoarding grain. Raynal demanded 300 *livres* of ransom from the lawyer's nephew and claimed that he would offer the money to the poor. After seeing the chevalier de Borel, commander of the National Guard, confer with municipal officials, Raynal assembled a crowd and stormed town hall. The protesters declared to the officials that Raynal was the popularly acclaimed mayor of Mende and that they wanted the 300 livres at once. Raynal then distributed the money as he liked, while crowds invaded private homes and extorted payments from the well-to-do. Raynal and his accomplices were arrested that night.[23]

A graver subsistence revolt broke out in August 1790, as peasants from the region of Carcassonne and the Black Mountain damaged the Canal du Midi and halted traffic. They detained a merchant in a tower of the commune located outside of Carcassonne, called la cité, where medieval walls still stand today. The rebels marched the merchant over to the administrators of the Aude the next day. The administrators tried to explain that free trade served the general interest. But the crowd became numerous and restless, and warned them that they would pay with their heads if they set the merchant free. The administrators wrote to the National Assembly a few days later that the peasantry stubbornly clung to the belief that the free circulation of grain was unlawful. The mayor of Carcassonne complained that the peasants saw their administrators as agents of the old regime.[24] Members of the departmental directory wrote to the National Assembly a month later:

> The people have inflicted enormous damage on the canal; the most seditious find safe haven from judicial pursuits and our decrees by taking refuge in la cité and closing the portals ... We have unanimously deliberated to address the king and the National Assembly and demand the demolition of the walls and towers of la cité of Carcassonne.[25]

Administrators of the Aude complained repeatedly between 1790 and 1792 that the financial toll of maintaining troops along the Canal du Midi to protect grain shipments from upper to lower Languedoc made it impossible for them

---

23   AN F7 3381/13; ADH B21627.
24   ADA 1 L165, pp. 14–17, 23–4.
25   ADA 1 L204. Carcassonne's current residents, who depend on revenue generated by tourism to la cité, are fortunate this request went unheeded.

to cover other governmental expenses. The worst incident occurred in August 1792, when thousands of peasants descended on Carcassonne to halt traffic along the canal. They broke into a public building and laid hold of two elected official. They tied one to the back of a horse and covered him with blows as the horse dragged him along. The other, a wealthy lawyer and the executive officer (*procureur-général-syndic*) of the department, was executed for having upheld free trade over the past two years.[26]

3   Social Strife over the Establishment of the New Regime

More common than these subsistence riots were revolts in which peasants and artisans strove to put an end to fiscal and seigneurial burdens. The economic crisis made these levies particularly onerous, and the collapse of royal authority permitted the lower classes to resist. At the same time, the well-to-do residents were anxious to restore order under the institutions legislated by the National Assembly. They aspired to hold state office and serve the new national order, and thus had little tolerance for seemingly irrational revolts against fiscal bureaus. Revolutionary regimes used coercion to break the peasantry's resistance to taxation.

Historians accord far less attention to this conflict over the establishment of state institutions than they do to revolts against the seigneurial regime. Le Roy Ladurie maintains that the anti-seigneurial character of the Revolution distinguished it from seventeenth-century movements against the fiscal agents of the crown. Charles Tilly argues that in eighteenth-century Languedoc, popular protest began to evolve into modern forms of conflict involving issues of class rather than opposition to the state. Instead of resisting taxation as they had prior to Louis XIV, artisans fought merchants, the lower classes seized grain, and smallholders and farm labourers battled proprietors. John Markoff shows that rural inhabitants generally called for outright abolition of the seigneurial regime in their cahiers de doléances, whereas they called for reform and equality when discussing taxes. 'Their taxation grievances reveal a sense of France beyond the local community … One sees here, I think, an emerging concept of citizenship at work; individuals, equal in their moral worth, are all to be assessed in accordance with some principle of equity'. Markoff argues that the peasant movement revealed a crystallisation of the revolutionary mentality after the fall of 1789, as subsistence

---

26   AN H1/748/100, pp. 132, 894; ADA L409, L410.

and fiscal revolts receded in the face of a general assault on the seigneurial regime.[27]

These scholars correctly stress the egalitarian charge of the peasant movement. We will see in the following section that rural communities participated in hundreds of illegal acts to put an end to seigneurial privileges. Yet it would be a mistake to regard the fiscal revolts as crude legacies of the absolutist past and as retrograde phases of the Revolution. That, of course, was the view of the revolutionary leaders. But the rural communities saw the tax system as the primary injustice. Quantitative analysis of 748 parish cahiers reveals over 2,000 grievances against taxes and less than 600 against seigneurial rights. Seven of the ten grievances, which parishes most commonly ranked at the top of their lists, were against taxation. The highest average ranking for a grievance against the seigneurial regime, the lords' right to raise pigeons, was fourteenth. Many parish cahiers did not even mention the seigneurial regime.[28]

The peasantry's collective actions highlight this preoccupation with state taxation. The data on popular rebellions of the old regime show 346 against tax farmers between 1661 and 1699 and 1,233 between 1760 and 1789. Peasants fought against seigneurs 85 times from 1661 to 1699 and 246 times from 1760 to 1789. The evidence presented in Chapters 1 and 2 suggests that common subjects of Languedoc harboured at least as much antipathy toward tax collectors as they did toward seigneurs in the last decades of the old regime. Table A.5 of the Appendix shows that peasants engaged in 100 illegal acts against taxation in the departments of old regime Languedoc between 1789 and 1794.[29]

One could argue that people have bemoaned taxes since time immemorial and still do today. One could argue that resistance to taxation was a residue from a bygone age before the state had impressed its institutions upon the peasants' way of life. Such arguments, however, ignore a basic attribute of the absolutist state. We saw in Chapter 1 that the soil was fragmented into an entanglement of landholdings, most of which belonged to the peasants. The share of the Languedocian soil made up of peasant tenures ranged from about 20 percent of the Toulousain to over 50 percent of the southern Massif central. Plots of land gave the peasants a degree of autonomy. They did not totally rely on large proprietors and merchants for land and employment.

Most peasants, of course, did not own enough land to secure complete autonomy. Demographic growth of the eighteenth century eroded the viability of their holdings and forced them to seek tenancies, employment, share-

---

27 Markoff 1996, pp. 12–13, 108, 291; Le Roy Ladurie 1974a, pp. 6–22; Tilly 1986, pp. 200, 388.
28 Markoff 1996, pp. 22, 30–2, 40–1, 43, 68, 101.
29 Nicolas 2002, pp. 56, 216.

cropping agreements, and material for cottage industry. Landowners and merchants reaped handsome profits from the peasants' labour. Yet they did not obtain all of their wealth from land rents and manufacturing. The nobility and bourgeoisie invested heavily in the manifest opportunities for authority, revenue, careers, and honours offered by the juridical and political relations of the old regime. Several decades of historiography show that the upper classes purchased tax farms, offices, seigneuries, and government annuities. They purchased noble titles in the hope of one day entering provincial estates and the royal court, where some of the greatest fortunes in the realm were made.[30]

The state took on an even greater role in the economic life of the country as a result of the Revolution. Purchases of church and émigré property added about one percent of the district of Toulouse and department of the Hérault, and almost two percent of the Haute-Loire, to the peasants' landholdings during the 1790s. Speculators and businessmen purchased many national lands and then resold them to the peasantry in smaller lots in the first decades of the nineteenth century. The peasants obtained an even greater portion of the soil by taking possession of lands belonging to the king and émigrés, and by establishing vineyards on land held on a communal basis. The peasantry had hesitated to clear scrublands for agriculture during the old regime because of the likelihood that lords would claim seigneurial rights over them. By destroying lordly authority during the Revolution, the peasantry was able to appropriate about 20 percent of the Aude during the 1790s. Moreover, the abolition of seigneurial rights and residual levies on the peasant tenures permitted rural inhabitants to establish full property rights over all their lands. The state presented the only means by which social elites could obtain wealth from this mass of national resources under peasant control.[31]

---

30 This historiography includes Lüthy 1998, vol. 2, pp. 9–10, 15, 17–18, 23; Porshnev 1963, pp. 112–13, 122, 563–6, 572; Althusser 1972, pp. 99–104; Anderson 1974, pp. 18–20, 47–8, 54–5, 97, 125–6, 138–9; Brenner 1985, pp. 213–327; Goubert and Roche 1984, vol. 1, pp. 66, 243, 356; Dessert 1984, pp. 43, 46, 59–60, 63, 316, 331, 341, 355, 367; Beik 1985, pp. 21, 245–78; Comninel 1987, pp. 195–6, 198, 200–3; Collins 1988, pp. 111, 122, 136, 144, 146, 155, 164, 214; Descimon and Jouhaud 1996, pp. 78, 155, 173, 189–90; Parker 1996, pp. 100–01, 263–5. For an analysis of the upper classes' use of state authority to secure income in Languedoc in the second half of the eighteenth century see Miller 2003, pp. 871–98.

31 Martin 1916, pp. 577, 582–3; Cambon 1951, pp. 33, 39, 51, 149, 152; Gallix 1951, pp. 28–31, 37–9, 105, 109; Brochier 1993, pp. 138–43; Bodinier, Teyssier, and Antoine 2000, pp. 220, 223, 368, 443; McPhee 1999, pp. 121, 132–3. Purchases of national lands may have pushed the peasantry's share of the soil from under 45 percent to about 50 (Andress 2004, pp. 245–6). Peter Jones argues that the Convention's decree of June 1793 ordering villages to divide their common lands permitted many peasants to obtain property (2003, p. 256).

Priests, jurists, merchants, proprietors, and other members of the bourgeoisie looked to the state for opportunity during the Revolution. We saw in Chapter 4 that in the political crisis of 1789, they demanded an end to the nobility's exclusive rights to the careers and revenues offered by the monarchy.[32] Bourgeois leaders throughout France thought their professional and economic futures hung in the balance as the Constituent Assembly redrew the administrative map. They bitterly quarrelled with one another in their efforts to convince the legislators to place administrative and judicial institutions in their towns. In the Ardèche, a decree of August 1790 dividing the department into three districts set off an outcry among patriots angered that the recasting of state institutions reduced the number of tribunals. The townspeople accused their legislators of selfishly favouring their own towns and friends in the allocation of state institutions and jobs. The districts forbid public gatherings in an effort to halt the spread of disorder.[33]

The new regime reflected the bourgeois revolutionaries' eagerness to broaden the opportunities of serving the state. The Constituent Assembly increased direct taxation on property but reduced overall levels of taxation by eliminating most indirect taxes. Indirect taxation had become the heaviest fiscal burden of the eighteenth century. Despite this initial slackening of fiscal pressure on the country, the revolutionary governments increased spending in each of the first five years of the Revolution. It is true that they inherited much of this spending from the old regime. The Constituent Assembly agreed to fund the clergy and reimburse tens of thousands of venal offices. Revolutionary governments also had to meet the costs of war after 1792. Yet it is also true that much expenditure stemmed from the establishment of departments, districts, and municipalities. These employed more administrators and judges than had the institutions of the old regime.[34]

Revolutionary legislators envisioned a state that would offer fairness and opportunity to patriotic and talented citizens. Many former nobles and well-to-do commoners placed hope in the Revolution and did not understand the *menu peuple*'s failure to appreciate its institutions. The national legislatures consistently disregarded the aspirations of anyone who did not belong to the prop-

---

32 According to Emmanuel Sieyès, 'It would be superfluous to peruse the sword, the robe, the Church and the administration in detail to show that the third estate forms everywhere nineteen twentieths of them, with this difference that it is assigned to all that is truly laborious, to all the burdens that the privileged order refuses to take on. The lucrative and honorific posts are occupied by the privileged order alone' (1988, pp. 34–5).
33 Margadant 1992; Jolivet 1980, p. 198.
34 White 1995, pp. 242–3; Pinaud 1992, p. 344; Crouzet 1993, p. 110; Sutherland 2002, pp. 10, 13; Andress 2004, p. 137; Cardenal 1936, pp. 78, 84, 92, 102, 104–5, 110.

ertied, professional, and educated elite. Legislators saw popular grievances as misguided expressions of lumpen ignorance, criminality, and aristocracy liable to thwart their effort to endow France with rational institutions. Refusals to go along with the manifestly reasonable project of national regeneration seemed to stem from ignorance or malevolence. The governmental elite of the 1790s was determined to foist its fiscal legislation on peasants and artisans unwilling to pay what they had long regarded as unjust burdens.[35]

Montpellier offers a good example of these divergent aspirations. In August 1789, well-to-do residents elected 99 merchants, lawyers, and noble magistrates to regenerate the municipality. The delegates declared it their duty to jettison laws inherited from the feudal past and allow 'all interested parties capable of expressing a suffrage, without distinction of rank, station or birth' to write new laws assuring a fair distribution of municipal offices. They also complained that armed bandits forced their way through the tax bureaus at the border of Roussillon and brought salt and tobacco into the province in violation of regulations maintaining the collection of indirect taxes until new fiscal laws were in place. They published urgent regulations: 'Decrees of the National Assembly, approved by the king, maintain old regime taxes. We therefore order municipalities to protect collection'.[36]

Local authorities heeded the directives of the central government and attempted to force the people to pay. Necker wrote to the military commander of Languedoc in the middle of 1789, 'I received the letters which you did me the honour of writing ... to inform me of the execution of several individuals who were condemned to death ... for having devastated the bureau of the tax farm during the riot which took place in Sète'.[37] Elected officials of Béziers sent companies of the Médoc regiment to seize a convoy of smuggled salt in the beginning of 1790. When a crowd encircled the soldiers, municipal leaders ordered them to fire, killing one person and wounding several others.[38]

Elsewhere in lower Languedoc, the tax farmers of Montpellier, Nîmes, and the southern Massif central reported that almost all of the municipal authorities of the region helped with the collection of fiscal receipts carried over from the old regime. The problem, according to the tax farmer of Beaucaire and Nîmes, was that 'Taxpayers, supported and inspired by enemies of the Revolution, seek to give a bad and false interpretation to the decrees passed by the National Assembly in maintaining that Languedoc's indirect taxes are

---

35   Andress 2004, pp. xvi, 122–3, 149, 164.
36   AN H1/748/292.
37   AN H1/1063.
38   AN H1/1453; Saurel 1898, vol. 1, pp. 233–4.

abolished'.³⁹ Several months later, in the fall of 1790, the treasurer of the departments of the former province reported the complaints of many receivers of direct taxes about the peasants' resistance. He went into detail about the upper Gard, where the peasants refused to pay the tax receiver and forced him to withdraw the garrisons. 'This revolution could become contagious and spread rapidly. I hope a response will come quickly'.⁴⁰

Administrators had more difficulties in upper Languedoc. The tax receiver in Grenade wrote to administrators of the Haute-Garonne toward the end of January 1791 that he was taking the mounted constabulary on rounds to back up fiscal officials and force the people to pay. He stated that this approach would overcome opposition and allow collection to proceed in the customary manner. The executive agent of the Haute-Garonne wrote to the district administrators of Muret in the fall of 1790 urging them to coerce the communes of the eastern part of the district to pay taxes. The minister of finances wrote to the Haute-Garonne in January 1791 of an insurrection in Rieumes and several other communes in the western part of the district of Muret. These peasants had not wavered from a deliberation taken in May 1789 to discontinue paying taxes. The departmental administrators then informed the local tax receiver that they were writing to the district of Muret,

> instructing it to take measures to clear obstacles that you have run into in the commune of Rieumes; we request that you designate the other communes that refuse to pay taxes, and you can be sure that we will not waste an instant in making them feel their error and in bringing them back to their duty.⁴¹

It was just as difficult for the authorities of the Haute-Garonne to collect indirect taxes due since 1789. The departmental administrators wrote to the minister of finances at the end of 1790 that revenue from the tax farms had evaporated. They wrote a month later, 'For about six months many people have refused to pay. The ... outrage has spread rapidly ... The people are excited and have learned to shake off the yoke of taxation'.⁴² The lower classes seem to have been disgusted with the destination of their tax payments. The administrators stated in the same letter that collection would proceed without obstacles, 'if a decree

---

39   ADH B9045.
40   AN H1/748/100, pp. 292, 296, 298.
41   Archives Départementales de la Haute-Garonne (ADHG) 1 L239. For the eastern part of the district of Muret see ADHG 1 L250.
42   ADHG 1 L239.

of the national assembly ordered that indirect taxes ... be set aside for charity workshops and aid to hospitals'.[43] But the national assembly did not make such a decree. Instead, the department published a proclamation summoning battle troops, the national guard, and the mounted constabulary to enforce collection and threatening those who resisted with punishment in accordance with the rigor of the law.[44]

Authorities of the Aude also used force to overcome resistance. Ten communities of the diocese of Carcassonne informed their tax receiver in the fall of 1789 that they would not pay. They threatened him with unspecified evils if he did not withdraw the garrison. The local military commander received a letter from Paris in December.

> You must judge ... what dangerous consequences it would be for ... finances if communities believed they had the right to refuse the payment of taxes ... The National Assembly has recognised by different decrees, notably that of last 26 September, how important it is to the maintenance of order and the reestablishment of credit that tax collection not be interrupted under any pretext.[45]

The letter urged the commander to gather information about the communities' demands and the effects they would have on other villages. It advised him 'to inform them that you are not disposed to tolerating their resistance and that you will oppose to it ... all the means at your disposal, and if in fact circumstances oblige, I urge you to take all suitable measures to compel these communities'.[46] A district tax receiver wrote to the department in the fall of 1790 that he was taking legal action against the inhabitants of Montlaur. He claimed that they refused to pay taxes even after he sent in the garrison. Troops invaded the Val-de-Dagne a year later, after the department expressed anxiety at seeing the inhabitants' refusal to pay taxes spread to nearby villages. The department sent troops into Belpech and Coustouge in 1792 to deal with tardy taxpayers. But the non-payment of taxes continued despite this military repression. In 1793, the executive agent of the Aude stated in the minutes of the departmental administration that 'malevolent individuals' spread the story that the National Assembly had abolished most taxes.[47]

---

43   Ibid.
44   Ibid.
45   AN H1/1063.
46   Ibid.
47   ADA 1 L165, L1339, L1344, L1411, L1455, L1474; McPhee 1999, pp. 103–4; *Procès-verbal de la session du Conseil du département de l'Aude, séant à Carcassonne, du 2 novembre 1793*, p. 499.

Repression had mixed results. Officials failed to collect all the sums assigned to the Haute-Garonne in seven of the first eight years of the Revolution. The one year they achieved a surplus was 1796, when inflation made the currency practically worthless. By contrast, the administrators of the Aude reported in 1793 that they began to have success collecting taxes. The department of the Hérault collected about half of its quota in the first two years of the Revolution but then recorded substantial surpluses over the next five years. The state had the most difficulty in the southern Massif central. The peasants' resistance reduced the tax yield in the Haute-Loire each year of the Revolution. Proceeds were tolerable until 1794 but then shrivelled to paltry levels between 1796 and 1798. The department attempted to replace exhortations with force in 1796 and 1797, garrisoning troops in rebellious cantons and billeting them in the homes of recalcitrants. But the revolts continued, and the department did not have enough troops to contain them. It renounced the use of force at the end of 1797 in an implicit acknowledgement of impotence. One local administrator wrote in the middle of 1796, 'Our peasants have only one thought: take advantage of the anarchy to emancipate themselves, totally if possible, from the payment of taxes'.[48]

Administrators faced similar difficulties in the rest of France. Governmental disarray made it possible for the populace to cease paying taxes after 1788. The Constituent Assembly only received a fraction of the fiscal receipts it legislated. Tax collection reached a low point in 1790, when fiscal yields fell to a little over a quarter of their level in 1788. Officials augmented receipts each year until 1793. But the depreciation of the currency then wreaked havoc on tax collection between 1793 and 1795. Legislators finally succeeded in establishing governmental authority in 1797. Fiscal receipts subsequently exceeded the levels of the 1780s. It took the state half as long to collect taxes in 1798 as it did before the Revolution. The re-emergence of state authority after 1798 was just as impressive as was its collapse in 1789. Historians have yet to recognise how adamant the state became about its fiscal prerogative.[49]

The efforts of administrators to increase tax receipts benefited well-to-do supporters of the Revolution. A good example is the district tax receivers who

---

48 As quoted in Delecambre 1943, p. 12. See also pp. 8–11, 292. For the collection of taxes in the Haute-Garonne, Aude and Hérault see ADHG 1 L701, L726; ADA L 612; ADH L 1617. For the Haute-Loire see Merley 1974, vol. 1, pp. 266, 268n, 269–70. Abbé Ch. Jolivet notes that the peasantry's resistance caused staggering arrears in tax collection in the Ardèche between 1789 and September 1793 (1980, pp. 142, 326, 334, 334n, 395).

49 Harris 1930, pp. 47, 175, 180; White 1995, p. 236n; Hincker 1988, p. 450; Crouzet 1993, pp. 96, 109, 122, 126, 214–15; Le Goff and Sutherland 1991, pp. 69, 72–3; Sutherland 2002, p. 7. See also pp. 10–11, 13.

gathered funds, made official disbursements, retained a percentage for themselves as remuneration, and forwarded the rest to the national treasury. These officials were necessary in a society where facilities for transfer were primitive and ready cash was scarce. We saw in Chapter 2 that their counterparts of the old regime, the 66 triennial diocese receivers of Languedoc, garnered about 650,000 livres a year for their services in the 1780s. Many of these offices had belonged to noble judges of the sovereign courts of Languedoc.[50]

The Constituent Assembly reduced the fees charged by the tax receivers of the old regime yet still left the fees at profitable levels. The district administrations received plenty of applications for the posts of receiver. The candidates had to raise a substantial security deposit and pay the requisite tax to join the electoral assemblies. Lists of receivers drawn up by the Aude and Haute-Garonne between 1790 and 1798 show that they were all well-to-do: merchants, rentier landowners, lower-level jurists of the old regime, revolutionary officials, a former diocese receiver, a deputy to the Estates General, and a public works contractor. The Constituent Assembly's guidelines allowed them to withhold 2.5 percent of receipts for their services. The eight receivers of the Haute-Garonne thus obtained an average of 3,700 livres in 1791, over 11,000 in 1795 and over 16,000 in 1796. The department of the Aude wrote a report in 1791 showing that its five receivers each made a further 2,000 from the sale of national lands. Resistance to taxation and the depreciation of the currency eroded these profits for much of the 1790s. But as the fiscal system improved, the revenue of tax receivers and the state grew in unison.[51]

Educated and propertied elites secured careers and revenues as a result of the growth of the state after 1789. The bureaucracy expanded to 250,000 employees, or five times its pre-revolutionary size, between 1792 and 1795. State payrolls swelled to include 670,000 officials by 1845. The British state, by contrast, employed fewer than 40,000 civil servants in the mid-nineteenth century. The salaries of civil servants at the apex of the French bureaucracy put them in the wealthiest tier of the population during the 1840s. The bourgeoisie of Paris invested five times more funds in state bonds than it did in company shares during this period. Investors undoubtedly sank more funds into private enterprise as the nineteenth century wore on. Yet it is generally recognised that the French bourgeoisie, composed to large extent of officials and lawyers, derived much more of its livelihood from the state than did its English or American counterparts.[52]

---

50   See Chapter 2, pp. xxx–xxx.
51   ADHG 1 L678; ADA L681; Schnerb 1933, pp. 237–8.
52   Church 1981, pp. 11, 72, 298; Cardenal 1936, pp. 78, 104–5. Vida Azimi writes that the number

The fiscal system underwriting the civil service and government bonds inherited regressive features from the old regime. While the legislation of the revolutionary period subjected all lands and individuals to the same taxes, it did not prevent the residents of the towns from thrusting an inordinate share onto rural communes. The peasantry obtained a measure of fairness with the drafting of cadastres measuring the value of properties over the course of the nineteenth century. Yet the cadastres were not completed until 1890. France shared the distinction, with Portugal, Spain, Serbia and Russia, of being the only European country to maintain a system of repartition for much of the nineteenth century. The state assigned quotas to communes and made their inhabitants collectively responsible. What is more, the state continued to raise about 50 percent of its revenue from indirect taxes levied on articles of consumption purchased by all citizens regardless of their wealth, just as it had prior to 1789. France had one of the most unfair tax systems in nineteenth-century Europe.[53]

4   The Seigneurial Regime, Peasant Revolts, and Counterrevolution

The peasant movement against the seigneurial regime presents one of the most difficult problems of interpretation for historians of the French Revolution. The peasants of Languedoc rebelled against their lords in times of fiscal pressure and dearth in the second half of the seventeenth century and then almost not at all after 1720. By contrast, they constantly rebelled against tax farmers in the second half of the eighteenth century.[54] Parish cahier written in the spring of 1789 expressed far more grievances against fiscal exactions than against seigneurial rights. Nevertheless, the peasant revolts of the revolutionary period evinced an unmistakably anti-seigneurial character. Table A.5 of the Appendix presents 316 illegal acts against the seigneurial regime in the departments of old regime Languedoc between 1789 and 1794. These acts amounted to almost 50 percent of all the popular revolts to take place in the region during the Revolution.

---

of state employees grew tenfold between 1792 and 1794 (1986, pp. 118, 130); Catherine Kawa states that the staff of government ministries grew 400 percent between the old regime and 1795–99 (1988, p. 189; Anderson 1992, p. 142; Zeldin 1973, vol. 1, pp. 60, 114, 116–17).

53   Bouvier 1973, pp. 82, 104; Schnerb 1973, pp. 238, 245; Schnerb 1933, pp. 55–6, 562; Marion 1927–31, vol. 5, pp. 14, 111–12, 230. Edward Berenson comments on the injustices of the tax system and the politicians who drew wealth from it (1992, pp. 67, 184).

54   Pélaquier 1990–91, pp. 7, 22.

Seigneurial levies did not amount to an overwhelming burden on the peasantry. Dues and tithes varied between villages and parcels – ranging from less than two percent of total production in the Vivarais to almost 20 percent of all produce in the Corbières – but usually amounted to well below 10 percent.[55] The seigneurial regime of Languedoc consisted primarily of political and honorific prerogatives. The jurisprudence of the old regime allowed seigneurs to enlist the authority of the courts and thrust their presence into rural communities. We saw in Chapter 1 that lords arraigned their villages before the Parlement of Toulouse on hundreds of occasions in the eighteenth century. It is worthwhile to review one of the Parlement's rulings to get a sense of what the seigneurial regime meant to the inhabitants of the region.

On 24 March 1783, de Mazade, seigneur and marquis of Avèze, seigneur of Saint-Bresson, Arre, Pommiers, Molières, Lafour, and Lovez, a swath of villages north and west of Montpellier and Nîmes in the present-day department of the Gard, brought his dependents before the Parlement of Toulouse to secure a set of privileges and prerogatives. The Parlement ordered the communities to present their annual tax registers to be examined and signed by the marquis's stewards. It ordered the confection of three keys to the communities' archives – containing titles, records of property sales, and maps of tax assessments – one key for the seigneurial judge, one for the communities' primary leaders (*premier consuls*), and one for the secretary-clerks (*greffiers*). The Parlement forbade bailiffs to deliver summons or decrees, to carry out seizures of property, or to perform any other acts without obtaining a letter from the seigneur d'Avèze. It gave the marquis the right to hold livestock caught in his woods, fields, moors, and other possessions until the owner paid him an indemnity. The Parlement accorded the marquis the right to publish the start of the wine harvest and have his grapes harvested two or three days before other proprietors harvested their grapes. It accorded him the right to appoint an agent to see to the payment of a portion of the harvest of certain crops in seigneurial dues (*tasque* or *champart*).

The ruling required the community leaders to notify the seigneurial stewards before holding assemblies, to inform them of the points of deliberation, including objections to the marquis's rights, and give them the presidency. It obliged the communities' secretary-clerks to record the minutes of assemblies and present them to the seigneurial stewards anytime the stewards might request them. It obliged the community leaders to bring all governmental instructions to Avèze before showing them to local priests and inhabitants. The

---

55   See Chapter 1, pp. xxx–xxx for data on seigneurial levies in Languedoc.

Parlement required the seigneurial judges to hold their proceedings in each of the châteaux where the marquis's prisons were located. It obliged each village to present a list of nine candidates from which Avèze would choose three community leaders.

The Parlement required these newly chosen consuls to wear a hood in a visit to the marquis d'Avèze's château, where they would offer an oath of loyalty in his hands. It forbade the inhabitants to engage in public merrymaking or dancing, to beat the drums or form crowds at the sound of musical instruments, without the marquis's permission. It obliged the inhabitants to tie up their animals, enclose their fowl, and refrain from cutting herbs along roads, ditches, and hedges between the 1 May and 1 August to protect the eggs of animals for hunting. The ruling gave the marquis the right to kill any dog or fowl caught in the fields.

The Parlement obliged the marquis's jurisdictional prosecutor and the communities' leaders to make sure that cabarets were closed during Sunday mass. It instructed the priests to follow a distinctive ceremonial procedure to recommend the marquis d'Avèze and his family in prayers, spray them in holy water and incense, and give them offerings, blessed bread, and candles during the services. It directed the community leaders to wear a hood to public events and yield to the precedence of the marquis's stewards. The Parlement ruled that on days of public ceremonies and festivals offered by the king, the seigneurial stewards and the community leaders would greet the marquis d'Avèze in his château and accompany him to the ceremonial bonfire (*feu de joie*), where he would do the honours of lighting the blaze.[56]

As this ruling suggests, the lords towered over rural society down to the end of the old regime. The crown made efforts to reduce seigneurial prerogatives and involve well-to-do peasants in village affairs in the 1770s and 1780s, but had only just begun the colossal task of overhauling the jurisprudence regulating the administration of the countryside, and probably never would have succeeded. Royal law originated in the feudal past and was laden with provisions for seigneurial prerogatives. We saw in Chapter 1 that lords used the law to secure hundreds of rulings from the Parlement of Toulouse, nearly identical to the one in favour of Avèze, over the course of the eighteenth century. And it seems that the frequency of these rulings was on the rise. A seigneurial offensive undoubtedly took place in eighteenth-century Languedoc. The lords profited from the extension of viticulture and the rising prices of wheat and woods within a carapace of political and honorific rights inherited from the feudal past.

---

56 ADHG B 1817.

It would be wrong, however, to search for a direct correlation between the imposition of seigneurial rights in the eighteenth century and the rural revolts of the Revolution. The National Assembly abolished all of the political and honorific prerogatives of lordship in response to uprisings against the seigneurial regime in many parts of the country, including 51 in Languedoc, after the fall of the Bastille in 1789. Stories arriving from Savoy and Dauphiné about an army of brigands commanded by the comte d'Artois and other aristocrats prompted the inhabitants of the Vivarias to take up arms in defence of the Revolution. They broke into châteaux and destroyed seigneurial titles, asserted use-rights over woods formerly protected by lordly rights, and forced a local seigneur to repay fines he had collected a short time ago.[57]

The peasants of the Albigeois and Castrais armed themselves in response to stories of brigands sweeping down from the area of Limoges. Once they heard that the crown had submitted to the demands of the National Assembly, they took the opportunity to enter about 10 châteaux of the Albigeois and Castrais, seize stores of grain, and repudiate customary dues.[58]

Revolts such as these led the National Assembly to abolish nearly all of the rights of the marquis d'Avèze and all of the other seigneurs of France on the Night of August 4, 1789. The legislation obliged peasant communities to go on paying seigneurial dues until they reimbursed the lords for the right to collect the dues. But in most parts of Languedoc, the dues were so derisory that the former lords probably did not even bother with the trouble of trying to collect them. On the whole, lordly rights ceased to exist in the province in the fall of 1789.

Even so, a legacy of distrust sporadically sparked violence over the following three years. The *sieur* Nègre, lord of Villetritouls in the diocese of Carcassonne, had insisted on collecting dues from the local peasantry despite the presentation of titles in 1761 proving that the village lay within the royal domains. In the first year of the Revolution, the departmental directory of the Aude received complaints from Nègre that the peasants of Villetritouls refused to pay the accustomed dues and then received a complaint at the end of 1790 that they had laid waste to his possessions. In 1782, the count of Clarac, lord of Buzet-sur-Tarn in the diocese of Toulouse, had taken local peasants before the Parlement of Toulouse and secured a long list of seigneurial prerogatives like the ones enjoyed by the marquis d'Avèze. According to a report sent from Toulouse to the National Assembly at the beginning of 1791, the peasants' suspicion that Clarac

---

57   Brugal 1883, pp. 339–41; Ado 1996, pp. 132–3; Jolivet 1980, pp. 131–9; Riou 1988, p. 165.
58   Cazals and Poitevin 1992, p. 184; Rascol 1961, p. 239; Godechot 1986, pp. 80–4; Castan 1980, p. 107.

and his associates plotted against the Revolution led them to set his château ablaze and shoot dead one of his guests.[59]

There were several other incidents of this sort in different parts of the region in the first years of the Revolution. But in general, the peasants had no need to run the risk of breaking the law and attacking their former lords, because the lords no longer enjoyed any onerous rights over them. The one part of the province where seigneurial dues did represent a heavy burden was the Aude. Seigneurs of this area of Languedoc had asserted their rights to dues, fines, common lands, political powers, and honorific privileges more frequently than did their counterparts in other part of the province. Figure 5.2 presents a geographic classification of the hundreds of assertions of seigneurial rights of the second half of the eighteenth century described in Chapter 1.

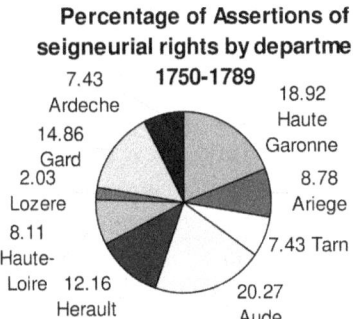

FIGURE 5.2
Assertions of seigneurial rights by department in old regime Languedoc

Significantly, the inhabitants of the Corbières region of the Aude paid about a fifth of their income in seigneurial dues and tithes, the highest such charges in the province.[60]

Between 1790 and 1792, the peasants of the Aude devised all sorts of subterfuge to avoid the law requiring them to go on paying dues to their former seigneurs. Their resistance spanned several years, took many forms, and eventually succeeded in uprooting the seigneurial regime from the department. It differed from the pattern of revolts common to other parts of the country – where the peasantry persistently took direct action against seigneurial property, as the national legislatures dragged their heels before finally abolishing all lordly rights in July 1793 – in that it was basically a movement of passive resistance. The peasants' refusals to heed the summons of the authorities of the

---

59   ADA 1 L165, p. 254; ADHG B1893, C4291; McPhee 1999, p. 51; Sabatié 1971, pp. 176–96.
60   McPhee 1999, p. 28.

Aude to fulfil their obligations to the former seigneurs make up almost 10 percent of all the popular revolts recorded in Table A.5 of the Appendix.[61]

In other parts of the province, the peasants worried more about the possible reestablishment of the political and honorific rights of lordship than they did about seigneurial levies. The king's attempt to emigrate in 1791 cast suspicion on former nobles in many parts of the country. Patriots feared that the nobles plotted with foreign armies to attack the country and restore the old regime. The lower classes frequently urged officials to search the nobles' residences and verify that they were not preparing to join royalist conspiracies. Patriots of the Gard and the southern Massif central were particularly responsive to such urgings, for as we saw in the previous chapter, nobles and clergymen organised armed encampments of counterrevolutionaries in this part of old regime Languedoc between 1790 and 1793. Many local residents thought they needed to destroy the nobility's capacity to cause harm.[62]

They got their opportunity at the end of March 1792, when 69 national guardsmen drowned in the Rhône while traveling from Villeneuve-lès-Avignon to Arles to help quell counterrevolutionary activity. The inhabitants of the Ardèche and Gard immediately blamed the accident on aristocrats. Peasants of the Ardèche stormed châteaux, pulled out fences, cut down trees, and wrecked the gardens of former nobles. In the Gard, they burned and pillaged châteaux, and built bonfires with titles and furniture, in 77 locations, including villages formerly subject to the marquis d'Avèze, during the month of April.[63]

The demographic geography of Gard was conducive to the politicisation of the peasantry. Many villages of the department had over 2000 inhabitants and a diverse population of professionals, shopkeepers, and peasants. These rural residents set up popular societies and communicated the political mood of the country to the peasantry. The clubs imparted fears about counterrevolution and the reinstatement of old regime privileges.[64] A report given by a commander of the national guard to the district of Sommières during the uprisings

---

61 McPhee 1999, pp. 61–3. The non-violent resistance, which characterised the peasant movement of the Aude, is the reason it does not appear in the surveys of the rural revolts. These surveys of the waves of peasant revolts in response to the hesitations of the revolutionary legislatures before abolishing all lordly rights are located in Ado 1996; Markoff 1996; Jones 1988.
62 Tackett 2003, pp. 150, 168–9, 169n.
63 Jolivet 1980, pp. 341–9. Deliberations of the department, districts, and popular societies of the Gard about the rural uprisings are found in ADG L44, L158, L418, L590, L1722, L1838, L2122. The most comprehensive description of these revolts is in Rouvière 1974, vol. 2, pp. 186–264.
64 Jones 1988, pp. 212–15.

of April 1792 gives a sense of the peasants' outlook. He stopped a crowd of three or four-hundred rebels arriving in Souvignargues and asked them the object of their mission, 'I was told that it was to knock down châteaux, because their masters are f ... aristocrats'. He urged the crowd to respect the law but was told that 'all aristocrats are guilty. They want to destroy the constitution and are trying to ruin us all by bringing in foreign troops ... They plan on making use of the châteaux, and it is therefore urgent to render them unusable'.[65]

The political fallout from this wave of anti-seigneurial violence revealed the involvement of popular societies and national guards. Clubs and administrators of Nîmes and the Gard blamed each other for having incited the uprisings. The fact is that none of the authorities made any effort to stop the violence until it began to threaten property rights. Peasants of the district of Uzès shared out the property of a lord accused of having usurped their land. Rebels taxed wealthy residents of the district of Le Vigan to bring down the price of grain and threatened a nobleman, accused of having enriched himself at their expense, with the arson of his house if he did not give them 100,000 livres. The general council of the Gard then posted an address aimed at reigning in the violence:

> Do you not see ... that in scaring and ruining proprietors and the rich, you make them unable to pay their taxes and thus deprive the Nation of a necessary resource; you chase from the state the capital that makes it prosperous, and you thus upset agricultural production, destroy manufacturing, condemn commerce to inaction, and plunge into indigence the people you believe to be serving?[66]

The revolts of the Ardèche and Gard suggest that the economy and culture of the old regime do not fully explain the anti-seigneurial movement. The general sentiment against taxation expressed in the popular uprisings of the eighteenth century and the parish cahiers de doléances did not foreshadow the prevalence of attacks on châteaux and seigneurial titles. The targets of the revolts developed in accordance with the political dynamics of the Revolution. Peasants perceived conditions in which they could pillage châteaux and burn seigneurial titles with impunity.[67]

A wave of revolt in the Ariège in fall of 1792 illustrates this relationship between anti-seigneurial revolts and the overall political context. The judges of the Parlement of Toulouse, the potentates of the region, declared their refusal

---

65 Rouvière 1974, vol. 2, pp. 191–2.
66 ADG L44 contains the quote. L158 and L1838 contain reports on threats to property.
67 Markoff 1996, pp. 15, 267–8, 273, 333.

of the Constituent Assembly's work in 1790. Two years later, patriots of the Ariège attributed a series of incidents to the intrigue of conservative administrative bodies. A mob organised by the municipality in Mirepoix, for example, chased down and beat citizens gathering to raise volunteers for the army. The imminence of war with Spain made many patriots fear that local nobles would side with the enemy in an effort to restore their former rights. Patriots got their chance to confront the perceived danger in August 1792, when a decree authorised communes to search the homes of suspects. The peasants then went from one château to another burning and pillaging between September and November. This wave of revolts was much smaller than the one that spread across the Ardèche and Gard in April 1792 yet bore a striking similarity to it. In both waves of revolts, national guards and notables participated in large numbers. Once order returned to the Ariège, moderates accused Séguier-la-Pique, a local administrator and an acquirer of national lands, of having been the instigator and leader of the uprisings.[68]

This pattern of revolt casts doubt on Alfred Cobban's argument that the leaders of the third estate sought to preserve seigneurial levies. He advanced this argument to refute the claim of Marxist historians that the bourgeoisie and peasantry allied against feudalism in 1789. Many wealthy commoners, the argument goes, owned seigneurial rights and sought to forestall their abolition. Thus, on the night of August 4, the National Assembly made dramatic declarations about the abolition of feudalism in order to calm unrest but retained seigneurial levies in the ensuing legislation.[69] However, the evidence from Languedoc shows that subsistence and tax revolts caused the revolutionary elite far more alarm than did the revolts against the seigneurial regime. While bourgeois legislators would not abandon established forms of property such as lordly rights, venal offices, and shares of tax farms, they rarely used state power to help the former seigneurs collect dues. The evidence from the Corbières, where the peasantry steadfastly refused to go on paying seigneurial dues, even after the National Assembly made clear that the dues were legally binding, indicates that the authorities did little to help the former lords enforce their remaining rights.[70]

Other incidents from the district of Toulouse suggest that the authorities tolerated or even encouraged opposition to the former seigneurs. Peasants denounced the baron de Miglos as a dangerous aristocrat after he sought to

---

68 Arnaud 1904, pp. 292–3, 347–54; Casteras 1911, pp. 32, 32n–33n.
69 Cobban 1965, pp. 43–8.
70 McPhee 1999, p. 63.

collect his seigneurial dues in February 1791. Authorities arrested him and transported him to Paris, where he was executed a few years later. Depuy de Sacère, lord of Escanecrabe, sent a steward into the homes of local peasants to demand the payment of dues in November 1789. He threatened to take recalcitrants to court, crush them with legal fees, and turn them out of their homes. But the authorities did nothing to back up his threats. Instead, they turned a blind eye as the peasants turned Sacère out of the village in a din of boos. He emigrated shortly thereafter.[71]

In conclusion, peasants showed ingenuity in the face of difficult economic circumstances of the eighteenth century. They responded to the strain of population growth on their landholdings by growing cash crops, taking on leases, producing textiles, hiring themselves out as labourers, and bringing new terrains under cultivation. The peasants brought about economic growth by dint of additional expenditures of manual effort. But the productivity of their labour did not improve and their standard of living remained much the same. The peasants actually became dependent on precarious markets for wine, textiles, and grain. As bread prices rose amid the collapse of royal institutions in 1788 and 1789, the peasantry seized stores of grain, destroyed fiscal offices, broke into the homes of elites, and demanded that they regulate the cost of basic goods in localities throughout Languedoc.

Economic insecurity heightened frustration with the burdens of taxation and the seigneurial regime. The peasants looked on taxation with more distaste than they did any other burden of the old regime. Yet taxation began sustaining a new regime in which many former nobles and wealthy commoners placed their hopes. The seigneurial regime did not unify the upper classes in the same way. When royal authority collapsed, the lords were unable to rally ruling groups to protect seigneurial prerogatives. While revolutionary officials employed the full force of the state to protect tax collection, they actually encouraged assaults on châteaux when they perceived a threat of counterrevolution. Anti-seigneurial violence thus constituted the most common type of disturbance between 1788 and 1793 and erupted in two waves of uprisings against châteaux and lordly titles in the Ardèche, Gard, and Ariège in 1792.

Much of the urban population – social strata including merchants, farmers, surgeons, workers, master craftsmen and shopkeepers – became politically active during these years. They shared the ambition of former nobles, wealthy wholesale merchants, jurists, landlords, and other elites to earn the honours and rewards of public careers by serving the state and nation. The elites prob-

---

71   Bastier 1975, p. 305.

ably would have maintained control over electoral assemblies and local administrations to the exclusion of the rest of the population had it not been for war and the continued rise in prices. Requisitioning grain, regulating prices, and arming the populace came to be seen as urgent necessities for the survival of the Revolution. While militants demanded the implementation of such policies, local elites saw them as threats to hierarchy and property. These divergent perspectives intensified political conflicts in the towns. These municipal politics of the 1790s are the subject of the next chapter.

CHAPTER 6

Politics and Class, 1792–99: Radicalism, Terror, and Repression

Until the end of 1792, popular revolts and resistance to taxation played havoc with the nine departments into which the National Assembly divided Languedoc. Counterrevolutionary uprisings persisted until the spring of 1793. These challenges to the constitutional order dominated local politics. Merchants, lawyers and former nobles, who embraced the constitution of 1791, represented stability and won the support of property owners in elections. Yet in 1793 and 1794, as the internal challenges to the constitutional order diminished, the social composition of local government changed, and many members of the upper classes faced proscription in the period known as the terror.

In the 1970s and 1980s, historians determined that the social relations inherited from the old regime had little to do with this radical interlude. Richard Cobb saw that the terror was the first instance of popular government in French history yet maintained that it was the work of coteries of militants, not a social movement. Certain individuals had the talent and temperament to conquer power on the local level and impose their vision of a revolutionary order. François Furet argued that the collapse of royal authority undid the social moorings of politics and permitted the militants of clubs and electoral assemblies to rally a political community around the ideology of equality and pure democracy. The underside of this ideology was the contention that its expected enemies, the privileged orders, plotted against the people. Revolutionaries used terror against imaginary opponents. Lynn Hunt finds that a 'new political class' of merchants, artisans, shopkeepers, clerks, and ex-priests rose to power in towns throughout France in 1793 and 1794. This class shared the fears of people across the Atlantic world that political organising outside of public assemblies harboured malevolent plots. The 'new political class' undertook an unprecedented project of transforming political language, rituals and organisations without the aid of any practical experience of politics under the old regime. Revolutionaries therefore had a particularly difficult time tolerating the emergence of political organising and ended up using terror to suppress it.[1]

---

1   Albert Soboul provided the dominant interpretation of the terror prior to Furet. He argued that a faction of the bourgeoisie allied with an ensemble of shopkeepers, artisans, and work-

This chapter takes up the issues addressed in this literature. It weighs the relevance of language, symbols, and political loyalties to the radicalisation of politics in the 1790s. The chapter evaluates the importance of individuals and social movements. Did the social relations of the old regime monarchy play any role in the radicalisation of politics in the 1790s? Did the economic context play a role?

In answering these questions, the first part of this chapter examines the circumstances in which urban residents became politically active. Master craftsmen, shopkeepers, farmers, surgeons, and workers hoped to play a role in public life. Their calls for political participation became insistent in 1792 and 1793, as spiralling prices threatened to dissipate their modest capital and as foreign monarchies threatened to dash all the hopes the Revolution had awakened. The lawyers, landlords and wealthy merchants in charge of local government feared that aggressive policies to surmount this crisis – regulating prices, requisitioning grain, and arming the populace – would undermine property and hierarchy. In 1793, when the Convention began to enforce these policies, notables in the successor departments of Languedoc resisted. The Convention consequently purged local governments and entrusted them to revolutionary enthusiasts found among the petty property owners of the towns. The second part of this chapter presents the extraordinary measures taken by these militants against former nobles, clergymen, and urban elites who seemed reluctant to sacrifice for the revolutionary cause. The third part analyses the militants' fall from power. Their authority depended on the central government rather than a coherent political and social movement. The Convention thus had no trouble pushing them off of the political stage, once it moved to restore moderate government in 1794.

1   The Challenges of Political Representation and Democracy

Although the nobility lost its privileged access to local government in the first years of the Revolution, political authority still did not extend very far beyond

---

ers, known as the sans-culottes, to defeat the aristocracy in 1793 and 1794. Political leaders fixed the price of life's necessities, even if this measure contravened the capitalist principle of private property, in order to maintain the support of the sans-culottes and assure the triumph of the bourgeois class as a whole. Once this interclass alliance vanquished the feudal nobility, it came apart at the expense of the sans-culottes in Thermidor (Soboul 1972, pp. 251, 254, 263). Cobb 1998, pp. 171–4, 220–1, 223–4, 227, 240; Furet 1981, pp. 22, 24–7, 48, 51; Hunt 1984, pp. 2, 12–13, 24, 32, 39–40, 43, 48–9.

a relatively small circle of wealthy landlords, jurists, and wholesale merchants. In 1792 and 1793, these political leaders faced mounting criticism from urban residents anxious about rising prices and the threat posed to the Revolution by foreign monarchies. We saw in Chapter 4 that noble judges of the Cour des Comptes, Aides et Finances of Montpellier rallied to the National Assembly and shared ascendancy in electoral assemblies with wealthy merchants in the department of the Hérault in the first two years of the Revolution. They set the tone for local politics through the Club of the Friends of the Constitution and Equality of Montpellier. The elections in the fall of 1792, held for the first time without property qualifications, hardly altered the departmental, district and municipal administrations, returning officials who had governed the Hérault since 1790.[2]

Protestants and wholesale merchants (*négociants*) took control of government in Nîmes and the Gard at the end of 1790 after the failure of the counterrevolutionary revolts led by nobles and clergymen. Wholesale merchants had the greatest fortunes in the entire region. They formed the most numerous professional category, followed by landlords (*bourgeois*), in the Society of the Friends of the Constitution of Nîmes in 1791. The membership of this club and the departmental administration overlapped through the summer of 1793.[3]

The well-to-do also controlled the departments of the Ariège and Aude. Active citizens meeting the property qualification to vote elected Bertrand d'Artiguières mayor of Foix, the capital of the Ariège, in 1790. He had been a field marshal of dragoons and a knight of St.-Louis before the Revolution. Other members of the municipality included a lawyer, who had opposed the doubling of the third and vote by head in the Estates General, and d'Artiguières's son, who had been a member of the aristocratic Estates of Foix. The Revolution was relatively uneventful in the Aude, with little counterrevolutionary activity and few Jacobin clubs. The merchant manufacturers, (*fabricants*) who oversaw much of the economic life of this textile-manufacturing region, shared local government with lawyers and old regime administrators.[4]

Jurists, merchants, manufacturers, and shopkeepers won election to the municipal council of Toulouse in 1790. The voters spurned the noble judges of the Parlement for opposing the Constituent Assembly. Wholesale merchants and lawyers made up the majority of the Literary and Patriotic Club of Toulouse

---

2 Archives Nationales (hereafter AN) H1/748/134, H1/748/292; Vialles 1921, p. 259n; Duval-Jouve 1974, vol. 2, pp. 19–20.
3 Gutherz and Huard 1982, pp. 222–3; Rouvière 1974, vol. 4, p. 307n.
4 Arnaud 1904, pp. 80, 151, 151n, 153, 187, 205–8, 293–5; McPhee 1999, pp. 106–7, 111; Fournier 1984, pp. 403, 413; Fournier and Péronnet 1989, pp. 110–11; Rives 1984, pp. 163–4.

in the middle of 1791. This governmental bourgeoisie, composed largely of barristers in the judicial city of Toulouse, assimilated the culture of the Enlightenment and rejected the Parlement's staunch resistance to change. Yet it did not wholeheartedly embrace the Revolution, because the Constituent Assembly had abolished the barristers' official association and all their formal honours and professional rights.[5]

These notables did not succeed in controlling the scope of political participation. Artisans, workers, and merchants gained a majority in the popular society of Toulouse in 1792. The club became exigent about revolutionary principles and began favouring direct democracy. The representative of the Convention made a member of the club, the lawyer Descombels from Castelsarrazin, executive agent (*procureur-général-syndic*) of the department in May 1793. Affluent merchants and lawyers faced the worrisome prospect of losing control of local government to socially inferior groups and outside forces.[6]

The relations of production of the regional textile industry underlay the political positions adopted by the inhabitants of the Gard. Wholesale merchants put raw material out to merchant manufacturers and artisans, and marketed the finished products. They had long sought to bring down the costs of production and enhance their profits by paying the producers as little as possible. The wholesale merchants enjoyed uncontested control over local government until November 1791, when residents of Nîmes formed a second political club. The membership fee of six *livres*, as opposed to twenty-four for the Society of the Friends of the Constitution, facilitated the participation of merchants, artisans, and workers of modest means. A letter sent to the Legislative Assembly in May 1792 shows that many members could hardly sign their own name. Alarmed by this unprecedented political mobilisation, the well-to-do residents of Nîmes sought to amalgamate the popular society into the original club and re-establish their hegemony.[7] According to the popular society's refusal,

> It is ... the desire to educate ourselves in speaking a language of simplicity, readily understood by everyone, that gave birth to our society ... All these flowered speeches, which are like the enchanted orchestra of genius and

---

5 AN H1/748/134; Berlanstein 1975, p. 169; Nelidoff 1996, pp. 147, 164. For information on Toulousain clubs see Archives Départementales de la Haute-Garonne (ADHG) L4543, L4552, L4553.
6 ADHG L4548, L4552, L4553; Nelidoff 1996, pp. 200, 233, 237; Berlanstein 1975, p. 175.
7 Lewis 1978, p. 54; Gutherz and Huard 1982, p. 224; Pouthas 1934, p. 112. Anne Marie Duport's research shows that journeymen, master craftsmen, and merchant manufacturers of the silk industry made up most of the members of the popular society. Lawyers and liberal professionals were largely absent from the club's membership (Duport 1987, pp. 105–6).

taste ... are not suited for the people, they usually throw it into a stupid ecstasy, from which it only comes out to applaud imitatively what it did not understand.[8]

The two clubs began to disagree on issues in April 1792 during the wave of assaults on châteaux, titles, and other properties analysed in the previous chapter. The departmental administration accused the popular society of inciting the unrest. The popular society refuted the accusation but made known that certain châteaux owners were monarchist oppressors unworthy of sympathy. Two months later, the popular society defied the royal veto and the express wishes of the departmental administration by sending volunteers to the camp of federated militias gathering in Paris to defend the Revolution. The popular society favoured a republic while local officials continued to support a constitutional monarchy headed by Louis XVI. After the establishment of the Republic in November 1792, the Friends of Liberty and Equality, formerly Friends of the Constitution, redoubled their efforts to fuse the two clubs. The representative of the Convention urged the popular society to acquiesce. But the popular society made fusion contingent upon the preservation of its title and a purge of the moderates. Its conditions sharpened discord and divided the inhabitants of the region into adversarial camps.[9]

Patriots contested the notables' control over electoral assemblies and municipal administrations in the Ariège at the end of 1790. They deemed the election of September 1791 to the Legislative Assembly a victory for democrats, popular societies, and opponents of the refractory clergy. Still, in 1792 the departmental directory, and many of the districts, municipalities, and tribunals, remained reluctant to embrace the ardent revolutionary positions of the patriots. The department favoured likeminded municipalities in the allocation of funds for gendarmes, markets and roads, and allowed ruffians to harass patriotic merchants. The patriots labelled these officials 'aristocrats' for tolerating refractory clergy, and for identifying with constitutional monarchy and its proponents like Lafayette.[10]

These disputes took place within a context of economic insecurity. Grain prices increased in the second half of the eighteenth century and then climbed sharply in 1788 and 1789. Prices stabilised in Toulouse between the fall of 1789 and the summer of 1791, but then began to rise, until a rapid rise between

---

8   Quoted from Rouvière 1974, vol. 2, pp. 74–5. See also vol. 2, p. 78.
9   Archives Départementales du Gard (ADG) L47, L158, L415, L1089, L1838, L2122, L2123; Lewis 1978, p. 53; Rouvière 1974, vol. 3, pp. 30, 34, 34n, 37–8.
10   Arnaud 1904, pp. 187, 205–8, 249–50, 292–5, 324–5.

August 1792 and May 1793 made grain almost three times as expensive as it had been in the summer of 1791. Conditions were particularly grim in the Hérault and Gard, where the inhabitants had long relied on grain imports. Bad harvests in the regions from which the inhabitants normally purchased grain, the bankruptcy of local administrations, and the disruption of shipments by rebellious crowds made dearth a real possibility in 1792 and 1793. The crisis was exacerbated by the collection of food for the troops mobilised against the monarchies of Austria and Spain.[11]

Economic insecurity increased the townspeople's frustration with moderate officials. The popular society of Toulouse created a committee of subsistence and called on authorities to control prices at the beginning of 1793. Local leaders, however, held firm to the tenets of economic liberalism. The municipality of Nîmes ignored repeated petitions of workers and the popular society for affordable grain and higher wages in 1792 and 1793. The popular society wrote to affiliated clubs of the Gard in November 1792 that the Society of Republicans, made up almost entirely of wholesale merchants and landlords, favoured constitutional monarchy and looked to the coming elections as a chance to establish an aristocratic republic. Yet they failed to break the moderates' grip on the region. Lawyers, landowners, and wholesale merchants enjoyed the support of the central government and had the means to influence electoral assemblies. Some of Nîmes's wealthiest merchants won election to the municipality.[12]

In the Ariège, disputes became violent amid the growing likelihood of war with Spain in 1791 and 1792. Popular societies denounced the reluctance of the departmental administration to requisition grain for the army and the refusal of several municipalities to ask well-to-do residents to help billet troops. Departmental administrators expressed anxiety in a letter to the minister of the interior in June 1792,

> Popular societies, affiliated with the Jacobin club in Paris, continually issue incendiary writings and calumnious denunciations scorning the constituted powers ... These societies carry the ignorant and credulous people to insurrection ... If their proceedings continue to be tolerated, we will no longer be able to vouch for public tranquillity, and France will soon be devoured by the horrors of anarchy.[13]

---

11   Frêche and Frêche 1967, pp. 74–5; Johnson 1986, pp. 39–41.
12   ADG L47; Sentou 1967, pp. 466, 469; Lewis 1978, p. 54; Pouthas 1934, p. 118; Rouvière 1974, vol. 3, pp. 37–8; Gutherz and Huard, 1982, p. 225.
13   Arnaud 1904, pp. 308–9. See also pp. 294–5, 300–1.

The dreaded insurrections took place two months later. The lower classes of Pamiers accused the municipal government of embezzling funds destined for military volunteers. They took power in a violent insurrection, killing one municipal official and pillaging the houses of two others. The mayor Guillaume Malroc of Mirepoix had owned a seigneurial domain, an ennobling office, and a judgeship in the seneschal court prior to the Revolution. Fearing that the efforts of local patriots to mobilise support for the war would undermine public order, Malroc declared martial law and distributed arms to his partisans. The district and nearby municipalities accused Malroc's administration of collaborating with foreign monarchies and former seigneurs, and called the inhabitants of the countryside to arms in support of the patriots. They forced Malroc to flee and jailed members of the municipal council. A similar uprising overthrew the municipal government of Foix headed by the former knight of St.-Louis and field marshal of dragoons, Bertrand d'Artiguières. Democrats later won election to all levels of government in the Ariège in December 1792.[14]

Wholesale merchants, landowners, and jurists remained at the head of the other eight departments of Languedoc until they joined the movement, labelled federalist, against the events of 31 May and 2 June 1793 in which an alliance of the Parisian crowd and the group of deputies known as the Mountain expelled elected representatives from the Convention. The Club of the Friends of the Constitution and Equality of Montpellier called for assemblies in the cantons of the Hérault to mobilise resistance. Those who attended these assemblies believed that deputies allied to the mob would never establish a stable constitutional order. They formed a committee of public safety and elected as president Jean-Jacques-Louis Durand – the mayor of Montpellier, the former president in the Cour de Comptes, Aides et Finances, and owner of 120,000 francs of bonds. The committee assigned Albisson, a judge of the district tribunal and a former official of the Estates of Languedoc, the task of drafting a protest. He demanded the reintegration of the expelled representatives, the abolition of the revolutionary committee and the extraordinary criminal tribunal of Paris, the restoration of the situation before the Mountain's coup, and a trial of the responsible parties before a jury of the nation. Durand, Albisson, and other local federalists controlled the department until the end of July 1793, when they realised the futility of their cause and retracted their protests.[15]

---

14 Arnaud 1904, pp. 318–19, 347–50, 356; AN F7 3654, F7 3654/1; Cazanave 1991, pp. 47, 50; Ado 1996, pp. 313, 319.

15 Paul Hanson provides a useful map of the departments that embraced federalism (1989, pp. 8–9, 12). Gégot 1984, p. 239; Gégot 1988, p. 105; Duval-Jouve 1974, vol. 2, pp. 61, 65, 69–70, 79n.

The municipality of Toulouse convoked electoral assemblies at the beginning of June to oppose the Convention. The attendees placed a few merchants and a dozen barristers in charge. They denounced the cabals in the Convention and the spread of lawlessness. Descombels, however, had the general council of the Haute-Garonne decline proposals for raising an armed force, and the popular society of Toulouse supported the Convention. The federalist revolt did not go beyond innocuous declarations, because Toulouse did not have much manufacturing and lacked a wealthy bourgeoisie with the social weight to mobilise a movement.[16]

By contrast, the wholesale merchants of Nîmes cracked down on club militants and popular protests even before the events of 31 May and 2 June. The moderate Society of Republicans made a disparaging allusion to the popular club in April 1793, when it refused to associate with people suspected of promoting anarchy. A month later, the departmental administration of the Gard suspended the right of assembly after agitation among rural labourers for higher pay. It then began to organise and arm a militia to protect property owners and prevent the Convention from being captured by Parisian militants.[17]

The news of the seizure of power by these militants, allied to the Mountain, prompted local officials to call an assembly of the communes of the Gard. The assembly declared, 'you who want peace and order, to arms. You who have properties, to arms, or soon they will be devastated: you who want to pass on the fruits of your hard work to your children ... to arms'.[18] The assembly used the local militia to intimidate the partisans of the Convention. The militia blocked the doors of the popular society and seized its papers. But while the militia effectively dispersed its adversaries in the Gard, it amounted to a feeble force in comparison to the army of the Republic. The militia consisted of 600 soldiers, who melted away the moment news arrived of the advance of regular units toward the Gard in mid-July.[19]

The insubordination of the local authorities led the Convention to look below the stratum of notables for officials willing repress its opponents and mobilise men and resources for war. The Convention's representative Joseph Antoine Boisset sought to stimulate the zeal of the officials of the Hérault by

---

16   ADHG L67, L283; Berlanstein 1975, p. 174; Nelidoff 1996, pp. 233, 237; Lyons 1978, pp. 41, 46, 52; Sentou 1967, p. 477.
17   ADG L2125; Pouthas 1934, pp. 126–7. According to Duport, wholesale merchants, financiers, bankers, and rentiers of the Gard took up arms against the Convention, because they feared that the national political drift to the left threatened their property (1987, p. 88).
18   ADG L51.
19   ADG L47, L3137; Gutherz and Huard 1982, p. 228.

recruiting surgeons, apothecaries, artisans, and shopkeepers into the Popular Society of the Friends of the Constitution of Montpellier in October 1793. The club's minutes show that it staffed the local administration, received solicitations for state employment, and examined applications for certificates of civic-mindedness (*certificats de civisme*) required to receive pay from public treasuries. Boisset named members of the popular society and local administrative bodies to a committee of surveillance. The committee's minutes show that it purged the National Guard and examined the qualifications of new recruits. It replaced trained judges with farmers, surgeons, and merchant manufacturers. Boisset actually had to temper the committee's zeal so as to preserve the reputation and authority of the local judiciary.[20]

These measures altered the social composition of the administration. Wholesale merchants, lawyers, and landlords dominated the assemblies of the canton of Montpellier held in June 1793 to challenge the Mountain. Tax rolls and the list of the creditors of the diocese show that almost 80 percent of the members of the assemblies belonged to Montpellier's wealthiest class of residents. Wholesale merchants and jurists controlled the municipality of Montpellier prior to 1793, whereas artisans and shopkeepers controlled it in the fall of 1793. Over 75 percent of the municipality belonged to the wealthiest class of residents prior to June 1793, whereas the percentage fell to 20 at the end of 1793.[21]

The representatives on mission Marc Antoine Baudot and Guillaume Chaudron-Rousseau purged the district of Toulouse, and the judiciary and department of the Haute-Garonne, and charged Descombels with naming new officials. Descombels replaced 25 municipal officials of Toulouse with merchants, artisans, and shopkeepers in the fall of 1793. The tax assessments of municipal officials fell over 25 percent between the first years of the Revolution and the period known as the year II lasting from 22 September 1793 to 21 September 1794. Michel Athanaze Malpel, 90 percent of whose 150,000 francs was in real estate, was a lawyer and municipal magistrate, and was related to a noble judge of the Parlement of Toulouse, prior to 1789. He became a municipal official in 1790 and the executive agent of the department in 1791. The

---

20   Archives Départementales de l'Hérault (ADH) L5528, L5761, L6213; Laurent and Gavignaud 1987, p. 176; Gégot 1988, pp. 241–3; Gégot 1974, vol. 1, pp. 94–113, 123, 126, 146, 176, 206–9; Duval-Jouve 1974, vol. 2, pp. 123.

21   Wealthy residents appear among the top 7.5 percent of taxpayers according to the capitation rolls of 1789, among the creditors of the diocese, among those paying the forced loan of 190,000 livres decreed by the department in April 1793, and/or among the 187 individuals paying the highest patriotic contribution in 1789 and the municipal revolutionary tax of 1793: AN H1/748/289, H1/748/292; ADH L 3471; Delpuech 1954, p. 51 and the following pages.

Jacobin club accused him of leniency toward suspects and refractory priests, and the representative Chabot replaced him with Descombels in 1793. Voters elected Marc Derrey, a judge in the seneschal court of Toulouse prior to 1789, to municipal office in 1790 and to the post of mayor in 1792. He was arrested for federalism and executed in 1794. His lands were worth almost 150,000. Conversely, the wholesale merchant Groussac, mayor during the year II, had a fortune of 5,200, all of it moveable property. The take-over of local government by merchants, surgeons, and artisans like Groussac must have seemed like a social revolution to the jurists of the Toulousain bourgeoisie.[22]

The representatives on mission to the Gard did not alter the social composition of the administration as rapidly or as thoroughly. Rovère reopened the popular society of Nîmes and closed the moderate club of French Republicans in the fall of 1793. Yet he continued to staff the municipal council with wholesale merchants and lawyers. Local militants expressed their displeasure, and the Convention replaced Stanislas Joseph François Xavier Rovère with Jean Borie, a representative from the Lozère, in January 1794. The social composition of the administrative bodies then changed. Landlords and lawyers continued to run the department, but artisans and merchants gained control over the districts and municipalities of Uzès and Nîmes.[23]

The representatives on mission to the Ariège staffed the local government with their supporters even though the department had never wavered in its support for the Convention and the war. The representatives Raymond Gaston and Joseph-Pierre-Marie Fayau purged the popular societies of Foix and Tarascon in April 1793. They then allowed their own handpicked members to name a new district administration. In the fall of 1793, the representatives Pierre Paganel, Chaudron-Rousseau, and Baudot appointed members of the popular society of Pamiers to a revolutionary committee of the department and required them to obtain approval for all of their acts. Agents of the central government (*commissaires civils*) enforced the committee's work, going from town to town, purging municipalities and popular societies, and arresting suspects. Several popular societies wrote to the Convention in November 1793 that the representatives and their agents sent bogus reports about the political climate of the Ariège to justify authoritarian measures. The popular societies claimed that the representatives spread lawlessness and disrespect for property. Chaudron-Rousseau, however, had influence in the Committee of Public

---

22 ADHG L209, L511, L4548; Hunt 1984, p. 169; Berlanstein 1975, p. 176; Sentou 1969, pp. 178, 225, 264–5.
23 ADG L 139; Lewis 1978, pp. 71–2; Gutherz and Huard 1982, pp. 230, 235.

Safety, which confirmed his authority and permitted him to redouble the number of purges in the beginning of 1794.[24] He sent a letter to Paris in March:

> I dissolved and recreated the popular society of Mirepoix; aristocrats and especially ignorance infested the former. Imagine, citizen colleagues, that it thought itself a fraction of the sovereign and, as such, superior to the delegates of the National Convention. The new one will not fall into this error. It will not harbour any aristocrats, and will unite all the lights of Mirepoix with the most active patriots.[25]

Representatives on mission left the administration of the Aude alone for several months after the federalist crisis despite the repeated calls of Carcassonne's Jacobin club for government intervention. The representative Jacques Joseph François Cassanyès finally overhauled the committee of surveillance and integrated many artisans in November 1793. Artisans made up a third of the municipal council of Carcassonne during the year II. But toward the end of April 1794, Chaudron-Rousseau carried out new purges and put loyal shopkeeper/merchants (*commerçants*) in the committee of surveillance and merchant manufacturers in the departmental administration. He accused the council of Carcassonne of incompetence and replaced its artisans with well-to-do merchants. A delegation from the popular society woke Chaudron-Rousseau at one in the morning on 17 May to rebuke his dictatorial manner and his alliance with the local notables. Chaudron-Rousseau responded to this insubordination by purging the popular society's leading members.[26]

2 Revolutionary Policies and Personalities

The merchants, artisans, and petty property owners, who entered local government in the wake of the federalist crisis between the fall of 1793 and the end of the summer of 1794, used their power to tyrannise former nobles, priests, and members of the middle classes suspected of lacking generosity for their fellow citizens and enthusiasm for the Republic. In Carcassonne, the surveillance committee arrested women and workers for crimes such as religious zeal and refusing to drink to the republic in the spring of 1793. But after the feder-

---

24 Arnaud 1904, pp. 380–1, 383, 392–3, 417–18, 423–6, 430–1, 443, 446, 450–1, 462–7, 490–2.
25 Arnaud 1904, p. 487.
26 Archives Départementales de l'Aude (ADA) L392, L394, L2123; Fournier 1984, p. 422; Fournier and Péronnet 1989, p. 119; Rives 1984, p. 169.

alist crisis, the authorities arrested nobles rather than workers. They not only detained people for symbolic acts, like wearing the white label of monarchy, but also for selling grain above the maximum prices on essential goods legislated by the Convention. The surveillance committee of Le Vigan in the Gard welcomed denunciations of shopkeeper/merchants suspected of selling wood and grain above the maximum prices. Solon Reynaud, representative to the Haute-Loire, heeded the request of the popular society of Le Puy and set up a public granary. Registers drawn up for the representative Baudot in Toulouse at the end of September 1793 state that a levy on 'the rich, recognised for being aristocrats, selfish, constitutional monarchists (*feuillants*), moderates and federalists' would subsidise bread for sans-culottes, workers, and patriots. Breaches of the maximum prices represented almost a third of the accusations received by the revolutionary committee of Toulouse.[27]

Revolutionaries may have endeavoured to ensure townspeople a measure of economic security but did nothing to develop a movement for social equality. The only group to advocate the socialisation of property was Gracchus Babeuf's Conspiracy of Equals, which only had a handful of followers, most of whom were attracted by the insurrectionary side of the program. Conflicts between radicals and moderates in southern France in 1793 and 1794 did not mobilise the mass of peasants and wage earners. Textile workers and day labourers, paying a meagre capitation tax of two livres or less, comprised almost 45 percent of Montpellier's taxpayers in 1789, yet never played any role in government. The lower classes ceased having a bearing on the course of the Revolution with the ebb of popular uprisings at the end of 1792.[28]

Revolutionaries were concerned above all with what Hunt terms, 'the language of national regeneration, the gestures of equality and fraternity, and the rituals of republicanism'. Hunt argues that the Revolution invented 'the mobilizing potential of democratic republicanism and the compelling intensity of revolutionary change'.[29] The Republic signified a break with the nobility's privileged access to government. It offered civic standing and public responsibility to merchants, artisans, surgeons, farmers, and workers. Revolutionaries set great store by a person's political allegiance, because it carried a message about

---

27   ADA L392, L1153, L2124; Archives Municipales de Toulouse (AMT) 2 G 8; Gorlier 1955, p. 241; Chanon 1988, p. 144. Lyons shows that after Thermidor in the year III, when authorities returned to economic liberalism, mortality rates in Toulouse's popular quarter of St.-Cyprien mounted 40 percent higher than they had been in the difficult year of 1789, and to the highest level of the entire period from 1789 to 1813 (Lyons 1978, pp. 120–1, 124–5).
28   AN H1/748/292; Johnson 1986, pp. 258–60; Hunt 1984, pp. 198, 225.
29   Hunt 1984, p. 15.

their right to take part in government. According to the minutes of the popular society of Montpellier in the wake of the federalist crisis, 'The mayor has always had liaisons with aristocrats of the area, and patriots have always looked at him suspiciously, because he only came to their café to announce with affectation news unfavourable to the republic'. The popular society claimed that 'Bonnefout, former royal attorney (*procureur*) of Montpellier, [was] fairly well known under the old regime and the new regime for his villainy and his care to arouse troubles and dissensions in the commune'.[30] The municipality of Mauguio denounced the justice of the peace Fermaud for counterrevolutionary opinions disconcerting to patriots. The surveillance committee of Béziers accused the justice of the peace Gottis père of aristocracy for using his home as a meeting place for the least civic-minded people.[31]

This zealous attachment to the Republic came across in the *affaire des galettes*, the most dramatic event of the Revolution in the Hérault. On 1 April 1794, as dearth threatened the area of Montpellier, the municipality ordered the inhabitants to bring all their flour and grain to a public depot. The next night, a boy bread maker on patrol saw light in a baker's shop and suspected a violation of the measures taken to cope with the shortages. He looked through the keyhole to verify his suspicion and then informed a municipal officer. The officer uncovered a clandestine network of bakers working for private individuals. The popular society accused the offenders of starving the people to create nostalgia for the old regime. Raisin Pagès, public prosecutor of the criminal tribunal, charged three women and nine men – merchants, bakers, jurists, and a farmer – with aristocracy and complicity with émigrés for their involvement in the ring. The popular society convinced the tribunal to hold a public trial in the municipal auditorium for the people to see. The tribunal sentenced four to death and three to prison. The executions were carried out in the Promenade du Peyrou, the square recently embellished by the bishops and barons of the Estates of Languedoc to honour royal absolutism and glorify the city of their meetings.[32]

The Convention's reliance on popular societies to prosecute the war and suppress internal enemies in the wake of the federalist crisis allowed ardent radicals of the Haute-Garonne to organise a revolutionary army and impose their vision of a new regime on the inhabitants of the Southwest. The radicals at the helm of the revolutionary army were François Hugueny, Joseph-Alexis Blanchard, and Claude-Louis Gélas. Hugueny had been a councillor in the seneschal

---

30 ADH L5528.
31 ADH L3219, L5791, L5645.
32 Duval-Jouve 1974, vol. 2, pp. 164–9; Gégot 1984, pp. 244–5; Catalan 1902, pp. 47–50, 53.

court of Auch prior to the Revolution. He joined other judges of the region in resisting the crown's suppression of the Parlement of Toulouse in 1788. Voters elected him mayor of Beaumont and president of the district tribunal in 1790. Descombels appointed him president of the departmental tribunal in 1793.[33]

Blanchard and Gélas came from modest backgrounds. Blanchard worked for the chamber of commerce of Toulouse as a clerk and represented the association of writing-masters in the municipal assemblies held in the first half of 1789 to call for reform of the Estates of Languedoc. His participation in the electoral assemblies of 1790 earned him no more than a clerical position under a justice of the peace. Gélas was an expert on feudal titles and a proprietor of vineyards near Beaumont. The district of Toulouse offered him a lacklustre bookkeeping position after 1789. Blanchard and Gélas caught the eye of authorities by their enthusiastic interventions in the popular society. Hugueny made Blanchard his principal agent for carrying out policies in the fall of 1793. The representative on mission appointed Gélas to the committee of surveillance and commissioned him to survey fortresses on the Spanish frontier. Gélas then received the task of organising the revolutionary army of the Haute-Garonne.[34]

Hugueny, Blanchard and Gélas led the revolutionary army into Grenade in October 1793. The army was made up of about 700 farmers and artisans from Beaumont and Toulouse. The National Assembly had chosen Grenade over Beaumont for the district capital in 1790. Hugueny asked the soldiers to free Grenade of fanaticism, 'a monster vomited by despotism'.[35] The army incarcerated officials felt to be lacking public spirit, billeted troops with suspects, and turned the property of affluent individuals over to pillage. One commander had a detachment loot the home of his former employer, the marquis de Bélesta. Gélas compelled Madame de Nougarède of Beauzelle to fix supper for his troops and take part in the meal so they could mock and insult her. The army set up a grain depot to receive an eighth of the harvest of neighbouring cantons. Hugueny and Paganel wrote to the local authorities, 'None can claim the right to eat bread while others have none'.[36]

Members of the army intended above all to see Grenade submit to the Republic they embodied. Grenade's committee of surveillance attempted to control the requisitions of grain and other materials for Toulouse and the army. It came out against the nomination of a candidate from Beaumont, a relative of Hugueny, for the revolutionary tribunal of Toulouse. Gélas was furious. He

---

33   Cobb 1955, p. 29; Lyons 1978, pp. 60–2; Duboul 1891, pp. 15–16, 18–19, 37.
34   AN H1/748/291; ADHG 1 L 548, 1 L 559; Duboul 1891, pp. 58–60.
35   Quoted from Gérard 1991, p. 173.
36   Gérard 1991, p. 177. See also pp. 167, 170–1.

went to town hall and blustered, 'even if I were a hundred leagues away, I would come back to exterminate Grenade, to pulverise it, even if need be, against the authority of the Convention; I would raze the town to the ground and leave no brick standing, if I learned, after my departure, that the municipality remained in a state of apathy'.[37] Hugueny then took the municipal officers into the temple of reason (formerly the Cathedral before the arrival of the revolutionary army) and carried out a new purge. Hugueny and Blanchard used the temple of reason to hold public meetings at which they tried to outdo each other's rhapsodies for the Mountain and invectives against suspects. An army spokesman warned the peasantry that failure to work on Sundays and respect the ten-day week of the republican calendar would result in arrest. Soldiers charged a crowd arriving in Grenade for Sunday mass. On 29 November 1793, the army surprised a congregation in a church, snatched books from the lectern, ripped them apart, and forced the faithful to dance around the altar at gunpoint.[38]

Jean-François Baby, a thirty-five-year-old wholesale merchant and property owner, brought the same brand of politics into the Ariège. He was the executive agent of Tarascon in March 1792, when the department asked him to organise quarters for troops being mobilised for war. Administrators soon learned with alarm that Baby billeted all the troops in the homes of the well-to-do. His revolutionary tirades were another source of alarm. News of the king's flight in 1791 prompted him to comment that this shameful separation of the monarch from the nation undoubtedly overjoyed the enemies of the Revolution. 'But the heaven watching over the safety of this empire, in foiling their manoeuvres, has sent their black homicidal plots to hell'.[39] General irritation with Baby led soldiers and members of the popular society to rip a liberty tree out of his yard and throw it in the Ariège River after he departed for the Spanish frontier to help organise the war effort in 1793.[40]

Baby, however, enjoyed the favour of Marc-Guillaume Vadier, one of the Ariège's deputies to the Convention and a member of the committee of general security. Baby represented the Ariège in Paris at the formal acceptance of the Constitution of the Year II and then returned to the department to work with the Convention's representatives on mission in the fall of 1793. On 30 October, Vadier wrote to the representatives Baudot and Chaudron-Rousseau, lauding their efforts to 'extract this beautiful country from the state of apathy and numbness in which it has been plunged. The public spirit has not been able

37 Duboul 1891, pp. 89–90. See also p. 84.
38 AMT 2 I 33; Gérard 1991, pp. 168–9, 173–4; Duboul 1891, p. 93; Lyons 1978, pp. 60–1.
39 Arnaud 1904, p. 245. See also pp. 300–1. Cobb 1987, p. 218; Casteras 1891, p. 270.
40 Arnaud 1904, pp. 392–3.

to pierce the crust of prejudice and ignorance in a country abandoned to the priests, to the crooks, and to the haughtiness of some insolent country nobles'. Vadier exhorted Baudot and Chaudron-Rousseau 'to foil factions' and 'punish traitors'.[41]

Baby drew up lists of hundreds of suspects and would have added many more, he argued, in a letter sent to Chaudron-Rousseau in July 1794, had Vadier accorded him more time. He dismissed the municipal officers of Mirepoix for their reluctance to draw up lists of suspects and replaced them with Gabriel Clauzel, a bankrupt wholesale merchant disinherited by his father. Clauzel had used the National Guard to invest the Episcopal palace of Mirepoix and harass the bishop in 1790. He earned the enmity of the affluent residents the same year by composing precise rolls for the patriotic contribution to tax their wealth as much as the law permitted. Clauzel prepared lists for Chaudron-Rousseau to purge the municipality, the revolutionary committee, and the popular society. A deputy of the Convention wrote to Chaudron-Rousseau right before Thermidor to commend Clauzel's work in the committee of surveillance of Mirepoix, where 'his presence alone frightens the enemies of the new regime'.[42]

Baby led a detachment of the revolutionary army of the Haute-Garonne into the Ariège at the end of October 1793. He guided soldiers to the high valleys near Tarascon, reputedly infested with aristocrats and priests escaping to Spain. Soldiers climbing into a mountain pass spotted people hiding behind trees. Baby ordered the cannonries to fire, and an innocent peasant boy was killed. Baby consoled his men by claiming that they had fired for the good cause and indemnified the father by levying a tax on the nearest town's four richest residents. The army then obliged the municipality of Vic-Dessos to draw up a list of fanatics and aristocrats. These had to pay for their own transportation to the authorities in Montauban, the rich defraying the cost of the poor. Baby had the fathers and grandparents of soldiers at the front take turns guarding the less dangerous suspects so that, in his words, 'each poor sans-culotte could savour the sweet pleasure of reducing the property of aristocrats to rubble'.[43] The revolutionary soldiers forced the priest of Rabat to disavow everything he had ever told fellow villagers about Christianity and then turned his house over to pillage. Baby obliged the commune of Saurat to write to the Convention, 'that it was renouncing all religious cults, except liberty, reason and philosophy'.[44]

---

41   Quoted from a letter printed in Tournier 1896, pp. 193–5. Arnaud 1904, pp. 417–18.
42   Quoted from a letter printed in Tournier 1896, pp. 184–5. See also Arnaud, 1904, pp. 427–8, 602, 603n; Cazanave 1991, pp. 54–7; Casteras 1891, pp. 271–2.
43   Arnaud 1904, pp. 438–9; Casteras 1891, pp. 122–3, 271, 273–4.
44   Arnaud 1904, pp. 440, 514.

Thermidorian propaganda meant to discredit the militants of the year II may have influenced the histories from which the foregoing account is taken.[45] What is clear is that the heavy-handed policies of Baby and his associates created resentment among local residents. On 17 December 1793, Fabre d'Églantine read to the Convention a letter written to his fellow deputy Pierre Joseph Cambon by the municipality of St.-Girons. The letter complained of the dictatorial conduct of the Convention's agents in the Ariège. The Convention then prepared decrees to arrest Baby and disband his detachment. But Vadier intervened, defended the Convention's agents, and had the decrees suspended.[46]

After Thermidor, Vadier could do nothing to protect Baby from the enmity of local residents. Baby had become such a pariah that the national agent Fauré was dismissed just for waving hello to him in the prison of Foix. Baby wrote to the committee of legislation of the hopelessness of obtaining a fair trial in the Ariège. His plea bought him time until the amnesty of November 1795. Baby left prison to suffer the harassment of the local priests and find his property in ruins. He fled to Paris and asked the Council of Five Hundred for an indemnity. After failing to obtain a hearing, he began spreading imprecations against the Directory and Councils and joined Babeuf's Conspiracy of Equals. Baby took part in the Jacobins' attempt to win over the troops stationed at Grenelle and was arrested again, this time to be executed, in September 1796. In the words of Cobb, 'Baby was not a man made for a life in peaceful times'.[47]

Revolutionaries such as Clauzel and Baby left an indelible impression on succeeding generations. According to Alexis de Tocqueville, 'Revolutionaries of a hitherto unknown breed came on to the scene: men who carried audacity to the point of sheer insanity; who baulked at no innovation and, unchecked by any scruples, acted with an unprecedented ruthlessness'.[48] If they issued from a 'special breed of men', then none was of as pure a race as Michel Courbis, the old regime prosecutor in the seneschal court of Nîmes. He became a municipal councillor in 1791, the executive agent of the district in 1792, and then head of the popular society. Courbis had to flee during the federalist crisis, as the upper classes cracked down on local militants.[49]

But the Mountain's consolidation of power brought Courbis back to Nîmes as mayor and head of the committee of surveillance in the fall of 1793, and

---

45 Baby's exploits as leader of the revolutionary army of the Haute-Garonne in the Ariège are found in the works of Arnaud (1904).
46 Tournier 1896, pp. 99–100.
47 Cobb 1987, p. 221. See also Cobb 1995, p. 34; Arnaud 1904, pp. 555, 555n, 604–5.
48 Tocqueville 1955, p. 157.
49 ADG L3137; Gutherz and Huard 1982, pp. 232–3.

afforded him the opportunity to impose his idea of a revolutionary order on the inhabitants of the region. Courbis seems to have opposed the extremes of economic inequality. He wrote a letter in February 1794 instructing an agent to sell some of his rural property so that he would adhere to 'the current principles, which do not permit a sole individual to have an immensity of terrain'.[50] But most of Courbis's ideas about revolution were repressive. He detained about 300 people in the fall of 1793 until the complaints of his victims' families led the representative Boisset to arrest him and disband the committee of surveillance. Boisset accused the committee of violating liberty and Courbis of becoming a dictator. Courbis believed that Boisset's policy of moderation and his amnesty for federalists were harmful to the Republic. He wrote to a fellow citizen in February 1794 'that the federalists, like the émigrés and the refractory priests, are ferocious beasts and enragés who must be extirpated if we do not wish to perish. They are incurable. It is a combat to the death'.[51]

Many of Nîmes's politically active residents shared Courbis's idea of revolution. The popular society wrote to the Committee of Public Safety of the people's confidence in Courbis and their disapproval of the representative Boisset. The government responded by replacing Boisset with Borie in January 1794. Borie entrusted public security to the committee of surveillance, freed Courbis from prison, and permitted him to become mayor once again in March. Courbis then launched a reign of terror.[52]

Nîmes was one of only five cities granted an autonomous operation of the terror after the Convention brought all suspects to Paris in the spring of 1794. The authorities of the Gard arrested almost 4,000 people in 1793 and the year II, and three quarters of these between March and August 1794 during Courbis's second stint as mayor of Nîmes. They executed 166 people, 0.81 percent of all of the victims of the terror in France. Local revolutionaries targeted former nobles and members of the bourgeoisie more than they did the lower classes. This repression of the upper classes was common to departments such as the Gard that had seen armed resistance to the Republic. Nobles, landowners and clergymen of the region had taken up arms for orthodox Catholicism between 1790 and 1793. The Protestant commercial elite had revolted against the Jacobin Convention in the summer of 1793. The militants of the

---

50   ADG L3137; Fajon 1867, p. 123; Laurent and Gavignaud 1987, pp. 181, 187–8, 190; Gutherz and Huard 1982, pp. 232–3.
51   ADG L152; Laurent and Gavignaud 1987, pp. 181, 187–8.
52   ADG L138; Laurent and Gavignaud 1987, p. 190; Gutherz and Huard 1982, p. 233.

Gard therefore targeted both Protestant and Catholic members of the upper classes. Courbis and his henchmen executed 87 Catholics, 47 Protestants and a Jew.[53]

TABLE 6.1 Percentage of those arrested in the Gard in 1793 and the year II classified by social and professional group

Profession	Percentage of arrested
Nobles	20.4
Ecclesiastics[a]	15.8
Workers[b]	12.7
Farmers	12.1
Artisans/shopkeepers[c]	11.3
Revolutionary officials[d]	8.4
Merchants and manufacturers	6.5
Liberal professionals[e]	5.5
Clerks[f]	5.2
Military officers	3.5

a Priests, canons, monks, nuns, etc.
b Domestics, joiners, workers, dyers, bargemen, etc.
c Shoe repairmen, butchers, tailors, innkeepers, apothecaries, etc.
d Tax collectors, agents of sections, *étapiers*, mayors, presidents of the criminal tribunal, etc.
e Lawyers, notaries, royal attorneys, old regime judges (*conseillers*), engineers, etc.
f Schoolmasters, *gardes des salins*, organists, former tithe collector, etc.

The committee of surveillance, which conducted this repression, consisted of five stocking makers (*faiseurs de bas*), three merchants and manufacturers, a

---

53 The other eight departments of Languedoc saw 1.53 percent of all the executions in France during the terror (Greer 1966, pp. 23–4, 26, 40, 145–7). Le Roy Ladurie and Lewis argue that while patriotic Protestants and merchants fought with Catholic landowners, magistrates, and clergymen for control of the Gard in the first years of the Revolution, the elite of both religions then united against a seemingly murderous liberty, destructive of property and industry in 1792 and 1793. The upper classes of both religions were therefore targets of the terror (Ladurie 1967, pp. 102–3 and Lewis 1978, pp. 75–6). The data in Table 6.1 come from a list compiled by Rouvière 1974, vol. 4, pp. 419–600. About 20 percent of the victims were women. The data in Table 6.2 come from a list found in Fajon 1867, pp. 44–7.

TABLE 6.2 Percentage of those executed in the Gard during the Terror classified by profession

Profession	Percentage of victims
Landlords[a]	13.5
Ecclesiastics[b]	7.5
Workers[c]	13.5
Farmers	3.8
Master craftsmen/shopkeepers[d]	19.5
Government officials[e]	13.5
Wholesale merchants	6.8
Liberal professionals[f]	14.3
Clerks[g]	6
Military officers	.7
Volunteer	.7

a Includes at least five nobles.
b Priests, protestant ministers, *ex-chartreux, frère chartreux*, former abbot.
c Masons, joiners, porters, tanner, *amidonier*, etc.
d Printer, *fayencier*, leather merchant, merchant, silversmith, etc.
e Justices of the peace, president of the departmental directory, former inspector of military convoys, vice-president of a district, district judge, etc.
f Mostly lawyers, but also notaries, an architect, *géometre*, and engineer.
g Includes a master of dance, master of music, maître de l'école, gendarme, etc.

bookbinder, a mechanic, a launderer, and a cloth worker (*apprêteur d'étoffes*). One of its lists of suspects, a page drawn up at the end of April 1794, contained about 100 names from the tenth section of Nîmes. The committee divided the names into two columns, one on the left entitled 'the rich' with many merchants and landlords, and one on the right with many farmers, bakers, merchants, and textile workers. It wrote one of three notations next to each entry: moderate, constitutional monarchist, or aristocrat.[54]

The revolutionary tribunal decided the fate of people appearing on these types of lists. The president of the tribunal was Courbis's brother-in-law, a

54 ADG L189, L3138.

former royal attorney. The other six judges included an auctioneer, a notary, an ex-priest, a silk worker, an apothecary's son, and a well-to-do farmer. It was alleged after Thermidor that the judges would take counsel in Courbis's home, overlooking the law court and town square, before going into session, and return afterwards for dinner and drinks to watch the execution of those they had condemned. Courbis and his guests would then go down to the square and dance a farandole around the guillotine. The allegation must have had some basis, for Courbis claimed in his defence that the guillotine stood next to a liberty tree and that he danced around the tree to set a proper example for the people on the weekly day off of the republican calendar.[55]

3   Thermidor

Courbis and other leaders of the terror took measures to stabilise the price of basic goods like bread and firewood, but did not promote the participation of peasants and wage earners in politics. Their authority came from political networks centred in Paris rather than social movements in the departments. Once the Convention called a halt to the extraordinary policies used to wage all-out war, local militants fell from power without a struggle. Former nobles, federalists and affluent landowners regained office in the fall of 1794 and pushed artisans and shopkeepers out of the political arena.

A few examples demonstrate the trend. André Rech, the defendant of those accused of complicity with émigrés in the affaire des galettes, took over the post of public prosecutor of the Hérault in February 1795. Pierre Montels, a wealthy royal attorney prior to 1789 and a member of Durand's municipality during the federalist revolt, became mayor of Montpellier in March 1795. His administration comprised many wholesale merchants, landlords, notaries, and attorneys. About 65 percent of the municipal officers belonged to the wealthiest class of residents. Resignations and replacements further reduced the number of artisans and shopkeepers in the municipal council over the following three months. The propertied classes of Montpellier and the Hérault then sought to punish the former militants of the revolutionary tribunal and surveillance committee responsible for the affaire des galettes. They would have put the terrorists to death had it not been for the amnesty of the year IV.[56]

---

55   Rouvière 1974, vol. 4, pp. 184–5, 187–8; Pouthas 1934, pp. 152–3, 167; Fajon 1867, pp. 58, 123.
56   Gégot 1984, p. 248; Gégot 1974, vol. 1, p. 218; Duval-Jouve 1974, vol. 2, pp. 238–9; Catalan 1902, pp. 53–4. Data in Table 6.3 come from AN H1/748/292; Duval-Jouve 1974, vol. 2, pp. 120–1, 214.

TABLE 6.3   Percentage of members of the municipal council of Montpellier classified by social and professional group

Professions	January 1791 (based on 33)	October 1793 (based on 31)	February 1795 (based on 40)
Wholesale merchants	36[a]	3	35
Noble judges of the Cour des Comptes, Aides et Finances	12	0	5
Other noblemen	3	0	0
Doctors/architects	15	3	7.5
Royal attorneys and notaries	12	3	15
Landlords	9	0	7.5
Master craftsman/shopkeeper	9	58	22.5
Surgeons	3	10	5
Farmers and gardeners	0	16	0
Stockbroker (*agent de change*)	0	3	2.5
Worker	0	3	0

a   One wholesale merchant, Chaptal, was also a chemist. Another, Jean Allut, was also a landlord.

Landlords and jurists replaced the artisans and shopkeepers in the municipal council of Toulouse after Thermidor. Pierre Roussillou, a wholesale merchant of drapes and a deputy to the Estates General, was the mayor of Toulouse from July to November 1795. He left a bequest of almost 180,000 francs. Jean Joseph Janole was a lawyer in the Parlement, a member of municipal councils in 1791 and 1792, and a judge in the district tribunal during the federalist crisis. He hid during the year II and re-emerged in October 1795 to become the public accuser of the departmental tribunal. He arrested Vadier, the Ariégeois deputy to the Convention, at the end of 1795. Janole and other Thermidorians sponsored a religious revival and encouraged royalist youths to harass local Jacobins.[57]

Nevertheless, merchants, master craftsmen, and shopkeepers regained control of Toulouse when the Directory held elections. The average tax assessment of the municipal councillors between 1795 and 1799 stood at only 45 percent of

---

57   Sentou 1969, pp. 166–7; Nelidoff 1996, pp. 243–4; Schlumberger 1971, pp. 271–2, 277. Data in Table 6.4 come from AN H1/748/134; ADHG L511.

TABLE 6.4 Percentage of members of the municipal council of Toulouse classified by social and professional group

Profession	January 1790 (based on 56)	January 1794 (based on 39)	July 1795 (based on 48)
Jurists[a]	30	5	16
Master craftsmen/shopkeepers	18	28	14.5
Wholesale merchants (négociants)	16	25.5	31
Landlords	12.5	5	10
Liberal professionals[b]	10.5	2.5	4
Merchants (marchands)	3.5	7.5	0
Farmers and gardeners	3.5	5	4
Manufacturers	3.5	2.5	0
Nobles	3.5	0	0
Military officers	3.5	0	0
Workers	2	10	2
Surgeons	0	5	0
Clerks[c]	0	2.5	4

a   Includes lawyers, royal attorneys, judges and notaries.
b   Includes professors, doctors, and public-works contractors/engineers.
c   Appraiser (of metallic money), assessor, master writer.

its level immediately after Thermidor. Even the councillors of the year II had higher tax assessments than did those of the Directory period. Revolutionaries of Toulouse did not claim many victims during the year II and did not create vengeful enemies. Jacobins consequently did not cause much alarm when they won elections after 1795. Toulouse became a revolutionary stronghold under the Directory. Notables did not regain political power until after Napoleon's coup. In 1802, the 600 highest taxpayers of the Haute-Garonne, over 60 percent of whom were landlords, monopolised all levels of the local government.[58]

Socially predominant groups also regained control of the southern Massif central. Delmas, the mayor of the Ardèchois town of Aubenas prior to the year II, reappeared at the end of 1794 and arrested Jacobins for chasing refractory priests, welcoming women into the popular society, opening public schools, and fostering a cult of reason. The same notables who held public office in the Ardèche between 1789 and 1791, including many former nobles, won elections

---

58   Hunt 1984, pp. 159, 169; Schlumberger 1971, pp. 282–3; Bouyoux 1958, pp. 317–18, 325.

during the Directory, as the political climate drifted toward moderate republicanism and monarchism. In Le Puy-en-Velay, capital of the Haute-Loire, the artisans who had run the municipality during the year II lost their posts to lawyers, doctors, landlords, and merchants in March 1795. Quatrefages de Laroquète, a member of the Constituent Assembly, regained a post in the municipal council of Le Vigan in the Gard after having lost the post of mayor to a surgeon during the year II.[59]

Nîmes went through tragic events after Thermidor. Jean Boudon, a bourgeois farmer, club militant, and judge in the revolutionary tribunal, rose to defend Robespierre and Saint-Just when the popular society met on 19 Thermidor. The other members shouted him down and refused to let Courbis speak. Boudon stood up again, shouted, 'I'll die for my country', and shot himself in the head.[60] It was a cry of despair, for the local elite was determined to avenge the torments it had suffered during the year II. Protestant and Catholic bankers, wholesale merchants, and landlords regained control of Nîmes in 1795 and facilitated the work of royalist murder gangs. They allowed a mob to enter the prison and massacre Courbis and two judges of the revolutionary tribunal. The minister of justice wrote to the executive agent of the civil and criminal tribunal of the Gard in March 1796 criticising the local authorities for the violence. 'Nothing has been spared to assure these execrable crimes a scandalous and reprehensible impunity'.[61] The Gard and the Southeast suffered the bloodiest reaction in France after Thermidor. White terrorists, as the reactionaries were known, chose their victims more methodically than had Jacobins and sans-culottes. They killed more people than had their terrorist predecessors of the year II.[62]

4   Making Sense of the Sans-Culottes' Year in Power

Current scholarship on the Year II stresses the revolutionaries' rhetoric of national regeneration and their unprecedented effort to achieve democracy and equality. The revolutionaries assumed that good citizens stated their views openly and that political organising outside of public assemblies could only have nefarious ends. The revolutionaries failed to appreciate the difficulties they faced in seeking to transform their polity and society. They ascribed their

---

59   Jolivet 1980, pp. 553, 555; Riou 1988, pp. 174–6; Bayon-Tollet 1982, pp. 365, 367; Gorlier 1955, p. 236.
60   Lewis 1978, p. 77. See also pp. 79, 85.
61   ADG L3138; Lewis 1978, pp. 79, 85; Gutherz and Huard 1982, p. 240.
62   Cobb 1998, pp. 182, 187–8.

setbacks to the deeds of malevolent plotters and used state power to terrorise suspected enemies.[63]

This explanatory model seems particularly applicable to the governmental assemblies of Paris. It makes sense of the letters written from the Convention by Vadier to his agents in the Ariège applauding their efforts to rid the department of schemers and aristocrats suspected of extinguishing civic virtue and leading the people astray. It also makes sense of the affaire des galettes of Montpellier in which authorities beset by a subsistence crisis executed women and shopkeepers for so-called aristocracy and collusion with émigrés.

Nevertheless, the current scholarship cannot account for most of the radicalism described in this chapter. Anxiety about political organising had little to do with Gélas's desire to subject a noblewoman to the abuse of his revolutionary soldiers or his threats to the municipality of Grenade for failing to acquiesce to their authority. Suspicion of plots does not account for the pleasure Baby and the members of the revolutionary army appear to have taken in humiliating the priests and well-to-do residents of the Ariège.

Certain militants just about corresponded to those denounced by the Thermidorians as '*buveur de sang*'. They seem to have genuinely enjoyed the bloodshed and violence. They seem to have made a conscious effort to promote an image of ferocity and inspire fear in the local population. What the militants had in common was not social class – their numbers were too limited and backgrounds too heterogeneous – but temperament: a desire to conquer power on the local level, cleanse the administration of old regime elements, and fill it solely with patriots. The sans-culottes did not have a coherent programme (the word programme probably is not even applicable to their sundry ideas) and did not think of themselves as a national movement. The only reason they ever came to power in the first place was the Convention's need for allies to enforce divisive policies and fend off the dangers of foreign and civil war in the fall of 1793. The militants usually came to the attention of the Convention as a result of their demeanour, dedication and ability to manipulate assemblies. Their rift with the Convention in 1794 stemmed from irreconcilable visions of revolution. The sans-culottes' militancy disaggregated political authority, while the rulers in Paris sought to centralise it.[64]

Still, the evidence presented in this chapter suggests that the politics of the terror did not come down solely to individual temperaments. The leaders of the terror we have examined were jurists, clerks, landowners, and business-

---

63   For current scholarship, see Furet 1981, pp. 14–15, 26–7; Hunt 1984, pp. 27, 43, 49, 55–6.
64   Cobb 1998, pp. 172, 175, 218, 220–1, 223–4, 227, 238, 240, 242.

men, and the officialdom that followed them consisted of shopkeepers, master craftsmen, merchants, farmers, surgeons and workers. Those who rounded up suspects and partook in the adventures of the revolutionary army came from the petty-bourgeois middling strata.

These militants had shared a hopeless exclusion from the old regime spheres of wealth and privilege. We saw in Chapters 1 and 2 that bishops, seigneurs, office holders, and nobles appropriated the economic surplus of Languedoc and put their power on view in public ceremonies. The monarchy left the impression of a regime given over to private interests and pretentious displays.[65] The Revolution created an opportunity to break with this system, and to open meaningful responsibilities and prominent positions to commoners. The first years of Revolution, however, only opened the government to notables. Wealthy merchants, lawyers, landowners and former nobles had the education, wealth and connections to lead assemblies and carry elections. After the initial excitement of Revolution, the notables sent the petty-bourgeois middling types back to their routine lives as bookkeepers, engineers, postal clerks, and schoolteachers.

Frustration with the failure of the Revolution to open positions to wider spheres of the population turned into anxiety amid war and inflation in 1792 and 1793. Local administrators were reluctant to fix prices, requisition grain, and arm the populace. The well-to-do classes saw such policies as a threat to property and order. They allowed inflation to threaten the modest economic status that merchants, artisans, and shopkeepers had achieved. The authorities seemed willing to allow the petty-bourgeois middling strata to sink into the mass of peasants, day labourers, and indigents. They seemed willing to allow foreign monarchies to dash all the hopes the Revolution had raised.

Ardent expressions of revolutionary commitment, then, had a basis in social conditions. Many merchants, clerks, surgeons, farmers, and workers coveted positions of public responsibility. When they sensed that the local notables aimed not only to keep them subordinate, but also to allow their modest capital to dissipate and the Revolution to end, then their hopes for a better life turned sullen. In Nantes, the lawsuits and counter-litigation arising out of the atrocities committed during the terror evince a virulent and pathological political language. The officials accused one another of debauchery, sexual perversity, and unspeakable acts of cruelty.[66]

---

65   Shovlin 2000, pp. 577–606.
66   Baczko 1994, pp. 136, 162.

In the departments of old regime Languedoc, revolutionary militants exalted the new regime that permitted them to participate for the first time in government, and they inflicted fantastic punishments on anyone suspected of sympathising with the old regime that had excluded them. In the Haute-Garonne, judges and clerks such as Hugueny and Blanchard won a following by belligerently flouting the religious practices of the old regime. A bankrupt businessman like Clauzel found myrmidons to assist him in bullying the bishop of Mirepoix. Artisans and shopkeepers joined the jurist Courbis in celebrating a public campaign of executions against landlords, liberal professionals, and moderate officials of the Gard. Such militancy can be read as the obverse corollary of the public ceremonies of the old regime. Of course, not everyone excluded from the positions of authority of the monarchy went on to become a terrorist. But one cannot account for the demeanor of the ones who did without taking the old regime into consideration.

The revolutionary militants could not translate such class anger into a political program. Members of the petty-bourgeois middling strata had no wish to mobilise the urban and rural masses for the redistribution of property. They actually arrested many women, farmers, artisans, and workers on suspicions of hoarding and sympathy for the monarchy. Had the pillage of tax offices, the raids on markets, and the disrespect for property, so widespread in the first years of the Revolution, continued into 1793, then the jurists, merchants, and landowners, who directed the terror, probably would not have spoken out so stridently against inequality. Thus, when members of the Convention decided that the perilous circumstances of 1793 had passed, they had no trouble shoving the terrorists off the political stage, for the terrorists had not built a social movement around their positions in the revolutionary government of the former province of Languedoc.

Conclusion

The foregoing story of popular uprisings and terror shows that the upper classes of Languedoc, as in France as a whole, proved incapable of controlling the political evolution of the country. The nobility did not take responsibility for defending the interests of property owners. In the first years of the Revolution, many nobles of Toulouse, Nîmes, and the southern Massif central tried to uphold the prerogatives of the church and king. Likewise, the liberal nobles, wealthy merchants, jurists, and property owners, who dominated local government between 1790 and 1793, did not instill confidence in their will to mobilise men and resources against economic collapse and the foreign monarchies threatening the Revolution. When the Convention began to conscript the population, requisition grain, and control prices in the summer of 1793, the authorities of all nine departments of the former province of Languedoc, except the Ariège, came out in opposition.

The efforts of royalists, in the first years of the Revolution, to maintain the authority of throne and altar cast a pall over provincial society. Voters removed nobles and clergymen of the Haute-Garonne, the Gard, and the southern Massif central from office in the first years of the Revolution. In 1792, militants encouraged peasants to pillage châteaux in the areas of the Ardèche, Gard and Ariège, where royalists organised against the Revolution. Between the fall of 1793 and the first half of 1794, during Languedoc's interval of popular government, revolutionaries inflicted humiliating punishments on former nobles, priests, and well-to-do townspeople suspected of egotism and sympathy for the monarchy. The militants persecuted proportionally more former nobles, clergymen, and government officials than they did other social groups.

Why did the nobles and propertied classes of the Third Estate first lose control over local politics and then become the enemy of the revolutionaries? The reflections of Montesquieu and Tocqueville suggest that the answer is to be found in the politics and society of the old regime. They argued that monarchy, as a form of government, encouraged the nobles to set themselves apart as an order with distinctive privileges and interests. Montesquieu maintained that monarchy encouraged the nobles to seek official preferments and titles rather than to practice civic virtue. Codes of honour, the very principles of monarchical government, inspired the nobles to distinguish themselves from commoners through the pursuit of glory and applause. Tocqueville held that the monarchy's centralisation of power broke down customary solidarities and created a country of self-seeking individuals indifferent to the public good. For the nobles, royal centralisation led to 'the growth of all the vices to which they

[were] congenitally prone and, indeed incite[d] them to go still further on the way to which their natural bent incline[d] them'.[1]

Tocqueville argued that whereas the English gentry paid taxes, improved its landholdings, and ran the administration and government, French nobles, in exchange for privileges, allowed the king to build an independent administration. The French nobility sold its property to commoners and became an unproductive caste prizing its titles above all else.[2] Tocqueville no doubt exaggerated these trends. Together with bourgeois proprietors, nobles owned most of the land of Languedoc. They asserted control over as many parcels of land as they could in order to take advantage of the rising agricultural prices of the eighteenth century.

Though Tocqueville did not perceive the nobles' inclination to seek profit, he did provide an insightful analysis of their relationship to the national economy. Like other landlords residing in the towns, the nobles turned their properties over to the peasantry in exploitative sharecropping agreements. The dense and growing population of peasants, with parcels of land too small to assure their livelihood and absorb all of the labour power of their family members, encouraged property owners to seek economic gain from the relatively low cost of human energy. Proprietors did not have to invest in pasture, fertiliser, fodder crops, and farm animals, because they could count on profits from the peasantry's tendency to intensify its labour and compete for leases and employment. Similarly, merchants obtained stable returns from putting textile production out to peasant households anxious to gain value from their family members' capacity to work and maintain their standard of living. Languedocian merchants invested the returns in venal offices, titles, annuities, seigneurial domains and land. They did not accumulate capital or sustain economic development.

To be brief, rather than constructively develop a common project to encompass the aspirations of rural inhabitants, the upper classes instead drew their economic surpluses to the towns. Instead of winning the social clout accruing to leaders of a common economic destiny, the nobles caused resentment by taking the fruits of the peasants' labour. Contrary to the impression of his contemporaries, Tocqueville stated that peasant landownership was a fact of the old regime rather than a result of the Revolution. Yet the peasants did not enjoy undisturbed tenure of their parcels of land. They were burdened by a stratum of parasitic seigneurs residing in the towns. The peasants therefore regarded the

---

1 Tocqueville 1955, p. xiii; Montesquieu 1949, vol. 1, pp. 23–5, 29–32.
2 Tocqueville 1955, pp. 26–7, 70, 79–81, 83, 98–9, 123.

nobles as enemies rather than benefactors, and rose up to destroy their privileges when the circumstances permitted in 1789.[3]

My point is that the dense population of smallholders encouraged those enjoying a certain degree of wealth to invest in the privileges and prerogatives embedded in the laws and institutions of the old regime rather than in agrarian and manufacturing enterprises. Privileges and prerogatives permitted the upper classes to benefit from the rising prices and economic growth of the eighteenth century. Peasant sharecroppers and smallholders increased the production of grain for the market in the Toulousain and Lauragais. They cleared lands for vineyards in Mediterranean Languedoc and developed sericulture in the region of Nîmes and the southern Massif central. Peasants and rural artisans churned out textiles for merchants of Carcassonne, Montpellier, and Nîmes. Landlords used seigneurial prerogatives to assert rights to the output of the newly cleared lands, to levy resources on peasant production, and to monopolise lucrative forest products. Seigneurs drew on their influence in the judiciary to obtain advantages during grape harvests, eliminate use-rights on their fields, and lift restrictions on the grain trade.

The laws and institutions of the monarchy afforded the upper classes further means of obtaining wealth beyond this domination of landed property. Nobles and other affluent landowners invested in titles, tax farms, venal offices, and government bonds. These components of the old regime channelled much of the wealth of Languedoc into the private fortunes of the elite. Of course, many venal offices did not generate much revenue for their owners. Judgeships were investments in an honourable profession. Military commands offered the opportunity to win honour defending the realm and overseeing public order. Municipal councils permitted local elites to enjoy prominent ranks in the official ceremonies attended by the people.

Tocqueville argued that the nobles set great store by these types of privileges. Exclusive rights and honours were the only things that set them apart from other men of property. Outward signs of rank gave meaning to the noble order.[4] Economic gain did not provide much satisfaction without a corresponding advancement through the official ranks of the monarchy. As nobles benefited from the economic growth of the eighteenth century, they used their seigneuries, judgeships, and the Estates of Languedoc to parade their standing in public events and enforce formal rituals in honour of the church and the king. The nobility relied on the absolutist state for wealth and status.

---

3 Tocqueville 1955, pp. 26, 31, 70, 83, 123, 203–4.
4 Tocqueville 1955, pp. 78, 81, 89.

CONCLUSION

I have argued in this book that the political system of the old regime, a system of royal sovereignty conferring governmental honours to nobles and facilitating their accumulation of wealth, shaped the conflicts of the 1780s and 1790s. The argument owes a great deal to Tocqueville's insight that nobles preserved a sense of their liberty even though they allowed the king to centralise power. They served the king out of honour and affection, not constraint.[5] But in the eighteenth century, it became nearly impossible for the nobles to serve the king as they would have liked. The king needed revenue to counter England's escalation of the imperial rivalry in North America, the Caribbean, India, and Europe. The king's efforts to draw additional revenue from the economy left less leeway for the nobility to serve in an honourable and affectionate manner.

Since the 1990s, scholars have analysed the political culture and language of the old regime to explain the opposition to royal absolutism that emerged in the second half of the eighteenth century. Historians have shown that the king's magistrates resisted his decrees after 1750 by invoking concepts such as the inviolability of the law and the sovereignty of the nation. Their opposition to royal edicts contributed to a sea change in political culture and discourse. A barometer of the change was the multiplication of professional writers and the proliferation of political literature. By the last decades of the old regime, writers appealed to 'public opinion' for the legitimacy of their views. Even royal ministers published decrees and pamphlets aimed at winning the reading public to their side. They unintentionally helped establish the public as the legitimate judge of national issues. The cultural and linguistic transfer of sovereignty from the king to the nation set the Revolution in motion.[6]

This scholarship sheds light on political developments in Languedoc. The language and culture of the period shaped the perspectives of policymakers. The king and his ministers sought to improve the provincial administration and augment the fiscal take by broadening participation in public affairs. Rulings of the royal council stripped lords of seigneurial rights so as to encourage industrious peasants to participate in local government. The crown modified town councils to extend administrative responsibility to urban residents. The king and his ministers sought the approval of public opinion to diminish the tax exemptions of the privileged classes.

But the political language and culture of the period proved inimical to policies formulated by a sovereign monarch. Many nobles would relinquish their privileges to a constitutional and representative government, not to arbit-

---

5 Tocqueville 1955, pp. 119–20.
6 For a discussion of this scholarship see pp. xxx–xxx of the introduction.

rary regime. In 1788 and 1789, the nobility rallied a broad movement of clergymen, townspeople, and well-to-do villagers to make the Estates of Languedoc representative. Freely elected provincial estates would inhibit the coercive tendencies of the regime.

My argument is that there was a social basis to this revolutionary crisis. Royal policies called into question the rights of lordship and office holding on which the nobility relied for wealth, status, and careers. The crown's desperate search for credit led it to an archaic and aristocratic institution, the Estates of Languedoc, to raise funds for the American War of Independence. In the 1770s and 1780s, the crown raised more loans through the Estates of Languedoc than it did through any other institution apart from the Hôtel de Ville of Paris. The monarchy collaborated ever more closely with the bishops, barons, and agents of the Estates in the administration of Languedocian resources. The monarchy extended the Estates' jurisdiction to the affairs traditionally regulated by lords and office holders. The majority of provincial nobles saw this policy as an illegitimate and coercive infringement of their distinctions, immunities, and privileges.

Thus financial exigencies led the crown to close off avenues for public service, at the same time as its reformers sought to involve wider strata of the population in the administration of the provinces. Instead of winning support from public opinion, the crown's policies alienated its traditional supporters. The transfer of administrative jurisdiction over towns and villages from office holders and seigneurs to the oligarchs of the provincial estates threatened the vital interests of the greater part of the provincial nobility. The king's subjects acquired ideas for constitutional renovation and discourses for political participation from the culture of the period. But it is unlikely that the subjects would have turned the culture and discourses against the regime had the nobles not faced threats to their positions in the seigneurial regime and royal administration.

Tocqueville believed that the nobles' idea of liberty prepared them to resist despotism but not to create a stable government afterward. They were unable to shape public opinion, because their idea of liberty did not join them to other royal subjects in common interests. Their privileges caused resentment.[7] Lords and magistrates repeatedly clashed with the intendant and the Estates of Languedoc in the 1770s and 1780s over exclusive rights to seigneuries, municipal magistracies, venal offices and tax privileges, which burdened the rest of the population. It was therefore difficult for the nobles to convince common

---

7 Tocqueville 1955, pp. 142, 203–4.

subjects that they would defend the interests of society as a whole. When the breakdown of royal authority in 1789 freed common subjects from the obligation to respect the nobility's prerogatives and privileges, they struck out on their own path and came to see the nobility as the enemy.

The path taken by the revolutionaries led straight to the levers of state power. According to Tocqueville, the monarchy had so enthralled the French with its power that the revolutionaries could hardly conceive of a liberal polity. They assumed that the state should have an officialdom and bureaucracy with unlimited power to mould the lives of the citizenry.[8] In 1788 and 1789, the leaders of the third estate of every constituency and town of Languedoc contested the nobles' privileged access to public office. Priests denounced the bishops' control over the wealth and authority of the clergy. Between 1791 and 1793, merchants, artisans, farmers and workers of Toulouse, Nîmes, and the Ariège sought to participate in political affairs. The upper classes' reluctance to share governmental responsibility during the emergencies of foreign invasion and economic collapse unleashed ten months of terror across the region in 1793 and 1794.[9]

Tocqueville's analysis, then, helps explain why the urban middle classes fought against the nobility to obtain state power. Yet it does not fully explain the revolutionary impulse. François Furet argued that for all of the lucidity of Tocqueville's analysis, it does not account for the nobility's evolution as a class. Tocqueville conceived of classes in static terms. He thought the nobles' power was coterminous with their autonomous feudal governance of the countryside. Tocqueville assumed that as the crown replaced the nobility as the sovereign between the fifteenth and seventeenth centuries, the nobility must have declined as a class. Furet argued that Tocqueville was unable to notice the nobles' integration into the power structures of the monarchy through appointments to key positions such as the intendancies and through the purchase of venal offices.[10]

Montesquieu, by contrast, believed that monarchical government could not exist without the nobility. Monarchy presupposed intermediate powers, such as venal offices, seigneurial jurisdictions, ecclesiastical authorities, and respected judges. Montesquieu argued that monarchs could not rule effectively without them. Princes seeking to free their rule from the intermediate powers laid the basis for despotism or popular government. And since despotism did

---

8   Tocqueville 1955, pp. 57, 60, 167.
9   Edward Berenson draws out this aspect of Tocqueville's theory, highlighting the influence of undivided sovereignty on the political conceptions of revolutionaries (Berenson 1995).
10   Furet 1981, pp. 144, 155.

not have a strong nobility to lead the people, it was prone to sedition, extremism, social disarray, and revolution.[11]

In sum, Montesquieu argued that kings had to come to terms with the feudal past to rule effectively. Recent research on the absolutist state substantiates this argument. David Parker shows that Louis XIV sponsored a revival of feudal law. Royal jurists uncovered precedents for the king to assert suzerainty over all of the lands of the realm. Louis XIV brandished his right of eminent domain to force the nobility to pay for exemptions from his seigneurial rights. He gave the nobles a lesson in feudal law, which they used to enforce rights over peasant communities during the eighteenth century. William Beik's research on Languedoc shows that Louis XIV integrated nobles into his project of state building by coordinating their vested interests. Louis XIV assured bishops and barons control over the Estates of Languedoc and less lofty nobles control over town governments, seigneuries, and other institutions of the feudal past. He sold hundreds, perhaps thousands, of venal offices to the province's wealthy subjects. Though venality of office post-dated feudalism, it confirmed the same principle: private ownership over portions of public authority.[12] As Montesquieu discerned, nobles enjoyed real power. It was not the independent military power of the feudal period, but an intermediate power inscribed in the laws and customs of the monarchy, and upheld by its forces of order.[13]

The monarchy, then, sustained a profoundly traditional order, steeped in privilege and hierarchy. It prevented public opinion from accumulating the innovative power ascribed to it by Jürgen Habermas. Public discussion of the concerns of townspeople, Habermas maintains, developed outside of the constraints of royal authority in the press, cafés, academies, and literary societies of the eighteenth century. These institutions generated a public sphere of rational critical debate, a public opinion, which gained legitimacy at the expense of royal absolutism.[14] In Languedoc, many nobles recognised the legitimacy of public opinion. Like other educated elites, they believed that public servants should hold office by election rather than by right. Nobles joined in patriotic festivities to celebrate the fall of royal absolutism in the summer of 1789. They won elections to lead national guards and administrations in most parts of Languedoc in 1789 and 1790. They had gained practical experience of government during the old regime, and property owners therefore looked to them for

---

11   Montesquieu 1949, vol. 1, pp. 15–18, 55–6.
12   Blaufarb 2016, pp. 2, 9–10, 50, 151.
13   Parker 200, pp. 60–96; Beik 1985, pp. 13, 15, 29, 31, 67–8, 140, 335–6.
14   Habermas 1989, pp. 54, 84, 86–7.

leadership, as peasants and artisans ransacked châteaux, resisted taxation, and showed general disregard for the law.

Nevertheless, an irreducible stratum of the nobility and clergy did not recognise the legitimacy of public opinion and did not relinquish the rights it had enjoyed under the monarchy. Abbots, bishops, seigneurs and magistrates of Toulouse, Nîmes and the southern Massif central recoiled before the prospect of collaborating as equals with well-to-do Protestants and commoners in political assemblies. They did not respect elected officials whom they had long seen as inferiors. These nobles and clergymen came out in favour of the exclusive prerogatives of the king and Catholicism. Many of them took up arms in the Gard, Lozère, Ardèche, and Haute-Loire between 1790 and 1793. Only force could vanquish these elites. The use of force broke down rational critical debate and paved the way for its disappearance in the lawlessness, repression, and terror of 1793 and 1794.

Furet contended that a proper analysis of revolutionary politics must put aside the social and economic context. He argued that the collapse of royal authority undid the social moorings of politics and made ideology the arbiter of power. Once the ideology of equality and pure democracy filled the political space left by the collapse of royal authiroty, the Revolution proceeded to its tragic dénouement in the terror. Jacobins believed that the people could only obtain liberty and equality after vanquishing resistance. They therefore imagined that nobles, or anyone else who held office, plotted against the people.[15] Scholars sympathetic to this argument could find evidence to support it in this book. Ideology prompted the deputies of the Convention and their local commissioners to try to cleanse the departments of old regime Languedoc of priests and moderates suspected of inhibiting the emergence of a revolutionary culture.

Yet ideology was not the sole cause of radicalisation. When militants of 1793 and 1794 accused jurists, clergymen, former nobles, and wealthy merchants of aristocracy and monarchism, they drew on specific memories. The seigneurial regime, the local judiciary, the tax farms, and the provincial estates had allowed the upper classes to lay claim to economic resources. Royal institutions permitted seigneurs, magistrates, and bishops to wield power in the king's name and display their rank in public ceremonies. In 1792 and 1793, townspeople did not really believe that these potentates continued to run the government. Rather, they associated the revolutionary elite's reluctance to extend political participation beyond the well-to-do, and its reluctance to adopt measures to fend off

---

15   Furet 1981, pp. 18, 22, 24–6, 36–7, 51, 54, 56, 70.

royalist armies and economic hardship, with the governance they knew from the old regime. Master craftsmen, merchants, farmers, and workers identified the revolutionary elite of 1790–93 with the self-seeking pursuit of distinction characteristic of monarchy. Revolutionary militants punished anyone suspected of trying to monopolise public office and turn a profit on economic difficulties.

The peasants also longed to lay the old regime to rest. They resisted taxation and destroyed official registers and fiscal bureaus, as public authority crumbled in 1789. Revolutionaries had to use force to achieve the acceptance of a new governmental edifice. There has not been much research on the popular resistance to taxation in the 1790s. Historians focus on the frustrations with seigneurial rights and tax privileges. They generally assume that peasants embraced, or at least tolerated, the state and that they acted to abolish anachronistic inequalities in civil society. For Tocqueville, the peasant revolts precipitated a sudden advance toward modern society's equality of conditions. They completed the long process initiated by the monarchy of eroding the nobility's privileges and prerogatives. Georges Lefebvre maintained that the nobles carried out an 'aristocratic reaction' to recover the rights they had lost to the establishment of the absolutist state in the seventeenth century. Peasant revolts brought this reaction to an abrupt end. They destroyed retrograde privileges and laid the groundwork for modern class relations based on property.[16]

The grievances and actions of the peasants of Languedoc belie this reading of the state as a neutral, modernising power, which steamrolled the particular rights of the old regime. Rather, as this book has made clear, the absolutist state absorbed the elites of all three estates into its governing structures, permitting them to benefit from the tax collection. The peasants' determined resistance to taxation in the Haute-Garonne and Aude in 1789 and 1790, and in the Haute-Loire throughout the revolutionary decade, seems reasonable when one bears in mind the social and political relations of the period.

The peasants' resistance to taxation did not gain any support among the revolutionary authorities. Legislators recast the entire administration, expanding the number of posts and opening state service to hundreds of thousands of merchants, jurists, and landowners. Much of the bourgeoisie obtained a stake in the state. The seigneurial regime concerned a fraction of the upper classes, which became increasingly identified with counterrevolution, while taxation, the lifeblood of a strong state, concerned all who invested in state bonds, aspired to government careers, and had property to defend. Well-to-do

---

16   Tocqueville 1955, pp. 26–7, 29–30, 79, 121; Lefebvre 1947, pp. 131–51.

townspeople believed that constitutional government would offer opportunity to men of education and talent. They thought that popular resistance to taxation stemmed from ignorance and self-interest. Revolutionary leaders saw their project through this class-tainted lens. They allowed anti-seigneurial revolts to intimidate suspected opponents of the Revolution but dealt with violations of tax laws by invading villages, billeting troops in homes, and sending peasants and artisans to the gallows.

The Revolution no doubt improved the peasants' lives. Research on the department of Puy-de-Dome in central France shows that the fiscal system established during the Revolution maintained inequalities yet constituted a significant improvement over the old regime. Townspeople continued to pass an inordinate share of the burden onto the countryside, especially its poor regions, yet reduced iniquities in the allotment of taxes among village landowners. Legislators obliged large proprietors to pay taxes and granted the poor a measure of relief. David Andress argues that the abolition of seigneurial authority lessened the burdens weighing on the peasantry. The average lifespan of the French increased from 30 to 40 years, and the share of children reaching age 15 increased from half to two thirds, in the generation after 1790. These gains did not result solely from medical improvement, for no comparable gains were registered in other countries during the same period. The peasantry unanimously supported the abolition of the seigneurial regime. The rebels of the Vendée, for instance, opposed conscription and the persecution of their religious leaders, but had no desire to restore lordly rights.[17]

Whether the Revolution paved the way for gains in agricultural productivity is another matter. Roger Price and Peter Jones argue that agricultural capitalism emerged slowly. The peasants continued to produce for domestic consumption and local markets well into the nineteenth century. Methods of cultivation in most parts of the country resembled those of the seventeenth and eighteenth centuries. Jean-Laurent Rosenthal argues that the abolition of seigneurial privileges established absolute property in the place of private rights of eminent domain and thus brought a measure of calculability to agrarian ventures. The reform of legal codes and the establishment of an expeditious judiciary did away with interminable lawsuits and permitted proprietors to go forward with profitable drainage projects. These improvements began to bear fruit after 1860. George Grantham's research advances a different chronology of agricultural improvement. Basing his calculations on the growth of the number of agricultural constructions in the first half of the nineteenth century, Grantham

---

17 Schnerb 1933, pp. 555–6, 562; Andress 2004, pp. 245–6, 256–7.

argues that buoyant demand from the towns prompted farmers to invest in agriculture, augment productivity and accumulate capital. After these decades of growth, the sharp decline in world market prices after 1870 led to a decline in rural investment.[18]

Grantham's evidence, however, is just as indicative of the growth of the rural population as it is of the productivity of agriculture. The research of Emmanuel Le Roy Ladurie on the cadastres of Languedoc shows that the rural population continued to grow all the way up until 1870. It seems logical that the growing number of rural households accounts for the growing number of agricultural buildings. Moreover, Grantham uses a low figure of about eight million workers in his calculation of agricultural productivity, whereas the actual rural population amounted to nearly 28 million. Many of these millions worked in agriculture part time on small plots, in family sharecropping ventures, in breaks from textile manufacturing, and in other irregular intervals. Adding these labourers would lower the estimates of agricultural productivity.[19]

Lastly, Grantham includes land clearances in his estimate of the capital stock. Historians have long interpreted the farming of hardscrabble as evidence of the peasants' efforts to extract more income from the land rather than of investment in agriculture. The peasants brought hillsides, scrublands, and commons under cultivation to obtain revenue from cash crops such as vines. They introduced subsistence crops such as maize, potatoes, and chestnut trees, which gave them the security to obtain revenue selling wheat and silk on the market. These innovations expanded the economy.[20]

Yet they did not transform the technical aspects of farming. Across France, crop yields fluctuated within a limited range from 1700 until well into the nineteenth century without ever breaking through to an advanced phase of growth. Land clearances and new crops augmented output but did not develop the economy. A population's standard of living improves when it obtains more income from its exertions. A close look at the economic lines to which the peasants of eighteenth-century Languedoc were attracted – vines, sericulture, maize, etc. – reveals that they all required intensive work. The peasants become involved in the lines in which their reserves of family labour gave them an advantage. Yet they did not thereby obtain greater returns for their time working, improve their standard of living, or develop the economy. Moreover, all the drudgery

---

18 Price 1981, pp. 42–92; Jones 1988, pp. 257–8; Rosenthal 1992, pp. 17–18, 83, 87–9, 94–6, 133–5, 173; Grantham 1996, pp. 41, 52–7.
19 Le Roy Ladurie 1974, pp. 5, 247, 309, 311.
20 Grantham 1996, pp. 49, 52–3, 56. For Grantham's figures on the agricultural workforce (Marchand and Thélot 1997, pp. 31, 174, 178).

involved in land clearances undermined the ecological balance of the husbandry. Woods, bushes, and greenery on the hillsides retained water and kept the temperature above freezing. Once the peasantry cleared this vegetation away, vines and olive trees were recurrently wiped out by frosts, and entire harvests by rainstorms. The prefect of the Aude wrote in 1818 that local hillsides had been left without wood, soil, pasture, or water, and had become totally unsuited to agriculture.[21]

Property rights and land clearances thus did not propel the economy to higher levels of productivity. Jean Meuvret argues that fear of dearth formed the basis of the rural economy. Peasants planted grains on all types of soils all over the realm. Languedoc saw an expansion of polyculture – including additional arable, sericulture, potatoes, maize, vineyards, chestnuts and cottage textile production – from 1730 or 1740 until about the end of the 1800s. Such extensive farming did not increase the standard of living of rural inhabitants. The keys to development in the region between Albi, Toulouse and Carcassonne in which the soil and topography were suited to the latest forms of husbandry were the reduction of the cultivated surface, the extension of pasture, the farming of fodder crops, and the replacement of human energy with animals. Elsewhere, the keys were the abandonment of arable in favour of specialisation in lines such as viticulture. The rural population slowly began to specialise in this way between the 1840s and 1860s, during the belle époque and the 1920s. When family farmers began to make more rational use of the rural geography in the 1960s, France emerged as one of the leading agricultural producers on the planet. Family farms provided the motor for the economic take-off, which made France an industrial power under de Gaulle and Pompidou.[22]

Although the Revolution did not drastically alter the rural economy, it did strengthen the state. The Constituent Assembly increased levels of taxation in many parts of the country, and successive regimes imposed heavy fiscal burdens to finance the revolutionary wars. Donald Sutherland argues that if one includes under the rubric of feudalism all of the levies imposed by instances of public authority, whether lords or the state, then one discovers an increase of feudal exactions during the Revolution. Tax rates did not increase all that much in some regions such as Mayenne and the area around Dunkirk, but doubled

---

21   Morineau 1971, pp. 61, 63, 70, 86, 321; McPhee 1999, pp. 121, 132–3, 144–5, 175–6. For the economic limitations of land clearances and labour-intensive farming see Miller 2009, pp. 1–30 and Miller 2004, pp. 1–17. For a similar type of labour-intensive, ecologically damaging sort of economic growth in China see Brenner and Isett 2002, pp. 609–62.
22   Meuvret 1987, vol. 2, pp. 11, 36–8, 168–9, 206–8, 215; Perry and Girard 2002, pp. 226–7; Audisio 1993, p. 16; Wylie 1974, pp. 360–70; Miller 2019.

in upper Normandy and upper Maine, and grew by over half in Île-de-France. Tax rates generally grew by staggering amounts between the 1790s and 1800s. 'If the weight of an energetic fiscality overwhelmed what benefits there were to the abolition of feudal dues and the tithe – that is, if feudalism was indeed nationalised' then, Sutherland calculates, the peasantry actually yielded more revenue to public authorities as a result of the Revolution.[23]

The Restoration and the July Monarchy received more tax revenue than had the Napoleonic regime on account of the overall growth of the economy. State budgets grew substantially, while actual rates of taxation diminished. The regimes of the nineteenth century continued the long-drawn-out process of writing cadastres for an equitable distribution of taxes. They also reduced the number of civil servants in the fiscal bureaucracies. But in spite of these reforms, the French state still maintained a comparatively iniquitous tax system and employed a far larger proportion of civil servants than did its British or American counterparts. The bureaucracy grew by leaps and bounds in the half century following the Revolution.[24]

After Napoleon III's coup put an end to the Revolutions of 1848, Karl Marx realised that the Revolution of 1789 had not established a totally modern and liberal state. The nineteenth-century French state was more than just a guardian of economic liberty and property. Marx developed this idea toward the end of *The Eighteenth Brumaire*.

> The executive power with its enormous bureaucratic and military organisation, with its ingenious state machinery, embracing wide strata, with a host of officials numbering half a million, besides an army of another half million, this appalling parasitic body, which enmeshes the body of French society like a net and chokes all its pores, sprang up in the days of the absolute monarchy ... The seigneurial privileges of the landowners and the towns became transformed into so many attributes of state power, the feudal dignitaries into paid officials and the motley pattern of conflicting medieval plenary powers into the regulated plan of a state authority whose work is divided and centralized as in a factory.[25]

Marx argued that the state drew its sustenance from the smallholding peasantry. The material reproduction of rural households and the inadequacy of the transportation network divided the countryside into independent and isolated

---

23   Sutherland 2002, p. 11. See also pp. 3, 7, 10, 13 and Andress 2004, pp. 137, 139, 244.
24   Marion 1927–31, vol. 5, 14–15, 21, 110–12, 229–30.
25   Marx 1963, pp. 121–2.

families. The peasants were incapable of uniting in resistance to the state despite all they had in common. They stagnated economically and intellectually. 'The great mass of the French nation is formed by the simple addition of like entities, much as a sack of potatoes consists of a lot of potatoes huddled into a sack'.[26]

Edward Berenson shows that Marx's verdict on the peasants was not entirely correct. Marx ignored their ability to innovate and increase production, their involvement in markets, and the variety of their productive activities.[27] Marx did not mention the challenge they mounted to the parasitic state in the Revolution of 1789. Peasants destroyed the seigneurial regime in thousands of uprisings in many parts of France between 1789 and 1793. The destruction of the seigneurial regime altered the nature of political authority, making it less personal and more abstract. Of course, the prevalence of sharecropping in the nineteenth century maintained a direct and personal exploitation of the rural masses. Yet it was worlds away from its old regime complement of lordship. Seigneurs had had the legal right to choose village leaders, preside over village assemblies, receive pledges of loyalty, and display their eminence in religious ceremonies. In destroying the seigneurial regime, the peasantry laid the basis for a uniform code of laws, which eliminated feudal customs and attitudes, and disseminated new ways of thinking.

Thus, as Lynn Hunt argues, the Revolution had a far greater effect on politics than it did on the economy and social structure. The revolutionaries bequeathed to future generations the belief that political engagement could regenerate government and society. They brought the ideologies of liberalism, conservatism, republicanism, and even proto-socialism into the political arena as agents of transformation. The peasant revolts played a role in extending this belief in politics to wide strata of the population. They destroyed the private rights to public authority belonging to seigneurs, clergymen and municipal oligarchies, and turned the people's dealings with government into a general affair involving the national state. The peasant revolts thereby made ideology accessible to portions of the citizenry that had long thought about politics in local and personal terms. Rural inhabitants began to take stock of economic and political structures, and the means of transforming them. During the Second Republic, the political perspective of large portions of the peasantry extended beyond the village. The peasants of many departments embraced democratic socialism and resisted Napoleon III's coup.[28]

26   Marx 1963, pp. 123–4.
27   Berenson 1987, pp. 213–29.
28   Hunt 1984, pp. 12–13, 212–13, 221; Margadant 1979, pp. 11–28, 138–61.

Marx's negative assessment of peasant politics seems far more applicable to 1789 than to 1848. The absolutist system did not prepare the peasants to think about politics in anything but personal and local terms. Peasants displayed a close perception of the way in which local landlords, often office holders in the financial system, imposed burdens on the poor and weak. But they did not display a capacity to organise themselves and impose their interests on the nation as a whole. The peasant uprisings petered out at the end of 1792. Former nobles and other large landowners eventually re-established order, respect for property, and their control over the state. By the end of the revolutionary decade, the state collected more revenue than had the monarchy, and collected it more promptly. The state emerged from the maelstrom of revolution stronger and more bureaucratic than it had ever been under the absolute monarchy.

Appendix

The 73 assertions of lordly rights referred to on page xxx and Table 1.2 on page xxx listing rulings favourable to lords were tabulated from incidents found in the following sources: Archives Nationales H1/748/177, H1/748/178, H1/748/179, H1/748/180, H1/940, H1/942/2, H1/1054, H1/1063; H1/1105; Archives Départementales de l'Hérault B9973, C458, C959, C2002, C2340, C2919, C6724; C6726, C6802, C6870, C6879, C6887; Archives Départementales de l'Aude 5 C 9; Archives Départementales du Gard C1194, C1197, C1198, C1199; C1200; Archives Départementales de la Haute-Garonne B1816, B1817, B1859, B1866, B1893, C2161; Archives Départementales du Tarn B601, B705; Archives Municipales de Toulouse AA312; Larguier 1989, pp. 368–70; Amanieu 1959, pp. 146, 148, 176–7; Arnaud 1904, pp. 34–5, 35n., 131–3; Bastier 1975, pp. 56–7, 253; Bernard 1971, p. 132; Bonnet 1988, p. 300; Bonnet and Marquié 1980, p. 72; Borrel 1944–46, pp. 186–7; Bru 1989, p. 17; Castan 1980a, pp. 69, 78–80, 154; Castan 1980, pp. 89, 95; Castan 1982, p. 16; Cazanave 1991, pp. 47–8; Contrasty 1990, pp. 219, 241; Delouvrier 1990, p. 222; Delouvrier 1896, pp. 212–13; Delouvrier 1892, pp. 211, 219–20; Escudier 1905, pp. 198–200; Fayet 1970, p. 197; Fournier 1994, vol. 1, pp. 275–6, 314; Fournier 1975, p. 339; Frêche 1975, pp. 537–8; Pasquier and Galabert 1925, p. 34; Gigou 1981, pp. 86–7; Gigou 1978, pp. 107–8, 120–1; Godechot 1951, pp. 85–6; Grenier 1964, p. 45; Grillou 1979, pp. 32–3; Laffon 1992, p. 53; Lavigne 1875, p. 175; Hindie Lemay 1991, p. 939; Marquié 1993, p. 248; Martin 1984, pp. 137–8; McPhee 1999, pp. 22, 51, 56; Merley 1974, vol. 1, pp. 157–8; Nègre 1970, pp. 191, 214–16, 234–5; Négri 1988, pp. 64, 67–71; Nicolas 2002, p. 181; Pélaquier 1996, vol. 1, pp. 95–6, 541; Plandé 1944, p. 159; Puget 1990, p. 143; Reynier 1952, pp. 6, 8 Reynier 1943–51, pp. 285, 330–1; Roux 1988, p. 25; Sabatié 1971, pp. 176–96; Sabatier 1988, pp. 176–7; Saumade 1908, pp. 79–80, 417–19, 442–55, 555; Saurel 1898, vol. 1, p. 110; Segondy 1949, pp. 181, 343–4; Terrenq 1970, pp. 60–2, 64–8; Montaugé 1869, pp. 108–9; Yché 1985, pp. 72, 75–7.

Table A.1: Recipients of 5,347,859 *Livres* reimbursed by the Estates of Languedoc in 1786 for loans taken out for the king every year since 1775

Paris and Versailles

Nobles[1]	1,760,620
Middle classes[2]	1,472,583
Ecclesiastic establishments	24,000
Boursiers du College Cholets	20,000
Abbey and prior	19,000
Doctor of the king	15,000
Captives and slaves of house of mercy	800

Loan contracts reimbursed to individuals next to whom no geographic location was listed

Royal military school	610,000
Nobles	59,500
Commoners	53,600

Loan contracts reimbursed to individuals residing neither in the capital nor in Languedoc

Commoners[3]	132,525
Nobles[4]	92,200
Ecclesiastic establishments	33,900
Bishop, Canon, and prior	24,000

---

1 Includes robe nobles and parlementaires, a *secrétaire du roi*, and others.
2 Includes, lawyers, *bourgeois*, priests, and others.
3 Includes a priest and a non-noble former military commander.
4 Includes a secrétaire du roi.

Toulouse

Nobles[5]	257,623
Commoners[6]	55,400
Ecclesiastic establishments	8,000

Languedoc

Nobles	143,758
Commoners[7]	76,800
Ecclesiastic establishments	68,900
Canon	9,000

Montpellier

Nobles[8]	227,700
Commoners[9]	122,450
Canons	9,000
Ecclesiastic establishments	7,000

Nîmes

Noble	6,000
One investor from Geneva	10,000
One investor from Gand	6,000

---

5   Includes many parlementaires.
6   Includes lawyers and the treasurer of Toulouse.
7   Includes lawyers and priests.
8   Includes many nobles of the robe of the Cour des Comptes, Aides et Finances and the Bureau of Finances. Also includes a secrétaire du roi, the intendant, and M. de Joubert (treasurer of the Estates).
9   Includes a *négociant*, a *procureur*, a receiver of domains, the diocese receiver, the first Drogman to the French ambassador to the Porte, and priests.

Table A.2: Creditors of the diocese of Montpellier

Creditors[a]	Number
Abbots, pastors, priests, canons, *hôpitaux*, etc.	80 (29.2% of those for whom we know the profession and/or status, 12% of the total)
Joubert, Treasurer of the Estates of Languedoc	1
Presidents, Correctors, Councillors, etc. of the *Cour des Comptes, Aides et Finances*	28 (10.2%, 4%)
Treasurers of France of the Bureau des Finances	7
Nobles	96 (including 7 knights de St.-Louis) (35%, 14%)
Marshals and captains of infantry, cavalry, etc.	6
Prosecutors/attorneys, lawyers, notaries, councillors in the presidial, the *juge mage*	25 (9.1%, 3.7%)
Professor of law, architect, and doctors	7
Tax receiver	1
Landlord (*bourgeois*)	1
Controlleur des postes	1
Wholesale merchants, *parfumeur*, apothecary	4
Former surgeon major	1
Financier	1
Consuls of Matelles	1
College of surgery	1
Régentes	3
Spinner, bookstore owner, cook, shoe repairman, etc.	8 (2.9%, 1%)
Farmers (*ménager* and *jardinier*)	2

a   The diocese had a total of 674 creditors. We know the status or profession of 274.

Table A.3: Creditors of the diocese of Toulouse, 1787 and 1788

Title of creditor	Amount of interest received annually	Total credits on the diocese of Toulouse
Nuns, a chapel, *maisons de charité*, priests, and *hôpitaux*	35,583	732,930
Treasurer of the Estates of Languedoc	577	11,541
Barons of the Estates	8,500	161,000
Syndic generals of the Estates	1,300	26,000
Magistrates, Parlement	7,550	149,733
Secrétaire du roi	407	8,135
Noble lawyer, former *capitoul* and treasurer of Toulouse	300	6,000
Nobles	15,616	327,620
Lawyer, syndic of diocese of Toulouse	190	3,520
Sub-delegate of the intendant	100	2,000
Syndic of the diocese of Albi	1,060	21,200
Diocese tax receiver	4,655	68,005
Master of music	600	12,000
Lawyers	2,592	55,162
Landlords (*bourgeois*)	1,250	25,000
Non-nobles, no profession	3,400	76,530
Inn keeper	233	8,000
Magistrate, *cour des comptes*, Paris	450	15,000
Noble, Paris	312	10,400
Nuns and a seminary, Auch, Béarn, Agen	8,890	167,908
Total	93,565	1,887,684

The diocese also reimbursed *l'oeuvre du Bouillon* of the parishes of la Daurade, St.-Etienne, and St.-Sernin 15,400 *livres*, *la maison de charité* of the parish of la Daurade 17,000, a lawyer 6,000, and the receiver of *tailles* 19,000 in 1788.

Table A.4: Classification of professions for five Languedocian villages

Sérignan (Hérault) 1777 (percentages based on 308 households)

Agricultural workers	Fishermen	Artisans/Shopkeepers	Small landowners	Liberal professionals	Bourgeois rentiers	Civil servants
50.3	10.4	12.7	14	3.9	7.1	1.6

Saint-Eulalie 'aux Bois' (Aude) 1793–97 (61)

Agricultural workers	Fishermen	Artisans/Shopkeepers	Small landowners	Liberal professionals	Civil servants
34.4	4.9	41	8.2	4.9	6.6

Belpech (Aude) 1790 (385)

Agricultural workers	Tenant farmers and sharecroppers	Peasant landowners	Innkeepers, merchants and surgeons	Artisans	Lawyers and doctors	Bourgeois rentiers
39.7	13.5	23.6	1.8	18.4	1.6	1.3

Belpech (Aude) 1791 (455)

Agricultural workers	Tenant farmers and sharecroppers	Peasant landowners	Innkeepers, merchants and surgeons	Artisans	Lawyers and doctors	Bourgeois rentiers
35.2	1.3	45.3	2.6	13.6	1.3	.7

Bram (Aude) 1806 (227)

Agricultural workers	Peasant landowners	Artisans	Merchants and shopkeepers	Liberal professionals and civil servants	Bourgeois rentiers
46.7	23.3	23	3.1	2.6	1.3

Vébron (Lozère) beginning of eighteenth century (232)

Peasant proprietors	Agricultural workers and sharecroppers	Artisans	Shopkeepers
36.6	29.7	28.4	5.2

Vébron (Lozère) 1841 (300)

Peasant proprietors	Agricultural workers and sharecroppers	Artisans	Shopkeepers
26.7	45.3	23.3	4.7

Sources for Table A.4: Molinier 1968, p. 51; Nègre 1970, pp. 249–51; Cazanave 1989, p. 193; Jacquemay 1986, pp. 339–40; Poujol 1981, p. 43.

Table A.5: Peasant revolts in the departments of old regime Languedoc

HAUTE-GARONNE 9.01% of the acts of lawlessness in former province

YEAR→ ISSUE INVOLVED IN REVOLT↓	Pre 14 July 1789	Post 14 July 1789	1790	1791	1792	1793	1794
SEIGNEURIAL REGIME/TITHES		3	10	2	3	1	
USE-RIGHTS			1			1	1
TAXATION		6	6	1			
SUBSISTENCE	1	3		1	8	4	1
CLASS/PROPERTY					3	2	

ARIÈGE 4.96%

YEAR→ ISSUE INVOLVED IN REVOLT↓	Pre 14 July 1789	Post 14 July 1789	1790	1791	1792	1793	1794
CLASS/PROPERTY		1			6		
SUBSISTENCE		1	1				
SEIGNEURIAL REGIME/TITHES	1	2	5	1	11		
USE-RIGHTS					2		
TAXATION		1					

TARN 10.4%

YEAR→ ISSUE INVOLVED IN REVOLT↓	Pre 14 July 1789	Post 14 July 1789	1790	1791	1792	1793	1794
SEIGNEURIAL REGIME/TITHES	1	11	9	7	2		
STATE AUTHORITY			2				
SUBSISTENCE	2	5	1		3	3	3
CLASS/PROPERTY			1	2	4		
TAXATION		3					
USE-RIGHTS				3			
ANTI-CLERICAL					5		

APPENDIX

AUDE 27.17%

YEAR→ ISSUE INVOLVED IN REVOLT↓	Pre 14 July 1789	Post 14 July 1789	1790	1791	1792	1793	1794
SUBSISTENCE	3	4	9	2	4		
CLASS/PROPERTY		1	2		1		
TAXATION		18	8	3	2	4	
SEIGNEURIAL REGIME/TITHES		18	37	16	17	15	
USE-RIGHTS	1	2	3	3	1		
STATE AUTHORITY					1		

HÉRAULT 6.52%

YEAR→ ISSUE INVOLVED IN REVOLT↓	Pre 14 July 1789	Post 14 July 1789	1790	1791	1792	1793	1794
CLASS/PROPERTY				2	1		
SEIGNEURIAL REGIME/TITHES	1			3	2	2	
SUBSISTENCE	10	3			3	1	
TAXATION	1	6	3	2			
STATE AUTHORITY				1			
USE-RIGHTS			1				

HAUTE-LOIRE 2.02%

YEAR→ ISSUE INVOLVED IN REVOLT↓	Pre 14 July 1789	Post 14 July 1789	1790	1791	1792	1793	1794
SUBSISTENCE	2	1					
TAXATION	1	2		2	1	1	1
SEIGNEURIAL REGIME/TITHES		1		1			

LOZÈRE 6.37%

YEAR→ ISSUE INVOLVED IN REVOLT↓	Pre 14 July 1789	Post 14 July 1789	1790	1791	1792	1793	1794
CLASS/PROPERTY		1		2	2		
SEIGNEURIAL REGIME/TITHES				2	3	7	2
SUBSISTENCE	2	1		2			
TAXATION	1	2		6	1	2	1
USE-RIGHTS		1		3			

GARD 20.81%

YEAR→ ISSUE INVOLVED IN REVOLT↓	Pre 14 July 1789	Post 14 July 1789	1790	1791	1792	1793	1794
SUBSISTENCE	5	3			4	1	
CLASS/PROPERTY					12		
TAXATION		3	2	2			
SEIGNEURIAL REGIME/TITHES	2		4	4	77		1
USE-RIGHTS			3	1	1	1	
STATE AUTHORITY			2	1	5		

ARDÈCHE 12.73%

YEAR→ ISSUE INVOLVED IN REVOLT↓	Pre 14 July 1789	Post 14 July 1789	1790	1791	1792	1793	1794
SEIGNEURIAL REGIME/TITHES	1	16	2	1	11	1	
SUBSISTENCE	2	2		2			
PROPERTY/CLASS		5	2	1	8		
TAXATION	1	5			1	1	
USE-RIGHTS		1	5		8		
ANTI-CLERICAL		2			4		

Sources for Table A.5: Archives Nationales H1/748/100, H1/1063, H1/1105, H1/1453; F7/3651, F7/3652/1, F7/3654, F7/3677/4, F7/3681/9, F7/3681/13, F7/3681/14,

APPENDIX

F7/3691, Archives Départementales de la Haute-Garonne C 291; 1 L 239, 250, 268, 701; Archives Départementales de l'Aude 1 L 97, 133–135, 165, 401, 409, 410, 610, 1339, 1344, 1411, 1455, 1474, 1482, 1726, 2507; Archives Départementales de l'Hérault C47, 64, 74, 2925–2927, 5438, 5439, 5441, 6690; L 51, 531; B9045, 21627, Archives Départementales du Gard L44, 158, 418, 420, 590, 1722, 1838, 2122; Archives Municipales de Toulouse 2 I 7, 2 I 5; Archives Départementales du Tarn B 805; Ado 1996, pp. 102, 132–3, 248–9, 269–70, 270n; Albiousse 1978, pp. 231–3; Allaire 1990, pp. 134–5; Appolis 1950, p. 354; Arnaud 1904, pp. 133–4, 169–71, 171n, 214, 347–54; Astor 1980, pp. 176–7; Azema et al. 1999, pp. 179–80; Bastier 1975, pp. 304–6; Bourderon 1954, pp. 165–6; Bru 1989, p. 35; Brugal 1883, pp. 343–5; Castan 1980, pp. 107–8, 110; Cazals and Poitevin 1992, pp. 168, 184, 192; Chauvet 1967, p. 291; Combes 2000, pp. 56–7; Contrasty 1990, pp. 243–4; Delon 1922, pp. 42–4, 46–8, 50–3, 55–60; Delouvrier 1896, pp. 219–20; Descadeillas 1939, p. 13; Domenge-Dusfour 1924, pp. 54, 71; Dutil 1905, p. 99; Duval-Jouve 1974, vol. 2, pp. 76–7; Faury 1983, pp. 227, 231; Fayet 1970, p. 230; Georges Fournier 1990, pp. 27, 31–2, 35; Péronnet and Fournier 1989, p. 104; Laurent and Gavignaud 1987, pp. 90, 92, 132–43; Gégot 1984, pp. 233–4; Godechot 1986, pp. 83–4, 94–6; Gorlier 1955, pp. 210, 220, 227–8, 230–1, 241, 255; Grenier 1964, pp. 44–5; Jacquemay 1986, p. 107; Jolivet 1980, pp. 138–9, 200–4, 326, 331, 338, 343–8, 350–1, 393–4; Larguier 1989, p. 140n; Lavigne, 1875, p. 223; Lyons 1978, p. 129; Martin 1984, p. 212; Maury 1919, pp. 200–1; McPhee 1999, pp. 50–1, 59–60, 63, 66, 76, 80, 83–6, 88–90, 103–4; Mercadal 1973, p. 61; Merley 1974, vol. 1, pp. 265–9, 307; Péronnet and Castex 1989, p. 88; Picheire 1966, p. 53; Pouthas 1934, pp. 110–1; Rascol 1961, pp. 239–40, 245; Reynier 1943–51, p. 335; Riou 1988, pp. 165, 167–8; Rossignol 1890, pp. 32, 41–3, 58, 71, 83; Rouvière 1974, vol. 1, pp. 73n, 220–2, 378–9, vol. 2, pp. 186–264, vol. 3, pp. 19, 89; Saurel 1898, vol. 1, pp. 233–4; Viala 1909, p. 65; Vitalis 1956, pp. 295–8.

Bibliography

Manuscript Sources

National Library of France
Collection Joly Fleury

Departmental Archives of the Aude
Series B: judicial records of the seneschal court of Carcassonne
Series C: papers from the old regime intendancy, documents concerning the provincial administration
Series L: documents from the revolutionary period 1789–99

Departmental Archives of the Gard
Series C: papers from the old regime intendancy, documents concerning the provincial administration
Series L: documents from the revolutionary period 1789–1799
Series IV E: records of the inspectors of commerce

Departmental Archives of the Haute-Garonne
Series B: judicial records of the Parlement of Toulouse
Series C: papers from the old regime intendancy, documents concerning the provincial administration
Series L: documents from the revolutionary period 1789–1799

Departmental Archives of the Hérault
Series A: administrative and judicial affairs of the old regime
Series B, 1 B, 2 B: tribunals and jurisdictions (Cour des Comptes, Aides et Finances, royal tribunals, and seigneurial tribunals)
Series C: papers from the old regime intendancy, documents concerning the provincial administration
Series L: documents from the revolutionary period 1789–1799
Series E: communal and family archives, seigneuries
Series 2E: records of notaries

Department Archives of the Tarn
Series B: judicial records of the seneschal court of Castres
Series C: papers from the old regime intendancy, documents concerning the provincial administration

Municipal Archives of Toulouse
Series AA: administrative and economic affairs of the old regime
Series BB: documents from the municipal government of the old regime
Series 2G: documents from the revolutionary period in Toulouse
Series 2I: administration and subsistence in Toulouse during the Revolution

National Archives
Series B: elections and voting
Series F1: ministry of the interior: general administration
Series F4: ministry of the interior; general accounting
Series F7: general administration and law enforcement
Series F11: subsistence
Series H1: correspondence between the controller general of finances and the authorities of Languedoc
Series P: Paris Court of Accounts

Printed Primary Sources

Albisson, Jean 1780, *Loix municipales et économiques de Languedoc*, 7 Volumes, Montpellier: Rigaud & Pons.

Archives parlementaires de 1787 à 1860: recueil complet des débats législatifs & politiques des chambres françaises, imprimé par ordre du Sénat et de la Chambre des deputes; 1re série, t. IX discours du 24 septembre 1789; John Boyd Thacher Collection.

1775, 'Arrêt de la cour du parlement, du 18 mars 1771, qui fait inhibitions & défenses de mettre à éxecution, dans son ressort, aucuns actes émanés des Juges établis par lettres-patentes du 23 janvier, & édit de Février derniers', in *Recueil des réclamations, remontrances, lettres, arrêts, arêtes, et protestations des parlements, cour des aides, chambres des comptes, bailliages, présidiaux, élections, au sujet de l'Édit de décembre 1770, des conseils supérieurs, la suppression des parlements, & c.*, 2 Volumes, Amsterdam.

1788, *Arrêté des habitans de la ville de Mende, capitale du Gévaudan*, Mende.

M.B. ... M ... Avocat au Parlement de Languedoc, members de diverses academies 1788, *Voeu du Tiers-État et réclamations particulières du pays des Cévennes, sur son admission & ses doléances aux États généraux, en conséquence des deliberations unanimes prises par vingt-cinq communautés*, Nîmes: Chez les libraires associés.

Ballainvilliers, Simon-Charles-Sébastien Bernard 1989 [1788], *Mémoires sur le Languedoc; suivis du Traité sur le commerce en Languedoc de l'intendant Ballainvilliers (1788)*, Montpellier: L'Entente bibliophile.

Barante, Claude-Ignace Brugière de, prefect of the Aude 1802, *Essai sur le département de l'Aude adressé au ministre de l'Interieur*, Carcassonne: Chez G. Gareng, imprimeur de la préfecture.

Boutaric, François de and Théodore Sudre 1751 [1745], *Traité des droits seigneuriaux et des matières féodales*, Toulouse: G. Henault et J.-F. Forest.

Diderot, Denis 1971, 'Observations sur l'Instruction de S.M.I. aux députés pour la Confection des lois', in *Textes politiques*, Paris: Editions Sociales.

Domairon, L. 1920, '"Montpellier en 1760" d'après le "Voyage en Languedoc"', in *Inventaires et documents*, Montpellier: L'Administration municipale.

Donnadieu, Jean-Pierre (ed.) 1989, *Etats généraux de 1789: sénéchaussées de Béziers et Montpellier (procès verbaux et cahiers de doléances)*, n.p.: S.l.: Archives départementales de l'Hérault.

Du Pont de Nemours, Pierre Samuel 1913–23, 'Mémoire sur les municipalités', in *Oeuvres de Turgot et documents le concernant, avec biographie et notes*, edited by Gustav Schelle, 5 Volumes, Paris: F. Alcan.

Edme-Jacques, Genet and Théophraste Renaudot (eds.), *Recueil des Gazettes de France, Supplément de la Gazette du 5 décembre 1761*, Paris.

Fajon, Hippolyte (ed.) 1867, *Pièces et documents officiels pour servir à l'histoire de la Terreur à Nimes et dans le département du Gard l'an 11 de la République francaise, une et indivisible*, Nimes: Soustelle.

France.; Sénat.; France.; Chambre des députés.; France.; Assemblée nationale (1871–1942) 1787–, *Archives parlementaires de 1787 à 1860*, Paris.

Larguier, Gilbert (ed.) 1989, *Cahiers de doléances Audois*, Carcassonne: Association des Amis des Archives de l'Aude.

'Le 9 février 1771, le parlement de Toulouse arrêta qu'il seroit écrit au roi. La lettre fut rédigée ainsi qu'il suit' 1775, in *Recueil des réclamations, remontrances, lettres, arrêts, arêtes, et protestations des parlements, cour des aides, chambres des comptes, bailliages, présidiaux, élections, au sujet de l'Édit de décembre 1770, des conseils supérieurs, la suppression des parlements, & c.*, 2 Volumes, Amsterdam.

'Montpellier en 1768' 1920, in *Inventaires et documents*, Montpellier: L'Administration municipale.

Montesquieu, Charles de Secondat 1949 [1748], *The Spirit of the Laws*, translated by Thomas Nugent, New York: Hafner Press.

Necker, Jacques 1784, *De l'administration des finances de la France*, 3 Volumes, [Paris].

Pasquier, Félix and François Galabert (eds.) 1925, *Cahiers paroissiaux des sénéchaussées de Toulouse et de Comminges en 1789*, Toulouse: Impr. Et Librairie Édouard Privat.

Picot de Lapeyrouse, Philippe 1789, *De l'administration diocésaine en Languedoc, pour Server d'instruction aux députés de cette province aux États-Généraux*.

Procès-verbal de la session du conseil du département de l'Aude, séant à Carcassonne, du 2 novembre 1793.

1789, *Rapport de Messieurs les commissaires nommés par déliberation des États de Languedoc, du 18 janvier 1788; Précédé d'une lettre des commissaires des trios ordre du diocese d'Alais à M. l'Évêque d'Alais; et suivi d'une lettre du Roi à M. l'Archevêque de Narbonne.*

Schelle, Gustave (ed.) 1913–23, *Oeuvres de Turgot et documents le concernant, avec biographie et notes*, Paris: F. Alcan.

Sieyès, Emmanuel 1988 [1789], *Qu'est-ce que le Tiers État?* Paris: Flammarion.

M. l'Abbé de Siran, Vicaire Générale de Mende, Abbé d'Issoire 1789, *Véritable et fidèle procès-verbal des assemblées tenues en Gévaudan, pour, ou sous le prétexte de la restauration de la chose publique.*

M. l'Abbé de Siran, Vicaire Générale de Mende, Abbé d'Issoire 1789, *Lettre de M. l'Abbé de Siran, Vicaire Général de Mende, député du pays de Gévaudan, à M. le Comte de Bannes d'Arejan, baron des Etats de Languedoc, nommé par le cour député de cette province, et en cette qualité notable.*

M. l'Abbé de Siran, Vicaire Générale de Mende, Abbé d'Issoire 1789, *Plan patriotique, proposé au Gevaudan pour la deputation aux États Généraux.*

'Trésorier' 1782–1832, in *Dictionnaire encyclopédique des finances*, in *Encyclopédie méthodique, ou par ordre de matières*, edited by M. Démeunier, Volume 4, Paris: Chez Panckoucke.

Vic, Claude de, Joseph Vaissette and Ernest Roschach (ed.) 1876, *Histoire générale de Languedoc avec des notes et les pièces justificatives par dom Cl. Devic & dom J. Vaissete*, 15 Volumes, Toulouse: E. Privat.

Young, Arthur 1969 [1792], *Travels in France during the Years 1787, 1788, and 1789*, edited by Jeffry Kaplow, Garden City: Doubleday.

Secondary Works

Ado, Anatoli 1996, *Paysans en Révolution: terre, pouvoir et jacquerie 1787–1794*, Paris: Société des Etudes Robespierristes.

Albiousse, Lionel D' 1978 [1903], *Histoire de la ville d'Uzès*, Marseille: Laffitt Reprints.

Allaire, Roger 1990 [1911], *Histoire de la ville de Bédarieux*, Nîmes: C. Lacour.

Allen, Robert 1992, *Enclosure and the Yeoman: The Agricultural Development of the South Midlands, 1450–1850*, Oxford: Oxford University Press.

Allen, Robert 2000, 'Economic Structure and Agricultural Productivity in Europe, 1300–1800', *European Review of Economic History*, 3: 1–25.

Althusser, Louis 1972, *Politics and History: Montesquieu, Rousseau, Hegel and Marx*, translated by Ben Brewster, London: New Left Books.

Amanieu, René 1959, 'Une personalité toulousaine de la fin du xviiie siècle: Philippe Picot, seigneur de Lapeyrouse', *Annales du Midi*, 71: 143–92.

Anderson, Perry 1974, *Lineages of the Absolutist State*, London: New Left Books.
Anderson, Perry 1992, *English Questions*, London: Verso.
André, Louis 1894, *Essai sur l'histoire de la Révolution en Lozère*, Marvejols: A. Guerrier.
Andress, David 2004, *The French Revolution and the People*, London: Hambledon Continuum.
Appolis, Emile 1936, 'Une assiette diocésaine en Languedoc à la fin de l'Ancien Régime', *Comité des Travaux historiques et scientifiques de la section d'histoire moderne et contemporaine*, 5–58.
Appolis, Emile 1950, 'Une longue querelle au sujet des droits d'usage', *Annales historiques de la Révolution française*, 353–7.
Appolis, Emile 1951, *Un pays languedocien au milieu du XVIIIe siècle. Le diocèse civil de Lodève. Etude administrative et économique*, Albi: Impr. coop. du Sud-Ouest.
Arnaud, Gaston 1904, *Histoire de la Révolution dans le Département de l'Ariège (1789–1795)*, Toulouse: E. Privat.
Astor, Jacques 1980, *Histoire de Servian*, Servian, France: Ville de Servian.
Aubin, Gérard 1989, *La seigneurie en Bordelais au XVIIIe siècle d'après la pratique notariale: 1715–1789*, Rouen: Université de Rouen.
Audisio, Gabriel 1993, *Des paysans: XVe–XIXe siècle*, Paris: A. Colin.
Azema, Xavier, Pierre Carles et al. 1999, *Entre Coulazou et Mosson, 10 villages 10 visages*, Nîmes: Lacour.
Azimi, Vida 1986, 'Le personel administratif des comités des assemblées révolutionnaires: approche d'une administration révolutionnaire', *Mémoires de la société pour l'histoire du droit et des institutions des anciens pays bourguignons, comtois et romands (Dijon)*, 43: 105–9.
Baczko, Bronislaw 1994, *Ending the Terror: The French Revolution After Robespierre*, translated by Michel Petheram, Cambridge: Cambridge University Press.
Baehrel, René 1961, *Une croissance: la Basse-Provence rurale (fin xvie siècle–1789): Essai d'économie historique statistique*, Paris: S.E.V.P.E.N.
Baker, Keith 1990, *Inventing the French Revolution: Essays on French Political Culture in the Eighteenth Century*, Cambridge: Cambridge University Press.
Bastard d'Estang, vicomte de, Henri Bruno 1857, *Les parlements de France; essai historique sur leurs usages, leur organisation et leur autorité*, 2 Volumes, Paris: Didier et cie.
Bastier, Jean 1975, *La féodalité au siècle des lumières dans la région de Toulouse: 1730–1790*, Paris: Bibliothèque nationale.
Bayon-Tollet, Jacqueline 1982, *Le Puy-en-Velay et la Révolution française*, Saint-Etienne: Université de Saint-Etienne, Centre d'histoire régionale.
Béaur, Gérard 1984, *Le marché foncier à la veille de la Révolution: les mouvements de propriété beaucerons dans les régions de Maintenon et de Janville de 1761 à 1790*, Paris: Editions de l'Ecole des hautes études en sciences sociales.

Beik, William 1985, *Absolutism and Society in Seventeenth-Century France: State Power and Provincial Aristocracy in Languedoc*, Cambridge: Cambridge University Press.

Beik, William 2009, *A Social and Cultural History of Early Modern France*, Cambridge: Cambridge University Press.

Bell, David 1994, *Lawyers and Citizens: The Making of a Political Elite in Old Regime France*, New York: Oxford University Press.

Bercé, Yves Marie 1974, *Histoire des croquants: étude des soulèvements populaires au XVIIe siècle dans le sud-ouest de la France*, 2 Volumes, Genève: Droz.

Berenson, Edward 1987, 'Politics and the French peasantry: The Debate Continues', *Social History*, 12: 213–19.

Berenson, Edward 1992, *The Trial of Madame Caillaux*, Berkeley: University of California Press.

Berenson, Edward 1995, 'Revolutionizing Theory – Theorizing Revolution: State, Culture, and Society in Recent Works on Revolution', in *Debating Revolutions*, edited by Nikki Keddie, New York: New York University Press.

Bergasse, Jean-Denis 1989, 'Noblesse au village pendant la Révolution: un cas à Cessenon', in *Municipalités et révolution dans l'Hérault*, edited by Geneviève Gavignaud Fontaine, Jean Nougaret, and Jean-Claude Richard, Montpellier: Association Etudes sur l'Hérault.

Berger, Alain and Frédéric Maurel 1980, *La viticulture et l'économie du Languedoc du XVIIIe siècle à nos jours*, Montpellier: Editions du Faubourg.

Bergin, Joseph 1985, *Cardinal Richelieu: Power and the Pursuit of Wealth*, New Haven: Yale University Press.

Berlanstein, Leonard 1975, *The Barristers of Toulouse in the Eighteenth Century*, Baltimore: Johns Hopkins University Press.

Bernard, R.J. 1971, 'Les communautés rurales en Gévaudan sous l'Ancien Régime', *Revue du Gévaudan, des Causses et des Cévennes; Bulletin de la société des lettres, Sciences et Arts de la Lozère*, 110–65.

Bien, David 1978, 'The Secrétaires du Roi: Absolutism, Corps, and Privilege Under the Ancien Regime', in *Vom Ancien régime zur französischen Revolution: Forschungen u. Perspektiven = De l'ancien régime à la révolution française*, edited by Ernst Hinrichs, Eberhard Schmitt, and Rudolf Vierhaus, Göttingen: Vandenhoeck und Ruprecht.

Bien, David 1987, 'Offices, Corps, and a System of State Credit: The Uses of Privilege Under the Ancien Regime', in *The French Revolution and the Creation of Modern Political Culture*, 4 Volumes, edited by Keith Baker, Oxford: Pergamon Press.

Bien, David 1994, 'Old Regime Origins of Democratic Liberty', in *The French Idea of Freedom: The Old Regime and the Declaration of Rights of 1789*, edited by Dale Van Kley, Stanford, CA: Stanford University Press.

Biloghi, Dominique 1998, *Logistique et Ancien Régime: de l'étape royale à l'étape Languedocienne*, Montpellier: UMR 5609 du CNRS-ESID, Université Paul Valéry Montpellier III.

Biloghi, Dominique 1993, 'À la confluence de l'histoire militaire et de l'histoire sociale: les entrepreneurs de l'étape générale en Languedoc au XVIIIe siècle', in *Société, politique, culture en Méditerranée occidentale, XVIe–XVIIIe siècles: mélanges en l'honneur du professeur Anne Blanchard*, edited by Anne Blanchard, Montpellier: Université Paul Valéry, Centre d'histoire moderne.

Blanc, Dominique 1984, 'Différences culturelles et privilèges de la ville', in *Histoire de Carcassonne*, edited by Jean Guilaine and Daniel Fabre, Toulouse: Privat.

Blaufarb, Rafe 2002, *The French Army 1750–1820: Careers, Talent, Merit*, Manchester: Manchester University Press.

Blaufarb, Rafe 2016, *The Great Demarcation: The French Revolution and the Invention of Modern Property*, New York: Oxford University Press.

Bloch, Marc 1931, *Les caractères originaux de l'histoire rurale française*, Oslo: H. Aschehoug.

Bloch, Marc 1966, *French Rural History: An Essay on its Basic Characteristics*, translated by Janet Sondheimer, Berkeley: University of California Press.

Bodinier, Bernard, Eric Teyssier and François Antoine 2000, *L'événement le plus important de la Révolution: la vente des biens nationaux (1789–1867) en France et dans les territoires annexes*, Paris: Société des études robespierristes.

Bois, Guy 1976, *Crise du féodalisme: économie rurale et démographie en Normandie orientale du début du 14e siècle au milieu du 16e siècle*, Paris: Presses de la Fondation des Sciences Politiques.

Bonnet, Jean Louis 1988, 'Le comte de Belle-Isle, Baron de Lézignan (1719–1761)', in *Histoire de Lézignan*, edited by Joseph Euzet, Carcassonne: Société d'études Scientifiques de l'Aude.

Bonnet, Jean Louis and Claude Marquié 1980, 'L'ancien régime (vers 1500–1789)', in *Histoire des pays d'Aude*, Carcassonne: CNDP, C.D.D.P. de l'Aude.

Bonney, Richard 1978, *Political Change in France under Richelieu and Mazarin, 1624–1661*, Oxford: Oxford University Press.

Borrel, Chanoine 1944–46, 'Les tribulations d'une chatelaine', *Mémoires de la Société des arts et des sciences de Carcassonne*, 7, 3: 185–94.

Bosher, J.F. 1970, *French Finances 1770–1795: From Business to Bureaucracy*, Cambridge: Cambridge University Press.

Bossenga, Gail 1986, 'From Corps to Citizenship: The Bureaux des Finances before the French Revolution', *Journal of Modern History*, 58: 610–42.

Bossenga, Gail 1991, *The Politics of Privilege: Old Regime and Revolution in Lille*, Cambridge: Cambridge University Press.

Boüard, Michel de 1970, *Histoire de la Normandie*, Toulouse: Privat.

Bourderon, H. 1954, 'La lutte contre la vie chère dans la généralité du Languedoc au xviiie Siècle', *Annales du Midi*, 25–6: 155–70.

Bousiges, Richard 1988, *Un village cévenol pendant la Révolution: Saint-Florant de 1789–1795*, Salindres: Librairie Occitane.

Bouton, Cynthia 1993, *The Flour War: Gender, Class, and Community in Late Ancien Régime French Society*, University Park: Pennsylvania State University Press.

Bouvier, Jean 1973, 'Le système fiscal français du xixe siècle: étude critique d'un immobilisme', in *Deux siècles de fiscalité française, xixe–xxe siècle*, edited by Jean Bouvier, Jacques Wolff, and Robert Schnerb, Paris: Mouton.

Bouyoux, Pierre 1958, 'Les "six cents plus imposés" du département de la Haute Garonne en l'an x', *Annales du Midi*, 70: 317–27.

Brennan, Thomas 2006, 'Peasants and Debt in Eighteenth-Century Champagne', *Journal of Interdisciplinary History*, 37, 2: 175–200.

Brenner, Robert 1976, 'Agrarian Class Struggle and Economic Development in Pre-Industrial Europe', *Past Present*, 70: 30–75.

Brenner, Robert 1985, 'The Agrarian Roots of European Capitalism', in *The Brenner Debate: Agrarian Class Structure and Economic Development in Pre-Industrial Europe*, edited by T.H. Aston and C.H.E. Philpin, Cambridge: Cambridge University Press.

Brenner, Robert 1997, 'Property Relations and the Growth of Agricultural Productivity in late Medieval and Early Modern Europe', In *Economic Development and Agricultural Productivity*, edited by Amit Bhaduri and Rune Skarstein, Cheltenham: Edward Elgar Publishing.

Brenner, Robert 2001, 'The Low Countries in the Transition to Capitalism', in *Peasants into Farmers? The Transformation of Rural Economy and Society in the Low Countries (Middle Ages–19th Century) in Light of the Brenner Debate*, edited by Peter Hoppenbrouwers and Jan Luiten van Zanden, Turnhout: Brepols.

Brenner, Robert 2003 [1993], *Merchants and Revolution: Commercial Change, Political Conflict, and London's Overseas Traders, 1550–1653*, London: Verso.

Brenner, Robert and Christopher Isett 2002, 'England's Divergence from China's Yangzi Delta: Property Relations, Micro-economics, and Patterns of Development', *Journal of Asian Studies*, 61: 609–62.

Brewer, John 1989, *The Sinews of Power: War, Money and the English State, 1688–1783*, London: Unwin Hyman.

Brochier, André 1993, *La vente des biens nationaux dans le département de la Haute Loire (1791–1808)*, Le Puy: Edition des Cahiers de la Haute-Loire, Archives départementales de la Haute-Loire.

Bru, Henri 1989, *1789–1799: la Révolution dans le Tarn*. Albi: Centre départemental de documentation pédagogique du Tarn.

Brugal, Simon 1883, 'La jacquerie dans le Vivarais: de 1789 à 1793', *Revue de la Révolution*, 338–48.

Bruguière, Michel 1989, 'Les receveurs généraux sous Louis XVI: fossiles ou précurseurs?', in *Histoire économique et financière*, Volume 1, Paris: Imprimerie nationale.

Brunet, Pierre 1960, *Structure agraire et économie rurale des plateaux tertiaires entre la Seine et l'Oise*, Caen: Société d'impressions Caron.

Brunet, Roger 1965, *Les Campagnes toulousaines, étude géographique*, Toulouse: Association des publications de la Faculté des lettres et sciences humaines.

Cambon, Paul 1951, *La vente des biens nationaux pendant la Révolution dans les districts de Béziers et de Saint-Pons*, Montpellier: Imprimerie spéciale du Paysan du midi.

Canonge, Pierre 1990, *Montpellier à la fin de l'Ancien Régime: description économique, sociale, religieuse et politique*, Nîmes: C. Lacour.

Cardenal, Louis de 1936, 'Le "citoyen" de 1791 payait-il plus ou moins d'impôts que le "sujet" de 1790?', *Comité des travaux historiques et scientifiques. Section d'histoire moderne et contemporaine*, 22: 61–110.

Castan, Nicole 1980, *Les criminels de Languedoc: les exigences d'ordre et les voies du ressentiment dans une société pré-révolutionnaire, 1750–1790*, Toulouse: Association des publications de l'Université de Toulouse-Le Mirail.

Castan, Nicole 1980a, *Justice et répression en Languedoc à l'époque des lumières*, Paris: Flammarion.

Castan, Nicole 1982, 'Les rivalités à l'interieur des communautés rurales en Languedoc à la fin du XVIIIe siècle', *Études sur l'Hérault*, 4–5: 39–43.

Castan, Yves 1969, 'Attitudes et motivations dans les conflits entre seigneurs et Communautés devant le Parlement de Toulouse au XVIIIe siècle', in *Villes de l'Europe méditerranéenne et de l'Europe occidentale du Moyen Age au XIXe siècle; actes du colloque de Nice (27–28 mars 1969)*, edited by Antonio Marongiu, Paris: Les Belles Lettres.

Casteras, Paul de 1891, *La société Toulousaine a la fin du dix-huitième siècle: (L'ancien régime et la révolution)*, Toulouse: E. Privat.

Casteras, Paul de 1911, *La révolution en province. Révolutionnaires et terroristes du département de l'Ariège 1789 – an VIII*, Toulouse: Impr. Vialelle et Perry.

Catalan, Paul 1902, *La justice révolutionnaire à Montpellier et dans le département de l'Hérault en 1793 et 1794*, Montpellier: G. Firmin, Montane et Sicardi.

Cavanaugh, G.J. 1974, 'Nobles, Privileges, and Taxes in France: A Revision Reviewed', *French Historical Studies*, 8: 681–2.

Cazals, Antoine-Lucien 1883, *Une page de l'histoire du Lauragais, ou, Histoire de la ville et de la communauté de Montesquieu-sur-Canal depuis les temps les plus anciens jusqu'à nos jours*, Toulouse: Chez les principaux libraires classiques.

Cazals, Rémy 1983, *Les révolutions industrielles à Mazamet, 1750–1900*, Paris: La Découverte/Maspero.

Cazals, Rémy 1994, 'Le grand siècle industriel', in *Histoire de Carcassonne*, edited by Jean Guilaine and Daniel Fabre, Toulouse: Privat.

Cazals, Rémy and Michel de Poitevin 1992, 'Campagnes et villes, Désert et Lumières (1685–1789)', in *Histoire de Castres, Mazamet, la Montagne*, edited by Rémy Cazals, Toulouse: Privat.

Cazals, Remy and Jean Valentin 1984, *Carcassonne ville industrielle au 18ème siècle*, Carcassonne: Service educatif des Archives de l'Aude.

Cazanave, Jean 1991, 'Ambitions familiales à Mirepoix (Ariège) de 1788 à 1795', in *Révolution Et contre-révolution dans la France du Midi (1789–1799)*, edited by Jean Sentou, Toulouse: Presses Universitaires du Mirail.

Cazanave, Jean 1999, *La transition Révolutionnaire à Belpech:* [*1789–1800*], Toulouse: Editions de la Municipalité de Belpech.

Chandaman, C.D. 1975, *The English Public Revenue, 1660–1688*, Oxford: Clarendon Press.

Chanon, Georges 1988, 'Le Jacobinism. Du club des Jacobins aux sociétés populaires', in *La Haute-Loire et la Révolution française*, edited by Jacques Barlet, Neysac, Saint Julien Chapteuil: Editions du Roure.

Chartier, Roger 1969, 'L'académie de Lyon au XVIIIe siècle: étude de sociologie Culturelle', in *Nouvelles études lyonnaises*, edited by Chartier et al., Geneva: Librairie Droz.

Chartier, Roger 1991, *The Cultural Origins of the French Revolution*, translated by Lydia Cochrane, Durham, NC: Duke University Press.

Chaussinand-Nogaret, Guy 1970, *Les financiers de Languedoc au XVIIIe siècle*, Paris: S.E.V.P.E.N.

Chauvet, Maurice 1967, *Pages d'histoire du Languedoc*, Nice: Éditions la Lambrusque.

Cheney, Paul 2010, *Revolutionary Commerce: Globalisation and the French Monarchy*, Cambridge, MA: Harvard University Press.

Chéron, André and Germaine de Sarret de Coussergues 1963, *Une seigneurie en Bas Languedoc, Coussergues et les Sarret*, Bruxelles: Hayez.

Church, Clive H. 1981, *Revolution and Red Tape: The French Ministerial Bureaucracy, 1770–1850*, Oxford: Clarendon Press.

Clark, Gregory 1999, 'Too Much Revolution: Agriculture in the Industrial Revolution', in *The British Industrial Revolution: An Economic Perspective*, edited by Joel Mokyr, Boulder, CO: Westview Press.

Clay, Christopher 1984, *Economic Expansion and Social Change*, 2 volumes, Cambridge: Cambridge University Press.

Cobb, Richard 1955, *Les armées révolutionnaires des départements du midi (automne et hiver de 1793, printemps de 1794)*, Toulouse: Cahiers de l'Association Marc Bloch de Toulouse. Etudes d'histoire méridionale.

Cobb, Richard 1987, *The People's Armies: The Armées Révolutionnaires, Instrument of the Terror in the Departments, April 1793 to Floreal Year II*, translated by Marianne Elliott, New Haven: Yale University Press.

Cobb, Richard 1998, *The French and their Revolution: Selected Writings*, New York: The New Press.

Cobban, Alfred 1965, *The Social Interpretation of the French Revolution*, Cambridge: Cambridge University Press.

Coleman, D.C. 1977, *The Economy of England, 1450–1750*, London: Oxford University Press.

Collins, James 1988, *Fiscal Limits of Absolutism: Direct Taxation in Early Seventeenth-Century France*, Berkeley: University of California Press.

Collins, James 1995, *Classes, Estates, and Order in Early Modern Brittany*, Cambridge: Cambridge University Press.

Comninel, George 1987, *Rethinking the French Revolution: Marxism and the Revisionist Challenge*, London: Verso.

Combes, Anacharsis 2000 [1887], *Histoire de la ville de Castres et de ses environs pendant la Révolution française*, Nîmes: Lacour.

Contrasty, Jean 1936, *Histoire de la cité de Rieux-Volvestre et de ses évêques*, Toulouse: Sistac.

Contrasty, Jean 1990 [1922], *Histoire de Saint-Jory*, Paris: Res universis.

Cornwall, Julian 1954, 'Farming in Sussex, 1540–1640', *Sussex Archaeological Collections*, 92: 48–92.

Crafts, N.F.R. 1985, *British Economic Growth During the Industrial Revolution*, Oxford: Clarendon Press.

Crouzet, François 1985, *De la supériorité de l'Angleterre sur la France: l'économique et l'imaginaire, XVIIe–XXe siècles*, Paris: Librairie académique Perrin.

Crouzet, François 1993, *La grande inflation: la monnaie en France de Louis XVI à Napoléon*, Paris: Fayard.

Darnton, Robert 1995, *The Forbidden Best-Sellers of Pre-Revolutionary*. New York: W.W. Norton.

Daudet, Ernest 1881, *Histoire des conspirations royalistes du midi sous la revolution (1790–1793) d'après les publications contemporaines, les pièces officielles et les documents inédits*, Paris: Hachette & cie.

Davidson, Neil 2012, *How Revolutionary were the Bourgeois Revolutions?* Chicago: Haymarket Books.

Dawson, Philip 1972, *Provincial Magistrates and Revolutionary Politics in France, 1789–1795*, Cambridge, MA: Harvard University Press.

Delecambre, Etienne 1943, *La vie dans la Haute-Loire sous le Directoire: état social et économique, institutions et vie privée*, Rodez: Impr. P. Carrière.

Delon, Pierre J.–B. 1922, *La Révolution en Lozère*, Mende: Impr. Lozérienne.

Delouvrier, Alphonse 1892, *Histoire de Notre-Dame-des-Vertus de Paulhan*, Montpellier: Impr. Grollier.

Delouvrier, Alphonse 1896, *Histoire de Saint-Chinian-de-la-Corne et des ses environs (Hérault)*, Montpellier: Grollier.

Delouvrier, Alphonse 1990 [1896], *Histoire de la vicomté d'Aumelas et de la baronnie du Pouget*, Gignac: Bibliothèque.

Delpuech, Joseph-Pierre-Gabriel 1954, *Montpellier à la veille de la Révolution*, Montpellier: Impr. de P. Déhan.

Dermigny, Louis 1967, 'De la révocation à la Révolution', in *Histoire de Languedoc*, edited by Philippe Wolff, Toulouse: Privat.

Descadeillas, René 1939, *Le fédéralisme méridional pendant la Révolution: le comité civil et militaire de Narbonne (24 avril 1793–9 nivose an II)*, Carcassonne: Impr. et lithographie E. Roudière.

Descimon, Robert and Christian Jouhaud 1996, *La France du premier XVIIe siècle: 1594–1661*, Paris: Belin.

Dessert, Daniel 1984, *Argent, pouvoir et société au Grand Siècle*, Paris: Fayard.

Dion, Roger 1959, *Histoire de la vigne et du vin en France*, Paris: Imprimerie Sévin et Cie.

Domenge-Dusfour, C 1924, *Les subsistances dans le district de Montpellier de 1788 à l'an V*, Montpellier: Imprimerie de la Manufacture de la charité.

Donnadieu, Jean-Pierre 1995, '"Projet d'une nouvelle constitution pour la province de Languedoc" – 1789', in *Les Assemblées d'Etats dans la France méridionale à l'époque moderne: actes du colloque organisé par le Centre d'histoire moderne en 1994*, edited by Anne Blanchard, Henri Michel, and Elie Pélaquier, Montpellier: Université Paul Valéry, Centre d'histoire moderne.

Doyle, William 1988 [1980], *Origins of the French Revolution*, Oxford: Oxford University Press.

Doyle, William 1996, *Venality: The Sale of Offices in Eighteenth-Century France*, Oxford: Clarendon Press.

Doyle, William 1999 [1980], *Origins of the French Revolution*, 3rd edition, Oxford: Oxford University Press.

Dubédat, Jean-Baptiste 1885, *Histoire du Parlement de Toulouse*, Paris: A. Rousseau.

Duboul, Alex 1890, *La fin du Parlement de Toulouse*, Toulouse: F. Tardieu.

Duboul, Alex 1891, *L'armée revolutionnaire de Toulouse: épisode d'une rivalité de clochers*, Toulouse: Imp. F. Tardieu.

Dupâquier, Jacques 1988, *Histoire de la population française*, 2 Volumes, Paris: Presses Universitaires de France.

Duport, Anne Marie 1987, *Terreur et révolution: Nîmes en l'an II, 1793–1794*, Paris: Touzot.

Durand, Yves 1971, *Les fermiers généraux au XVIIIe siècle*, Paris: Presses Universitaires de France.

Dutil, Léon 1905, 'La circulation des grains dans l'Aude à l'époque révolutionnaire', *La Révolution française*, 97–113.

Dutil, Léon 1911, *L'état économique du Languedoc à la fin de l'ancien régime (1750–1789)*, Paris: Hachette & cie.

Duval-Jouve, Joseph 1974 [1879–81], *Montpellier pendant la Révolution: I–II*, 2 Volumes, Marseille: Laffitte Reprints.

Dziembowski, Edmond 1998, *Un nouveau patriotisme français, 1750–1770: la France face à la puissance anglaise à l'époque de la guerre de Sept ans, Oxford: Voltaire Foundation.

Egret, Jean 1955, 'Les origines de la Révolution en Bretagne (1788–1789)', *Revue Historique*, 213: 189–215.

Egret, Jean 1970, *Louis XV et l'opposition parlementaire, 1715–1774*, Paris: A. Colin.

Escudier, Adrien 1905, *Histoire de Fronton et du Frontonnais*, Toulouse: Imprimerie Douladoure-Privat.

Falgairolle, Edmond 1897, *Vauvert pendant la Révolution Française*, Nîmes: Lavagne Reyrot.

Faucher, Benjamin 1948, *Etat civil et documents cadastraux: répertoire numérique des sous séries IVE et VE et des documents analogues conservés aux archives communales*, Toulouse: Impr. et libr. E. Privat.

Faury, Jean 1983, 'L'entrée dans la politique moderne (1789–1848)', in *Histoire d'Albi*, edited by Jean-Louis Biget, Toulouse: Privat.

Fayet, Jean-Loup 1970, *Un village en Bas-Languedoc Marseillan*, Montpellier: Imprimerie Dehan.

Félix de la Farelle, F. 1841, *Études historiques sur le consulat et les institutions municipales de la ville de Nismes, suivies d'un mémoire sur son pass industriel*, Nismes: Ballivet et Fabre.

Félix, Joël 1999, *Finances et politique au siècle des Lumières: le ministère L'Averdy, 1763–1768*, Paris: Comité pour l'histoire économique et financière de la France.

Figeac, Michel 1996, *Destins de la noblesse bordelaise (1770–1830)*, 2 Volumes, Bordeaux: Fédération historique du Sud-Ouest.

Forster, Robert 1960, *The Nobility of Toulouse in the Eighteenth Century*, Baltimore: Johns Hopkins Press.

Fossier, Robert 1968, *La Terre et les hommes en Picardie jusqu'à la fin du XIIIe siècle*, 2 Volumes, Paris: B. Nauwelaerts.

Fournier Georges 1975, 'Communautés rurales en Bas Languedoc au XVIIIe siècle', in *Communautés du Sud: contribution à l'anthropologie des collectivités rurales Occitanes*, edited by Daniel Fabre and Jacques Lacroix, 2 Volumes, Paris: Union générale d'éditions.

Fournier Georges 1978, 'Aspects économiques et sociaux de la Révolution dans quelques communes du Languedoc de 1789 à l'an III', in *Économie et société en Languedoc-Roussillon de 1789 à nos jours*, Montpellier: Université Paul Valéry.

Fournier Georges 1984, 'Structures sociales et révolution dans quelques villes languedociennes', *Annales du Midi*, 96: 401–32.

Fournier Georges 1990, 'Paysans dans l'action révolutionnaire dans l'Aude et la Haute-Garonne', in *Colloque National des 1er et 2 décembre 1989 à Montauban en mars 1990*, [Montauban]: Comité du Bicentenaire de la Révolution dans le Montalbanais.

Fournier Georges 1994, *Démocratie et vie municipale en Languedoc du milieu du XVIIIe au début du* XIXe *siècle*, 2 Volumes, Toulouse: Association les Amis des Archives de la Haute-Garonne.

Fourquin, Guy 1964, *Les campagnes de la région parisienne à la fin du Moyen Âge: du Milieu du* XIIIe *au début du* XVIe *siècle*, Paris: Presses Universitaires de France.

Frêche, Georges and Geneviève Frêche 1967, *Les Prix des grains, des vins et des légumes à Toulouse (1486–1868), extraits des Mercuriales, suivis d'une bibliographie d'histoire des prix*, Paris: Presses Universitaires de France.

Frêche, Georges 1971, 'Compoix, propriété foncière, fiscalité et démographie historique en pays de taille réelle (XVIe–XVIIIe siècles)', *Revue d'histoire moderne et contemporaine*, 18: 321–53.

Frêche, Georges 1974, *Toulouse et la région Midi-Pyrénées au siècle des Lumières vers 1670 1789*, Paris: Cujas.

Fruhauf, Christian 1980, *Forêt et société: de la forêt paysanne à la forêt capitaliste en pays de Sault sous l'Ancien Régime: vers 1670–1791*, Paris: Éditions du C.N.R.S.

Furet, François 1981, *Interpreting the French Revolution*, translated by Elborg Forster, Cambridge: Cambridge University Press.

Furet, François and Ran Halévi 1996, *La Monarchie républicaine: la constitution de 1791*, Paris: Fayard.

Gallix, Maurice 1951, *La vente des biens nationaux pendant la Révolution dans les districts de Montpellier et de Lodève*, Montpellier: Impr. spéciale du Paysan du Midi.

Garden, Maurice 1970, *Lyon et les Lyonnais au* XVIIIe *siècle*, Paris: Les Belles Lettres.

Gauchet, Marcel 1989, *La Révolution des droits de l'homme*, Paris: Gallimard.

Gebhart, Monique and Claude Mercadier 1967, *L'Octroi de Toulouse à la veille de la Révolution*, Paris: Bibliothèque nationale.

Gégot, Jean-Claude 1974, *Le personnel judiciaire de l'Hérault, 1790–1830*, 2 Volumes, Montpellier: Centre d'histoire contemporaine du Languedoc méditerranéen Roussillon, Université Paul Valéry-Montpellier III.

Gégot, Jean-Claude 1984, 'Une Révolution tranquille? (1789–1799)', in *Histoire de Montpellier*, edited by Gérard Cholvy, Toulouse: Privat.

Gégot, Jean-Claude 1988, 'Chaptal et le fédéralisme dans l'Hérault', in *Chaptal*, edited by Michel Péronnet, Toulouse: Privat.

Gérard, Pierre 1991, 'L'armée révolutionnaire de la Haute-Garonne', in *Révolution et contre-révolution dans la France du Midi (1789–1799)*, edited by Jean Sentou, Toulouse: Presses Universitaires du Mirail.

Geraud-Parracha, Guillaume 1957, 'Le commerce des vins et des eaux-de-vie en Languedoc sous l'ancien régime', Dissertation, Montpellier.

Gigou, Emile 1978, *Une cité au pays d'Oc de Posquières à Vauvert*, Paris: Anthropos.

Gigou, Emile 1981, *Les conquérants de la costière*, Paris: Anthropos.

Girardot, Auguste Théodore 1845, *Essai sur les assemblées provinciales: et en particulier sur celle du Berry, 1778–1790*, Bourges: Vermeil.

Godechot, Jacques 1951, 'Réaction féodale et paysans "républiquains" en 1770', *Annales historiques de la Révolution française*, 121: 85–6.
Godechot, Jacques 1986, *La Révolution dans le Midi-Toulousain*, Toulouse: Privat.
Godechot, Jacques and Suzanne Moncassin 1965, 'Structures et relations sociales à Toulouse en 1749 et en 1785', *Annales historiques de la Révolution française*, 37: 129–69.
Gorlier, Pierre 1955, *Le Vigan à travers les siècles: histoire d'une cité languedocienne*, Montpellier: Editions de la Licorne.
Goubert, Pierre 1959, *Familles marchandes sous l'ancien regime: les Danse et les Motte, De Beauvais*, Paris: S.E.V.P.E.N.
Goubert, Pierre 1970 [1966], *Louis XIV and Twenty Million Frenchmen*, translated by Anne Carter, New York: Vintage Books.
Goubert, Pierre and Daniel Roche 1984, *La société et l'Etat* in *Les français et l'Ancien Régime*, Volume 1, Paris: A. Colin.
Gouron, Marcel 1939, *Les étapes de l'histoire de Nîmes: (causeries faites à l'École Antique de Nîmes)*, Nîmes: n.p.
Goy, Joseph and Anne-Lise Head-Köenig 1969, 'Une expérience: les revenus décimaux en France méditerranéenne, XVIe–XVIIIe siècles', *Etudes Rurales*, 36: 66–83.
Gramsci, Antonio 1971, *Selections from the Prison Notebooks*, edited and translated by Quintin Hoare and Geoffrey Nowell Smith, New York: International Publishers.
Grantham, George 1996, 'The French Agricultural Capital Stock, 1789–1914', *Research in Economic History*, 16: 37–83.
Greer, Donald 1966, *The Incidence of the Terror During the French Revolution: A Statistical Interpretation*, Gloucester, MA: P. Smith.
Grenier, Antoine 1964, *Florensac à travers les ages*, Béziers: thèse de l'édition de Béziers.
Grillou, Etienne 1979, *Verfeil en toulousain*, Verfeil: Amis du Vieux Verfeil.
Gueniffey, Patrice 2000, *La politique de la Terreur: essai sur la violence révolutionnaire, 1789–1794*, Paris: Fayard.
Gutherz, Xavier and Raymond Huard 1982, *Histoire de Nîmes*, La Calade, Aix-en Provence: Edisud.
Habermas, Jürgen 1989, *The Structural Transformation of the Public Sphere: An Inquiry into a Category of Bourgeois Society*, translated by Thomas Burger, Cambridge, MA: MIT Press.
Hamscher, Albert 1976, *Parlement of Paris after the Fronde*, Pittsburgh: University of Pittsburgh Press.
Hanson, Paul 1989, *Provincial Politics in the French Revolution: Caen and Limoges, 1789–1794*, Baton Rouge: Louisiana State University Press.
Harris, Robert 1979, *Necker, Reform Statesman of the Ancien Régime*, Berkeley: University of California Press.

Harris, Seymour Edwin 1930, *The Assignats*, Cambridge, MA: Harvard University Press.
Harvey, David 2010, *A Companion to Marx's Capital*, London: Verso.
Havinden, Michael 1961, 'Agricultural Progress in Open-Field Oxfordshire', *Agricultural History Review*, 9: 66–79.
Heller, Henry 2006, *The Bourgeois Revolution in France, 1789–1815*, New York: Berghahn Books.
Higonnet, Patrice 1971, *Pont-de-Montvert: Social Structure and Politics in a French Village, 1700–1914*, Cambridge, MA: Harvard University Press.
Hill, Christopher 1982 [1961], *The Century of Revolution 1603–1714*, New York: Norton.
Hincker, François 1988, 'De l'impôt à la contribution', in *L'Etat de la France pendant la Révolution: 1789–1799*, edited by Michel Vovelle, Paris: Editions La Découverte.
Hincker, François 1989, *La Révolution francaise et l'economie: décollage ou catastrophe?* Paris: Editions Nathan.
Hindie Lemay, Edna 1983, 'Physiocratie et renouveau à l'Assemblée Constituante, 1789–1791', *Transactions of the 6th International Congress on the Enlightenment*, Oxford: Voltaire Foundation.
Hindie Lemay, Edna 1991, *Dictionnaire des Constituants: 1789–1791*, 2 Volumes, Paris: Universitas.
Hoffman, Philip 1996, *Growth in a Traditional Society: The French Countryside, 1450–1815*, Princeton: Princeton University Press.
Hoffman, Philip, Gilles Postel-Vinay, and Jean Laurent Rosenthal 1999, 'Information and Economic History: How the Credit Market in Old Regime Paris Forces Us to Rethink the Transition to Capitalism', *American Historical Review*, 104: 69–94.
Hood, James 1971, 'Protestant and Catholic Relations and the Roots of the First Popular Counterrevolutionary Movement in France', *Journal of Modern History*, 43: 245–75.
Horwitz, Henry 1977, *Parliament, Policy, and Politics in the Reign of William III*, Manchester: Manchester University Press.
Huang, Philip 1990, *The Peasant Family and Rural Development in the Yangzi Delta, 1350–1988*, Stanford: Stanford University Press.
Hudson, David 1972, 'The Parlementary Crisis of 1763', *Canadian Journal of History*, 7: 97–117.
Hudson, Pat 1992, *The Industrial Revolution*, London: E. Arnold.
Hunt, Lynn 1984, *Politics, Culture and Class in the French Revolution*, Berkeley: University of California Press.
Hurt, John 2002, *Louis XIV and the Parlements: The Assertion of Royal Authority*, Manchester: Manchester University Press.
Jacquart, Jean 1974, *La crise rurale en Ile-de-France 1550–1670*, Paris: A. Colin.
Jacquemay, Claude 1986, *En Lauragais sous la Révolution et l'Empire: Bram*, Bram, France: n.p.

Jaurès, Jean 2015, *A Socialist History of the French Revolution*, abridged and translated by Mitchell Abidor, London: Pluto Press.

John, A.H. 1965, 'Agricultural Productivity and Economic Growth in England, 1700–1760', *Journal of Economic History*, 25: 19–34.

Johnson, Christopher 1995, *The Life and Death of Industrial Languedoc, 1700–1920*, New York: Oxford University Press.

Johnson, Christopher 2015, *Becoming Bourgeois: Love, Kinship and Power in Provincial France, 1670–1880*, Ithaca: Cornell University Press.

Johnson, Hubert 1986, *The Midi in Revolution: A Study of Regional Political Diversity*, Princeton: Princeton University Press.

Jolivet, Charles 1980 [1930], *La révolution dans l'Ardéche, 1788–1795*, Marseille: Laffitte Reprints.

Jones, Colin 2003, *The Great Nation: France from Louis XV to Napoleon*, London: Penguin.

Jones, E.L. 1967, 'Introduction', in *Agriculture and Economic Growth in England, 1650–1815*, edited by E.L. Jones, London: Methuen.

Jones, E.L. 1968, 'The Agrarian Origins of Industry', *Past and Present*, 40: 58–71.

Jones, Peter 1979, 'The Rural Bourgeoisie of the Southern Massif Central: A Contribution to the Study of the Social Structure of *Ancien Régime* France', *Social History*, 4: 65–83.

Jones, Peter 1985, *Politics and Rural Society: The Southern Massif Central, c. 1750–1880*, Cambridge: Cambridge University Press.

Jones, Peter 1988, *The Peasantry and the French Revolution*, Cambridge: Cambridge University Press.

Jones, Peter 1989, 'A Response to Hilton Root, "The Case Against Georges Lefebvre's Peasant Revolution"', *History Workshop Journal*, 28: 103–6.

Jones, Peter 2003, *Liberty and Locality in Revolutionary France: Six Villages Compared, 1760–1820*, Cambridge: Cambridge University Press.

Jouanna, Arlette 1989, *Le devoir de révolte: la noblesse française et la gestation de l'Etat moderne, 1559–1661*, Paris: Fayard.

Kagan, Richard 1975, 'Law Students and Legal Careers in Eighteenth-Century France', *Past and Present*, 68: 38–73.

Kaiser, Thomas 1994, 'Property, Sovereignty, the Declaration of the Rights of Man, and the Tradition of French Jurisprudence', in *The French Idea of Freedom: The Old Regime and the Declaration of Rights of 1789*, edited by Dale Van Kley, Stanford: Stanford University Press.

Kawa, Catherine 1988, 'L'appareil d'état', in *L'Etat de la France pendant la Révolution: 1789–1799*, edited by Michel Vovelle, Paris: Editions La Découverte.

Kerridge, Eric 1967, *The Agricultural Revolution*, London: Allen & Unwin.

Kettering, Sharon 1978, *Judicial Politics and Urban Revolt in Seventeenth-Century France: The Parlement of Aix, 1629–1659*, Princeton: Princeton University Press.

Kettering, Sharon 2001, *French Society 1589–1715*, Harlow: Longman.
Krause, Sharon 1999, 'The Politics of Distinction and Disobedience: Honor and the Defense of Liberty in Montesquieu', *Polity*, 31: 469–99.
Kwass, Michael 2000, *Privilege and the Politics of Taxation in Eighteenth-Century France: Liberté, Égalité, Fiscalité*, Cambridge: Cambridge University Press.
Kwass, Michael 2014, *Contraband: Louis Mandrin and the Making of the Global Underground*, Cambridge. MA: Harvard University Press.
Labrousse, Ernest 1933, *Les prix* in *Esquisse du mouvement des prix et des revenus en France au XVIIIe siècle*, Volume 1, Paris: Librairie Dalloz.
Labrousse, Ernest 1944, *La crise de l'économie française à la fin de l'ancien régime et au début de la revolution*, Paris: Presses Universitaires de France.
Labrousse, Ernest 1966, 'The Evolution of Peasant Society in France from the Eighteenth Century to the Present', in *French Society and Culture since the Old Regime*, edited by Evelyn Acomb and Marvin Brown, New York: Holt, Rinehart and Winston.
Laffon, F.G. 1992 [1890], *Histoire de Saint-Orens-de-Gameville*, reprint, Paris: Res Universis.
Lamouzèle, Edmond 1910, *Essai sur l'Administration de la Ville de Toulouse à la fin de l'Ancien Régime (1783–1790); d'après les Procès-Verbaux du Conseil général du Conseil politique et des commissions*, Paris: Giard & Brière.
Larguier, Gilbert 1989, *1789 dans la sénéchaussée de Limoux suivi du texte intégral du cahier de doléances de Raymond Ribes, subdélégué de l'intendant*, Limoux: Comité limouxin du bicentenaire de la Révolution française et de la Déclaration des droits de l'homme.
Larguier, Gilbert 1996, *Le drap et le grain en Languedoc: Narbonne et Narbonnais 1300–1789*, 3 Volumes, Perpignan: Presses Universitaires de Perpignan.
Larguier, Gilbert and Joan Thirsk (eds) 1999, *La terre et les paysans en France et en Grande-Bretagne de 1600 à 1800*, Paris: Ellipses.
Laurent, Robert and Geneviève Gavignaud 1987, *La Révolution française dans le Languedoc Méditerranéen 1789–1799*, Toulouse: Bibliothèque historique Privat.
Laurent, Robert and Geneviève Gavignaud 1989, 'La Révolution municipale dans le département de l'Hérault 1789–1790', in *Municipalités et révolution dans l'Hérault*, edited by Geneviève Gavignaud Fontaine, Jean Nougaret, and Jean-Claude Richard. Montpellier: Association Etudes sur l'Hérault.
Lavigne, B. 1875, *Histoire de Blagnac: sa baronnie, ses barons, ses chateaux, non prieuré, ses églises*, Toulouse: Capdeville.
Lefebvre, Georges 1947, *The Coming of the French Revolution*, translated by R.R. Palmer, Princeton: Princeton University Press.
Lefebvre, Georges 1963 [1954], *Études sur la Révolution française*, Paris: Presses Universitaires de France.

Lefebvre, Georges 1982 [1973], *The Great Fear of 1789: Rural Panic in Revolutionary France*, translated by Joan White, Princeton: Princeton University Press.

Legay, Marie-Laure 2001, *Les états provinciaux dans la construction de l'état moderne, aux xviie et xviiie siècles*, Genève: Droz.

Legay, Marie-Laure 2003, 'Le credit des provinces au secours de l'état: les emprunts des états Provinciaux pour le comte du roi (France, xviii siècle)', in *Pourvoir les finances en province sous l'ancien régime: journée d'études tenue à Bercy le 9 décembre 1999*, edited by Françoise Bayard, Paris: Ministère de l'économie, des finances et de l'industrie, comité pour l'histoire économique et financière de la France.

Le Goff, T.J.A. and D.M.G. Sutherland 1991, 'The Revolution and the Rural Economy', in *Reshaping France: Town, Country and Region during the French Revolution*, edited by Alan I. Forrest and Peter Jones, Manchester: Manchester University Press.

Le Goff, T.J. A 1999, 'How to Finance an Eighteenth-Century War', in *Crises, Revolutions and Self-Sustained Growth: Essays in European Fiscal History, 1130–1830*, edited by W.M. Ormrod, Margaret Bonney, and Richard Bonney, Stamford: Shaun Tyas.

Lemarchand, Guy 1989, *La fin du féodalisme dans le pays de Caux: conjuncture économique et démographique et structure sociale dans une région de grande culture de la crise du xviie siècle à la stabilisation de la Révolution, 1640–1795*, Paris: C.T.H.S.

Lemarchand, Guy 1990, 'Troubles populaires au xviiie siècle et conscience de classe: une preface à la Révolution française', *Annales historiques de la Révolution française*, 279: 32–48.

Lepetit, Bernard 1988, *Les villes dans la France moderne (1740–1840)*, Paris: Albin Michel.

Le Roy Ladurie, Emmanuel 1966, *Les paysans de Languedoc*, 2 Volumes, Paris: S.E.V. P.E.N.

Le Roy Ladurie, Emmanuel 1967 [1962], *Histoire du Languedoc*, Paris: Presses Universitaires de France.

Le Roy Ladurie, Emmanuel 1974, *The Peasants of Languedoc*, translated by John Day, Urbana: University of Illinois Press.

Le Roy Ladurie, Emmanuel 1974a, 'Révoltes et contestations rurales en France de 1675 à 1788', *Annales: économies, sociétés, civilisations*, 29: 6–22.

Lewis, Gwynne 1978, *The Second Vendée: The Continuity of Counter-Revolution in the Department of the Gard, 1789–1815*, Oxford: Clarendon Press.

Lyons, Martin 1978, *Revolution in Toulouse: An Essay on Provincial Terrorism*, Bern: Lang.

Lilti, Antoine 2005, *The World of the Salons: Sociability and Worldliness in Eighteenth-Century Paris*, translated by Lydia Cochrane, New York: Oxford University Press.

Lucas, Colin 1973, 'Nobles, Bourgeois, and the Origins of the French Revolution', *Past and Present*, 60: 84–126.

Lüthy, Herbert 1998 [1959], *La banque protestante en France de la révocation de l'édit de Nantes à la Révolution*, 2 Volumes, Paris: Ecole des hautes études en sciences sociales.

Marchand, Olivier and Claude Thélot 1997, *Le travail en France, 1800–2000*, Paris: Nathan.
Marczewski, Jean 1952, *Le revenu national*, Paris: cahiers de l'ISEA.
Margadant, Ted 1979, *French Peasants in Revolt: The Insurrection of 1851*, Princeton: Princeton University Press.
Margadant, Ted 1992, *Urban Rivalries in the French Revolution*, Princeton: Princeton University Press.
Marinière, G. 1958, 'Les marchands d'étoffe de Toulouse à la fin du XVIIIe siècle', *Annales du Midi*, 70: 251–308.
Marion, Marcel 1927–31, *Histoire financière de la France depuis 1715*, 6 Volumes, Paris: Rousseau.
Markoff, John 1996, *The Abolition of Feudalism: Peasants, Lords, and Legislators in the French Revolution*, University Park: Pennsylvania State University Press.
Marquié, Claude 1993, *L'industrie textile carcassonnaise au XVIIIe siècle: étude d'un Groupe social: les marchands-fabricants*, Carcassonne: Société d'études scientifiques de l'Aude.
Marraud, Mathieu 2000, *La noblesse de Paris au XVIIIe siècle*, Paris: Ed. du Seuil.
Martin, Clément 1984, *Histoire de Montolieu*, Toulouse: Eché.
Martin, Ernest 1900, *Histoire de la ville de Lodève depuis ses origines jusqu'à la Révolution*, Montpellier: Serre.
Martin, Henri 1916, *Documents relatifs à la vente des biens nationaux: district de Toulouse*, Toulouse: É. Privat.
Maury, P. 1919–20, 'Les finances de la ville de Toulouse pendant les premières années de la Révolution', *Annales du Midi*, 31/32: 196–212.
Marx, Karl 1844, 'On the Jewish Question', in *Deutsch-Französische Jahrbücher*.
Marx, Karl 1963 [1898], *The Eighteenth Brumaire of Louis Bonaparte*, New York: International Publishers.
Mathias, Peter and Patrick O'Brien 1976, 'Taxation in Britain and France, 1715–1810: A Comparison of the Social and Economic Incidence of Taxes Collected for the Central Governments', *The Journal of European Economic History*, 5: 601–50.
McPhee, Peter 1999, *Revolution and Environment in Southern France: Peasants, Lords and Murder in the Corbières*, Oxford: Oxford University Press.
Mercadal, Paul 1973, *Montasruc-La-Conseillère et ses environs. Montastruc-la Conseillère et ses environs: Azas, Buzet-sur-Tarn, Garidech, Gemil, Roqueserière, Saint-Jean Lherm*, Montastruc-la-Conseillère, France: n.p.
Meiksins Wood, Ellen 2012, *Liberty and Property: A Social History of Western Political Thought from Renaissance to Enlightenment*, London: Verso.
Merle, Louis 1958, *La métaire et l'évolution agraire de la Gâtine poitevine de la fin du Moyen Age à la Révolution*, Paris: S.E.V.P.E.N.
Merley, Jean 1974, *Texte* in *La Haute-Loire de la fin de l'Ancien Régime aux débuts de la Troisième République*, Volume 1, Le Puy: Cahiers de la Haute-Loire.

Mettam, Roger 1988, *Power and Faction in Louis XIV's France*, Oxford: Basil Blackwell.

Meuvret, Jean 1987, *La production des céréales et la société rurale* in *Le problème des subsistances à l'époque Louis XIV*, Volume 2, Paris: Éditions de L'École des Hautes Études en Sciences Sociales.

Meyer, Jean 1966, *La Noblesse bretonne au XVIIIe siècle*, 2 Volumes, Paris: S.E.V.P.E.N.

Michel, Henri 1980, *Hérault* in *Grands notables du Premier Empire*, edited by Louis Bergeron and Guy Chaussinand-Nogaret, Volume 5, Paris: Centre national de la recherché scientifique.

Miller, Stephen 2003, 'Absolutism and Class at the end of the Old Regime: The Case of Languedoc', *Journal of Social History*, 36: 871–98.

Miller, Stephen 2004, 'Economic Growth in Eighteenth-Century France: A Review of the Evidence with Regard to Languedoc', *Journal of the Oxford University History Society*, 2: 1–17.

Miller, Stephen 2009, 'The Economy of France in the Eighteenth and Nineteenth Centuries: Market Opportunity and Labour Productivity in Languedoc', *Rural History*, 20: 1–30.

Miller, Stephen 2019, 'Peasant Farming in Eighteenth and Nineteenth-Century France and the Transition to Capitalism Under Charles de Gaulle', in *Case Studies in the Origins of Capitalism*, edited by Xavier Lafrance and Charles Post, Cham: Palgrave Macmillan.

Minovez, Jean-Michel 2012, *L'industrie invisible: les draperies du Midi, XVIIe–XXe siècles: essai sur l'originalité d'une trajectoire*, Paris: CNRS éd.

Minovez, Jean-Michel 2012a, *La puissance du Midi: drapiers et draperies de Colbert à la Révolution*, Rennes: Presses Universitaires de Rennes.

Mokyr, Joel 1977, 'Demand vs. Supply in the Industrial Revolution', *Journal of Economic History*, 37: 981–1008.

Mokyr, Joel 1999 [1985], 'Editor's Introduction: The New Economic History and the Industrial Revolution', in *The British Industrial Revolution: An Economic Perspective*, edited by Mokyr, Boulder, CO: Westview Press.

Molinier, Alain 1968, *Une paroisse du bas Languedoc: Sérignan 1650–1792*, Montpellier: Impr. Déhan.

Molinier, Alain 1985, *Stagnations et croissance: le Vivarais aux XVIIe–XVIIIe siècles*, Paris: Ecole des hautes études en sciences sociales.

Molinier, Alain 1988, 'Économie et société des temps modernes', in *Histoire du Vivarais*, edited by Gérard Cholvy, Toulouse: Privat.

Moote, A. Lloyd 1971, *The Revolt of the Judges: The Parlement of Paris and the Fronde 1643–1652*, Princeton: Princeton University Press.

Morère, G.B. 1991 [1899], *Histoire de Saint-Félix-de-Caraman: baronnie des États de Languedoc. Première ville maitresse du diocèse de Toulouse*, Toulouse: APAMP, Association pour la promotion du patrimoine archéologique et historique en Midi-Pyrénées.

Moriceau, Jean-Marc 1994, *Les fermiers de l'Ile-de-France: l'ascension d'un patronat agricole, XVe–XVIIIe siècle*, Paris: Fayard.

Morineau, Michel 1971, *Les faux-semblants d'un démarrage économique: agriculture et démographie en France au XVIIIe siècle*, Paris: A. Colin.

Mousnier, Rolland 1979, *The Institutions of France under the Absolute Monarchy, 1598–1789*, translated by Brian Pierce, 2 Volumes, Chicago: University of Chicago Press.

Nègre, André 1970, *Histoire de mon village: Sainte-Eulalie 'aux bois'*, Caen: Ozanne.

Négri, Jean-Marie 1988, *Poussan en Languedoc: nos seigneurs et notre histoire*, Nîmes: Lacour/Colporteur.

Nelidoff, Philippe 1996, *La municipalité de Toulouse au début de la Révolution*, Toulouse: Presses de l'Université des sciences sociales de Toulouse,

Nelidoff, Philippe 1996a, *Société albigeoise et préparation des États-Généraux de 1789*, Toulouse: Presses de l'Université des sciences sociales de Toulouse.

Neveux, Hugues 1975, 'Déclin et reprise: la fluctuation biséculaire (1340–1560)', in *Histoire de la France rurale*, Volume 2, edited by Emmanuel Le Roy Ladurie, Paris: Seuil.

Nicod, Jean-Claude 1971, 'Les séditieux en Languedoc à la fin du XVIIIe siècle', in *Recueil de mémoires et travaux de la société d'histoire du droit et des institutions des anciens pays de droit écrit*, 8: 145–65.

Nicolas, Jean 2002, *La rébellion française: mouvements populaires et conscience sociale (1661–1789)*, Paris: Seuil.

Nielidov, Philippe 1989, 'États-Généraux et particularismes locaux', *Revue du Tarn*, 136: 593–609.

Niélidow, Philippe 1989, 'La preparation des États-Généraux de 1789 à Albi', *Annales du Midi*, 101: 27–37.

Overton, Mark 1996, *Agricultural Revolution in England: The Transformation of the Agrarian Economy, 1500–1850*, Cambridge: Cambridge University Press.

Parker, David 1980, *La Rochelle and the French Monarchy: Conflict and Order in Seventeenth-Century France*, London: Royal Historical Society.

Parker, David 1996, *Class and State in Ancien Régime France: The Road to Modernity?* London: Routledge.

Parker, David 2003, 'Absolutism, Feudalism and Property Rights in the France of Louis XIV', *Past and Present*, 179: 60–96.

Pascal, Camille 1994, 'Bipolarisation sociale dans la ville d'Ancien Régime: le sixain Saint Croix de Montpellier, 1665–1788', *Revue d'histoire moderne et contemporaine*, 41: 396–417.

Pélaquier, Elie 1990–1, 'Les mouvements anti-fiscaux en Languedoc d'après les archives de la cour des comptes, aides et finances de Montpellier (1660–1789)', *Annales du Midi*: 5–29.

Pélaquier, Elie 1996, *De la maison du père à la maison commune: Saint-Victor-de-la-Coste, en Languedoc (1661–1799)*, 2 Volumes, Montpellier: Université Paul Valéry, Montpellier III.

Péronnet, Michel 1990, 'Jean Arnaud de Castellane, évêque-comte du Gévaudan', in *Entre adhésion et refus: la Révolution en Lozère 1789–1799. Actes du colloque tenu aux Archives Départementales de la Lozère le 4 août 1989*, edited by Benjamin Bardy, Jean-Paul Chabrol, and Hélène Duthu, Mende: Conseil général.

Péronnet, Michel and Jean Castex 1989, *La Révolution dans la Haute-Garonne 1789–1799*, Le Coteau: Horvath.

Péronnet, Michel and Georges Fournier 1989, *La révolution dans le département de l'Aude, 1789–1799*, Le Coteau: Horvath.

Perry, D.L.L. and Pierre Girard 2002, *France Since 1800: Squaring the Hexagon*, Oxford: Oxford University Press.

Petot, Jean 1958, *Histoire de l'administration des ponts et chaussées, 1599–1815*, Paris: Librairie M. Rivière.

Peyriat, André 1990 [1982], *Histoire de Saint-Hippolyte-Du-Fort*, Nîmes: C. Lacour.

Picheire, Joseph 1966, *Histoire d'Agde*, Lyon: P. Bissuel.

Pinaud, Pierre-François 1992, 'Un example de technique financière: histoire du budget et des dépenses, 1789–1830', *Revue historique*, 287: 339–63.

Plandé, Romain 1944, *Géographie et histoire du département de l'Aude*, Grenoble: Editions françaises nouvelles.

Poitrineau, Abel 1979 [1965], *La vie rurale en Basse-Auvergne au xviiie siècle (1726–1789)*, Marseille: Laffitte.

Porshnev, Boris 1963, *Les soulèvements populaires en France de 1623 à 1648*, Paris: S.E.V. P.E.N.

Potter, Mark 2000, 'Good Offices: Intermediation by Corporate Bodies in Early Modern French Public Finance', *The Journal of Economic History*, 60: 599–626.

Potter, Mark 2003, *Corps and Clienteles: Public Finance and Political Change in France 1688–1715*, Aldershot: Ashgate.

Potter, Mark and Jean-Laurent Rosenthal 1997, 'Politics and Public Finance in France: The Estates of Burgundy, 1660–1790', *Journal of Interdisciplinary History*, 27: 577–612.

Poujol, Robert 1981, *Histoire d'un village Cévenol: Vébron*, Aix-en-Provence: Édisud.

Pouthas, Charles-Hippolyte 1934, *Une famille de bourgeoisie française de Louis XIV à Napoléon*, Paris: Librairie Félix Alcan.

Price, Roger 1981, *An Economic History of Modern France, 1730–1914*, London: Macmillan.

Puget, Jean 1990, *Talairan en Corbières*, Carcassonne: Association des amis des archives de l'Aude: Fédération audoise des oeuvres laïques: Société d'études scientifiques de l'Aude.

Puntous, T. 1909, *Les états particuliers du diocèse de Toulouse aux XVIIe et XVIIIe siècles*, Paris: V. Giard et E. Brière.

Ramet, Henri 1935, *Histoire de Toulouse*, Toulouse: Tarride.
Rascol, Pierre 1961, *Les paysans de l'Albigeois à la fin de l'Ancien Régime*, Aurillac: Impr. moderne.
Rebillon, Armand 1932, *Les états de Bretagne de 1661 à 1789. Leur organisation. – L'évolution de leurs pouvoirs.–Leur administration financière*, Paris: Éditions A. Picard.
Reynier, Élie 1943–51, *Histoire de Privas*, 3 Volumes, Aubenas: Société de l'Imprimerie Habauzit.
Reynier, Élie 1952, 'Puissance d'un agent seigneurial: le notaire Alexandre-Philippe Lacrotte', *Revue du Vivarais*, 56: 6–13.
Richet, Denis 1974, 'L'Élite, out le mensonge des mots', *Annales E.S.C*, 29, 1: 49–72.
Richet, Denis 1991, *De la Réforme à la Révolution: Études sur la France moderne*, Paris: Aubier.
Riley, James 1986, *The Seven Years War and the Old Regime in France: The Economic and Financial Toll*, Princeton: Princeton University Press.
Riou, Michel 1988, 'Politique et société sous la Révolution et l'Empire', in *Histoire du Vivarais*, edited by Gérard Cholvy, Toulouse: Privat.
Riou, Michel 1990, 'Religion et révolution dans le département de l'Ardèche', in *Religion, révolution, contre-révolution dans le Midi 1789–1799: colloque international tenu à Nîmes les 27 et 28 1989*, edited by Anne Marie Duport, Nimes: Editions J. Chambon.
Rioufol, Maxime 1904, *La Revolution de 1789 dans le Velay*, Le Puy: Impr. G. Mey.
Rives, Jean 1984, 'Une ville peu révolutionnaire (1789–1800)', in *Histoire de Carcassonne*, edited by Jean Guilaine and Daniel Fabre, Toulouse: Privat.
Rives, Paul 1885, *Etude sur les attributions financières des états provinciaux et en particulier des états de Languedoc aux dix-huitième siècle*, Paris: E. Thorin.
Root, Hilton 1987, *Peasants and King in Burgundy: Agrarian Foundations of French Absolutism*, Berkeley: University of California Press.
Root, Hilton 1989, 'The Case Against George Lefebvre's Peasant Revolution', *History Workshop Journal*, 28: 88–102.
Rosenthal, Jean-Laurent 1992, *The Fruits of Revolution: Property Rights, Litigation, and French Agriculture, 1700–1860*, Cambridge: Cambridge University Press.
Rossignol, Élie-A 1890, *Histoire de l'arrondissement de Gaillac (Département du Tarn) pendant la Révolution de 1789 à 1800*, Toulouse: A. Chauvin.
Rouvière, François 1974 [1887], *Histoire de la Révolution française dans le département du Gard*, 4 Volumes, Marseille: Laffitte.
Roux, Michel 1988, 'Révolution et bouleversements administratifs dans le Massif Central', in *La Haute-Loire et la Révolution française*, edited by Jacques Barlet, Neysac, Saint Julien-Chapteuil: Editions du Roure.
Sabatié, Françoise 1971, 'Stagnation démographique, réaction seigneuriale et mouvements révolutionnaires dans la région de Toulouse: le cas de Buzet-sur-Tarn', *Annales historiques de la Révolution Française*, 204: 176–96.

Sabatier, Gérard 1988, *Le vicomte assailli: économie rurale, seigneurie et affrontements sociaux en Languedoc des montagnes (Velay, Vivarais, Gévaudan), aux XVIIe et XVIIIe siècles*, Saint-Vidal: Centre d'étude de la vallée de la Borne.

Saint-Jacob, Pierre de 1960, *Les paysans de la Bourgogne du nord au dernier siècle de l'Ancien Régime*, Paris: Belles Lettres.

Saumade, G. 1908 *Une petite commune rurale du Languedoc sous l'Ancien régime: Fabrègues, 1650–1792*, Montpellier: 'L'Abeille', Impr. coopérative ouvrière.

Saurel, Ferdinand 1898 [1894–96], *Histoire religieuse du département de l'Hérault pendant la révolution, le consulat et les premières années de l'empire*, 4 Volumes, Montpellier: Chez tous les libraires.

Savey, Suzanne 1969, 'Essai de reconstitution de la structure agraire des villages de Sardan et d'Aspères (Gard) sous l'Ancien Régime à l'aide des compoix', *Annales du Midi*, 81: 41–54.

Schelle, Gustave. 1888, *Du Pont de Nemours et l'école physiocratique*, Paris: Librairie Guillaumin et Cie.

Schlumberger, Michèle 1971, 'La réaction thermidorienne à Toulouse', *Annales historiques de la Révolution française*, 204: 265–83.

Schneider, Robert 1989, *Public Life in Toulouse 1463–1789: From Municipal Republic to Cosmopolitan City*, Ithaca: Cornell University Press.

Schneider, Robert 1989a, 'Crown and Capitoulat: Municipal Government in Toulouse 1500–1789', in *Cities and Social Change in Early Modern France*, edited by Philip Benedict, London: Unwin Hyman.

Schnerb, Robert 1933, *Les contributions directes à l'époque de la Révolution dans le département du Puy-de-Dome*, Paris: F. Alcan.

Schnerb, Robert 1973, 'Les vicissitudes de l'impôt direct de la Constituante à Napoléon', in *Deux siècles de fiscalité française, XIXe–XXe siècle*, edited by Jean Bouvier, Paris: de Gruyter Mouton.

Secondy, Louis and Jeanne Segondy 1980, *Pignan en Languedoc: contribution à l'histoire des communautés languedociennes*, n.p.

Segondy, Jean 1949, *Une ancienne châtellenie royale du Saint-Ponais: Cessenon-sur-Orb: la seigneurie, la communauté, le consulat, la paroisse*, Montpellier, Impr. De la Charité.

Sentou, Jean 1967, 'Révolution et contre-révolution', in *Histoire du Languedoc*, edited by Philippe Wolff, Toulouse: Privat.

Sentou, Jean 1969, *Fortunes et groupes sociaux à Toulouse sous la Révolution (1789–1799)*, Toulouse: E. Privat.

Sewell, William 1994, *A Rhetoric of Bourgeois Revolution: The Abbé Sieyes and What is the Third Estate?* Durham, NC: Duke University Press.

Shovlin, John 2000, 'The Cultural Politics of Luxury in Eighteenth-Century France', *French Historical Studies*, 23: 577–606.

Shovlin, John 2000a, 'Toward a Reinterpretation of Revolutionary Antinoblism: The Political Economy of Honor in the Old Regime', *The Journal of Modern History*, 72: 35–66.

Shovlin, John 2003, 'Emulation in Eighteenth-Century French Economic Thought', *Eighteenth-Century Studies*, 36: 224–30.

Skocpol, Theda 1979, *States and Social Revolutions: A Comparative Analysis of France, Russia, and China*, Cambridge: Cambridge University Press.

Smith, Jay 1996, *The Culture of Merit: Nobility, Royal Service, and the Making of Absolute Monarchy in France, 1600–1789*, Ann Arbor: University of Michigan Press.

Smith, Jay 2005, *Nobility Reimagined: The Patriotic Nation in Eighteenth-Century France*, Ithaca: Cornell University Press.

Soulier, André 1993, *Le Languedoc pour l'héritage: les paysages économiques du Bas Languedoc de la fin de l'Ancien Régime aux années 1930*, Montpellier: Presses du Languedoc. Max Chaleil Editeur.

Soboul, Albert 1958, *Les campagnes montpelliéraines à la fin de l'Ancien Régime; propriété et cultures d'après les compoix*, Paris: Presses Universitaires de France.

Soboul, Albert 1964, 'De la Bastille à la Gironde: [1789–93]', in *Histoire de la Révolution française*, Volume 1, Paris: Gallimard.

Soboul, Albert 1972, *The Sans-Culottes: The Popular Movement and Revolutionary Government 1793–1794*, translated by Remy Ingris Hall, Garden City, NY: Anchor Books.

Stone, Bailey 1994, *The Genesis of the French Revolution: A Global-Historical Interpretation*, Cambridge: Cambridge University Press.

Sutherland, D.M.G. 2002, 'Peasants, Lords, and Leviathan: Winners and Losers from the Abolition of Feudalism 1780–1820', *Journal of Economic History*, 62: 1–24.

Swann, Julian 1995, *Politics and the Parlement of Paris under Louis XV, 1754–1774*, Cambridge: Cambridge University Press.

Swann, Julian 2003, *Provincial Power and Absolute Monarchy: The Estates General of Burgundy, 1661–1790*, Cambridge: Cambridge University Press.

Tackett, Timothy 1986, *Religion, Revolution, and Regional Culture in Eighteenth-Century France: The Ecclesiastical Oath of 1791*, Princeton: Princeton University Press.

Tackett, Timothy 1996, *Becoming a Revolutionary: The Deputies of the French National Assembly and the Emergence of Revolutionary Culture (1789–1790)*, Princeton: Princeton University Press.

Tackett, Timothy 2003, 'Collective Panics in the Early French Revolution, 1789–1791: A Comparative Perspective', *French History*, 17: 149–71.

Taylor, George V. 1967, 'Non-Capitalist Wealth and the Origins of the French Revolution', *American Historical Review*, 72: 469–96.

Teschke, Benno 2003, *The Myth of 1648: Class Geopolitics and the Making of Modern International Relations*, London: Verso.

Teisseyre-Sallmann, Line 1980, 'Urbanisme et société: l'exemple de Nîmes aux XVIIe et XVIIIe siècles', *Annales*, 35: 965–86.

Teisseyre-Sallmann, Line 1980, 'Urbanisme et société: l'exemple de Nîmes aux XVIIe et XVIIIe siècles', *Annales*, 1995, *L'industrie de la soie en Bas-Languedoc: XVIIe–XVIIIe siècles*, Paris: Ecole des Chartres.

Teissier Du Cros, Ch. 1944–48, 'L'impôt de l'équivalent du Languedoc dans les Dernières années de l'Ancien Régime', *Annales du Midi*, 290–325.

Teyssier, Patrice 1988, 'Les justices seigneuriales dans le Velay à la fin de l'Ancien Régime', in *La Haute-Loire et la Révolution française*, edited by Jacques Barlet Neysac, Saint Julien-Chapteuil: Editions du Roure.

Terrenq, Raymond 1970, *La vie communale à Baziège*, Toulouse: Impr. toulousaine.

Théron de Montaugé, M. 1869, *L'agriculture et les classes rurales dans le pays toulousain depuis le milieu du dix-huitième siècle*, Paris: Librairie agricole de la maison rustique.

Thirsk, Joan (ed.) 1967, *Agrarian History of England and Wales*, Volumes 4 and 5, London: Cambridge University Press.

Thirsk, Joan (ed.) 1978, *Economic Policy and Projects: The Development of a Consumer Society in Early Modern England*, Oxford: Clarendon Press.

Thomas, Louis 1936, *Montpellier ville marchande: histoire économique et sociale de Montpellier des origines à 1870*, Montpellier: Librairie Valat.

Thomson, J.K.F. 1982, *Clermont-de-Lodève 1633–1789: Fluctuations in the Prosperity of a Languedocien Cloth-Making Town*, Cambridge: Cambridge University Press.

Tilly, Charles 1986, *The Contentious French*, Cambridge, MA: Belknap Press.

Tocqueville, Alexis de 1955, *The Old Regime and the French Revolution*, translated by Stuart Gilbert, Garden City, NY: Doubleday.

Tournier, Albert 1896, *Vadier, président du Comité de sûreté générale sous la terreur: d'après des documents inédits*, Paris: Ernest Flammarion.

Trouvé, Claude-Joseph 1818, *Essai historique sur les États-généraux de la province de Languedoc, avec cartes et gravures*, Paris: F. Didot.

Tudez, Maurice 1934, *Le Développement de la vigne dans la région de Montpellier du XVIIe siècle à nos jours*, Montpellier: Imprimerie de la Presse.

Tulippe, Omer 1934, *L'habitat rural en Seine-et-Oise essai de géographie du peuplement*, Paris: Sirey.

Van Kley, Dale 1984, *The Damiens Affair and the Unraveling of the Ancien Régime 1750–1770*, Princeton: Princeton University Press.

Velde, François R. and David R. Weir 1992, 'The Financial Market and Government Debt Policy in France, 1746–1793', *The Journal of Economic History*, 52: 1–39.

Venard, Marc 1957, *Bourgeois et paysans au XVIIe siècle: recherche sur le rôle des bourgeois parisiens dans la vie agricole au sud de Paris au XVIIe siècle*, Paris, S.E.V.E.N.

Viala, Louis 1909, *La question des grains et leur commerce à Toulouse au dix-huitième Siècle (de 1715–1789)*, Toulouse: E. Privat.

Vialles, Pierre 1921, *Études historiques sur la cour des comptes, aides et finances de Montpellier*, Montpellier, Impr. Firmin et Montane.

Vidal, Henri 1979, 'Les attaques contre les États de Languedoc à la veille de leur disparition', *Recueil de mémoires et travaux publié par la société d'histoire du droit et des institutions des anciens pays de droit écrit*, 10: 219–28.

Vidal, Jacques 1960, *L'équivalent des aides en Languedoc*, thèse de droit, Montpellier.

Vitalis, J. 1956, 'Une émeute des journaliers agricoles de Saint-Nicolas-de-la-Grave en mars, 1793', *Annales historiques de la Révolution française*, 28: 295–8.

Weber, Max 1927, *General Economic History*, translated by Frank Knight, Glencoe, IL: The Free Press.

White, E.N. 1995, 'The French Revolution and the Politics of Government Finance, 1770–1815', *The Journal of Economic History*, 55: 227–55.

Wolfreys, Jim 2007, 'Twilight Revolution: François Furet and the Manufacturing of Consensus', in *History and Revolution: Refuting Revisionism*, edited by Mike Haynes and Jim Wolfreys, London: Verso.

Wrightson, Keith 1982, *English Society 1580–1680*, New Brunswick, NJ: Rutgers University Press.

Wrigley, E.A. 1985, 'Urban Growth and Agricultural Change: England and the Continent in the Early Modern Period', *Journal of Interdisciplinary History*, 15: 683–728.

Wylie, Laurence William 1974 [1957], *Village in the Vaucluse*, Cambridge, MA: Harvard University Press.

Yché, Julien 1985 [1916], *Etude historique sur Gruissan*, Gruissan, Narbonne, France: J. Pauc.

Zeldin, Theodore 1973, 'France 1848–1945', in *Ambition, Love and Politics*, Volume 1, Oxford: Clarendon Press.

Index

Affaire des galettes 173, 181, 185
Agde 67, 85n25, 112n16, 124, 140
Aigues-Mortes 29
Aiguillon, the duc d', military governor 91
Airolles, Joseph II 40
Albi
    Administration 114
    Bourgeoisie 112n16, 119–120
    Economy 22, 30, 132, 137, 199
    Fiscal administration 55n27, 70, 119, 207
    Nobility 106–107, 117–118, 128
    Revolts against seigneurs 154
    Seigneurial regime 32–33, 41, 85n25, 87
    Subsistence revolts 119–120, 139
Albisson, Jean 65, 167
Alco, Bonnier d', President of the cour des comptes, aides et finances of Montpellier 126
Alès 29, 54, 58, 68–69, 85n25, 121
Alet 137
Alzon, Vicomte d' 86
American War of Independence 79, 192
Anderson, Perry 6, 12n35, 76n11
Andress, David 197
Aniane 82
Aragon 18
Ardèche (*département*) 122–123, 129, 145, 149n48, 156–159, 183, 188, 195, 212
Arejan, M. le comte de Bannes d' 68n58, 69
Ariège (*département*) 129, 157–159, 163, 165–167, 170, 175–177, 185, 188, 193, 210
Arles 156
Arre 152
Artiguières, Bertrand d' 115, 163, 167
Artois 53, 72, 78
Artois, comte d' 154
Aspe, d', president of the Parlement of Toulouse 116
Pierre d'Astruc 59
Aubais, Emmanuel François d'Urre, marquis d' 68
Auch 174, 207
Aude (*département*)
    Bourgeoisie 115, 149–150, 163, 171
    Economy 25, 136–137, 139n17, 144, 196, 199, 208–209

Popular revolts during Revolution 211
Revolts against seigneurs 154–156
Revolts against taxation 148
Subsistence revolts 141
Austria 166
Avèze, de Mazade, marquis d' 152

Babeuf, Gracchus 172, 177
Baby, Jean-François 175–177, 185
Ballainvillier, intendant of Languedoc 53n25, 136
Bannes, châteaux de 123
Bassy, countess de 98
Bastille 121, 154
Baudot, Marc Antoine 169–170, 175–176
Beaucaire 59, 146
Beaumont 174
Beauvau, Prince de, military governor of Languedoc 91
Beauzelle, Madame de Nougarède de 174
Bédarieux 30, 84, 111, 115, 138
Beik, William 5n13, 7, 63, 194
Belbèze, M. Jean François Denis d'Albi de 39
Bélesta, marquis de 174
Belle Époque 199
Belpech 32–33, 54, 148, 208
Bérat 83–84
Berenson, Edward 151n53, 193n9, 201
Bernis, cardinal de, archbishop of the Albi 67, 69n62, 106, 117–119, 128
Béziers 29, 37, 82, 84, 86, 97n54, 110–111, 114n19, 132, 134, 146, 173
Bezousse 85
Bien, David 62
Biffy, Comte de, military general 95, 125n47
Bize 138
Black Mountain 29, 74, 138, 141
Blanchard, Joseph-Alexis 173–175, 187
Boisset, Joseph Antoine 168–169, 178
Bordeaux 20–21, 36
Borie, Jean 170
Bouchet, Prior du 70
Boudon, Jean 184
Bouloc 70
Boussairolles père, Jacques-Joseph 55

Boutaric, François de   37
Boutonnet   48
Brenner, Robert   4, 24n7, 31n27, 99, 101–102, 199n21
Bretx et Thil   39
Brienne, Loménie de   69n62, 107
Brittany   27, 63, 66–67, 69, 78, 91, 97, 107–108
Bureau of finances   34, 54, 88, 95, 125, 205n9, 206
Burgundy   15n42, 20, 53, 63, 66–72, 78, 80–81, 97, 101n64, 107–108
Buzet-sur-Tarn   41, 154

Cahiers de doléances
   Agriculture   136
   Bourgeoisie   111–112
   Judiciary   47–48
   Nobility   37, 113–114, 116, 124
   Participatory government   110
   Seigneurial regime   31n29, 33–34, 38, 142–143, 151, 157
   Taxation   54–55, 57–60, 70, 74, 142–143, 151
Cahuzac   85
Calonne, controller general   21, 54, 83–84
Cambacérès, Jean-Jacques Régis de   37
Cambon, Pierre Joseph   177
Cambrésis   78
Canal du Midi   21, 29, 64, 132, 141–142
Canourgue, Place de la, Montpellier   126
Capendu   68
Capens   54
Capitation   52–53, 61, 95, 97, 118–119, 125–126, 169n21, 172
Capitouls (Toulouse municipality)   54, 90, 93, 115–117
Carcassonnais   *see Carcassonne*
Carcassonne
   Agriculture   199
   Bourgeoisie   112n16, 171
   Fiscal system   53, 59
   Manufacturing   29–30, 138, 190
   Nobles   37
   Peasant revolts against taxation   148
   Seigneurial regime   18, 40, 68, 82, 86, 154
   Subsistence revolts   139, 141–142
Caribbean   191
Jacques Joseph François Cassanyès   171

Castelnaudary   82, 137
Castelnau-d'Estrétefonds   31n29, 32
Castrais   *see Castres*
Castres   111, 112n16, 113, 120, 137–138, 154
Catellane, Jean Arnaud de   67
Catherine the Great   8
Cévennes   111, 132, 138
Chalabre   138
Castries, maréchal de   68, 69n62, 95
Catholicism   60, 89, 107, 120–124, 129, 178–179, 184, 195
Chamalières, Prior of   70
Charrier's Catholic army   123
Chaudron-Rousseau, Guillaume   169–171, 175–176
Choiseul, royal minister   64, 77
Cintegabelle   110
Clarac, comte de   41, 154
Clarensac   34
Clauzel, Gabriel   176–177, 187
Clubs (political)   127, 156–157, 163–178, 183–184
Claris, M. de, president of the cour des comptes, aides et finances of Montpellier   98
Cobb, Richard   161, 177
Cobban, Alfred   158
Combe, M. Jean Pierre de la   87
Committee of Public Safety   127, 170, 178
Constituent Assembly   *see National Assembly*
Conti, prince de   68
Contrôle des actes (royal tax)   56–58
The Convention
   Bourgeoisie   162, 164–165, 167–169, 188
   Nobility   120, 127
   Peasantry   144n31
   Representatives on mission   171
   Revolutionary armies   175–177
   Sans-culottes   16, 172–173
   Thermidor   181–182, 187
Corbières region of Languedoc   31, 33–34, 115, 135, 152, 155, 158
Council of Five Hundred   *see The Directory*
Courbis, Michel   177–179, 181, 184, 187
Cour des comptes, aides et finances, Montpellier
   Fiscal system   54–56, 58–59, 89, 97, 99
   Income   45–46, 61

Jurisdiction   49–50, 80, 96, 98, 100, 105, 112
Municipality of Montpellier   95
Nobility   67–68, 74, 120, 125, 205–206
Revolutionary politics   108–109, 121, 124, 126–127, 163, 167, 182
Seigneurial regime   18, 34–35, 37
Cournonterral   142
Coustouge   148
Cuxac   111

Dauphiné   107, 154
Davidson, Neil   8, 10
De Gaulle, Charles   199
Derrey, Marc   170
Descombels   164, 168–170
Diderot   8–10
Dillon, archbishop of Narbonne   57, 64, 69, 71, 79, 96, 109
The Directory   177, 182–184
Dufaur-Coaraze, Sieur Comte   83–84
Dunkirk   199
Durand, Jean-Jacques-Louis   167, 181

Eaux et forêts (waters and forests courts)   35
Églantine, Fabre d'   177
Émigrés   117, 144, 156, 159, 173, 178, 181, 185
England   8, 10–12, 23–24, 26, 29, 31, 51–52, 77, 101–102, 138–139, 150, 189, 191, 200
Enlightenment   3, 164
Équivalent (indirect tax farm)   52, 57–58, 60
Escanecrabe   159
Estates General   11, 14, 33, 47, 92, 111–114, 116–117, 122, 150, 163, 182
Étapiers (military contractors)   60, 125n48, 179
Eu, count d'   61

Fabre, François-Xavier   61
Fabrègues   54, 97
Fanjaux   83
Fayau, Joseph-Pierre-Marie   170
Federalists   167, 168, 170–173, 177–178, 181–182
Fitz-James, duc de   91
Flanders   53, 68, 72, 108
Florensac   68
Foix   115, 163, 167, 170, 177
Froment, François   122

Froment, Pierre   89, 122
Fronton   84
Fumel, Jean Felix, Henri de   66–67
Furet, François   15n42, 161, 185n63, 193, 195

Gabelle (salt tax)   55, 58–59, 90, 115
Gard (*département*)
    Bourgeoisie   121–122, 124, 157, 163–164, 166, 168, 170, 187–188
    Counterrevolution   123, 184, 195
    Economy   136
    Peasant revolts   212
    Peasant revolts against seigneurial regime   129, 156, 158–159
    Peasant revolts against   147
    Seigneurial regime,   152
    Terror   172, 178–180
Garonne river   115, 139
Gaston, Raymond   170
Gaul   36
Gélas, Claude-Louis   173–174, 185
Générac   70
Germanic tribes   36
Gévaudan   67, 70, 112n16, 113n18, 123
Gincla, Rivals de   53
Ginestas   99
Glorious Revolution of 1688   11
Gorsse, Raymond, syndic of the Estates of Languedoc   120
Goubert, Pierre   4–5
Goudet, Prior of   70
Gramsci, Antonio   7–8, 11
Grantham, George   197–198
Grazac, Prior of   70
Grenade   147, 174–175, 185
Groussac, mayor Toulouse, Year II   170
Gruissan   54
Guy, M. de Verdier de Port de   70

Habermas, Jürgen   194
Hainaut   68
Haute-Garonne (*département*)
    Bourgeoisie   117, 168–169, 173–174, 176, 177n45, 183, 187–188
    Fiscal administration   149–150
    Peasant revolts against taxation   147, 196, 210
Haute-Loire (*département*)   121, 124, 144, 149, 172, 184, 195–196, 211

Heller, Henry   3
Hérault (*département*)   124, 127, 144, 149, 163, 166–168, 173, 181, 208, 211
Hobbes, Thomas   44
Hoffman, Philip   132
Hugueny, François   173–175, 187
Hunt, Lynn   161, 172, 201

India   191
Industrial Revolution   31, 139, 199
Ile-de-France   26–27, 41, 102n66, 132, 200

Jacobins   163, 166, 170–171, 177–178, 182–184, 195
Jalès   123–124
Janole, Jean Joseph   182
Joly, Pierre   56
Jones, Peter   197
Jonquières et Saint-Vincent   33
Joubert, Laurent-Nicolas de   61
Joubert, Philippe-Laurent de   60–62, 69n62, 95, 125n48, 205n8, 206
July Monarchy   138, 200

knights of the royal military order of St.-Louis   70, 113, 115, 120, 121n34, 163, 167, 206

La Calmette   38
Lafour   152
Lamoignon, royal minister   107
Lamothe, Mme. De   34
Lanta, baron de   70
Lapeyrouse, Picot de   56, 70n65, 103–104
Laroquète, Henry Quatrefages de   121n34, 184
Lartigue, André de   117
Lastours, Joseph de   120
Latour, François Jacques Campan de   59
Latourzelle, count of   113
Launac   48
Lauragais   29, 32, 34, 56n30, 85n25, 112n16, 132, 190
Lavaur   85n25, 137
Le Cailar   85
Lefebvre, Georges   10, 15n42, 20, 130, 196
Legay, Marie-Laure   65
Legislative Assembly   164–165

Le Puy-en-Velay
  Bourgeoisie   109, 112n16, 121, 124, 172, 184
  Economy   25, 28n20, 30–31
  Nobility   70–71, 123
  Seigneurial regime   83
  Taxation   53n25, 54
Le Roy Ladurie, Emmanuel   25, 142, 179n53, 198
Levant   29, 138
Levenalet   138
Le Vigan   121n34, 157, 172, 184
Lille   108
Limoges   154
Limoux   83, 97, 111n12, 112n16, 113, 114n19, 138
Lissac   110
Lodève   30, 54n26, 58, 66, 70n65, 85n25, 112, 138
Louis XIV   7, 12, 56, 64, 76–77, 95, 130, 134, 137, 142, 194
Louis XV   7, 69n62, 77, 91
Louis XVI   7, 92, 165
Lovez   152
Lozère (*département*)   123, 170, 195, 209, 212
Lunel   29

Machault, royal minister   63
Upper Maine   200
Malbois, César de   34
Malpel, Michel Athanaze   169
Malroc, Guillaume   167
Marguerittes, Baron de   121–122
Markoff, John   142
Marvéjols   83
Marxism   3, 6, 8, 10, 158, 200–202
Mauguio   173
Maupeou, royal minister   49, 91
Maurel, Jean-Marie de Bancalis de   18–19
The maximum   172
Mayenne   199
Mazamet   30, 56, 58, 138
McPhee, Peter   131
Mediterranean   21, 28, 41, 64, 132–134, 190
Mende   53–54, 59, 67, 83, 111–113, 140–141
Meplès, Serres de, president of the Cour des comptes, aides et finances of Montpellier   124
Meuvret, Jean   199
Midi-Pyrénées   24n8, 32, 137
Miglos, baron de   158

Mirepoix   32, 54, 83, 111n12, 114n19, 115n20, 158, 167, 171, 176, 187
Molières   152
Monestier, abbey of   70
Montal, vicomtesse de   35
Montauban   176
Montbrun   66
Montels, Pierre   181
Montesquieu   1–2, 6, 16, 36–37, 42, 85–86, 103, 113, 188, 193–194
Montgaillard   85
Montlaur   148
Montolieu   138
Montredon   61
The Mountain   *see The Convention*
Muret   147

Nantes   186
Napoleon   138–139n17, 183, 200
Napoleon III   200–201
Narbonnais   *see Narbonne*
Narbonne   22, 28–29, 54, 87, 99, 113, 133–135, 139
National Assembly
   Administrative reform   16, 145, 150, 161, 174
   Bourgeoisie   131, 142, 145, 164, 184
   Capitalism   3, 8, 10
   Nobility   15, 104, 106–107, 116–117, 122–124, 126–129, 157–158, 163
   Revolts against seigneurs   154, 158
   Revolts against taxation   145–146, 148–149, 199
   Subsistence revolts   141
Necker, Jacques   53, 56, 58, 79, 96, 111, 146
Nemours, Du Pont de   9n27, 77
Nérestang, marquis de   83
Nîmes
   The Arena of Nîmes   64, 66
   Bourgeoisie   88–89, 111–112, 120, 123–124, 157, 163–164, 166, 168, 170, 177, 193
   Counterrevolution   122, 184
   Manufacturing   29–30, 138–139
   Nobility   16, 107, 121, 128–129, 188, 195
   Office holders   58–59
   Parlement of Toulouse   88–89, 92
   Peasantry   28, 38, 126, 190
   Revolts against taxation   55, 146

Seigneurial regime   33–35, 61–62, 70, 85n25, 152
Taxation   54, 205
Terror   178, 180
Nîmois   *see Nîmes*
Niquet, de, first president of the Parlement of Toulouse   91
Noailles, Jacques Barthelemy   59
Normandy   27, 81, 98, 200

Octrois (municipal indirect tax)   59–60, 90

Paganel, Pierre   170, 174
Pagès, Raisin, public prosecutor of the criminal tribunal of Montpellier   173
Pamiers   47, 167, 170
Paris basin   *see Ile-de-France*
Parker, David   24n7, 74n72, 99–100, 194
Parliament   12, 51, 77
Peccais   55
Penitent Blanc, church of the, Niîmes   122
Périgord, Count of (military governor)   44, 49, 53, 65, 69n62, 71, 91, 103, 108, 112
Perpignan   87
Peyrou, Promenade du   64–65, 173
Pezouls, Roche de   121
Physiocracy   8–9, 13, 20–21
Pignan   28, 54
Plaisance   82
Poitou   26
Polignac, comte de   67, 69n62, 71, 80
Pommiers   152
Pompidou, Georges   199
Popular societies   *see (political) clubs*
Portalès, M. de   42
Portugal   151
Pouget   86
Poussan   34
Pouzilhac   31n29, 32–33
Prédial courts   *see seneschal courts*
Prévôté (royal military tribunal)   38
Price, Roger   197
Protestants   16, 60, 74, 88–90, 107, 120, 122–124, 128–129, 163, 178–180, 184, 195
Provence   81
Puivert, president of the Parlement of Toulouse   49
Puy-de-Dome   197

Quesnay, François   8
Quillan   56

Rabat   176
Rabestens   83
Raynal, Joseph   140–141
Rech, André   181
Rennes   91, 108
Representatives on mission   169–171, 174–175
Rességuier, M. de   34, 86
The Restoration   200
Revolt of the armed masks   37, 57
Revel   85
Reynaud, Solon   172
Rhône river   156
Rieumes   147
Rieux   25n10, 54, 83, 85n25, 140
Riley, James   51
Rochegude   48
Rochegude, marquis de   119–120
Rohan Chabot, Madame de   68
Rome   117
Rosenthal, Jean-Laurent   197
Rouairoux   68
Roussillon   146
Roussillou, Pierre   182
Rousson   57
Rovère, Stanislas Joseph François Xavier   170
Royal domains   12, 41, 55–56, 76, 88, 103, 125n48, 154, 194, 205n9
Royal Military Academy   79
Russia   8, 151

Sacère, Depuy de   159
St.-Ambroix   38
St.-Barthélémy legion of Toulouse's National Guard   116
Saint-Bresson   152
St.-Cyprien neighborhood of Toulouse   115–116, 172n27
St.-Didier   83
St.-Chinian   59
St.-Denis   111, 123
Ste.-Anastasie   70
Ste.-Eulalie   82, 208
Saint-Félix-de-Caraman   34, 85
St.-Gervais   111
St.-Girons   177

St.-Hilaire d'Ozilhan   70
St.-Hippolyte-Du-Fort   121
St.-Jory   70
St.-Michel-de-Vax   87
St.-Papoul   54
St.-Pierre-de-Rivière   47
St.-Pons   59, 138, 140
Saint-Priest (intendant of Languedoc)   55
Saint-Sernin   48, 207
St.-Thibéry   85
St.-Ursule monastery of Nîmes   90
Saint-Victor-de-la-Coste   31n29, 32–33, 54, 73n71
Saissac   85
Salles   85
Salons   6, 34
Salze, Pierre-Joseph de   113
Sandricourt, Monseigneur Vermandois de St.-Simon Rouvoy de   67
Sans-culottes   161–162n1, 172, 176, 184–185
Sardan   136
Saurat   176
Sault region of Languedoc   21
Sauve   85
Savoy   154
Second Republic   201–202
Secourieu   34
Séguier-la-Pique   158
Sénéchas   31n29, 32
Seneschal courts
  Bourgeoisie   117, 121, 167, 170, 173, 177, 206
  Income   44–46
  Jurisdictional rights   38, 50
  Municipal government   88–89, 92, 95, 120
  Religion   47
  Seigneurial regime   18, 35, 82–84, 90
  Taxation   59
Serbia   151
Sète   61, 68, 96, 146
Seven Years War   64, 77, 90
Sieyès, Emmanuel Joseph   10, 145n32
Siran, abbey de   69, 113n18
Sommières   61, 156
Southern Massif central
  Bourgeoisie   111–112, 156, 183
  Counterrevolution   16, 128, 188, 195
  Economy   24n8, 25, 29, 74, 107, 120, 132, 134, 136, 143, 190

Nobility   129
   Revolts against taxation   146, 149
   Seigneurial regime   33, 38
   Subsistence revolts   139
Souvignargues   157
Spain   21, 29, 117, 138, 151, 158, 166, 174–176
Surveillance committees   169, 171–174, 176–179, 181
Sutherland, Donald   199–200

Tackett, Timothy   129
Taille (direct tax levied on commoners)   5, 50, 53, 63, 74, 97, 125
Taille réelle   see taille
Tarascon   170, 175–176
Tarn (*département*)   117, 120, 128, 210
Taussac   84
Terraube, Monseigneur de Gallard de   70
Terray, controller general   53, 58, 91
Terror   169, 170–171, 175, 177–179, 182–185, 195
Tharaux   84
Thermidor   161–162n1, 172n27, 176–177, 181–184
Tilly, Charles   142
Tocqueville, Alexis de   50, 63, 130, 177, 188–193, 196
Toulouse-Lautrec, count de   68, 117–118
Tour-Maubourg, Marquis de la   109
Tournon   130
Turgot, controller general   9n27, 48, 77

United States   151, 200
Uzès   22, 29, 32, 38, 48, 54, 57, 70, 73n71, 74, 84, 111, 121, 157, 170

Vachon, Georges François de   67
Vadier, Marc-Guillaume   175–177, 182, 185
Vagnas   85
Val-de-Dagne   148
Vauvert   121
Vendée   197
Vénézobre   74
Versailles   7, 21, 33, 35, 52, 69, 69n62, 71–72, 74, 80, 83, 93–94, 98, 100, 204
Vias   85
Vic-Dessos   176
Villasavary   86
Villefloure   40
Villeneuve-de-Berg   38
Villeneuve-lès-Avignon   156
Villetritouls   154
Villiers, marquis du   110
Vingtièmes   52–53, 63, 91, 97–98, 103, 108
Vivarais
   Counterrevolution   123
   Economy   24n8, 25, 28–30, 73, 132, 136
   Revolts against seigneurs   121
   Seigneurial regime   32–33, 37–38, 85n25, 152
   Taxation   54, 57, 70, 97
Vizille   107

Weber, Max   51

The Year II   see The Terror
Young, Arthur   28n20, 29, 64

Zébel, dame Rouch de   86

www.ingramcontent.com/pod-product-compliance
Lightning Source LLC
Chambersburg PA
CBHW071234070526
44583CB00017B/2173